Also by Kate Williams

England's Mistress: The Infamous Life of Emma Hamilton

Becoming
Queen Victoria

Becoming
Queen Victoria

The Tragic Death of Princess Charlotte

and the Unexpected Rise of Britain's Greatest Monarch

KATE WILLIAMS

Ballantine Books
New York

Biography
VICTORIA
2010

Published in the United States by Ballantine Books,
an imprint of The Random House Publishing Group,
a division of Random House, Inc., New York.

BALLANTINE and colophon are registered trademarks of Random House, Inc.

This work was originally published in hardcover in the United Kingdom by Hutchinson,
a member of The Random House Group Limited, London, in 2008.

Library of Congress Cataloging-in-Publication Data

Williams, Kate.
[Becoming queen]
Becoming Queen Victoria : the tragic death of Princess Charlotte and
the unexpected rise of Britain's greatest monarch / Kate Williams.
p.   cm.
Originally published as: Becoming queen. London : Hutchinson, 2008.
Includes bibliographical references and index.
ISBN 978-0-345-46195-7
eBook ISBN 978-0-345-52193-4
1. Victoria, Queen of Great Britain, 1819–1901—Childhood and youth. 2. Charlotte Augusta,
Princess of Great Britain, 1796–1817. 3. Charlotte Augusta, Princess of Great Britain, 1796–1817—
Influence. 4. Princesses—Great Britain—Biography. 5. Queens—Great Britain—Biography.
6. Great Britain—Kings and rulers—Succession. I. Title.
DA555.W55 2010
941.081—dc22   2010013227

Printed in the United States of America on acid-free paper

www.ballantinebooks.com

2 4 6 8 9 7 5 3 1

First U.S. Edition

Book design by Virginia Norey

Contents

PART ONE

1796–1817

Charlotte: The Queen Who Never Was

INTERLUDE

1817–20

Drunken Dukes

PART TWO

1820–37

Little Victoria

PART THREE

1837–41

The Young Queen

The Family of Princess Charlotte
and Princess Victoria

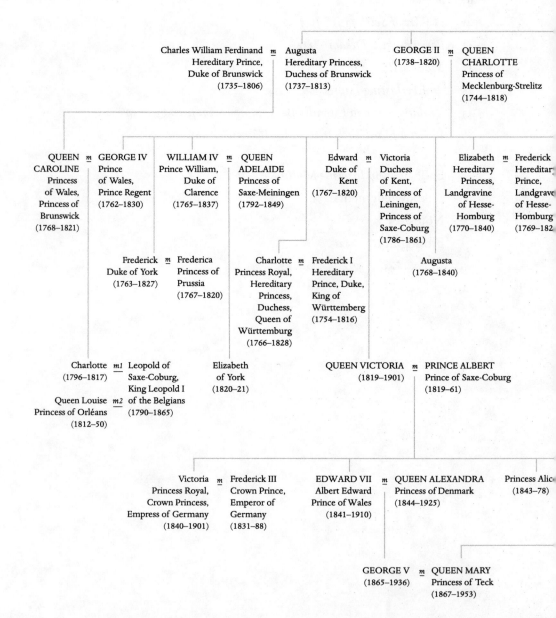

GEORGE I _m_ SOPHIA DOROTHEA
(1660–1727)   Princess of Zell
               (1666–1726)

GEORGE II _m_ QUEEN CAROLINE
(1683–1760)   Princess of Ansbach
               (1683–1737)

Augusta _m_ Frederick
Princess of Wales   Prince of Wales
Princess of   (1707–51)
Saxe-Gotha
(1719–72)

Henry _m_ Lady Anne Horton   William Henry _m_ Maria   Caroline Matilda _m_ Christian VII
Duke of   Duchess of   Duke of Gloucester   Duchess of   Queen of Denmark   King of Denmark
Cumberland   Cumberland   (1743–1805)   Gloucester,   (1751–75)   (1749–1808)
(1745–96)   (1743–1808)   Countess Dowager
                                                   of Waldegrave
                                                   (1739–1807)

Ernest _m_ Frederica   Adolphus _m_ Augusta   Sophia   Alfred   Mary _m_ William   Sophia
Duke of   Princess of   Duke of   Duchess of   (1777–1848)   (1780–82)   Duchess of   Frederick   Matilda
umberland,   Mecklenburg-   Cambridge   Cambridge,   Gloucester   Duke of   of Gloucester
King of   Strelitz   (1774–1850)   Princess of   (1776–1857)   Gloucester   (1773–1844)
Hanover   (1778–1841)   Hesse-Cassel   (1776–1834)
1771–1851)   (1797–1889)

                    Augustus   Octavius   Amelia
                    Duke of Sussex   (1779–83)   (1793–1810)
                    (1773–1843)
                    _m1_ Lady Augusta Murray
                        (1762–1830)
                    _m2_ Lady Cecilia Buggin
                        (1793–1873)

George V _m_ Queen Marie   George _m_ Louisa   Augusta _m_ Frederick   Mary _m_ Francis
King of   Princess of   Duke of   Fairbrother,   Hereditary   Hereditary   Adelaide   Duke of Teck
Hanover   Saxe-Altenburg   Cambridge   Mrs. Fitzgeorge   Princess,   Prince,   Duchess   (1837–1900)
1819–78)   (1818–1907)   (1819–1904)   (1815–90)   Grand Duchess   Grand Duke of   of Teck
                                                             of Mecklenburg-   Mecklenburg-   (1833–97)
                                                             Strelitz   Strelitz
                                                             (1822–1916)   (1819–1904)

Prince Alfred   Princess Helena   Princess Louise   Prince Arthur   Prince Leopold   Princess Beatrice
(1844–1900)   (1846–1923)   (1848–1939)   (1850–1942)   (1853–84)   (1857–1944)

List of Illustrations

Becoming
Queen Victoria

Introduction

꧁꧂

The English like Queens.

The Dowager Duchess of Saxe-Coburg
on hearing of the birth of her
granddaughter, Princess Victoria

The English do indeed like queens. Queen Victoria is England's longest-reigning monarch, having ruled for sixty-three years and two hundred sixteen days. Elizabeth II seems well on the way to ruling for sixty years, after weathering more challenges than many monarchs in history. I was born into a unique conjunction of female prime minister and monarch. To a child growing up in the 1980s, women ruled. Female heads were on coins and notes, criminals were incarcerated at Her Majesty's pleasure, and the queen's armed forces fought a female politician's wars.

Accustomed as we are to the long reign of Elizabeth II, a queen seems a perfectly welcome outcome for the present-day British. However, in the late eighteenth century, the situation was very different. Queen Anne's unhappy reign cast a long shadow, and female monarchs were seen as unreliable and untrustworthy. But with a mad king and a debauched prince regent in power, the English changed their mind about queens. They invested their hope for a stable future in a princess: Charlotte, daughter of the prince regent. She was young and pretty, apparently liberal in her views, and sympathetic to the general public. She gave the country hope throughout the rigors of the Napoleonic Wars, during an age when monarchs across Europe were being swept off their thrones. When she and her child died, the English despaired. They believed they were doomed to rule by the prince regent and his hedonistic brothers, including the buffoonish Duke of Clarence and the evil Duke of Cumberland.

Then, within a few years, Victoria appeared, the bearer of a slightly ridiculous anglicized version of a French name, given to her because the prince regent hoped she would always remain a minor princess. Few thought she would ever be queen.

In order to be queen, Victoria had to navigate prejudices, the unfriend-liness of her relations, and her mother's quest for power. We have a vision of her as dreary and stolid, the embodiment of stoic virtue and repressively moralistic views. But as a girl, she was passionate, impulsive, and eager for gaiety.

The idea of Victoria—young, fresh, liberal, and seemingly concerned with the plight of her people—kept the British hopeful throughout the largely appalling reigns of George IV and William IV. When she became queen at the age of eighteen years, three weeks and three days, an era of drunken, selfish kings who cared only for their own privilege came to a much-needed end. The profligate sons of George III had pushed a portion of the population closer to revolution than at any time since the English Civil Wars. Had the next king after William been his brother the universally detested Ernest, Duke of Cumberland—a notorious blackguard suspected of blackmail, incest, and murder—then the fate of the monarchy might have been spectacularly different.

This book tells the story of the transition of the monarchy to its mod-ern form and explores how the survival of the institution we know today was in part due to Charlotte and Victoria. The pages that follow tell the tale of two heirs to the throne, young women growing up in the palaces of St. James's and Kensington, forced to negotiate a tricky path between their own desires and the demands of duty to court and country. Both would have to battle against their parents and the intrigues of the court, one dying tragically, the other becoming a veritable symbol of Britishness and an apotheosis of queenship. This is their story.

Prologue

Kensington Palace, London, June 20, 1837

The Duchess of Kent had been praying for years that King William IV, George IV's brother and successor, would die before her daughter Victoria reached the age of eighteen. She wanted to be regent in order to secure riches and power for herself and her beloved adviser, John Conroy. The king hated the duchess, and he was grimly intent on holding on to power. Victoria turned eighteen on May 24, and the king finally stopped fighting to live.

Less than a month later, on June 20, the princess was woken in her bed and told she had important visitors. Still in her nightgown, she made her way downstairs to the sitting room below to receive the archbishop of Canterbury and Lord Conyngham, the Lord Chamberlain. Her mother was determined to enter with her, but Victoria told her firmly to wait outside. As she walked into the room, the two men knelt gravely before her and pronounced that King William had died.

Victoria was queen of England.

The duchess was listening at the door, hugging herself with excitement and dismissing her daughter's sudden flare of resistance as a mere tantrum. She had no doubt that she would be able to control every aspect of Victoria's life. The duchess had devoted every moment of the past eighteen years to positioning herself as the real power behind the throne, spying on her daughter relentlessly, forcing her to share a bedroom with her, and inspecting all her diaries and correspondence.

Victoria had very different ideas. As soon as her eminent visitors had departed, she issued her first command as queen: She wished to spend an hour alone.

From that point, she meant to make clear, she would rule alone.

And yet Victoria herself would not have existed if it had not been for the death of Princess Charlotte, daughter of George IV, the queen who never was. Her short life and sudden death changed the course of British royalty forever.

A portrait of George III and Queen Charlotte hangs in Kew Palace, in West London. Surrounded by rosy, happy children, they appear the ideal jolly, vital eighteenth-century family. After Queen Anne died without issue in 1714, George, elector of Hanover, had become the very unpopular George I of England. The first Hanoverian monarch was fifty-second in line to the throne, hardly spoke English, and had little interest in his country, but he was the nearest Protestant. He was repeatedly threatened by the sons of James II, the deposed Stuart king, but by the second half of the eighteenth century, it looked as though the monarchy was safe. The thrifty George III was beloved for his moral rectitude, his plain speaking, and his fondness for staying at home in England with his submissive, fecund queen.

Although the king became infamous for his bouts of mental illness and for losing America, he has been esteemed for his easy fertility and thirteen children. But behind the seeming harmony of the portrait lay a family that was one of the most unhappy and chaotic in history. George's tyrannical behavior toward them shaped the future of the British monarchy for more than a hundred years, indeed perhaps coming close to prompting its end. His daughters became bitter spinsters and his sons hopeless rakes, detested by the country for their irresponsible behavior and shocking debts. By 1817, the entire complement of thirteen children had produced only one legitimate child among them: Charlotte, daughter of George, Prince of Wales. When she died, the position was even more untenable: so many offspring and not one heir among them.

These apparently hearty, affectionate princes and princesses had failed spectacularly to marry or procreate successfully, thanks to a combination of their father's tyranny and their own selfishness.

Queen Charlotte was just eighteen when she gave birth in 1762 to her first child, a "strong, large and pretty boy," George, Prince of Wales. Delighted by his procreative skills, the king did not hold back. By September 1766, the twenty-one-year-old queen was the mother of three sons and heavily pregnant with her next child. Six girls and seven boys were finally produced (two more boys died young), with the youngest, Amelia, born in 1783.

George III had been exasperated by his failure to control the unwieldy marriages of his siblings. He was absolutely determined to control his offspring and produce docile, restrained princes and princesses who would marry whom he pleased. The children were given a strict timetable of lessons from seven in the morning until three in the afternoon, when they dined. There were no days off for birthdays, and there were harsh punishments if the children failed to live up to expectations. One of the princesses recalled how Princes George and Frederick were "held by their tutors to be flogged like dogs with a long whip." The king liked to see his family around him of an evening, but life was never informal: The children could seldom turn their backs on him, and the boys were hardly ever permitted to sit in the presence of the queen.

George, Prince of Wales, was the first heir born to a reigning monarch in twenty-five years. He truly felt the weight of parental expectation. Foibles that were tolerated in his brothers and sisters were severely chastised in him. The prince felt desperately unappreciated by his father, and he did not value the company of his mother and sisters. He bucked against his father's discipline, not least because he knew that the family much preferred his charming and handsome younger brother Frederick.

"He will either be the most polished gentleman or the most accomplished blackguard in Europe, possibly an admixture of both," declared one of his tutors when his charge was fifteen. The young prince was sociable, intelligent, loyal to his friends, and essentially kind. But his passions lay close to the surface—he was rash, hot tempered, often dishonest, and led by his emotions. He was also selfish and greedy. He careered through his late teens and twenties, chasing women, gambling, and borrowing money.

By the age of twenty-two, he was nearly £300,000 in debt, had been black-mailed by at least one disgruntled mistress, and was married illegally to a Catholic widow, Mrs. Fitzherbert, after a young curate had been freed from debtors' prison and paid £500 to conduct the ceremony.

The rest of the family was little better. As they lurched through their twenties, the princes horrified England with their spending, their wild behavior, and their preference for taking conspicuous mistresses rather than marrying. The Duke of York ignored his wife, leaving her alone in the country with her forty dogs and large menagerie, and indulged himself with several mistresses; the Duke of Clarence had ten children with the great comic actress Dora Jordan; the Duke of Kent also kept a mistress and ran up debts; the Duke of Sussex made an illegal marriage to Lady Augusta Murray, eleven years his senior, in 1793 in Naples; the Duke of Cumberland was hated for his cruelty and his extreme views. In short, Great Britain's most perfect family had become its most violently dysfunctional.

Part of the problem was the Royal Marriages Act. Infuriated by the secret unions of his siblings, George III decreed in 1772 that no descendant of George II (with the exception of the offspring of princesses married into other royal families) could legally marry without the consent of the sovereign and the approval of Parliament.

The six princesses led pitiful lives. The king adored his daughters and thought them exemplars of virtue in comparison to his rebellious sons. But he expected a payment in return for his affection: The princesses should remain at Windsor, confined to the society of the family, kept busy with painstaking embroidery and the reading of improving literature. Charlotte, the Princess Royal, was married to the Prince of Württemberg in 1797, but the others were not so fortunate. In November 1788, just when the king seemed to be edging toward finding husbands for his elder daughters, he collapsed into madness and had to be imprisoned and restrained at Kew Palace. The queen refused to leave Kew and was intent that her daughters would remain there with her. The king had recovered by early 1789, but the queen was embittered and miserable, and she wished the princesses to remain with her in retirement at Windsor. They began to resort to subterfuge and secret affairs.

For his sons, George III's collapse in late 1788 was an opportunity for freedom from his endless strictures. The Prince of Wales grasped the chance to take the position and riches he had desired for so long. He did everything he could to demand a regency and was not dissuaded even when the king soon returned to health. Despite the ire of the country, which regarded him as attempting to callously exploit his father's illness, the prince was determined to seize power and be his own man. Most of all, he wished never to take a legitimate wife. He had no desire to father the heir to the throne.

PART ONE

1796–1817

Charlotte: The Queen Who Never Was

1

ジ℃

"The Most Distressing Feelings
of My Heart"

The Prince of Wales was drunk. It was his wedding day, he was disgusted by his bride, and he was the most inebriated he had ever been outside of a brothel. He was in debt to the tune of over £500,000, and the only way to settle his obligations was to marry. But he was shocked by the ugliness of his wife-to-be, Caroline of Brunswick, and thought she smelled like a peasant. In the overheated, overdecorated Chapel Royal, dressed sumptuously in his customary high-fashion garb, the prince gritted his teeth, took another swig of porter, and tried to focus his mind on the showers of money he would receive.

The marriage of the thirty-two-year-old Prince of Wales had been a subject of debate for years. By 1794, ministers and courtiers were desperate for cheering news. Great Britain was mired in despond and recession. War with France had strained the country's finances and increased the price of imports, and the gentry lived in fear of the English mob setting off another French Revolution in England. "Never was there seen so gloomy a Birth-Day in this country as that of yesterday," bleated the *Morning Post* in January, referring to the queen's birthday. "Care and despondency seemed to sit on every brow, the affected smiles of Ministers shewed that disappointment and despondency resided in their hearts, and instead of being a day of joyous gratulations, a settled melancholy and dread apprehension for the safety of the Nation pervaded the Assembly."

The English needed a national event to lift their spirits, and the ideal solution was a royal wedding. But George was a demanding suitor. After nearly seventeen years of chasing the most beautiful women in London, he was easily bored, made unhappier by unlimited choice. Few, if any, of Europe's shy, bug-eyed princesses could have satisfied him. And yet, despite his own exacting standards, he was not the handsome young charmer he had once been. Perched on top of his flabby body was a round, rather saturnine face, and his once fine complexion had turned florid. Still, he had striking gray eyes, a mass of light brown hair, superb if flamboyant dress sense, and great charisma. When the heir to the throne was in the mood, no one could fail to be charmed by his exquisite manners and intensely flattering conversation.

The prince had always been hungry for affectionate sympathy. At the tender age of sixteen, he had fallen hopelessly in love with his sisters' twenty-three-year-old assistant governess, Mary Hamilton, besieging her with letters. Seven years later, in 1785, he staged an elaborate charade by pretending he was on his deathbed in order to persuade the devout Catholic widow Maria Fitzherbert to marry him. Blonde, bosomy, and beaky, she was the only woman who had resisted him sexually, but once he had married her and conquered her in bed, he lost interest. Relegated to the status of morganatic, unofficial wife, since George III had not sanctioned the union, Mrs. Fitzherbert was soon made miserable by her husband's philandering and spendthrift nature. As the diarist Thomas Raikes recorded, the prince was "young and impetuous and boisterous in his character, and very much addicted to the pleasures of the table." He courted other women and borrowed money from Mrs. Fitzherbert. And then, in 1793, the clever, unprincipled, and fascinating Lady Jersey began to exert her charms.

Born in 1753, the daughter of the Irish bishop of Raphoe, Frances Twysden was seventeen when she was married to the thirty-five-year-old Earl of Jersey. The prince first fell in love with her when she was twenty-nine and he twenty, but she batted him away. Twelve years later, however, once he was presiding over his own gilded court in St. James's, she was eager to charm him. At forty-one, she was nearly ten years his senior and already a grandmother, but she possessed, according to the diarist Nathaniel Wraxall, "irresistible seduction and fascination." The prince was soon captivated by her brittle, aloof glamour.

In the spring of 1794, the Court of Privileges decreed null and void the marriage of the prince's younger brother Augustus to Lady Augusta Murray. To the Prince of Wales, the court's decision seemed to give him permission to discard his wife in order to indulge himself with Lady Jersey. Catholic commoner Maria was even less suitable than the Protestant, aristocratic Lady Augusta. In June, when Mrs. Fitzherbert was dining with the Duke of Clarence and his mistress, Dora Jordan, she received an urgent letter. She opened it to find her lover informing her that their relationship was at an end. Her grief was only intensified by another letter, delivered a fortnight later, in which the prince justified his actions like a spoiled schoolboy. He, by contrast, thought he had acted very properly toward his unofficial wife. As he fussed to Captain Jack Willet Payne, friend and member of his household:

> *To tell you what it has cost me to write, and to rip up every and the most distressing feelings of my heart . . . which have so long lodged there is impossible to express. God bless you my friend; whichever way this unpleasant affair now ends I have nothing to reproach myself with.*

Opinion was sympathetic to Mrs. Fitzherbert, even though it was a time when Catholics were often reviled. The caricaturist Isaac Cruikshank produced an amusing cartoon of her fleeing in tears with her £6,000 annuity, as the prince fondles a skinny, wrinkly Lady Jersey. Still, the aristocracy did not waste too much time feeling sorry for the abandoned wife and hurried to flatter the new royal mistress.

Lady Jersey did not want her emotional prince falling in love with another Mrs. Fitzherbert or becoming dependent on the lady herself once more. She decided to secure her own position by encouraging her lover to enter into an arranged marriage. The prince was amenable to her persuasions, excited by the prospect of an expanded income on marriage, and payment of his horrific debts. In 1787, Parliament had been induced to pay off the most onerous sums and increase his allowance, but he had continued to spend wildly and his debts had shot up once more. By the time he fell in love with Lady Jersey, tradesmen were refusing to deal with him and creditors harassed him in the street. Finally realizing that Parliament would not bail him out again, the prince decided to marry and informed the king of his decision. He then promptly cast himself in the role of noble self-sacrificer, boasting how he had relinquished happiness and a love match to produce a royal heir. As he exclaimed when shown the list of possible candidates, "One damned German frau is as good as another."

Princesses across Europe were practicing their English, but sly Lady Jersey had her eye on one particular German frau. She encouraged her lover to think favorably of his first cousin, Princess Caroline Amelia Elizabeth of Brunswick-Wolfenbüttel. Six years younger than the prince at twenty-six, she was immature and, gossip had it, fat, tactless, and vulgar. She had been an indulged child in Brunswick, a small but licentious court where the duke's mistress was openly acknowledged. Then, as a teenager, she had been strictly disciplined, hardly ever allowed to dine with her mother, ordered upstairs if there were guests, and kept apart from her brothers. Thanks to such an upbringing, she was high-spirited, rebellious, attention seeking, and rude. She had thick blond hair, fair skin, and lively blue eyes, but her boisterous, abrupt manner had put off potential suitors. When George's mother, Queen Charlotte, heard some years previously that her brother Charles, Duke of Mecklenburg-Strelitz, was considering marriage with Princess Caroline, she had written him a bluntly dissuading letter:

> They say her passions are so strong that the Duke himself said that she was not to be allowed even to go from one room to another without her Governess, and that when she dances, this Lady is obliged to follow her for the whole of the dance to prevent her making an exhibition of herself by indecent conversations with men.

Now the queen kept her reservations to herself, for she knew how fond the king was of Caroline's mother, his sister, the Duchess of Brunswick.

The Duke of Wellington speculated that Lady Jersey had chosen clumsy Caroline, a woman of "indelicate manners, indifferent character, and not very inviting appearance from the hope that disgust for the wife would secure constancy to the mistress." Still, the prince had perhaps little choice: Few royal princesses in Germany were great beauties or had managed to grow up untainted by inbred madness or the sheer claustrophobia of tiny courts. On August 29, 1794, George wrote to his younger brother the Duke of York that all was over with Mrs. Fitzherbert and he was to marry Princess Caroline. He wrote to the Duke and Duchess of Brunswick asking for Caroline's hand, and they sent an eager reply, delighted to betroth their daughter to the heir to the richest throne in Europe when she had seemed lost to matrimony at twenty-six. The king suggested waiting until spring, but the prince was typically impatient. "We are all working and moving Heaven and earth to immediately send her over," he pronounced. As soon as the engagement was confirmed, the newspapers began to praise the young lady's great beauty and impeccable virtue. The government agreed to increase the prince's Civil List income from £60,000 to £100,000 a year and gave him £20,000 toward his wedding. He immediately devoted £5,000 of this to redecorating and furnishing Caroline's apartments in Carlton House.

The prince's envoy, James Harris, Lord Malmesbury, a discreet, experienced diplomat, had gained George's confidence when he had been British minister at the Hague. He set off to meet Caroline and escort her to London. When he arrived in Brunswick at the end of November, he was cautiously impressed by the future Princess of Wales:

> Pretty face—not expressive of softness—her figure not graceful—fine eyes—good hands—tolerable teeth, but going—fair hair and light eyebrows, good bust—short, with what the French call "des épaules impertinentes." Vastly happy with her future expectations. The Duchess full of nothing else—talks incessantly.

Malmesbury was also gratified by the princess's eagerness to please and her habit of asking for advice. "Her conversation was very right, she entreats me also to guide and direct her." He was, however, not much of a guide. "I recommend perfect silence on all subjects for six months after her arrival," he told her early on. The princess was soon infuriated by Malmesbury's diffident, somewhat impractical advice and cool demeanor. As she grew row-

dier and more aggressive, intent on catching his attention, his diary turned
into a litany of criticism. The princess, he complained, insulted or praised
without thinking and spoke wildly or excessively to impress, particularly
when she was nervous. He worried over her "light and flighty mind" and
reported: "My eternal theme to her is to *think before she speaks, to recollect
herself.*" Her impulsive character was most unsuited to that of the prince.
"With a steady man she would do vastly well, but with one of a different
description, there are great risks." Caroline's father was also concerned.
"She is not stupid," the duke sighed, "but she has no judgement." She
should be made aware that her role in England "would not be simply one
of amusement and enjoyment; that it had its duties, and those perhaps difficult and hard to fulfil." Free from illusions about the prince's character, he
urged the diplomat to instruct his daughter not to show jealousy at her husband's infidelities. Malmesbury did so, and told Caroline insistently that
"those of a very high rank have a high price to pay for it."

The problem was that the fastidious prince liked stylish, grown-up
women a few years his senior. Bouncy, boisterous Princess Caroline looked
and behaved like a child and had scant interest in fashion. The dressmakers
at Brunswick could hardly compete with those in London, the style capital
of Europe, but still, the princess seemed to have not the vaguest interest in
her appearance. Malmesbury quaked that his grubby, unfashionable charge
was to be married to one of the most immaculate dandies of the age,
whose debts to his tailor once hit more than £30,000. Indeed, Caroline later
declared that George "would make an excellent tailor, shoemaker or hairdresser but nothing else." Another man might have loved her for her open
demeanor, honesty, and genuinely kind heart. But the prince only valued
women who were exquisitely dressed and possessed of a perfect knowledge of etiquette. Jolly, girlish behavior held no appeal for him.

Malmesbury told himself that he could do nothing. He was in Brunswick only to collect the princess, not to report on her. In England, plans for
the wedding were moving ahead, the country was growing excited, and the
prince was eager to see his bride. One wonders, however, whether Malmesbury's diary was revised slightly with the benefit of hindsight and a desire
to justify his opinion, for he would have looked very foolish had he filled his
pages with praise. The old tale of the terrible incompatibility of the prince
and princess needs some tempering. It is unlikely that any other princess

would have made a more appropriate wife. The prince would have been better matched to a confident widow in her late thirties, but as heir to the throne he was supposed to marry a young virgin.

In late December, the princess finally set off for her new life, accompanied by her mother and Lord Malmesbury. She drove away radiant with anticipation and hope, watching the crowds waving wildly and listening to their cheers. Her enthusiasm was soon dampened. Malmesbury learned that troops were advancing across Europe. Holland was too dangerous to enter, and so he decreed that they would have to turn back and wait at Hanover. There they were forced to remain for two long, cold months while war raged. The Duchess of Brunswick complained and begged to return home, while Malmesbury, nervous about his reception in England, carped at the princess. He asked her lady-in-waiting to make it clear to her that "the Prince is very delicate and that he expects a long and very careful *toilette de proprete.*" He fretted that she had a trousseau full of rudimentary nightdresses and drawers. The prince liked ladies who wore delicate undergarments edged with Brussels lace.

Caroline laughed off his complaints about her inadequate lingerie and ignored his recommendations of regular baths. Malmesbury was beginning to understand that his mission was hopeless.

2

⸎

"I Find Him Very Fat, and Nothing as Handsome as His Portrait"

The London newspapers had continued to praise Princess Caroline's beauty, virtue, and stylishness. The usually scabrous James Gillray produced the caricature "The Lover's Dream," in which the prince grasps his pillow, absorbed in a dream, while the princess is borne toward him by angels. The king stands nearby, brandishing a large sack of cash. Starved of female glamour—for they had only the drab Queen Charlotte and her dowdy daughters—the British looked forward to the arrival of the lovely princess. The prince, however, had become distracted. He had fallen in love with the idea of himself as a great soldier and begged his father to allow him to take a position of command over the troops.

After months of bickering in Hanover, Caroline and her party set off for London in late March, arriving at Greenwich on the morning of Sunday, April 5, 1795. Dressed up, primped, and excited, Caroline looked eagerly around the riverbank for her escort, but there was nobody to meet her. Finally, after she had drummed her heels for an hour, she saw some ladies arriving, escorted by the 10th Light Dragoons.

Lady Jersey, who had intimidated the queen into giving her a position as

Caroline's Lady of the Bedchamber, had caused the delay by demanding extra time to prepare. She wanted the bride to be publicly humiliated. As soon as she arrived, she wasted no time in criticizing the princess's outfit and demanding that she change into an ugly and poor-fitting dress of white satin. Finally, when she announced that she would not sit facing the princess, as riding backward made her feel sick, Malmesbury told her un-equivocally that if she could not sit opposite Caroline, she should never have accepted the position of lady-in-waiting and would not be allowed to sit in the first carriage at all. Lady Jersey gave in and sat crossly with her back to the horses, shooting Malmesbury sour looks.

Caroline had heard gossip about the prince and Lady Jersey, and possibly even seen the lewd caricatures that had been circulated across Europe. She was hurt and angry, but not daunted. "I am determined never to appear jealous," she had told Malmesbury. "I know the Prince is leger [sexually fickle] and I am prepared on this point." She was confident that she would win against a mere lady-in-waiting.

Telling himself he had done all he could, Malmesbury escorted Caroline to St. James's Palace through cheering crowds. Beaming with happiness, Caroline managed an ungainly curtsy for her fiancé. As the prince politely raised her up, he recoiled in shock, horrified by her face, her ugly dress, and most of all, her pungent smell. He retreated in panic to a distant part of the room and fanned himself vigorously. "Harris, I am not well; pray get me a glass of brandy," he moaned to his valet. Malmesbury asked him if he should rather drink water. The prince swore at him and stormed out of the apartment, shouting, "I will go directly to the Queen." The bridegroom, performing like a great actor for Lady Jersey and the courtiers, was deter-mined that everyone should understand his awful sacrifice.

The princess stood open mouthed. "My God," she cried in French, "is the Prince always like that?" She was deeply disappointed. "I find him very fat, and nothing as handsome as his portrait."

Malmesbury promised her that the prince did not always behave so and would be very different later on that evening at the lavish welcome dinner. It would have been kinder had he said nothing. Caroline arrived to eat, de-termined to entertain her fiancé with her winning personality. Utterly ig-noring Malmesbury's earlier strictures that she should be elegantly quiet, she knocked back goblets of wine, told raucous jokes, and dropped coarse hints about Lady Jersey, who looked demurely at her plate. The prince suffered paroxysms of disgust, his initial dislike for his bride on the brink of blossoming into positive hatred.

The wedding was set for three days later. The prince drank, wallowed in self-pity, and indulged himself with thoughts of Mrs. Fitzherbert. He wished people to sympathize with his terrible distress. Few did. The newspapers hastened to assure their readers that Caroline was quite as lovely as reports had promised.

On Wednesday, April 8, the prince woke and prepared for his ordeal. The wedding was set for eight o'clock. While he was dressing, he received a letter from his father informing him that he would not be promoted to the rank of major general, a position he desperately desired. The king added that he had delayed answering the prince's letters until the arrival of the Princess Caroline. "Her amiable qualities will, I flatter myself, so fully engage your attention that they will divert it from objects not so pleasing to the nation." Consumed by anger, the prince drank as his valet dressed him, then gulped maraschino brandy on the short carriage journey from his luxurious home, Carlton House on Pall Mall, to the chapel at St. James's Palace. "Tell Mrs. Fitzherbert she is the only woman I shall ever love," he told the Duke of Clarence, seizing his brother's hand tearfully.

The chapel was adorned with fine crimson drapes and silver decorations, but the prince, pink faced and swaying, could hardly see them. To Lord Melbourne, he looked "like a man doing a thing in desperation; it was like Macheath going to execution; and he was quite drunk." Caroline, cheerful as ever, chattered to the Duke of Clarence as he escorted her up the aisle. She was weighed down by jewels and an ornate wedding dress of silver tissue and lace, robed over with velvet, an old-fashioned and deeply unflattering confection of hoops and giant bows which had been chosen by the queen. Following her were four aristocratic bridesmaids, in white satin decorated with silver foil and spangles, and bandeaux of white spangled crêpe topped with large ostrich feathers. The grandeur and glamour were wasted on her groom. So inebriated that he had to be held up by his ducal groomsmen, the prince twitched throughout the service and even leaped up in the middle of a prayer.

The uncomfortable atmosphere infected even the archbishop of Canterbury. When he asked whether either party knew of any cause or impediment to the marriage, he laid down his prayer book and stared hard, first at the king, then at the prince. Everybody knew about the prince's illegal wedding to Maria Fitzherbert. George burst into tears and looked, one equerry remarked, "like death and full of confusion, as if he wished to hide himself from the looks of the world." He stared hopelessly at the ever-supportive Lady Jersey when making his vows. After the service, the party walked to a reception in the queen's apartments in Buckingham House. The Duke of Leeds noted that the newlyweds hardly spoke, and he remarked on "the coolness and indifference apparent in the manner of the Prince towards his amiable bride."

The people of England were delighted by the marriage. "Never was public as well as private solicitude wound up to such a high pitch," exclaimed a journalist in *Bon Ton Magazine,* going on to lavish praise on Caroline, "whose virtues no less than her personal charms give her a lawful claim to love and esteem as to the admiration of the British nation in general." The streets and houses of London blazed with illuminations. The people had fallen in love with their royal family once more.

After a lengthy dinner at Buckingham House, the young couple retired to the bedchamber at Carlton House. Dead drunk, the prince fell into the grate and slept there for the entire night, his portly body splayed across the hearth. Next day, as a coachful of wedding cake was driven away from Carlton House, delicately parceled up for dignitaries and sent with the compliments of His Royal Highness, the bride and groom departed for their honeymoon. Their first stop was Windsor. George was still in a temper and refused to escort his wife to church or to promenade her around the castle terrace. The king offered his arm, and Caroline beamed at the onlookers, the epitome of a happy bride. The couple then continued their honeymoon at Kempshott, near Basingstoke, where to the princess's despair, her new husband and his courtiers lived like bachelors, "constantly drunk, sleeping and snoring in boots on the sofas . . . & the whole resembling a bad brothel more than a palace." Lady Jersey was the only woman in attendance.

"I flatter myself that you will have her turn out a very comfortable little wife," declared Princess Elizabeth to her brother, praising Princess Caroline's good humor and honesty. George, however, only made his wife more bitter and troublesome by neglecting her and insulting her. Parliament had

refused to boost his payment from the Civil List to the level he had expected, and the increase offered was put into the hands of a committee,
who would pay off his debts. In practical terms, the prince had to support
a wife on less money than he had had as a bachelor. Deciding that Caroline
was to blame for all his problems, he dismissed her maids of honor, although he expected her to continue to support Lady Jersey. He removed
chairs from her private dining room, saying he could not afford to pay for
them, and took back the pearl bracelets he had given her on their wedding
day, presenting them instead to his beloved Lady Jersey. In the eighteenth
century, when it was rare for a woman to own or inherit property or
money, her financial security was essentially tied up in her jewelry. "I fear it
is very bad," worried the Duchess of Devonshire. "The poor little Princess
is very ill used, as he certainly made her cry all the last ball."

The prince was squeamish about making love to his wife, and later asserted that he had sex with her only three times. He also confided to
Malmesbury that he did not think her a virgin, for she was bold and declared his manhood large, and "how should she know this without a previous means of comparison?" Worst of all, she was too dirty for him to bear.
She, in turn, hinted that he was impotent. Luckily for them both, Caroline
quickly conceived.

The country and the king were delighted by the news of a baby. Even
the prince was initially won over, writing from Brighton, where he and his
wife had retired to save money, that the mother-to-be was happy and content in his home, the Brighton Pavilion, and in "the best health and spirits
possible, excepting at moments a little degree of sickness." Soon, however,
the princess was feeling despondent. "I do not know how I shall bear the
loneliness," she wrote to a friend in Germany. The queen and her daughters did not visit her, and Caroline suspected that they disapproved of her.
Still worse, Lady Jersey was ruining her life. "I hate her, and I know she feels
the same towards me. My husband is wholly given up to her, so you can
easily imagine the rest." After the prince's brief excitement over the pregnancy had subsided, he returned to dwelling on his disappointment with
his wife. "We go on," he wrote to the queen, "aussi méchante, aussi médis-
ante et aussi menteuse que jamais"—as wicked, as slanderous, and as false
as ever. "I am surrounded by evil minds and everything I do is put into a bad
light," Caroline lamented. Lady Jersey reveled in the frequent occasions

when the princess muddled her words, stumbled over etiquette, or made smutty or tactless comments. The prince liked to hear his wife derided, and Lady Jersey liked to mock, so the pair passed pleasant evenings raking over the princess's many faux pas.

Euphoria about the royal wedding soon wore off. The war dragged on, soldiers were dying, and the people were hungry. When the king drove to Parliament, he was mobbed by furious Londoners screaming against their situation and the prime minister, William Pitt, "No war! No Pitt! No king! Bread, give us bread!" Some threw stones at his carriage windows. The prince blamed revolutionary sentiment in France, spouting: "Such shocking outrages and indignities might be thoroughly and radically prevented from ever happening again in future, & which are a disgrace to the age in which we live & can only be equalled by the enormities committed in a neighbouring kingdom, & owing in great measure to her pernicious example." He seemed unaware that his own wild spending and selfish behavior only fueled the people's antipathy.

3

"An Immense Girl"

On January 7, 1796, at twenty minutes past nine in the morning, Princess Charlotte Augusta arrived into the world at Carlton House, London. The prince burst into tears when the baby appeared, and wrote to his mother at quarter to ten:

> The Princess, after a terrible hard labour for above twelve hours, is this instant brought to bed of an immense girl, and I assure you notwithstanding we might have wish'd for a boy, I receive her with all the affection possible, and bow with due deference and resignation to the decrees of Providence.

"Papa is so delighted it is a daughter," wrote Princess Mary. "As you know, he loves little girls best." The king hoped that the baby would be the first of dozens of grandchildren and was optimistic that she would reconcile husband and wife. Princess Elizabeth reported that her father talked of "nothing but his grandchild, drank her health at dinner and went into the Equerries' room and made them drink it in a bumper." Isaac Cruikshank produced the caricature "Grandpappa in His Glory," showing the king spooning pap into the unwilling mouth of baby Charlotte, surrounded by drying nappies. The country rejoiced, briefly distracted from their resentment of the royal family. Another caricature showed how the populace celebrated: A debtor drinks to an early release from jail, a wet nurse and a milliner hope for employment, a member of a corporation jumps to make the announcement first, an artisan smiles that popery (that is, Mrs. Fitzherbert) has lost its influence, and a child and a farmer express simple delight. It was all so excitingly quick. As *The Morning Chronicle* slyly noted, the baby had arrived one day before the nine-month anniversary of the wedding.

While the country celebrated, the prince grew angry again, irritated by his wife's desire for more respect now that she was the mother of his child. Three days after his daughter's birth, the overwrought prince dashed off a sprawling will of over twenty-six pages, suddenly and sentimentally leaving all his worldly goods to the woman he had deserted, Maria Fitzherbert, addressing her: "My wife, the wife of my heart & soul." He entrusted his baby daughter to his parents and decreed that the Princess of Wales "should in *no way either be concerned in the education or care of the child, or have possession of her person*, for though I forgive her the falsehood and treachery of her conduct towards me, still the *convincing and repeated proofs I have received of her want of judgement and feeling, make me deem it incumbent upon me . . . to prevent by all means possible the child's falling into such bad hands as hers.*" As a final insult, he bequeathed all the princess's jewels to Princess Charlotte and left his wife only a shilling. "I had rather see toads and vipers crawling over my victuals than sit at the same table with her," he puffed.

The prince's pristine Carlton House had been invaded by a baby and armies of nurses. Little Charlotte was installed in a nursery headed up by Lady Dashwood, once Lady of the Bedchamber to Princess Elizabeth, who had been waiting on tenterhooks at Nerot's Hotel, ready to move in the minute the baby was born. She was assisted by the sub-governess, twenty-three-year-old Miss Frances Garth (sister of General Thomas Garth, equerry to the king), a nurserymaid and two assistants, and a robustly healthy wet nurse from Brighton, Mrs. Bowers. The nursery was run along stringent lines. No outsiders were permitted through its hallowed portals, and there was to be no contact between the nursery staff and the other servants in Carlton House. Mrs. Bowers was allowed to have three or four visitors one evening a week (presumably her family), and everybody had to be in bed by eleven o'clock. The baby princess would be moved to the room of Lady Dashwood when her own room was being cleaned, but she should not be out of the nursery after three p.m.

On February 11, the child was dressed up in a lace outfit chosen by the queen, and christened Princess Charlotte Augusta in the Great Drawing Room at St. James's Palace. Everybody agreed that the baby looked wonderfully healthy. She was named after the queen and the Duchess of Brunswick, who were also her godmothers. The king stood as godfather.

When Parliament refused to award him money on the birth of his heir, the Prince of Wales vented his anger on his wife by attempting to separate her from the child. She was allowed only one visit daily and forbidden ever to see the baby without a governess and a nurse being in constant attendance. For the rest of the time, he expected her to sit with Lady Jersey until he felt like going out with his mistress, leaving his wife alone. Caroline later claimed that she would die rather than relive those early miserable months in England.

The Princess of Wales struck up a secret friendship with the subgoverness, Miss Garth, who opened the nursery door to her when no one was looking. Although the prince had his apartments on the same floor, he visited the nursery so sparingly that he did not realize his wife was making clandestine visits. Caroline became so brazen that she began to take the little girl out driving in London, to the wild applause of the crowd.

The relationship between the prince and princess deteriorated even further as they began to use their child as a pawn in their battles. The prince was firmly eighteenth century in his outlook toward love: Great men married for social position and took a mistress for love, affection, and sex. Although Princess Caroline had seen her own father depend on his mistress, she had expected tenderness from her husband. Angry at his attempt to sideline her, she wrote to him in faulty French that she hated being shut up alone all day with his mistress. He replied furiously that Lady Jersey was simply a "friend" to whom he was "attached by strong ties of habitude, esteem and respect." Caroline sent a long reply: "It is very true that a few days before our marriage you took the trouble to destroy the rumours abroad concerning Lady Jerser [sic] and I did not hesitate to believe you. Would to God that nothing had dissipated that happy illusion." The prince was so angry at what he perceived as her insubordination that he sent her a biting letter telling her that he had lost all affection for her. He declared that they should no longer live together as man and wife. "Our inclinations are not in our power, nor should either of us be held answerable to the other because nature has not made us suitable to each other," he wrote. "Tranquil and comfortable society is, however, in our power; let our intercourse be restricted to that."

Princess Caroline sent the whole correspondence to the king and begged for his protection. The prince also wrote to his father, blaming his wife for spreading gossip that he had treated her harshly. He claimed that she had thwarted his every effort to live on good terms with her. "It would be now absolutely ruinous to my character and interest, as well as destructive to my peace of mind, for the rest of my life, to have further communication or intercourse of any kind with so dangerous a person as the Princess. I have only earnestly to supplicate your majesty to order measures for our final separation." When the king remonstrated with him, the prince shot off a desperate letter to his mother, blustering: "This worthless wretch will prove the ruin of him [the king], of you, of me, of every one of us." He accused his wife of relations with other men and judged her "a very monster of iniquity."

The king would not be persuaded.

> *You seem to look upon your disunion with the Princess as merely of a private nature, and totally put out of sight that as Heir Apparent of the Crown your marriage is a public act, wherein the King is concerned; that therefore a seperation [sic] cannot be brought forward by the mere inference of relations.*

He also noted that Parliament would make a settlement to Caroline and take it from the prince's jointure.

It was common knowledge that the prince was once more under Lady Jersey's spell. Gillray's "Fashionable Jockeyship" showed the prince riding piggyback on Lord Jersey, who carries him to his wife. The prince demands, "Buck! Buck! how many Horns do I hold up?" as the husband replies, "E'en as many as you please!" In one of Cruikshank's most shocking caricatures, the prince kicks the tea table to the ground while he shouts, "Marriage has no legal restraints on me! No legal tie can bind the will—'tis free & shall be so!" A behorned Lord Jersey peeps around the door, ushering the prince toward his supine mistress. Lady Jersey yielded to public pressure and resigned as Lady of the Bedchamber at the end of June, but the crisis was unstoppable. The prince simply installed his mistress, her husband, and her booty of bangles in the house next door and continued to see her as often as ever.

Everyone was discussing the prince's marital breakdown. Few had sympathy for him. "To be sure he has married a very foolish, disagreeable person," his brother, the Duke of Clarence, blabbed to a Mrs. Sutton at a ball in Richmond in September, "but he should not have treated her as he has done, but have made the best of a bad bargain, as my father has done. He married a disagreeable woman but has not behaved ill to her."

The injured wife attracted much public sympathy. *The True Briton* declared her "an amiable and accomplished personage who has been the object of so much unmerited ill-treatment." The journalist recommended that the English ignore the prince. "We have long looked upon his conduct as favouring the cause of Jacobinism and democracy in this country more than all the speeches of Horne Tooke and all the labours of the *Corresponding Society.*" The prince was single-handedly wrecking any remaining goodwill directed toward the monarchy.

When the princess attended the opera alone on May 28, 1796, *The Times* was stunned by her reception. "The house seemed as if electrified by her presence, and before she could take her seat, every hand was lifted to greet her with the loudest plaudits. The gentlemen jumped on the benches and waved their hats, crying out '*Huzza!*'" It was all quite overwhelming. "If the Princess will only afford the public a few more opportunities of testifying their respect for suffering virtue, we think it will bring more than one person to a proper reflection." Princess Caroline was only too eager to create opportunities for the public to adore her. On June 13, Charles James Fox was spectacularly reelected to his Westminster constituency. He was parading in triumph past Carlton House when the mob began calling for the little princess; promptly, declared *The Times,* "the sash of one of the upper windows was held up, and the Royal child showed to the populace, who gave three cheers." The prince spat venom at such reports, telling whoever would listen that his wife was determined to make the "poor little girl" an "instrument against her much injured father." Infuriated by his wife's habit of using Charlotte to achieve, as he put it, "worldly applause," the prince declared that she flashed the child around promiscuously to bolster her popularity. Her royal uncles and aunts also looked on in dismay. "I regret much the weakness of the mother," wrote the Princess Royal, "in making a plaything of the child, and not reflecting that she is a Princess, and not an actress."

The little girl seemed to enjoy the shouts of the crowds. But her nursery was in chaos. Her governess, Lady Dashwood, fell seriously ill in the summer and died in October 1796. The queen trawled through possible appointees, despairing of finding a successor. Finally, at the beginning of 1797, the elderly Maria, Countess of Elgin, was appointed. Six months later, Miss Garth left and was replaced by the youthful Ann Hayman. Charlotte had little consistency in her upbringing and was becoming nervous and unsettled. Unsurprisingly, after both her parents had shown little interest in her other than as a pawn in their bitter game, she was eager for attention and mercurial in her moods. Miss Hayman reported:

> My little charge was playing about. I took no notice of her at first, except to admire her great beauty and great likeness to the prince. She soon began to notice me; showed all her treasures and played all her little antics, which are numerous. She is the merriest little thing you ever saw—pepper hot, too: if contradicted, she kicks her little feet about in a great rage, but the cry ends in a laugh before you know which it is.

One of Miss Hayman's earliest duties was to take the child to visit the king on his birthday. Charlotte was initially a little grumpy with the king, but soon "recovered her good-humour and played with her grandpapa on the carpet a long while. All seemed to doat on her, and even the Prince played with her."

The prince had arranged to see his daughter when she was being dressed or at breakfast, but weeks would pass without a visit (perhaps the hours were too early for him). Miss Hayman wasted morning after morning, finely arrayed, hoping that the prince would arrive. She often had little idea whether he was at Carlton House or away. Piqued at his nonappearance, she struck up a friendship with the princess and encouraged her to take the child out in her carriage, displaying her to the cheering crowd. By the end of the year, the prince had dismissed her.

In the summer of 1797, Caroline left Carlton House and rented first a house in Charlton, near Blackheath, and then Montague House, a villa near Greenwich Park, which she adorned with garish decorations. She began to throw regular parties. Convinced that she was entertaining his political adversaries, the prince remonstrated to his father. The king informed Caroline that she could only receive society approved by the prince, which would mean very few people indeed. She was incensed, claiming to her husband that he treated her neither as his wife, nor as the mother of his child, nor as the Princess of Wales. "And I tell you that from this moment I shall have nothing more to say and that I regard myself as being no longer subject to your orders—or to your *rules.*" She announced she would invite whomever she pleased.

By the end of the year, however, the prince had become a little weary of fighting with his wife. He had broken off with Lady Jersey out of boredom, and he was considering courting Mrs. Fitzherbert, toward whom he knew Caroline had amicable feelings. He sent a cordial invitation to the princess to spend the winter with him at Carlton House. To his shock, she rebuffed the offer. The influential Sir Gilbert Elliot, later Earl of Minto, esteemed Caroline and begged her to reconsider and to reflect seriously on any step she might take if similar overtures were renewed, but "she said that she was a very determined person when once she had formed an opinion." She believed that her husband was attempting to befriend her because he wished for a loan from one of his relations. Whatever the truth, it was her last chance at reconciliation.

"God grant that you may be enabled to keep her in perfect ignorance of the unfortunate differences between her parents," wrote the Princess Royal, Charlotte's godmother, to Lady Elgin. "It gives me great pleasure to know that my dear little Charlotte is equally kind to both her parents; maybe, in the end, that little creature may itself serve as a sort of magnet to make them a little better." She was sadly deluded. The Prince and Princess of Wales were leading separate lives.

4

～❦～

"Fleas Are the Only Enemies
HRH Has"

Charlotte had been born into a world in transition. Between 1789 and 1830, the population of Britain rose from about ten million to sixteen and a half million, and there was a concomitant shift from countryside to town. With the enclosure of land, farming was becoming more centralized and mechanized, and the old-style tenant farmers eked out a living as laborers or tried their luck in the cities or the harsh factories that were springing up in the urban areas. There was still no organized relief for hunger or illness, and the typical man lived pitifully, particularly in the country and town slums, where life expectancy hovered around seventeen years. The poor were starving, and the rapidly expanding classes of clerks, lawyers, and merchants wanted more representation. Although Britain had the most enlightened political system in Europe, with regular parliaments and restraints on the power of the monarch, only one in ten men could vote. Thanks to George's madness and the extravagant behavior of his sons, the monarchy was deeply unpopular, considered a leech on the exchequer. The people dreaded the spendthrift, selfish Prince of Wales becoming king.

The heir to the throne grew into a pretty toddler with a fair complexion, a mass of fair curls, and big blue eyes. Dressed up in perfect little outfits, she was a precocious and engaging child who loved the limelight and knew how to charm her audience. Miss Hayman loved to show her off. On one occasion, a large crowd that had gathered in the park watched her and Charlotte drive twice up and down while the little girl "huzzaed and kissed her hand the whole time, and the people looked extremely delighted, running with the coach all the way." Later, Miss Hayman wrote, she performed the same from the window for a full hour to a great mob and all the procession of mail coaches. On holiday in Weymouth with the king and queen and her royal aunts, she amused the whole party with her prayers before bed. As Princess Elizabeth wrote to the Prince of Wales, the child usually announced, " 'Bless papa, mamma, Charlotte and friends,' but having been crueley [sic] bit by fleas the forgoing night, instead of *friends* she introduced *fleas* into her prayers." When Lady Elgin remonstrated with her to say "friends," Miss Hayman joked, "Why, Madam, you know we pray for our enemies & surely the fleas are the only ones HRH has, so she is perfectly right." Little Charlotte was most fond of her grandfather, who adored playing games with her and making jokes, but she was everybody's pet, as well she might be in a family of siblings in their twenties and thirties and not a legitimate child between them.

Charlotte's confident, bright ways charmed even her father. "She is getting to the age that amuses him, and he grows very fond of her," declared Miss Hayman. "The nurses take her to him without me generally when he breakfasts, and he spoils her dinner with a great piece of bread." The little girl learned how to perform in order to please the adults around her. By the age of three, she was dancing for her mother's parties and singing "God Save the King" and "Hearts of Oak" to the guests or to her grandfather and aunts.

The writer Hannah More came to visit the royal nursery and was captivated. Four-year-old Charlotte clasped More's hand and gave her a guided tour of Carlton House, making sure to show off her father's choicest pieces of furniture. She then sang and performed a short dance. More called her the "prettiest, most sensible and genteel a little creature you could wish to see." Five years later, she published her *Hints Towards Forming the Character of a Young Princess* and presented a copy to the queen. Young ladies, decreed More, did not devote sufficient time to serious matters. Wasteful and frivolous subjects should be discarded in favor of careful moral instruction and religious reading. Charlotte, however, was not the type of girl to settle to such a program of instruction. She was vivacious and warm, but also prone to tantrums, clinginess, and willful behavior. In an instant she could snap from easy blond prettiness to red-faced fury, kicking her heels and screaming hysterically at her governesses.

Charlotte's naughtiness was the consequence of her craving for love and attention. She had no brothers or sisters or cousins, and few potential playmates were deemed suitable for the prince's daughter. Her grandmother, aunts, father, mother, and even sometimes her beloved grandfather only seemed to take notice of her when she was performing like an actress or behaving like an angel. They made little attempt to play with her, amuse her, or catch her interest, and passed her to her governess the minute she grew fractious or demanding.

The prince was furious when he heard that her mother was showing her off. At Montague House, he stipulated, she must always dine alone. He far preferred his daughter to spend time with her five spinster aunts (his eldest sister, Charlotte, the Princess Royal, had been married to the hereditary Prince of Württemberg in 1797. Her first daughter died, and although no more children came, she kept the baby clothes she had brought over from England until her death). Augusta, Mary, Elizabeth, Sophia, and Amelia were locked up with their parents, with no diversions but sewing, playing music, and drawing, with, as the politician and diarist Greville wrote, their "passions boiling over." The older girls, heading into their forties, looked to be condemned to Windsor and embroidery forever. The two younger ones were both embroiled in secret scandals. In 1798, Princess Sophia fell in love with General Thomas Garth, the brother of Miss Garth and a favorite equerry of the king, who was thirty-three years her senior and so ugly that Greville dubbed him a "hideous old devil." Still, as one of the queen's ladies recalled, "the princess was so violently in love with him that everyone saw it. She could not contain herself in his presence." In August 1800, twenty-two-year-old Sophia gave birth secretly in Weymouth. Some declared that the father had been her own brother, the Duke of Cumberland, but the Princess of Wales, for one, was sure it was Garth. Sophia's child was baptized Thomas Garth and sent to the household of Major Herbert Taylor, then private secretary to the Duke of York. Amelia, the youngest daughter, a lovely, laughing, ruby-lipped young woman with a fine sweep of hair and a large bosom, was her father's favorite, and only thirteen years Charlotte's senior. At the age of nineteen she began a passionate affair with an equerry of her father, General the Honourable Charles Fitzroy.

The prince was ignoring his daughter and missing Mrs. Fitzherbert. His mode of charming was to lay violent siege, weeping and begging, and one target of his affections reported that he offered "vows of eternal love, entreaties, and promises of what he would do. I should make my own terms!!!" He moaned, clutched his heart, and then collapsed, an "immense, grotesque figure flouncing about, half on the couch, half on the ground." Mrs. Fitzherbert could not resist. "A Gentleman of high rank and MRS FITZHERBERT are once more *Inseperables* [sic]," proclaimed *The Times* on July 4, 1799. "When one is invited, a card to the other is a matter of course." The prince proved his love by engaging in a lengthy court battle to win his beloved the guardianship of a small girl, Minny Seymour, whom she had cared for after both the child's parents had died.

Charlotte was largely confined to her nursery, first at Carlton House and then also at Shrewsbury House, on Shooters Hill, near Greenwich, on the outskirts of London, close to her mother. Although naughty in private, she was handsomely behaved in public. For the New Year of 1803, a children's ball was given in her honor, and the little princess conducted herself beautifully. She "danced with great dignity and looked, if I may say so, what she really is born to be," praised Princess Mary.

Lady Elgin, Charlotte's dear "Eggy," was one of the few points of stability. The governess often found her position severely compromised by the warring parents and Princess Caroline's increasing friendship with the king. On one occasion, Caroline arrived at Shrewsbury House and told Lady Elgin that the king desired to see her and Charlotte before he left for Weymouth. Lady Elgin watched in horror as the king seized the eight-year-old in his arms, declaring to her that "he was to take Princess Charlotte to himself as the Prince wished it but he could say nothing yet." When Lady Elgin alerted the prince, he flew into a rage and became obsessed with the idea that his father was trying to kidnap Charlotte. Charles James Fox encouraged his worst fears: "The King may attempt to gain possession of the Princess Charlotte by violence or stratagem and take her to Windsor," he wrote. "Send immediately without a moment's delay for your daughter to

Carlton House." He recommended that the prince maintain "the possession of her person by all legal means." The Lord Chancellor adopted a
more mollifying position, suggesting that the prince should keep calm and
not give the episode too much thought. He believed that another bout of
the king's madness was imminent.

The Lord Chancellor was correct: The king was losing his mind. His dismayed wife and daughters watched the resurgence of the symptoms that
he had suffered in 1788: his habit of rushing everybody along for no reason
and speaking agitatedly, crying "hey" and "what what!" He veered between
excessive generosity—particularly to the Princess of Wales—and violent
anger. He was becoming increasingly cruel to the queen, bullying her and
declaring, as he had done in 1788, that his true love was the aged Countess
of Pembroke, whose beauty had made her very sought after in the court of
his youth. The queen was so afraid of him that she locked her door against
him at night, and the Prince of Wales began politicking wildly, in the hope
that his father would fall into complete madness. Throughout the king's illness, efforts were made to keep Charlotte apart from him, and so the little
girl lost her most indulgent friend in the royal family. Although he recovered his health in the early summer of 1801, he still suffered relapses and
bouts of hysteria until 1805, and Charlotte did not see him when he was ill.

In 1804, Lady Elgin resigned. She was in her sixties, plagued with gout,
and weary of the incessant politics of the royal family. She knew that she
had lost the prince's confidence after the unfortunate episode when the
king had threatened to seize his granddaughter. Charlotte was distraught
to lose her beloved Eggy. She had been her kind companion for as long as
she could remember. At the beginning of the following year, the king appointed the elderly and pusillanimous Dowager Baroness de Clifford as
governess to the nine-year-old girl. In the interim, Charlotte grew more rebellious and increasingly resentful at being bounced between her warring
parents.

5

The Mistress of Montague House

The Princess of Wales had turned Montague House into one of London's most popular venues. Every night she held court in her drawing room, dressed in exotic and outlandish outfits and surrounded by young, clever, and handsome men. Caroline may have held no charms for her husband, but she had a seductive appeal that other men could not resist. Many, such as William Pitt, were the king's own ministers. The painter Thomas Lawrence stayed overnight so that he could better complete her portrait, and George Canning, a twenty-nine-year-old politician who would later become prime minister, was a frequent visitor. Canning initially resisted what he called "the abundant and overpowering temptation to the indulgence of passion . . . which must have been dangerous, perhaps ruinous, to her who was the cause of it, and myself," but later became Caroline's lover. Admirers such as Canning adored her vivacity, but some were more dubious. "How the sea-captains used to colour up when she danced about, exposing herself like an opera girl," declared Lady Hester Stanhope, one of her erstwhile ladies-in-waiting. "I plainly told her it was a hanging matter, that she should mind what she was about." The princess blithely ignored warnings that she should behave with more caution.

One cold day in November, Charlotte, Lady Douglas, a lovely but impoverished woman with a talent for charming, was entertaining a friend in the parlor of her home on Blackheath Common when she realized that two ladies were ambling back and forth in front of the house, often hesitating by the gate, as if they wished to come in. The blonder of the two, stylish in a lilac satin pelisse and bright yellow half-boots, was obviously the Princess of Wales; the other looked as if she was her lady-in-waiting.

Unsure of what the princess expected, Lady Douglas went to the window and bobbed a low curtsy. The princess gave her a friendly nod. "You should go out," suggested the friend who was sitting with her in the parlor. "Her Royal Highness wants to come in out of the snow." Lady Douglas opened the door and Caroline bounced up. "I believe you are Lady Douglas, and you have a very beautiful child," she beamed. "I should like to see it." Explaining that her baby was still in London, for she was visiting Blackheath only briefly, Lady Douglas invited her illustrious caller into the parlor. Yellow boots flashing, the princess trundled gaily inside, plumped herself down on a chair, and began talking enthusiastically. After an hour, she shook hands and bustled out, leaving Lady Douglas and her friend in a state of shock.

The princess was quite charmed by her new acquaintance, and a painfully intense friendship began. Lady Douglas was soon an unofficial lady-in-waiting, spending most days at Montague House. Caroline simply could not leave her alone. She would burst into Lady Douglas's bedroom and grasp her friend in her arms, kissing her, praising her beauty, and declaring that she had never loved another woman so much. "Oh! believe me," she would exclaim, "you are quite beautiful, different from almost any Englishwoman; your arms are fine beyond imagination." She deluged her friend with promises of devotion and boasted wildly in the hope of impressing.

One day in the early summer of 1802, the princess arrived at Lady Douglas's house breathless with excitement. Coyly dropping her voice, she confided that she was with child. She told her stunned friend, who was herself heavily pregnant, that the baby had quickened at breakfast, and milk had flowed out of her breasts. She said she hoped it would be a boy, and if she was discovered, she would declare the prince the father, for she had slept two nights at Carlton House. It was all a story. Joke-loving Caroline had embarked on the most dangerous prank of her life. Sometime before, one Sophia Austin had come to visit the princess, asking for help. Her husband, Samuel, had lost his job at Deptford Dockyard (the 1802 Peace of Amiens had prompted the docks to fire many of their workers), and she had a new baby. Caroline had become desperate for a child, and she decided that the Austin infant would fit the bill. The page who interviewed Mrs. Austin suggested that the princess might like to adopt the child after he had been weaned. Mrs. Austin duly left little Willy at Montague ten days later. While he was being weaned, Caroline told her friend that she was pregnant.

When Lady Douglas called, the princess vowed that Willy Austin was her son. She insisted on looking after his every need. "I was entertained the whole morning by seeing [the child] fed, and every service of every kind performed for it by her Royal Highness the Princess of Wales," Lady Douglas marveled. She could not believe that the princess changed the child herself and tossed the dirty diapers onto the hearth. "From this time the drawing rooms at Montague House were literally in the style of a common nursery. The tables were covered with spoons, plates, feeding-boats [bottles] and clothes, round the fire napkins were hung to air, and the marble hearths were strewed with napkins which were taken from the child." Rumors quickly began that the princess's close friend, the naval officer Captain Thomas Manby, was the father.

The princess's friendships often commenced with a wild outpouring of passion and then soured and cooled. She was soon bored of Lady Douglas and began to discourage her from visiting. When Lady Douglas complained of neglect, Caroline flew into a rage. Making no effort to disguise her hand, she scribbled abusive unsigned letters that were accompanied by wild drawings of Lady Douglas in bed with Admiral Sir Sidney Smith, a frequent visitor to Montague House who was said to have been a lover of Caroline's. The Douglases demanded an audience with her, but she refused them. When the king appointed Caroline as the ranger of Greenwich Park in 1805, she decided to alleviate her debts by leasing out the various houses in the park to the Royal Naval School or using them to accommodate her own household. Sir John and Lady Douglas were given notice to leave their house.

Sir John demanded an explanation, and the princess called in her brother-in-law, the Duke of Kent, to mediate. In the course of the discussions, the Douglases enlightened the duke about the shocking poison-pen letters, which they had kept. The Duke of Kent managed to mollify them with his tact (and perhaps money). There was, after all, no concrete evidence that Caroline had actually written the letters, and moreover, to have Lady Douglas's name plastered across the newspapers in connection with an adulterous relationship would only ruin her reputation. The affair looked as if it would blow over, until the Prince of Wales heard the gossip and seized on the chance to disgrace his wife. On November 5, the prince met Lady Douglas at the house of Colonel McMahon in Mayfair. There, she told all, alleging that the princess had committed adultery and asserting that Willy Austin was the princess's child. She also told the prince that if she was found out, Caroline aimed to install Willy as first in line to the throne over Charlotte by declaring him the father. The prince was enthralled by the story. If it could be proved that Caroline had committed adultery, then she would be guilty of treason and eligible for the death penalty.

While all England was gripped by Horatio Nelson's astonishing victory against Napoleon's fleet at the Battle of Trafalgar on October 21 and the terrible tragedy of his bloody death as battle raged around him, the prince plotted to rid himself of his wife. Presented with the evidence, the king reluctantly authorized a secret commission of cabinet ministers to look into his daughter-in-law's behavior. On June 1, 1806, when Charlotte was ten, the "Delicate Investigation" began with an interrogation of the Douglases. The prime minister, the Lord Chief Justice, and other luminaries then interviewed the princess's servants about Caroline's gentleman guests, her size, and even the state of her sheets. A torrent of confusing secondhand and contradictory evidence followed. It was hard to ascertain whether or not possible lovers had stayed, or whether Caroline had been pregnant or just fat or padded, or whether her sheets had been stained with blood, which might confirm that she had given birth. Unfortunately for the prince, the princess's closest ladies, her dressers, and her doctors all declared that she had never been pregnant. Mrs. Sophia Austin gave a sworn statement that William was her son, and her words were backed up by the hospital register.

In mid-July, the commission concluded that there was no evidence to suggest that William Austin was Princess Caroline's child or that she had ever been pregnant since giving birth to Charlotte. Caroline was delighted, but was furious to find that many in society did not think her entirely guiltless. The report of the commission had revealed many unsavory anecdotes about her behavior, particularly with Captain Manby. The king refused to see her, declaring that "there have appeared circumstances of conduct on the part of the Princess which his Majesty could never regard but with serious concern." Incensed and aggrieved, Caroline began talking of publishing a book to defend herself. She declared to the prince that she was ready to expose to the world the affairs and peccadilloes of his sisters and to declare that the king allowed them liberties that he refused to her.

Charlotte could not remain ignorant of the terrible investigation. During the inquiry she was not allowed to see her mother, and her father was too busy for her. One day she was out with her governess, taking an airing in the park, when she spotted her mother. Caroline immediately turned her back and headed in the opposite direction. She was only obeying the command not to make contact with her daughter, but Charlotte was not to know. Distraught and angry, the ten-year-old dashed home and scrawled that her mother was a "monster" in the clutch of "pride and the Devil." With the word "Devil," she struck the paper repeatedly with her pen, exclaiming, "There, I do this to show how many devils there were that took hold of her!"

When Caroline was acquitted, the prince's popularity hit an all-time low. The public was scandalized by the way he had treated her and judged him cruel and ungallant for exposing his wife to such scrutiny. It also seemed very unfair that Caroline had not been allowed to defend herself in a proper inquiry. The prince was miserable and frustrated, unable to believe that all the evidence accrued was not enough to allow him to divorce his wife. All he could do was forbid her to visit Carlton House and decree that Willy Austin must leave the house whenever Charlotte was present.

In search of a distraction, the unhappy prince devoted his energies to seducing Isabella, Marchioness of Hertford, a tall, statuesque, and ambitious grandmother in her late forties. "He writes day and night almost, and frets himself into a fever," reported Lady Bessborough, "and all to persuade la sua bella *Donnone to live with him publickly!!* A quoi bon, except to make, *if possible*, a greater cry against him?" Lady Hertford soon acquiesced to his promises of passion, and she became a constant presence at Carlton House and Brighton Pavilion. Mrs. Fitzherbert had to watch her lovelorn husband trail after her grand, disdainful rival, whose heavy bosom trembled with his presents of jewels.

6

⚜

*Forming the Character of
a Young Princess*

In July 1804, the king decided to assume responsibility for Princess Charlotte's education. He decreed that he wished her to live at Lower Lodge, one of the many dwellings scattered through Windsor Great Park, three miles south of the castle, and be brought up mainly under his direction. The prince dissented. It took the whole of 1805 for them to agree that when her father was at home, which was usually during the summer, the little girl should live at Warwick House, a tall and poky seventeenth-century house at the end of an alley behind Carlton House, and spend the rest of the year with the king, the queen, and her aunts at Windsor. Even worse, from the point of view of the prince, the king took back the £5,000 a year that he had given to his son for Charlotte's education (the prince had hardly been spending it well) and decreed that the Princess of Wales should be allowed regular visits from her daughter. "It is quite charming to see the Princess and her child together," he declared.

Warwick House had previously functioned as accommodation for members of the Prince's household. The property was small and dilapidated, "miserably out of repair and almost falling to ruins," snorted a later governess. Charlotte had a drawing room, bedroom, and dressing room (which acted as her maid's bedroom) on the first floor, with a bedroom and sitting room for her governess nearby. The Princess of Wales was forbidden to visit.

Charlotte had been the only child in a houseful of adults, and now the king had plans to introduce even more elderly and middle-aged people to her life. He was quite clear that she should "both day and night be constantly under the eyes of responsible persons." Such a program of quasi surveillance was hardly the way to quash her tempestuous and rebellious nature. When Lady Elgin relinquished her young charge, she described her as quite perfect: "free from all fault whatever, both in character and disposition." She noted "that her mind was pure and innocent, and that her progress in learning had been uncommonly great." Anxious to avoid any suggestion that she had been too indulgent or lax in teaching her charge, Lady Elgin had lied. At the age of nine, Charlotte was lazy, slapdash, and unable to concentrate.

The king appointed Dr. John Fisher, bishop of Exeter, who had taught the princes, to superintend the child's education, assisted by Lady de Clifford. Small, thin, and irritable, Mrs. Alicia Campbell, widow of a governor of Bermuda, was to be sub-governess. Mrs. Udney, a gossipy, brassy woman who was prickly and fond of drink, was employed as assistant sub-governess. The Reverend George Nott was sub-preceptor, with responsibility for religious instruction, Latin, and ancient history; and there would be specialist instructors in music, dancing, drawing, writing, German, French, history, and geography. It was a punishing set of tutors for a girl with no love of learning.

Lady de Clifford took the easiest route with Charlotte and never tried to admonish or discipline her. The two became good friends. The little princess adored her indulgent nurse, Mrs. Gagarin, and respected Mrs. Campbell, but she detested Mrs. Udney, whom she called "Mrs. Nibs," believing her a vulgar gossip. She tried to avoid the pompous Dr. Fisher, whom she called "the Great UP" after his habit of ponderously emphasizing the last syllable of "bishop."

The bishop's assistant, Dr. Nott, took the princess for prayers and religious instruction from eight until nine every morning. She would then eat breakfast and have a walk before further lessons. Between half past one and three o'clock, she dressed in more formal attire and ate dinner, and was then allowed to play or go for a drive in the carriage. The hours after dinner were occupied with composition, music, and dancing, and then she would be allowed to play before going to bed at eight.

Charlotte's education was designed for a future queen. It was usually deemed quite sufficient for girls of her age to have a few accomplishments, along with some facts of history and geography learned by rote (knowledge of context was not necessarily required). In the 1790s, Mary Wollstonecraft had inveighed against the notion that girls should be lightly educated, but the tradition remained that they should not be too clever or bookish. Most were taught at home by their mothers, who tended to use traditional texts such as Goldsmith's *History of England*. A girl was to be educated to think conventionally, to entertain her husband, to foster social bonds through an ability to draw and play, to sew, and most of all to be a good—acquiescent—wife. As Hannah More wrote, girls should never dispute. The "liberty of private judgement" was fine, but "they should by no means be encouraged to contract a contentious and contradictory turn" and instead should foster a "submissive temper, and a forbearing spirit." Charlotte's future did not lie in sewing and obedience, and so her education was much more wide-ranging than that of the average girl.

The king hoped to make his granddaughter "an honour and comfort to her relations, and a blessing to the dominions over which she may hereafter preside." Unfortunately, the schoolroom soon collapsed into rivalry. Lady de Clifford quickly grew to hate the pompous, ever-critical Dr. Fisher, and the two argued constantly over who should control Charlotte's education. Not surprisingly, Charlotte failed to thrive and became even more rebellious, kicking against her strict program of learning. Dr. Nott was shocked by the princess's lack of diligence, her poor spelling, and her appalling handwriting. After a few months of teaching her, he was almost in despair. He returned her composition, complaining that there were fifty spelling mistakes, unreadable passages, and errors that a "common servant would have blushed to have committed." He begged her to reform.

> *Where, may I ask your Royal Highness, is this to end, or when are we to have the satisfaction of seeing your mind animated with a becoming pride and a generous resolution to improve? More than three*

months have passed, during which the most unremitting exertions
have been employed by those about you, and what is the progress you
have made? Let the enclosed paper speak. I shall only add that igno-
rance is disgraceful in proportion to the rank of the person in whom
it is found, and that negligence, when the means of improvement are
in our power, is criminal in the sight of the Almighty.

Charlotte felt genuine affection for the clergyman, and she never meant
to be cruel, but her hatred of being chained down and her fondness for having her own way made her a difficult pupil. As convinced of her own right-
ness as her father was of his, she continued to dash off her work lazily, if at
all. Even worse, she lied and passed on slanderous gossip. Only when Dr.
Nott collapsed with strain did she attempt to reform. "I shall labour to recover your health by my industry, and wish to please and make you happy,"
she wrote, overwhelmed by a contrition that subsided almost immediately.

Still, life at Warwick House was preferable to Lower Lodge, which the
little girl hated. She felt lonely and isolated there, and visits to her relations
at the chilly castle gave her scant pleasure. The queen, angry and irritated
by the king's unstable behavior, criticized her five daughters and upbraided
her granddaughter. Charlotte's greatest pleasure was playing with the
grandchildren of Lady de Clifford. She tormented the three little girls,
rolling them down hills into nettles and always winning at games of hide-
and-seek. Their brother, George, became her partner in crime, even sneak-
ing a strange mess on to Lady de Clifford's plate at lunch, much to the
governess's fury. "A pretty Queen you'll make," sniffed George to Charlotte.

In her free time, Charlotte relished visiting the shops with her governess, pretending to be one of Lady de Clifford's grandchildren and spending her own money on toys and jewelry. She was allowed £10 a week, an
astonishing sum for a child when a week's lodging, meals, and fires cost one
guinea and sixpence for a working man, four guineas for a man of fashion.
As she would do throughout her life, she showered her little friends with
gifts, presenting George Keppel, Lady de Clifford's grandson, with a pony
and an expensive watch, slipping him money when he asked for it, and
giving dolls to his sisters.

Charlotte could not understand why her father had tried to refuse to let her be brought up by the king, and then ignored her. She met him so infrequently that she fell into a nervous temper when she did. "You do not see Charlotte at all to advantage," the queen told her eldest son. "She is quite different with us, I assure you." He remained unconvinced. "You always say so, I know. It is very unfortunate, but she appears to me half in the sulks." For the prince, Charlotte was a bitter reminder of her boisterous and demanding mother. He liked women and girls who were docile and deferential, but even when Charlotte tried to seem sweetly cosseting, he paid her little attention. A letter survives that she wrote to him aged ten, begging for affection.

> Forgive me, my dearest papa, for writing to you when you have so much business, but I saw you so unwell last night that I could not help writing to see how you are. Believe me, my dearest papa, that my whole aim is to gain your regard and affection; if I should lose that, I shall be destitute of everything in this world most dear to me; but I trust that will never happen. Oh how I wish I could see more of you! but I hope I shall in time. I am sensible how irksome it must be to you to see me, feeling I can be no companion to you to amuse you when in health and spirits & am too young to soothe you when in affliction. Believe me, I am always truly happy when I do see you.

Despite the hours of labor expended on the letter, it seemed to make little difference. There is no recorded reply from the prince, and he continued to neglect her. Both he and his wife were spoiled, self-centered, and obsessed with the idea of themselves as victims. Their daughter came very low on their list of priorities.

Desperate for attention, the young princess became so melancholy that she decided to write her will, a sad act for such a small child. Like the prince leaving his goods to Mrs. Fitzherbert after his marriage, she bequeathed her belongings to express her anger with her father. She left her houses and jewels to her governesses and demanded that the king make Nott a bishop. Of the hated sub-governess Mrs. Udney, Charlotte wrote, "Nothing to Mrs. Udney for reasons."

When the prince heard of the will, he was incensed. Never one to experience pangs of guilt, he decided that the staff at Warwick House had been influencing his daughter against him, and discharged Mrs. Campbell. Dr. Nott, distraught with shame, took to his bed for weeks and was later forced to resign. "I shall ever remember your kindness and your good advice," wrote Charlotte to him sadly. Dr. Fisher, hastily attempting to shift attention from himself, told the prince that Mrs. Udney had shown her charge a shocking caricature of Emma Hamilton—Nelson's mistress, who was attempting to charm the prince—and explained the sexual innuendoes. Unfortunately for Charlotte, Mrs. Udney was not dismissed. The prince liked his exasperating daughter to be ruled by those she hated.

Months passed, and a tutor to replace Dr. Nott was not appointed. Charlotte fell behind, and her German master had to hint to the queen that the little princess was "losing a great deal of time." The queen, Charlotte told her mother, observed that it was "of little consequence" whether I learned more or less. This was too much for the twelve-year-old princess. "She means to keep me in ignorance so that she may govern me," Charlotte fumed. "But I am determined never to be governed by anyone of my own sex. I shall always be happy to hear your opinion, my dear mamma, but even you shan't govern me." Charlotte, like her father and mother, was fond of making declarations about her own character—as befitted a future queen. A new tutor was finally appointed a year after Dr. Nott left. Charlotte returned to her lessons, but with little enthusiasm.

At the end of 1806, the Duke of Brunswick, Caroline's aged father, died while battling Napoleon's forces. His kingdom was seized, and his widow set off to England to throw herself on the mercy of her brother. The duchess was one subject on which the queen and Princess Caroline were in assent: They detested her. The king, however, was delighted to see his sister once more, and she was thrilled to see England for the first time in forty-three years. Princess Caroline, who was living mostly at Kensington Palace, offered her mother Montague House. The Duchess of Brunswick soon settled her ample girth at Blackheath, and the prince declared that Charlotte should visit her grandmother for two hours on a Saturday, when her mother might be present.

In the summer of 1807, Charlotte had her first seaside holiday, in Weymouth, with her governesses and, to her great pleasure, without Dr. Fisher. The princess relished her freedom on the sands. British seaside resorts were enjoying a great renaissance, packed with aristocrats and gentility who could not travel overseas thanks to the wars raging across Europe. Emma Hamilton declared that all those at Weymouth neglected the heiress presumptive to goggle at herself and her daughter, "Nelson's angel." If that was the case, Charlotte perhaps enjoyed a little time out of the glare of constant scrutiny. The following year, on a visit to Bognor, she felt so relaxed that, according to one observer, she would amble down to town in the morning and gossip with the baker over his latest batch of hot morning rolls. She shared her grandfather's fascination with the lives of ordinary people, but happily lacked his obsession with protocol.

Charlotte looked like a Hanoverian princess, even though she was hoydenish and devoid of the requisite reserve. She was tall, statuesque (indeed, tending to fat), with pale skin, blue eyes, and her mother's fair hair. Lady Charlotte Bury, née Campbell, lady-in-waiting to the Princess of Wales, commented that she "had all the fulness of a person of five and twenty":

> *Princess Charlotte is above the middle height, extremely spread for her age; for her bosom is full, but finely shaped; her shoulders large, and her whole person voluptuous; but a nature to become soon spoiled, and without much care and exercise she will shortly lose all beauty in fat and clumsiness. Her skin is white, but not a transparent white; there is little or no shade in her face; but her features are very fine. . . . Her feet are rather small, and her hands and arms are finely moulded. She has a hesitation in her speech, amounting almost to a stammer; an additional proof, if any were wanting, of her being her father's own child; but in everything she is his very image. Her voice is flexible, and its tones dulcet, except when she laughs; then it becomes too loud.*

Charlotte had the "style and prestige that comes with royalty and power." But although she looked like an adult, she still behaved like a willful child. Lady Charlotte thought her "kind hearted, clever and enthusiastic" but also "capricious, self-willed and obstinate." She concluded that the princess's "faults have evidently never been checked, nor her virtues fostered." Visitors who met Charlotte at Carlton House or at one of her mother's parties were shocked by her poor posture and noisy behavior. At fourteen, the heir to the throne after her father was more tomboy than young lady, lolling on couches and stretching her legs out, showing her drawers, and deaf to the remonstrances of Lady de Clifford. "She is forward, dogmatical on all subjects, buckish about horses, and full of exclamations very like swearing," marveled Lady Glenbervie, lady-in-waiting to the Princess of Wales. She had the manners of her mother and the arrogance of her father.

Charlotte sauntered into her teens, continuing to scandalize the court with her antics. "I do not think her manner dignified, as a princess's ought to be, or indeed, as I should wish a daughter of mine to behave," declared Lady Albinia Cumberland, a Lady of the Bedchamber at Windsor. "She hates her 'Granny,' as she calls her—loves nobody except Princesses Mary and Sophia, goes swaggering about, and she twangs hands with all the men, is in awe of no one and glories in her independent way of thinking." She could be warm, friendly, and often charming, but she was oddly aggressive. Her playmate George Keppel declared that she liked to stride about and clench her fists like a boxer, even going so far as to pummel him. In great contrast to her retired, embroidering aunts, the princess was most content when petting her army of dogs or galloping across the park from Windsor. On one occasion, she terrified Lady de Clifford by taking the reins of the carriage and setting off at a wild gallop, ignoring her governess's screams and shouting, "Nothing like exercise!" The prince, however, was proud of his daughter's fearless riding and daring jumping. When he boasted to his friend Berkeley Paget of her skill on a horse, announcng that she could turn corners at a gallop, Paget politely replied that the princess must "have had pretty good nerves." "God damn you, isn't she my daughter?" came the reply.

Charlotte was an accomplished pianist with a passion for Mozart and Haydn. She was also a seeker after sensation. Lost in a hopeless infatuation with Lord Byron, she admired his portrait intensely, declaring that he had "something so very much above the common sort of beauty." She enjoyed the novel *The Sicilian Mysteries,* considering it "full of mystery and remarkably well worked up" (not for her were complaints like Lady Holland's that such books were "sad trash, abounding with the general taste for spectres, hobgoblins, castles, etc."). Young ladies with a taste for lurid fiction were ushered toward Jane Austen's books (and the prince also approved—he later ensured he was the dedicatee of *Emma*), for as one reviewer noted,

Pride and Prejudice had "no dark passages; no secret chambers; no wind-howlings in long galleries; no drops of blood on a rusty dagger." Attempting to seem like a docile young lady, Charlotte remarked she had learned her lessons from *Sense and Sensibility*. "I think Maryanne & me are very alike in disposition, that certainly I am not so good, the same imprudence, &c. however remain very like."

Rattled by his daughter's adult appearance, the prince clamped down on her freedoms. He refused to allow her to be confirmed, appear at court, or attend any gatherings but children's balls. If she went to the theater or opera, she had to sit at the back of the box and leave quietly before the end of the last act. He gave her £800 a year for dress, which was enough for a child but insufficient for the grown woman Charlotte appeared. She relied on the ingenuity of her maid and dresser Mrs. Louis to make her gowns seem more elegant and expensive than they were, and she began running up terrible debts. Although ready-to-wear garments had been advertised since the 1790s, nearly every English man and woman had their clothes and shoes made by specialists, and material was bought separately. Ordering dresses, therefore, could be a risk: They might not turn out quite as planned and thus would be thrust to the back of the closet. The costs of being a royal princess were high, especially as, like all her Hanoverian relations, Charlotte loved fine clothes.

It was not easy being future heir to the throne. Charlotte's deportment, health, learning, accomplishments, dress, and appearance were pointedly discussed and surveyed. Behavior or failings that would have been passed off as youthful phases in other children were in her the cause of ominous declarations about future character. It was her loss that she had no siblings to share the heavy weight of expectations. The prince had rebelled against his own strict upbringing, but now he inflicted a similarly punitive regime on his daughter, and was indeed a more controlling parent than his own father had ever been. Ill-disciplined, he imposed a rigid schedule on his daughter. Lazy, boastful, mendacious, and self-indulgent, he was always finding similar faults in his child. He was mercurial, veering wildly between excessive cruelty and emotional, tearful declarations, but he always expected her to be scrapingly obsequious to him. "I pity her that she is born to be a Queen," wrote Lady Charlotte Bury. "She would be a much happier being if she were a private individual."

7

Sex, Lies, and Scandals

No family was ever composed of *such odd people*," Charlotte mused, "I believe, as they all *draw different* ways, & there *have happened* such extraordinary things, that in any other family, either public or private, are never herd [*sic*] of before." She was right. The royals grew more ridiculous every year. In 1809, a handsome twenty-six-year-old woman stood in front of the six hundred MPs of the House of Commons and declared that the Duke of York, commander in chief of the army, had encouraged her to take bribes from men who wished for army commissions. Wearing an exquisite powder blue gown with a deep décolletage and carrying a white swan's-down muff, Mrs. Mary Anne Clarke was interviewed in the Commons by Spencer Perceval, chancellor of the exchequer, and infuriated him with her saucy answers. She claimed repeatedly that the duke had assisted her in selling commissions—and she had even pinned the names of those desiring promotions to the bed curtains in their home. "Mrs. Clarke," sighed William Wilberforce, "is elegantly dressed, consummately impudent and very clever."

Mary Anne was a low-born courtesan turned kept mistress who had attracted the duke, who was separated from his dog-obsessed duchess and always eager for comfort. He set Mary Anne up in a grand house near Portman Square furnished extravagantly with chandeliers, handsome sofas, and paintings. He also expected his mistress to be fabulously dressed and waited on by a full fleet of servants. His allowance was far too small to supply such luxury, and so Mary Anne began taking bribes.

The case in the House of Commons was deeply embarrassing for the royal family. The duke's puerile love letters were read out, and he was mocked as a corrupt, lovesick old fool. The duke had ended the relationship, and Mary Anne emerged as the heroine: a young mother who had been forced into selling commissions to accommodate her lover's wild demands and then been cavalierly abandoned. "The sensation in London about this nonsensical business is marvellous," sniffed the writer Charles Lamb. "Thousands of ballads, caricatures, lives, of Mrs. Clarke, in every blind alley." The day after the Mary Anne Clarke trial, the Drury Lane theater caught fire. "I think that even the dreadful calamity of the burning of Drury Lane will not be without its advantages," pronounced one woman, "if it makes people think and talk of something else."

It seemed as if the royal family could not plummet any lower in public opinion. There was a Prince of Wales who cared only about dragging his estranged wife's name through the mud; a host of spendthrift brothers, all leeches on the state; and five spinster sisters, two of whom had taken lovers from among their father's servants. And then soon after the Clarke affair, a yet more damaging scandal blew up around the Duke of Cumberland. The strangest royal brother of all, "Prince Whiskerandos" was painfully thin compared with his plump siblings. He had a sunken left eye that swirled but did not focus, a mustache, and long, catlike whiskers. His behavior was odder than his appearance. He was aggressive, and his language was often offensive. There were suggestions of dubious sexual practices, underworld contacts, and blackmail. To him, all women were fair game—young, old, married, or unmarried. He had tried to seduce his own sister, Princess Sophia, and even considered invading a nunnery to ravish the nuns when he was a young soldier. Charlotte dubbed him the "bottom of all evil" and was very afraid of him.

On the night of May 31, 1809, the duke claimed that he was woken at just before three in the morning by a saber slashing through his bed curtains. Screaming for his valet, Cornelius Neale, he leaped from his bed and dashed to the anteroom, sustaining a stab wound to the thigh. Armed with a poker, Neale advanced into the room, but it was empty; the duke's bloodstained sword lay on the floor. He called for the guard, and a search was begun. When they entered the room of Joseph Sellis, another valet to the duke, they found him dead in his bed, blood streaming from his slashed throat. The jury at the inquest declared that Sellis had killed himself after attempting to kill the duke, but rumors began circulating that the duke had murdered his valet in revenge for his attempt to end their homosexual affair.

The newspapers fizzed with gossip about the wayward brothers who succeeded only at plunging the monarchy into disgrace. Through it all, Charlotte was their one hope: the blue-eyed, golden-haired girl who seemed so spirited and innocent. The public took to idealizing her as the perfect princess: sweet, reserved, possessed of a kind heart, and entirely unlike her self-centered father.

Charlotte's youngest aunt, Princess Amelia, had began to suffer from a pain in her side. Her illness worsened despite various courses of medical treatment and bleedings. By 1810 she was in almost constant pain, hardly able to eat, retching repeatedly, and fainting. Although the doctors did not diagnose it as such, she was suffering from tuberculosis and dying at the age of twenty-seven. She begged Sir Henry Halford—her handsome doctor, always ambitious to keep on the right side of whoever held power in the royal family—to allow her to ask her father for permission to marry her beloved Charles Fitzroy. He refused, asserting that the king's mind would be utterly broken and his insanity would return. Heartbroken, Amelia went into a quick decline, and in late October her hand was apparently perfectly transparent. She died on November 1, with Princess Mary sitting by her bedside. She left her belongings to her maid and Charles Fitzroy.

The long, drawn-out death of Amelia was too much for the seventy-two-year-old king to bear. At the party to mark the golden anniversary of his accession, held at Windsor Castle on October 25, 1810, he was nervous and agitated, and some onlookers were frightened by his behavior. Specialist doctors were appointed, and by November 4 he was restrained in a straitjacket and locked away from his family, although everybody heard him wailing. He was, Charlotte wrote, "quite lost" and "takes no notice of anything that went on in his room, and knows no one." She could no longer rely on her grandfather to protect her against her father's demands.

Charlotte turned fifteen at the beginning of January 1811, after a cold and unhappy Christmas. The princesses were angry that their mother kept them in strict retirement while their father was ill. The queen was afraid of her husband, perpetually irritable with her daughters and still mourning Amelia, and she dreaded her son becoming regent. After a life spent waiting desperately for power, the prince was impatient to gain the pomp and financial resources of a king. He was in debt to the tune of more than £500,000, and he had great plans for how he would spend his money.

8

✣

Prince Regent

On February 6, 1811, the Prince of Wales was sworn in as prince regent at a meeting of the Privy Council. Charlotte had her grooms saddle up her horse and ride with her past the windows, eager to remind the councillors that the new regent had a daughter who was nearly grown up. The spotlight was easily snatched from the prince: He was bloated, sickly, and debauched, while she was young and full of life and optimism.

The Whigs had supported the prince for years in the expectation of spectacular rewards and the highest government offices. But no sooner had George become regent than he was grasped by an unfamiliar caution. His family and the royal doctor counseled that should the king recover his mind and find the Whigs in power, the shock might kill him. Plump Lady Hertford, a diehard Tory, took every opportunity to whisper in the prince's ear against them. Most of all, the prince was simply too lazy to concern himself with the complex political arguments and the infighting that would occur within the Whig party if they came to power. He had other matters occupying his mind, too: a splendid party to celebrate his regency. His father had been content to enjoy a retired life in drafty Windsor and drab ceremonials. The prince regent was determined to be a London-based ruler, a leader of fashion, style, and taste who put on superb entertainments.

The Tories remained in power, and the Whigs gasped at the betrayal by the prince. Their eyes began wandering in the direction of Princess Charlotte. Surely, they reasoned, the fat old regent could not continue in his position until his death; the country would not stand for it. Young, beautiful Charlotte must soon be queen.

After spending his youth plotting against his father and building circles of supporters around himself, the prince was paranoid that his daughter would do the same. Discomfited by her adult appearance, her boldness in company and her popularity with the Whigs, he tried to sequester her from view. But now that Charlotte was so much closer to the throne, she was keen to capitalize on the public hunger to see her and she begged her father to allow her to hear his speech in the House of Lords.

> *My dearest father is always so kind and indulgent to me that I feel emboldened in troubling him with a few lines. It would be a very high gratification to me (if you should see no impropriety) to hear your Speech in the House of Lords, for it is a subject very interesting to all, particularly so to me. . . . If, however, you should my dear father, find any objection to it or should disapprove, I shall give up all thoughts of it, perfectly satisfied that you have good reasons for denying me.*

The last thing the prince wanted was to have pretty, popular Charlotte displayed to all in the House of Lords, catching the attention of the press and disgruntled Whigs. He ensured that she stayed at home.

The regent promoted himself to the rank of field marshal (a grand title for a man who had never fought) and devoted himself to spending money, turning Carlton House into a fairy palace for the party to celebrate his regency. Frantic to attend, Charlotte poured out her bitterness to her former sub-governess, Miss Hayman, who had moved to the household of the Princess of Wales.

> *Only to tell you that the Prince Regent gives a magnificent ball on the 5th June. I have not been invited, nor do I know if I shall be or not. If I should not, it would make a great noise in the world, as the friends*

I have seen have repeated over and over it is my duty to go there; it is
proper that I should. Really I do think it will be very hard if I am not
asked.

The prince knew that the Whigs were circling his daughter and trying to
reach her through her "friends," and he did not want her flaunting her popularity as she had done at his investiture. He packed her off to Windsor to
stay with her grandmother and aunts.

The most powerful man in England was terribly busy. He was compiling
lists of guests, decorating his splendid house, and negotiating the purchase
of a Rembrandt for £5,000. He ordered poultry and then changed his mind
about the date, so that cheap surplus chickens and guinea fowl flooded
onto the market. Finally, after months of deliberations, it seemed clear that
the king would not recover for some time. Two thousand invitations were
hurriedly sent off, some to people who had already expired.

On June 19, 1811, the party to celebrate the regency lit up St. James's.
Ostensibly excused as an entertainment for Louis-Philippe, the exiled
claimant to the throne of France, the single night of entertainment cost an
estimated £120,000. After queuing in their carriages for hours along the
Mall, the splendidly attired guests, including many members of the exiled
French royal family, were crammed into the gardens at Carlton House.
Lady Hertford sat proudly at the top of the table, displaying the bosom that
showed off jewels so wonderfully. The queen did not attend. Adamant that
she could not enjoy company during the king's illness, she commanded the
royal princesses to remain with her in Windsor. Princess Caroline whiled
away the day at Kensington Palace, lonely because the prince had invited
her ladies-in-waiting. Mrs. Fitzherbert had also received an invitation, but
not to sit at the top table. She asked the prince to reconsider, and he refused. She stayed away, and they never spoke again.

The fete was the finest London had ever seen. Carlton House had been
spectacularly decorated with drapes, glittering decorations, and huge can-
delabra. There "was not a spot without some finery on it, gold upon gold,"
reported one visitor. The party began at nine, and at half past two in the
morning, the luckiest guests went to dine. There, puffed up in his field
marshal's uniform, the prince oversaw proceedings, perched in front of a
large fountain splashing into a long stream that ran the course of the two-

hundred-foot table and was bordered by banks of green moss and flowers. At the end was a model lake surrounded by tiny urns puffing sweet-smelling smoke. Gold and silver fish tinkled down under miniature bridges, but within a few hours most were floating dead on the surface of the water. The regent, attended by seven servers, reveled at the sight of the country's most distinguished aristocrats sitting below him, the de facto king of London. At nearly fifty, he was finally free.

"What think you of bubbling *brooks & mossy banks* at Carlton House," snorted the poet Percy Bysshe Shelley. "Nor will it be the last bauble which the nation must buy to amuse this overgrown bantling of Regency." Eager to show off further, the new regent threw open the doors of Carlton House to the public for three days after the celebration. Crowds poured in, trampling over one another in their eagerness to inspect the prince's fine interiors and expensive collections of art and furniture. On the final day, the press was so great that some of the women guests were squashed by the crowds, escaping into the grounds with their dresses half torn from their backs.

Charlotte spent the great day shut up in stuffy Windsor with the queen and the "old girls," just able to hear the wails of the king through the walls. She waited for letters and newspaper reports, hungering for every detail about the party. She was painfully bored. Every day at Windsor continued the same. "We go on vegetating as we have done for the last twenty years of our lives," sighed Princess Elizabeth.

9

The Nunnery

Have you many pleasant parties?" Charlotte wrote plaintively to a friend. "I assure you a little London news to such a country lady as I am is quite a charity." She hated being shut up in the "Nunnery," as Princess Sophia called it. Her only entertainment in the hotly barren months was a visit to Eton with the queen.

The queen had warmed to her granddaughter and encouraged her boisterous sense of humor. "Charlotte is not at all afraid of the Queen," wrote Princess Mary. "[S]he runs on from subject to subject and into all her jokes with the Q., just as she does with us, and stands over the Queen's chair & yesterday afternoon kept the Queen laughing from eight o'clock until 10." There was precious little else to laugh at. The worst of life at Windsor was not the cries of the mad king from his locked rooms, but the terrible bickering among the four princesses, desperate to escape their sorry imprisonment in the castle. For the forty-one-year-old Princess Elizabeth and her three middle-aged sisters, there was nothing but dull days of embroidery, with only female attendants for company (indeed, few aristocrats cherished the position of lady-in-waiting to such retired ladies). Charlotte noted gloomily, "The same thing each hour is marked out to the moment." She liked Princess Sophia, attracted by her gentle character and fascinated by the gossip that she had had an affair. But she hated her aunts Augusta, Elizabeth, and Mary, the family beauty, and carped back when they picked on her. The very sight of them infuriated her. As she wrote, "It will be dreadfully dul [*sic*] to be shut up for 5 hours in the royal menagerie, for the e[vening]s are so short that there is *no going out* after dinner, so they *work, work without* a word being utter'd."

The queen had noted nervously that there was no "great variety of amusement" at Windsor, but she hoped that she would be able to make "Charlotte's visit as little dull as circumstances will admit of." But the queen had scant concept of recreation outside of bleak rounds of embroidery. Charlotte was so lonely that she even enjoyed a visit from the coarse Duke of Cumberland. He busied himself teasing the governess, Mrs. Udney, first waltzing with Charlotte and then forcing the bosomy governess to waltz with him. Charlotte wrote, "[This] was a *most amusing scene* as you *can well conceive.*" She hoped to see more of the duke. "I am quite happy I am so good a scholar & trust that *ere long* we may waltz very often together." The duke did not come to see her frequently. He visited only to flirt with Mrs. Udney.

Charlotte had struck up a warm friendship with twenty-one-year-old Margaret Mercer Elphinstone, the daughter of Lord Keith. The princess had perhaps met Miss Elphinstone through her uncle, the Duke of Clarence, who had once retained Lord Keith in his household. Margaret, whom her friends called Mercer, was rich, pretty, intelligent, a Whig sympathizer, and eight years Charlotte's senior. The princess was soon pouring out her heart to her new friend, scribbling her exuberant letters littered with capitals and italics. She confided her wish to win her father's approbation and begged Mercer for help. "I shall regularly transmit to my *commander-in-chief* my plan of *operations,* my manouvers, my skirmishes &c," she bubbled. "If I *win* the *battle* & *obtain* THE flag, I will lay it at your feet, altho' you gave me yourself *my armour.*" She made sure to report to her friend when the prince came to dine, and whether he was "very kind to me" or "*hardly spoke to me* AT ALL, & when he did his manner was *so cold* that it was very distressing." She was thrilled when she received "3 boxes of prints" from Ragley, the country estate of Lady Hertford and her husband, a present from Lady Hertford that she took to be proof that she was "in high favour." Miss Elphinstone listened to Charlotte's often tedious confidences and advised her carefully. In return, she expected absolute loyalty and did not take kindly to the princess having other companions or expressing admiration for her governesses. Charlotte quickly learned that the way to please Miss Elphinstone was to imply that only she possessed her love and confidence.

Charlotte's careful recordings of when she was in favor with her father more closely resemble the hopeful utterances of a courtier than those of a daughter. All her efforts seemed worthwhile, though, when her father directed some of his famous charm her way. On one occasion the regent dined with her and told a series of "ridiculous jokes," climaxing by mocking Mrs. Udney's husband as *"the most hideous being that ever was seen"* and saying "that *no picture* or drawing *could convey* an adiquate idea of his ugliness, & that he was sure Mrs. Udney could not have liked him." Then, Charlotte reported: "[Between] the prince's *laughing,* her *crying,* her *apologies,* it was excellent. As to myself, I was near expiring—I *talked* as *much* & as *easily* as *ever* I *could."* The princess—apart from her beloved Mercer—far preferred the company of men.

Over the hot summer, London steamed. The waste of one million people oozed into the Thames and heated slowly under the broiling sun. The drunks sat outside and burned in the heat. In Windsor, Charlotte mooched about Lower Lodge, bored and restless, calling in tradesmen and fingering new silks or wrought bracelets. She bought generous presents for Miss Elphinstone and other friends and soon began to fall into debt.

The precocious princess was desperate for adventure. "George Fitz-Clarence is arrived from Portugal," she wrote to Miss Elphinstone. "I saw him the very day he arrived in town, much grown and looking very well." Seventeen-year-old Captain George, the eldest son of the Duke of Clarence by the beautiful actress Mrs. Jordan, was handsome, brave, and full of life. After sweet smiles, poignant glances, and friendly rides, Charlotte became infatuated with her dashing cousin. Sadly, however, he was soon called away to his regiment in Brighton. She was briefly despondent, but then a new admirer cantered into view. Lieutenant Charles Hesse, a handsome young officer in the Light Dragoons, had begun aiming cheekily suggestive grins her way. When she went out driving in her carriage in Windsor Great Park with Lady de Clifford, he drew up alongside on his horse and waved at her. Charlotte was soon in thrall to him. A suggestion that he was the son of the Duke of York by a German aristocrat served to intensify his charm.

Every morning Charlotte dressed carefully in case she might see Hesse, and then propped herself up smiling in her carriage, carefully arranged to show off her best side. On the days when he did not appear, her heart plunged. Finally, quite overwhelmed by passion, she confessed all to her mother. Princess Caroline listened sympathetically, then, to Charlotte's great surprise, volunteered to help by giving Hesse notes to pass to her daughter, thus providing the pair with a legitimate reason to meet. The young lovers exchanged letters and grasped every opportunity to grow closer.

Poor Lady de Clifford began to realize that her charge was passionately in love. Visions of a raving regent filled her confused mind. After six weeks had passed, she begged Charlotte to stop seeing Hesse and to give up riding out. The lovesick princess flew into a passion and vowed to see her admirer as much as she wished. She dashed to tell all to her mother in Kensington, who was only too pleased to stroke her hair and ask for every detail. The princess even offered to pass on her daughter's letters to Hesse and, still more surprisingly, gave Hesse a portrait of Charlotte without her daughter's knowledge. Delighted at finding a way of taking revenge against her estranged husband, Caroline declared that she could even arrange meetings for the pair. When Hesse's regiment left Windsor, Caroline offered to let him into her room through a secret door in the gardens. Charlotte was waiting nervously in the sitting room. Caroline, smiling broadly, threw open her bedroom door to the pair, pushed them in, and locked the door after them, crying, *"Je vous laisse, amusez vous."*

It does not seem as if anything very daring went on in the chamber (and Princess Caroline was probably listening at the door), but for young people in their position, the very act of holding hands in secret was seen as shockingly transgressive, and Charlotte was compromising her reputation terribly. They even exchanged rings. She was rebelling against her father, who had hidden her away at Windsor, and her spinster aunts, who seemed so dead to love.

Excited by her love affair, Princess Charlotte dashed about, buzzing with pent-up energy. Catherine, Grand Duchess of Oldenburg, wrote to her brother, the tsar, amazed to see the future queen of England march up to men and shake their hands. "At every motion it seems as tho' she were going to show her knee. She looks like a boy, or rather a ragamuffin. . . . She is ravishing, and it is a crime to have allowed her to acquire such habits."

The grand duchess thought Charlotte pretty, with lovely blue eyes, good teeth, and a pretty mouth and skin, but too fat, especially "about the hips." Charlotte was beginning to put on weight. There was little to do at Windsor other than eat and think of Hesse and ride out in the blazing sun hoping to catch a glimpse of him. "You are grown very fat and very much sunburnt," her grandmother told her crossly. "Oh Lord," the old lady said of a picture given to her by the Princess of Wales, "it's frightful, quite frightful."

Charlotte turned sixteen in 1812, after a chilly winter in which she felt like a *"shriveled lemon."* Her father celebrated her birthday by throwing a generous dinner at Carlton House. In fine spirits, the regent showed his guests all around his house before sitting down with them to the lavish spread. "I am never so happy," he declared drunkenly, tears rolling down his fat face, "as when in the bosom of my family." Charlotte felt as though she was "upon thorns" because she had to eat with him and then leave early to dine with her mother in Blackheath. Almost as soon as she had trotted out of the door, her uncles cracked open their largest bottles of port and began to get royally drunk.

The young princess was thrilled to be back in London. February 22 was to mark her first outing to the opera, preceded by a ceremonial dinner at Carlton House. The evening was a failure. Charlotte sat in her finery, endured a dull meal in the company of dreary politicians, then watched her father lurch into a drunken defense of his decision to retain his Tory ministers. Swearing and swaggering, he offered the Whigs an insultingly small part in a coalition government. As one guest, Thomas Granville, recorded:

> The Princess Charlotte rose to make her first appearance at the Opera, but rose in tears and expressed herself strongly to Sheridan, as he led her out, upon the distress which she had fled in hearing her father's language. Nor should it be forgot that, at the Opera, seeing Lord Grey

in the box opposite to her, she got up, and kissed her hand to him
repeatedly, in the sight of the whole Opera.

So began the myth of the lovely, tearful Charlotte and her allegiance to the Whigs. Lord Byron wrote a poetic response to the reports of the disastrous dinner:

> *Weep, daughter of a royal line,*
> *A Sire's disgrace, a realm's decay;*
> *Ah, happy! if each tear of thine*
> *Could wash a father's fault away.*
>
> *Weep—for thy tears are virtue's tears—*
> *Auspicious to these suffering isles:*
> *And be each drop in future years,*
> *Repaid thee by thy people's smiles.*

The poem was first published anonymously in the *Morning Chronicle*, but by February, Byron was publishing it under his own name. The nation was investing its hope in the sixteen-year-old princess, oddly eager to see a sheltered teenager become queen. For the public, she was every virtue personified: graceful, reserved, sensitive, charming, self-disciplined, and, most important of all, sympathetic to the Whigs.

The Whigs had been trying hard to attract the heir to the throne. Handsome, vain forty-eight-year-old Lord Grey, the lover of Georgiana, Duchess of Devonshire, for ten years and the father of her daughter, made every attempt to charm and flatter Charlotte. She was pleased to adopt a political position that differed from that of her father and uncles. Of her Tory uncle the Duke of York, she judged that their politics did not agree, "which could never make us quite easy together." She blamed her father's mistress for driving him into the arms of the Tories, writing crossly that he visited Lady Hertford *"every day & dines there every day."* The regent, although he had once been an ardent supporter of the Whigs, was angry about his daughter's passionate interest in his enemies and her mother's political supporters. He punished her by forbidding her to see Miss Elphinstone and ignored her every plea to him to change his mind.

On May 11, 1812, the prime minister, Spencer Perceval, was shot by a madman. The regent did not call an election but instead suggested that Lord Liverpool form another Tory government. The furious Whigs reviled the king, and caricatures of the prince as a self-indulgent, bloated joke began to fill the shops. When the Tory *Morning Post* tried to present him as a "conqueror of hearts" and—even—an "Adonis in loveliness," Leigh Hunt let fly in *The Examiner.*

> This "exciter of desire"—this "Adonis in loveliness," is a corpulent man of fifty!—in short, this delightful, blissful, wise, pleasurable, honourable, virtuous, true, and immortal prince, is a violator of his word, a libertine over head and ears in disgrace, a despiser of domestic ties, the companion of gamblers and demireps [courtesans], a man who has just closed half a century without one single claim on the gratitude of his country, or the respect of posterity!

Hunt and his brother, fellow editor of *The Examiner,* were promptly imprisoned for two years for libel.

"The print shops are full of *scurrilous caricatures* & infamous things relative to the Prince's conduct," Charlotte fretted. The prince's betrayals upset the Whigs, and his repeated, expensive renovations of Carlton House and Brighton Pavilion infuriated the public, who felt their high taxes funded only his pleasure. In April, George Cruikshank produced "Princely Predilections," a cartoon that shows the drunken regent confused between his Tory ministers and his old Whig friends. Lady Hertford controls him with a pair of reins intended for children. Princess Charlotte is also in the company, plump, overdressed, and weeping copiously. She is sobbing over her father and because of a snub from Arthur Wellesley, who makes an obscene gesture at her, his arm around Moll Raffles, his common mistress. Other caricatures were more childish. Charles Lamb dashed off a ridiculous poem on the prince for *The Examiner,* which began:

> Not a mightier whale than this
> In the vast Atlantic is;
> Not a fatter fish than he
> Flounders round the polar sea.

See his blubber—at his gills
What a world of drink he swills.

The poem ended:

By his bulk and by his size,
By his oily qualities,
This (or else my eyesight fails),
This should be the prince of Whales.

Stimulated by the comparison, Cruikshank produced "The Prince of Whales, or the Fisherman at Anchor," in which the regent was a monstrously fat fish, accompanied by an emollient mermaid Lady Hertford.

Relations between the regent and his daughter were worsening. When he drove out, the crowds stood silent, but they cheered Charlotte wildly and clapped her mother. The Whigs were stepping up their campaign to present Charlotte as the perfect monarch. As Lady Charlotte Bury reported at the beginning of the following year:

> There are in the newspapers, daily, long histories written, with intention to inflame the public with an idea of the Princess's [Caroline's] wrongs, and, above all, to make it clear that Princess Charlotte could reign tomorrow, if any circumstance was to unfit her father for so doing. This is the great part with the party out of office, and which men of ambition want to establish, in order to raise themselves.

Such reports naturally inflamed the regent into repressing his daughter. Charlotte looked like a woman and, unfortunately, rather like her mother. He saw her not as a young girl requiring guidance and support but as a rebellious force to be crushed and intimidated, and he was terrified by her popularity. In the summer of 1812, he decided to put her under what was essentially house arrest at Lower Lodge in Windsor, isolated from society, with her mother only allowed to visit her fortnightly.

"I confess I can no longer submit, it is too great a sacrifice to be demanded," Charlotte scribbled to Miss Elphinstone, begging her friend to disobey the order of the prince and write to her. "I detest everything that bears the name of *clandestine,* but I call this *not* so. I hold myself *absolved* from the promise that was *extorted* from me, not to hold any communication *whatever* with you. It is an unjust and cruel requisition." She was feeling wretched.

> *My residence is* deplorable & irksome, *deprived* now *of* all possibility *of seeing* any of my friends, surrounded by spies *that detail everything; & by people that can neither be* trusted *or* liked—a perfect prison. *When my thoughts are not occupied by studdy, it* ruminates *upon* everything *that is uncomfortable, & happiness fled.* Studdy, *from disliking it, you know, is now my greatest resource, as it passes away hours of ennui; indeed, the days appear to me as if they would never have an end.*

In sad contrast to her afternoons the previous year with Hesse trotting beside her, she was forced to ride out in the company of her dreary aunts. The rest of the time, she stayed in with her governesses. "How long I am *doomed* to remain in this infernal dwelling, I am *perfectly ignorant.*" The little household of women at Lower Lodge was cross, ill, and rubbing one another the wrong way. "I sleep but little, or suffer from severe headaches or colds," complained the princess. "A regular system of *persecution* seems to be *the thing.* I am *persecuted sometimes* (I cannot say often) by their officious civilities, by their *uncertain temper,* directions & advice." She had come to detest her Aunt Elizabeth, complaining that she had the potential to be a second Duke of Cumberland, having "all his dark propensities of deceit," and she disparaged Mary as "too great a repeater." Only Sophia was a true friend. "I can hardly believe she belongs to them—so wholly different is she in thoughts, opinions, manners," decided the sixteen-year-old. "Her nobleness and rectitude of mind renders her no favourite here. The constant scenes of intrigue, of tracasseries, she can but ill support." Her relations were cruel, and everything was dull. "The Bishop is here," she wrote crossly, "and reads with me for an hour or two every day from Mrs. Hannah More's *Hints for Forming the Education of a Young Princess:* this is I believe what makes me find the hours so long."

Charlotte had expected to enjoy more freedom as she grew older. Instead, her life became more miserable with every birthday. She was only two years off her majority, the age when she could rule alone, but she was still restrained by the narrow routine and isolation of Warwick House and Windsor that had been put in place in 1804, when she was eight. As her grandfather was incapacitated and her father constantly assailed by bouts of serious ill health, it was not entirely unlikely that she would become queen in two or three years' time. She was woefully unprepared to govern Britain, the most powerful country in Europe, if not the world. As she herself declared, "I have seen so little, &, I may add, nothing of the world as yet."

10

"Thinking that She Has
a Will of Her Own"

After the cancellation of two of her fortnightly visits, Princess Caroline grew agitated and demanded to see her daughter. She declared that she was ready to march down to Windsor and be turned away by the Queen. Determined to show herself to the world as a persecuted victim, the princess drove to Windsor and began banging on doors, crying out for Charlotte. "Though I begged hard," she bridled, "the stony-hearted old Queen would not let me see her."

When the regent heard of his wife's behavior, he was furious. He hurried to Windsor and summoned Charlotte to appear in front of a ridiculously pompous council of the queen, Princess Mary, and the prime minister, Lord Liverpool. He told his daughter that he knew she had received a letter from her mother complaining that she was badly treated, and he wanted Charlotte to give the letter to him. Charlotte answered that she had burned it and refused to give in, even as her father raged. Lord Liverpool threw up his hands over the triviality of the matter and returned to London to engage with more pressing matters of war.

When the story appeared in the papers the following week, the regent called his daughter to London, to be challenged by the same council. Angry and resentful, he was punishing Charlotte for her popularity and her mother's uncontrollable behavior. When Charlotte attended the opening of Parliament for the first time, at the end of 1812, she drove out to the cheers of the public, while her father was received in silence. He was so incensed that he told her she would not be allowed to the queen's Drawing Room to celebrate her birthday in January.

Tormented by an eye infection and aware that the regent was angry with her for allowing Hesse to flirt with Charlotte in Great Windsor Park, Lady de Clifford finally resigned in December. After persuading the queen, swollen with dropsy and perpetually angry, to allow her daughters out of Windsor, the regent decreed that his daughter should be accompanied to London by her aunts. But Charlotte did not want to be chaperoned by her aunts. She desired to be treated like an adult, attended by ladies-in-waiting, including her old friend Miss Elphinstone, rather than watched by shriveled old governesses. Princess Mary told her brother that Charlotte was "ready to receive any body you appointed as a Lady of the Bedchamber but never would *submit to obey any body* in the capacity of Governess."

On January 10, Charlotte wrote to her father requesting that she no longer be accompanied by a governess, and a copy of the letter was sent to Lord Liverpool. Her father flew into a rage and dashed to Windsor, with Lord Eldon, the chancellor, to berate Charlotte for her disobedience. "I know all that passed in Windsor Park," he thundered, referring to Charlotte's flirtations with FitzClarence and Hesse. "If it were not for my clemency," he continued, "I would have you shut up for life. Depend upon it, as long as I live, you shall never have an Establishment, unless you marry." Lord Eldon backed him up, pronouncing that Charlotte should be entirely subject to her father. "If she were my daughter, I would have locked her up," the chancellor declared, bold words from a man who had himself eloped with his wife. Charlotte was furious, later weeping to her aunt that she had been compared to the great-granddaughter of a collier (the chancellor's grandfather had been a coal transporter in Newcastle upon Tyne). She never spoke to Eldon again. The regent had long known about his daughter's flirtations with Hesse and had saved up the knowledge for the most crushing moment possible.

Obdurate, the regent appointed the Duchess of Leeds as Charlotte's governess. She only visited Warwick House in the afternoons, but that was more than enough for the princess, who thought her a dull, portly woman always complaining about her illnesses. When Charlotte misbehaved by showing off her ankles or gossiping during divine service, the duchess panicked, wept, vomited, and tossed all night at the prospect of having to admonish her charge. Charlotte had no respect for her and despised her fourteen-year-old daughter, Lady Catherine, whom she thought a "convenient spy upon everybody in the house" with her "way of walking so lightly that one never hears her."

Early in 1813, the dreaded Mrs. Udney left, and in her place a new governess was appointed whom Charlotte truly trusted and admired. Fifty-six-year-old Miss Cornelia Knight was a respected writer who had traveled abroad with her mother and lived in Naples with the exuberant ménage à trois of Sir William and Emma Hamilton and the married Lord Nelson. When the notorious threesome returned to England, Cornelia hurriedly separated herself and in 1805 became one of the queen's ladies, until the regent decided that he wished her to serve his daughter. After her spell with Nelson and Lady Hamilton, Miss Knight was adept at flattering overblown egos and used to exhibitionist behavior and temper tantrums. She was immediately sympathetic to Charlotte and shocked by the regent's aim to keep her in a "protracted infancy." Warwick House she thought a perfect convent, and the regent she judged to be tyrannical. She made sure always to imply that she was Charlotte's lady companion, in attendance rather than on guard.

Weary of attacking his daughter, the regent hinted that she might be allowed a freer life. He suggested that she and Miss Knight would dine with him at home, visit plays and the opera, entertain at Warwick House, and balls at Carlton House. He proposed a ball on February 5, which would not be a children's affair since young adults would also be invited. Charlotte was delighted at her father's seeming recognition that she was grown up, and excited when she heard that the handsome twenty-three-year-old Duke of Devonshire, son of the famous Georgiana and head of the most important Whig family in London, was to be her partner. She dressed carefully in a "superb dress of white lace richly embroidered in lama [lamé]" and "a profusion of diamonds," as well as the great ostrich feathers that denoted full court dress. To no avail. The Duke of Devonshire excused himself because of illness, and she was once again surrounded by old people. "All very magnificent, but such a lack of dancing young men and, indeed, women," remarked one guest, Mary Berry. Princess Mary refused to be usurped as the family beauty, and so, as Charlotte spat, she "opened the Ball, tho' it was given for me and was always the cupple above me, as jealous & ill-natured the whole night as she could be." The seventeen-year-old had been so isolated from the court that she had no idea of the identity of the guests, and she was grateful to Lady Jersey for keeping close by and slipping her the names of those who attended.

In spite of jealous Aunt Mary and guests she did not know, Charlotte danced until six in the morning and was—for the first time in a long time—happy. "The Queen and the whole pack of devils leave town," she gloated two days after the ball. Most wonderfully, her father had allowed her to re-main in London. She wrote to Miss Elphinstone, "I am fortunately to be rid of all I hate most, at least for a little while."

The Princess of Wales had been writing to her husband complaining that she was denied access to her daughter. He refused to answer, leading her to inquire if she was not the only subject in England whose plea would not reach the throne. She finally published a copy of her letter on February 10, 1813 in *The Morning Chronicle,* in which she begged him to pity "the deep wounds which so cruel an arrangement inflicts on my feelings . . . cut off from one of the very few domestic enjoyments left to me . . . the soci-ety of my child." Charlotte, she claimed, was isolated, shut up at Windsor, where she enjoyed "none of those advantages of society that are deemed necessary for imparting a knowledge of mankind." The "Regent's Valen-tine," as the letter became known, took England by storm. The public were seized with sympathy for their poor Princess of Wales. Canny manufactur-ers began to produce prints commemorating Caroline's victimhood, and there were even plates and cups made celebrating the oppressed wife.

The regent decided to conquer Caroline once and for all. He denied her access to Charlotte and announced that he would review the papers per-taining to the "Delicate Investigation." A committee of privy councillors, judges, the archbishops of Canterbury and York, and the Speaker of the House of Commons was appointed to decree "whether it was fit and proper that the intercourse between . . . Princess Charlotte and the Princess of Wales should continue under restriction and regulation."

Charlotte hid inside Warwick House, horrified by the prospect of another investigation. Eager to win the war of appearances, her father was being terribly friendly. "It is quite curious how much it is now the fashion of those about him to cry up the necessity of our being a great deal together, of seeing one another often, & alone, & how desirable & necessary it is for our mutual comfort," she lamented. "It makes one disgusted & distressed to a degree with all the falseness." Intent on clearing her name, Princess Caroline published a lengthy self-defense that she had sent the king in 1806. The regent, raging against her insurrection, printed his Law Officers Report. Charlotte was distraught to read the sordid details of her mother's imprudent behavior. "It really came upon me with *such a blow* & it staggered me so terribly, that I *never have* & shall *not ever recover* from it, because it sinks her so very low in my opinion."

Too distressed to venture out in her carriage, Charlotte refused a visit to the opera. Two of her female friends, the Misses Hervey, came to tell Charlotte that gossip was rife that she had had an affair with her cousin Captain George FitzClarence, and that she was hiding indoors because she was pregnant. Charlotte was shocked and embarked on proving that there was no truth in the story by showing herself around town. "If you have read in the papers that I have not been able to go out, that is a great lie, for there is not a day I do not drive in the Park till 5," she wrote to Miss Elphinstone. "But tho" *you are silent,* yet I feel you read *other things* in the papers wh. are infamous—so very bad that unless we were alone, I could not repeat them. *Some I think* will credit them." The circulation of such a terrible lie had made her miserable. "[Y]ou will find a great change with regard to my spirits, wh. are less infinitely than since we met last."

The inquiry concluded that Princess Caroline should continue to see her daughter under the same restrictions. "It leaves you just where you were before," sighed Charlotte. The prince's effort to punish his wife made her more popular than ever. She was applauded at the opera and besieged by letters of support. She was soon wishing for her husband's death and began creating wax dolls of him and prodding them with pins before burning them.

Charlotte asked if she could visit her mother in May for her birthday, and the prince sent her a kindly letter explaining that he would allow her to go, but he noted: "I confide so much in your own discretion, sense of propriety, & what you must feel is the delicacy of both our situations at the present moment, that you will see how desirable it is to make this merely a morning visit, & not to extend it to the hour of the day when you might be subjected to society . . . which I might not approve of." Charlotte was only allocated an hour, and the visit was unsatisfactorily formal. Still, even though she had been shocked by her mother's behavior, she thought her "ill used" and that she was "still more now than before." As she later said, "My mother was wicked, but she would not have become as bad as she was if my father had not been infinitely worse."

Worried by the exposure of her mother's affairs, Charlotte decided to end her correspondence with Hesse and wrote asking him to return the ring she had given him and other keepsakes. She begged Miss Elphinstone for help.

> *It is a subject not a little unpleasant to me to have to think of & recur to, & at the same time not a little anxious for me, as I have several trinkets wh. I should be in dismay at ever being seen. As to letters, I suppose he has kept them, that first setting out was a direct promise from both mutually to burn all letters, wh. I did most strictly, for certainly they were much too full of professions & nonsense not to have got him into a desperate scrape if ever seen.*

But faithful Miss Elphinstone had little success. Hesse was reluctant to restore the letters, answering only that he had them with him and that should he be killed, they should be sent to Miss Elphinstone, "without being seen by any person." Charlotte blamed her mother for enabling her private meetings with Hesse. Frantic, she even authorized her friend to confide in her father, Lord Keith, and enlist his help. If the letters were made public, they would wreck her reputation. Furthermore, if the Princess of Wales was revealed as encouraging the meetings between her daughter and an officer so corrupt that he would sell her letters, the Regent would have more ammunition to begin divorce proceedings.

In July, the Prince of Wales threw a fete at Carlton House to celebrate the Duke of Wellington's latest victory against the French forces at Vittoria. Charlotte's first official public appearance caused some stir. Captain Gronow, a young ensign in the 1st Foot Guards, was impressed.

She was a young lady of more than ordinary personal attractions; her
features were regular, and her complexion fair, with the rich bloom
of youthful beauty, her eyes were blue and very expressive, and her
hair was abundant, and of that peculiar light brown which merges
into the golden. In figure her Royal Highness was somewhat over
the ordinary height of women, but finely proportioned and well-
developed. . . . She created universal admiration, and may I say a
feeling of national pride, amongst all who attended the ball.

The princess had no shortage of admirers. The Duke of Sussex encouraged Augustus D'Este, his son by his morganatic wife, to try to woo the
princess. D'Este embarked on a charm offensive, riding next to her on her
drives and trailing behind her when she went to visit Kensington Palace. He
even sent a letter tumbling with the "most high-flown praises & formal
declaration of the most violent passion possible," sealed with a royal crest
(to which he had no right), to add to the insolence. Charlotte begged his father to tell him to stop.

Another man who dared do more than wave at her while she was out
driving was Lord Yarmouth, the thirty-six-year-old son of her father's mistress, Lady Hertford. She was delighted when he bought her a beautiful
white poodle, apparently confiscated from a French prisoner at Dartmoor,
which performed tricks for its mistress. Yarmouth, like any man at court
with half a brain, knew that the way to please Charlotte was by slandering
her relations. He sidled up to her at the Duke of York's birthday party and
whispered how Princesses Mary and Elizabeth were "intriguantes in every
way." He declared himself her "humble slave," the victim of a passion for
her that no one could equal, and suggested that he would help her to learn
how to manage her father. Charlotte responded cautiously: She believed he
had "by no means the same influence he used to have with the P."

The most celebrated suitor of all, however, was the young Duke of Devonshire, heir to the spectacular Chatsworth estate, Whig leader, and the
most eligible young man in England. Aristocratic mothers of single young
ladies wept to see him pay court to Princess Charlotte, and London
watched and wondered. "Young P. and her father have had frequent rows of
late," Henry Brougham, supporter of the Princess of Wales, wrote to fellow politician Thomas Creevey, "but one pretty serious one. He was angry

with her for flirting with the Duke of Devonshire, and suspected she was talking politics."

Every Whig aristocrat in London was trying to captivate Princess Charlotte, and the ambitious duke wanted to win her, even though he had damaged his chances somewhat by crying off her ball in February. He popped up when she went driving in the park, and he sent presents. The Whigs began to worry that he would turn Tory in order to court the princess officially. Although Charlotte liked to discuss Whig matters, she found him unattractive. The duke had not inherited his famous mother's charisma: He was stolid, pedantic, and dull. "His constancy is certainly unabated," she sighed to Miss Elphinstone. "I frequently have regretd [sic] its not being bestowed on others who would feel and appreciate it *much more* & *really* as *it would deserve*, & wh. I have not in my power to give him."

Charlotte enjoyed flirting with the duke because it was a way of teasing her father. When caricatures began to appear of Devonshire and Charlotte gazing into each other's eyes, the regent grew convinced that his daughter was plotting against him with the Whigs and considering Devonshire as a suitor. He dreaded her marrying an Englishman and then setting up a rival court to his own in London. He began to turn his thoughts toward marrying her off. If, he decided, she was married to a prince from another country, she would be forced to live abroad, and the public would soon forget her.

There were few royal fathers in Europe who did not hope that their sons might be considered by the prince regent as the husband of the heir to the English throne. The prince plumped for the twenty-year-old Hereditary Prince of Orange. Holland was an excellent diplomatic ally and, happily for the regent, Charlotte would be required to live there for the entire year. He informed his daughter of his plan, and made it clear that she would have to obey. "Charlotte must lay aside the idle nonsense of thinking that she has a will of her own," he told her governess. "While I live she must be subject to me as she is at present, if she were thirty or forty or even five and forty."

11

⚜

Violent Orange Attacks

Slender Billy," as the Prince of Orange was known by his fellow soldiers, had never cut much of a dash. He had fled to England with his family at the age of three, attended Oxford University, and joined the British Army, and in 1811 became Wellington's aide-de-camp. He was more hindrance than help. Although he had great courage, he made some reckless decisions, which resulted in the deaths of many of his men. He had returned to Holland in 1813 as crown prince, a short, skinny, and ugly youth with buck teeth and wispy blond hair, and a diffident and indecisive character. The prince regent had selected a suitor for his daughter whom he would be able to control.

After the fall of Napoleonic France, in the hope of creating a buffer state between France and Prussia, the Belgian provinces (formerly the Austrian Netherlands) and the Dutch provinces were placed under the rule of the House of Orange and dubbed the United Kingdom of the Netherlands. As the Belgian Catholic population still saw themselves as part of France and hated their Protestant neighbors, the rule of the House of Orange had to be enforced by the British Army. By marrying Charlotte to Slender Billy, the prince regent was making the clearest declaration that the United Kingdom of the Netherlands would survive and French domination would be no more.

Charlotte was unsure what to think of the Prince of Orange. She wished for her independence from her father, and she needed money, for she was in debt to the tune of £22,000. But she hated the idea of being married off to a foreigner she had never met, as her great-aunts and Aunt Augusta had been. As heir to the throne, she expected to have more say in her choice of husband. As she told Sir Henry Halford, the family's doctor and unofficial go-between, the public would hate to see "a future Queen of England marrying a *foreigner.*" She was, she declared, *"the publick property."* Arranged marriages could be disastrous (as that of her own parents showed) and seemed out of date: Charlotte, like thousands of other young girls across England, read the novels of Jane Austen and Fanny Burney and expected a love match. Most of all, she did not mean to leave the country, for she believed that if she moved overseas, her father would find it easier to divorce her mother and remarry, and then, in the words of Henry Brougham, "the young Princess's title to the throne [would] be gone."

And yet Charlotte liked the idea of being considered as a future bride, and it was certainly a great political alliance. She tried to imagine life with the prince. "Holland is a very odd place I believe, & in wh. society & everything else is quite different from any other place," she pondered. "Even now I *doubt* being *much* amused there. If [I] travel about & only remain there for a few weeks at a time, we *must see what* we *can do* to make it more *Londonish.*" She had heard that the prince seemed to have a kindly disposition, but she was dismayed by reports of his unprepossessing appearance and gauche manner. Many of her friends were skeptical. The Whigs wished the princess to stay single and in England, all the better to help their cause. Miss Knight was dubious about the Prince of Orange, as were the Duke of Sussex and Lady Jersey, whom Charlotte trusted. The Princess of Wales detested the Oranges, declaring them to be untrustworthy and violent.

Feeling confused, Charlotte began to flirt with her weak and ineffectual cousin the thirty-eight-year-old Duke of Gloucester, intending to use him as a weapon to needle her father. Nicknamed "Slice" and "The Cheese," the stodgy duke was devoid of imagination, but Charlotte thought that mar-

riage to him would be a popular choice. The Prince of Wales was whipped
into panic when he spotted her in intimate conversation with the duke at a
party, and dispatched a duchess to ensure the pair sat farther apart.

Charlotte was delighted by her success at irritating her father, declaring
the Duke of Gloucester an *"iron rod"* over the head of her father and his
stuffy courtiers. She teased one of her father's spies that if her father forbade her to marry the Duke of Gloucester, she would make a public avowal
that she would not marry anyone else. The prince blamed Miss Elphinstone and Lady Jersey for turning Charlotte against the House of Orange.
Suspecting that his old mistress might be meeting his daughter at the stu-
dio of the artist George Sanders, the prince demanded Charlotte be painted
at Warwick House, but Sanders declared that the light was wrong, and the
portrait was never completed.

The prince regent wished to introduce Charlotte to her future father-in-
law. He invited the Prince of Orange to his birthday celebrations at the
Royal Military College in Sandhurst. Unfortunately the birthday boy decided to celebrate the sunny weather by beginning to drink as early as possible. Soon the prince regent could hardly speak, and the royal brothers, as
well as the politicians, were dissolving into hysterical parodies of their former selves. The Duke of York fell over the back of his chair onto a wine
cooler and lay there, his head cut open, too drunk to do more than vaguely
wave his hands. When he attempted to sit up by grasping the tablecloth, he
pulled the crockery and cutlery on top of himself. Lord Liverpool, the
prime minister, later confessed that he hardly knew where he was, and the
Prince of Orange, father of Charlotte's suitor, lost both his coat and his
waistcoat and was spotted wandering around in just his shirt. When the
queen wished to leave, there was a frantic hunt for the regent, who was
eventually brought forward, utterly drunk. He "absolutely neither saw nor
spoke," as Charlotte noted, even when he was pushed forward to hand his
mother into her coach. The regent was not a particularly friendly drunk.
He practically shoved his daughter out of the way on his return to the
drinking table.

Charlotte decided not to see her putative fiancé, who had arrived in London with his father. She suspected that if she met him, it would be seen as
giving her tacit approval to the engagement. She carefully avoided any

event at which he would be present, and he departed to fight with Wellington's troops without meeting her.

As his daughter neared eighteen, the regent alternated threats with hon-
eyed promises. One moment he might tell her that she should "never be
persuaded or forced into any alliance" and that her potential grooms would
be invited to the country and she would be allowed to choose. Then he
would kick up his heels and rage at her that she must obey him. "I see he is
compleatly poisoned against me, & that he will never come round," Charlotte
complained after one such occasion. When she mentioned the Duke of
Gloucester, he lost his temper and accused her of addling her mind with
drink and flirting with other men, in words "so excessively indecent" that
she "hardly knew which way to look." He left her tearfully angry with him,
and she pronounced: "There does not live one who is a greater coward or a
greater hypocrite." The prince was keen to rid himself of his daughter. He
told Charlotte that she would have to meet her suitor. "My *torments* and
plagues are again beginning in spite of all promises made at Windsor," she
lamented. "I have had a *violent orange* attack this morning."

Sir Henry Halford was sent over to try, as Charlotte wrote, *"every argument of seduction* you can possibly conceive to *shake my firmness* & *turn my
head."* He told her that by "power, by riches, by liberty, by splendor, by pleasure, by society, & lastly by the *general* wish of the nation it would give universal delight." It was not an entirely unappealing prospect. No longer a
girl inhibited by governesses, she would be a rich, glamorous, respected
woman. But Charlotte refused, declaring that "3 or 4 years hence would
be quite time enough to think of such a thing." Her father, after all, had
delayed until he was thirty-two.

After much pressing, Charlotte changed her mind and agreed to meet
the Hereditary Prince of Orange when he arrived. "I am doing all that is
fair," she conceded, and "giving the young man a chance." The prince regent turned instantly into the most doting father, inviting his daughter to
dine at Carlton House and making a pet of her when she visited. On one
occasion, a group of ladies admired the diamond clasp he wore on his belt,
and he removed the ornament and gave it to Charlotte in front of the
whole company. Dazzled by her father's splendid company after the te-
dium of life at Warwick House, Charlotte began to wonder if marriage

with the Prince of Orange might not be worth it after all. However, she declared, as heiress presumptive, "I could not quit this country, as Queen of England *still less*." The prince, she decreed, would have to *"visit his frogs solo."*

The meeting between Charlotte and the prince was arranged for two days after he arrived. Miss Elphinstone spotted the young Dutchman when he arrived at Plymouth and thought him pleasing. Charlotte bubbled that she gave her friend permission to be in love with him for her own sake, "according to the old proverb, 'Love me, love my dog.' " The Prince of Wales suggested that she meet her suitor at an evening party at Carlton House, accompanied by the Duchess of Leeds, the Duke of Clarence, and Lord Liverpool. He declared that the grandees "would take off the glare of it, if it was put into the papers." In reality, he wanted witnesses. As he wrote, his daughter must be "decided that night one way or the other with [no] *hezitation.*"

Charlotte, agitated but lovely in violet satin trimmed with black lace, set out to meet the prince. Although pale, sickly looking, and rather short, her suitor made every effort to charm, and Charlotte was impressed by his good manners. Her father then ushered her into a private room and demanded her opinion. She hesitated; he groaned loudly, making full use of the hysterical talents that had once persuaded Mrs. Fitzherbert to submit to him. Touched by his seeming distress, Charlotte said that she had liked what she saw. He pounced on her answer as an assent to marriage, shouting, "You make me the happiest person in the world." He began weeping wildly, bellowing out his happiness so that all could hear. Charlotte was exhilarated, overwhelmed, and utterly outmanipulated. Determined not to miss a chance, the regent called in the Prince of Orange and, sobbing like a big blubbery whale, joined the couple's hands and blessed them. The princess was engaged to the Prince of Orange. Miss Knight was baffled. "I could only remark," she coughed, "that she had gained a great victory over herself."

12

ɔɛ

The Rising Sun

"It signifies nothing how they go on this day or that—in the long term, quarrel they must," wrote the politician Henry Brougham of the prince regent and his daughter. "He has not equality of temper, or any other kind of sense, to keep well with her, and she has a spice of her mother's spirit." Charlotte's supreme romance of love and hatred was with her father.

When the prince regent informed his daughter that she would be expected to live in Holland for at least half of the year and think herself "more a Dutch woman" when she was in Holland, Charlotte began to panic. "My soul is wrung to the bottom," she moaned. Dwelling on her vision of herself as her father's victim, she replayed the scene after dinner in her mind and decided she had been forced into an engagement. "I shall ever say," she wrote, "that the P. *used me ill and deceived me* throughout the whole affair."

And yet the newly engaged princess could not help but be excited by her family's approbation. Aunt Mary gushed to her about how happy she had made her father, and even the queen was pleased. As a reward for her obedience, Charlotte was finally allowed to be confirmed, and she took her first communion on Christmas Day. She loved being treated as an adult at last, and although she was concerned about her father's threats, her fiancé had, after all, said that "all his anxious desire" was to make her "as happy as was in his power." Perhaps he might agree to reside in England. And she was still elated by his suggestion that they might tour Europe after their marriage, a true temptation for a girl who had only ever visited Weymouth and its environs.

The year 1814 began with dark and freezing weather. The fog at the beginning of the year was so overwhelming that horses had to be led by lamplight, and many people were too afraid to go out in their carriages. The Thames froze over for the first time since 1788, and stalls were set up on it selling cakes, bread, ribbons, and trinkets, while people rubbed their hands near the spits roasting oxen. Charlotte enjoyed watching the crowds skating on the river and lining up in their carriages to watch the fair, but otherwise she was chilly, ill, and miserable, plunged into "*such a state of compleat stupidity & listlessness,*" that she could hardly think. "The cold literally has froze up every sence & faculty I possess."

After falling ill with prolonged stomach pains, the regent began to neglect his daughter once more. The newspapers were due to announce the engagement, and so there was no inducement to flatter Charlotte or give her diamond clasps. The frost turned to six weeks of heavy snow. Charlotte's life returned to the old routine of slow days at Warwick House, taking drawing lessons to fill the time and frittering away her money on excessively expensive jewelry for her friends, banking on Parliament awarding her a large sum when she married.

The Princess of Wales planned to give an evening dinner for her daughter's eighteenth birthday at her new house in Bayswater. Afraid that Caroline might gather Whig supporters for Charlotte, the regent decreed that his daughter could visit only in the morning. Charlotte did as she was told, and came away from her meeting in tears, full of sympathy for her mother, writing that she was "really oppressed and cruelly used." In the evening she saw her uncles, but the prince regent did not make an appearance. For him, the eighteenth birthday of his daughter was no reason to celebrate.

Charlotte was now old enough to rule England, but she felt cross, isolated, and very unlike a future queen. There had been no great change in her life. The dull days crawled past at Warwick House, as slow as before.

She found herself worrying about Hesse, whose regiment had been involved in a serious skirmish with the French. "Were anything to happen to our friend," she fretted to Miss Elphinstone, "I should feel it excessively, as it is impossible not to do so for a person one has been so intimate with."

The princess did not see her father until early March, when he called her to him to hear the reading of the letter from the king of the Netherlands asking for Charlotte's hand in marriage. She received a portrait of the prince and the staggering sum of £15,000 for jewels. But the glittering diamonds were a bribe: The prince expected her to spend six months of the year in Holland, and he would not be dissuaded.

The prince, wrote Lady Charlotte Bury, "wishes his wife to go with him to his own Dutch land; and so does the Prince Regent, who does not like a rising sun in his own. But report also whispers that the rising sun is aware of this, and will not consent to the marriage, unless she is allowed to shine in her own dominions." The Duke of Clarence paid a visit to the Dutch court and sent back reports that the ladies devoted their evenings to dreary rounds of sewing for soldiers.

Charlotte was sure that the only way to protect her position as heir was by remaining in England, thus ensuring that her parents did not divorce. Crowds shouted, "Never desert your Mother!" when she drove out, while hissing her father. She decided that she could agree to marry the prince but she would remain in England. Lord Grey, leader of the Whigs in the House of Lords, worried over the princess's "ability to support the attacks to which she will be exposed of all descriptions, both to cajole and to intimidate her; to allure her by promises and demonstrations of tenderness; and to subdue her by increased privations." Undeterred, Charlotte gathered her courage and wrote to her father.

> *When the marriage was proposed, I had not the slightest suspicion that my residence was not to be in England . . . and had I entertained any doubts on the subject, my consent would never have been given to the marriage. In this respect, I cannot change my opinion, and therefore I shall hope it will be stated as a condition in the treaty that I shall never be obliged to leave England contrary to my inclination, and at all events that my residence should previously and permanently be fixed in this country . . . I have written two letters to the*

> *Prince of Orange expressive of my resolution on this important sub-*
> *ject, and have not had the satisfactory answers I expected. I therefore*
> *apply to you, my dearest father and protector, trusting to your honour*
> *and affection.*

Whipped into an immediate fury, the regent informed his daughter that she would not see the marriage contract. Instead, he offered her £50,000 a year and told her that her eldest son would be educated in England since he would be heir to the throne. He made it very clear that he would be angry with her until she relented.

Less than a fortnight later, a servant went to Miss Knight and informed her that a young officer, Captain St. George, was at the door of Warwick House. She went down to receive the guest, only to find the Prince of Orange, who had just traveled over secretly from the Hague. He begged to see Charlotte, but she was still in bed and refused him. Undeterred, he sat down with a piece of paper and pleaded with her to change her mind:

> *Dearest Charlotte: I am extremely disturbed at your not wishing to see*
> *me; but I ask it once more as a particular favour that you will allow*
> *me to wait till you are up. If you insist on a refusal I must follow your*
> *wish and return at two o'clock. I am most desirous and anxious to be*
> *able to speak to you freely.*

Charlotte relented and came downstairs to speak to him. In the reception room, she told him how concerned she was that there was no home arranged for them in England. He promised to speak to her father.

The prince regent, however, was distracted. On April 9, England had heard the rousing news that the Allies had entered Paris and forced Napoleon to abdicate. Louis XVIII, the fat, gouty brother of the executed king, was to be put on the throne of France, and Napoleon was exiled to Elba. London lit up in celebration. The victory, the regent declared, could not have been won without his own "original and indefatigable endeavours." "Enjoy the triumph now, Prince of the mighty Isle," declared Robert Southey, the poet laureate. Few shared the prince's conviction that he was responsible. In one extravagant entertainment for the allied sovereigns, the crowd set upon the prince, attacking his carriage and demanding the where-abouts of Princess Caroline. The Prince ignored public opinion and de-voted himself to inviting the allied sovereigns, including newly crowned Louis XVIII and his wife, to London to celebrate the success, and planning magnificent balls.

On June 7, Tsar Alexander of Russia and the King of Prussia arrived in London with their commanders and courts for three weeks of victory cele-brations. The tsar's glamorous sister, the twenty-five-year-old Grand Duchess Catherine of Oldenburg, had already taken over the entire Pul-teney Hotel, on Piccadilly, at the regent's expense. The king and the tsar had planned to stay at Carlton House, but the tsar had been so infuriated by the regent and his habit of hogging the limelight that he hopped into his ambassador's coach and headed off to occupy the Pulteney with his sister.

Charlotte quite forgot the Prince of Orange, so entranced was she with the fascinating young tsar and his glamorous entourage. "The Emperor of Russia is my hero and everybody's hero," cooed Lady Charlotte Bury.

The Times marveled at how the hotel was "almost continually crowded with ladies and the juvenile branches of our distinguished families, who filled the great hall, the passageways and staircase, in constant succession, to have a glimpse of the Emperor." When the great man exited the hotel, he sometimes shook hands with some of the ladies, extending his palm del-icately through the rails of the staircase. "This caused such an emulation with the fair sex to obtain this honour, that some actually came at a consid-erable distance from the country to experience the gratification." Charlotte fell head over heels in love. "My ears are very ugly," she tinkled, "but I would give them both to persuade the Emperor to come to me to a ball, a supper, any entertainment that he would choose." But the tsar never paid a private call. He had sufficient female attention without offending the re-gent by visiting his daughter. Even worse, when he did encounter Char-lotte, he tried to persuade her to marry the Prince of Orange.

For three nights, London celebrated. The prince regent had pagodas and Chinese bridges erected in the parks, Hyde Park was taken over by drinking stalls and shops, and the theaters were jammed. The cows usually resident in Green Park dashed in terror into the streets. The city's finest besieged their dressmakers, the gentry were dizzy with parties, washerwomen struggled through piles of fine laundry, and traders worried that stocks of food might run dangerously low.

Charlotte, forbidden to attend any of the dinners, had to content herself with riding around St. James's in her carriage, hoping to be spotted by visiting dignitaries. To her fury, the Prince of Orange dashed to attend the balls and soirées from which she was barred. Sitting alone in Warwick House, she heard repeated stories of his drunkenness, and she began to grow very angry. The poor Prince of Orange might have grown up in England, but after a few years away, he was quite unable to keep up with the English passion for drinking. "The English," sniffed the Duke of Wellington of his army, "are fellows who have all enlisted for drink—that is the plain fact—they have all enlisted for drink." There were fifty thousand drinking houses in the country, not to mention thousands of unofficial gin parlors, and any gentleman worth his salt could easily knock back half a dozen bottles of port. The poor staved off the cold with lethally cheap spirits. Charlotte loved fun and parties, but she had a horror of drunkenness and hated those who indulged, such as Mrs. Udney. She had grown up seeing her father and uncles in pitiful states of inebriation, and she had hoped that her husband would not be similarly corruptible.

The princess finally achieved her desire: She was invited to a formal dinner at Carlton House. Surrounded by handsome young officers, it was impossible for her not to feel that her Prince of Orange was not much of a catch. He drank too much wine again and was soon flushed and confused. Charlotte's eye began to stray to the other young men, handsome in their freshly brushed dress uniforms and eager to please the heir to the throne. She soon spotted handsome, tall Prince Friedrich Wilhelm Heinrich August von Preussen, the thirty-five-year-old son of Prince Ferdinand, youngest brother of Frederick the Great. Unlike the gangly Prince of Orange, Friedrich, commonly known as August, was a smooth charmer. Unfortunately, he was also the black sheep of the Prussian royal family, and abandoned across Europe were his dozens of mistresses and a clutch of illegitimate children. He had fallen in love only once, with the beautiful Juliette Récamier, great beauty of Napoleonic France. Her failure to leave her husband turned him against women forever. By the time he met Charlotte, he was a cool and practiced philanderer.

Charlotte fell in love once more. She and August began to meet frequently, and he vowed to write when he returned to Prussia. With her father and uncles still distracted by their visitors, she was free to spend hours arranging herself in her finest gowns and waiting for his call. Even Miss Elphinstone knew nothing about the secret trysts, until she dropped round to Warwick House to be met by a flustered Miss Knight trying to send her away. Charlotte, she discovered, was ensconced upstairs, alone in her room with Prince August. Horrified, she cried that the prince should leave: Did they really think that no one would notice the furtive visits? The regent himself was just next door. Prince August was shown out, shamefaced, but within a day or two, he and Princess Charlotte were meeting in secret once more.

The princess was becoming passionately attached to August and had developed a real distaste for the Prince of Orange. She had come to find her fiancé gauche, weak, boring, and ugly. She told her mother: "I am sometimes obliged to turn my head away in disgust when he is speaking to me." The Princess of Wales was actively discouraging her daughter from marrying, piqued that those of her relations who had come to England to celebrate the victory had been too afraid of the regent's wrath to visit her. But preparations for the marriage were continuing apace. The queen had ordered Charlotte's bridal dress. Princess Mary warned her niece that once the grandees had left London, the prince regent intended to send for the Orange family and arrange an immediate wedding.

When Charlotte went to wish the tsar and his sister goodbye in their apartment at the Pulteney, the tsar took her into a private room and repeatedly told her that she should marry the Prince of Orange. Outside, the redoubtable Miss Knight protested that the princess was not allowed to be alone with any man. Charlotte finally emerged, only to hear that the Prince of Orange was waiting to see the tsar in an antechamber. In a panic, Charlotte and Miss Knight escaped down the back stairs. At the bottom, they bumped into Prince Leopold of Saxe-Coburg, a handsome twenty-three-year-old soldier in the tsar's entourage. Charlotte recognized him as a friend of Miss Elphinstone's. Beautifully dressed in the all-white uniform of the Russian cavalry, he was, it was clear from his badges, already a lieutenant general. Gallantly and rather daringly, he gave Charlotte his arm and offered to escort her and Miss Knight to their carriage. Charlotte played up to him coquettishly, suggesting he pay a visit to Warwick House. But she forgot him almost the minute her carriage started off toward Carlton House. She was addicted to Prince August.

Born in December 1790, Prince Leopold had been declared by Napoleon the handsomest man who had ever entered his Palace of the Tuileries. Unfortunately, he was quite impoverished, with an allowance of only £300 a year. The eighth child of Prince Francis of Saxe-Coburg, the son and heir of the reigning duke, he was as handsome and aspiring as the rest of his family, the greatest fortune hunters on the Continent. As Bismarck, the Prussian chancellor, later declared, the Coburg family was "the stud farm of Europe." They had to be: The territory of Coburg was barely four hundred square miles, or one and a half times the Isle of Wight, and contained only fifty thousand inhabitants. By the time of Leopold's birth, the family were so poor they could not afford to live in the ducal palace. In 1772, they had declared themselves bankrupt, with debts of a million thalers and an income of only seventy thousand. The emperor had to rescue them all. Luckily, the children proved handsome and resourceful, and charmed or married their way out of their backwater. Leopold's brother was in favor with the king of Prussia, and one sister, Victoire, for whom he would later conjure great plans, was married to the Prince of Leiningen. Another, Julia, married the Grand Duke Constantine, brother of the Russian tsar. His brother Ferdinand later wed Antonia de Kohary, only daughter of Prince Kohary and the richest heiress in the Austrian Empire. Like them, Leopold had a charming manner, dark good looks, and powerful sexual charisma. Thanks to his sister Julia, he became a favorite with the Russian court. He was made a cadet in the Imperial Guard at the tender age of five and a general when he was twelve, although he did not engage in actual combat. At seventeen, he visited Paris in an attempt to gain a position in Napoleon's entourage but instead began a passionate affair with Napoleon's lovely twenty-four-year-old stepdaughter, Hortense de Beauharnais, who had recently separated from her husband. There were tales that he had also been close to her mother, Josephine. "Here if you ask a lady to be seated, she goes to bed. That is the habit here," he decided.

Finally, in October 1813, young Leopold managed to fight against the French at a skirmish preceding the great Battle of Leipzig. On March 31, 1814, he marched into Paris with the Russian army, and then followed the tsar to London to celebrate the victory. Although he was only able to afford cheap lodgings over a grocer's shop in Marylebone, he was determined to make his mark. He cut a splendid figure in London in his uniform and became very popular with the ladies. Miss Elphinstone found him particularly appealing. Once she heard about the meeting on the hotel stairs, she decided that her new friend could be just the man to distract Charlotte from her obsession with August. It is also possible that some in the pay of the emperor of Austria, who had no desire to see Holland strengthened by the great alliance with Britain, had hoped to push handsome Leopold Charlotte's way.

Leopold brushed down his uniform and began to follow Charlotte when she rode out in the park. Just like Lieutenant Hesse, he waved at her, paraded behind her, and showed off his fine horsemanship. Finally, one evening, fired up by a few glasses of wine, he left the opera early to pay a visit. Full of confidence and high spirits, he effused endlessly to Charlotte about her beauty and grace, while she sat surprised, confused, and rather wishing he would go. She considered herself virtually engaged to Prince August. Leopold eventually took his leave, chastened but not deterred. He dashed off a letter to the prince regent explaining that Charlotte had asked him to visit and that he hoped he had not been forward in doing so without the permission of the regent. He avowed that he wanted to make a good impression in case he was asked to return. The regent paid little attention to the letter. It would never have entered his head to consider impecunious Leopold as a suitor.

In June, the regent finally allowed Charlotte to be presented at court at one of the queen's Drawing Rooms. Alas, he refused to allow her to dress at Warwick House, "lest it be thought that she be going in state." She had to travel in an ordinary outfit and change at Buckingham House (it had not then yet been transformed into a palace by John Nash). *The Lady's Magazine* rhapsodized about her "elegant petticoat of rich white satin with a superb border of the same and a wreath of silver laurel leaves," but the public were unable to admire the drape or the workmanship until Charlotte drove home after being handed into her carriage by the Prince of Orange.

On June 10, all the dignitaries, generals, and royals paid a great visit to the Ascot races. The Prince of Orange got hopelessly drunk with Prince Paul of Württemberg and made an exhibition of himself on the return journey by perching on top of a stagecoach. Charlotte felt it was the final straw. Six days later, she had made up her mind, but she had to plan carefully. She sent for her fiancé and told him that she could not leave England and that she expected to be able to invite her mother to their marital home whenever she wished. The prince refused, as she had expected. She then abruptly informed him that she was therefore forced to break off the engagement. Their relationship, she told him, was *"totally and for ever* at an end." She later asked Miss Knight to write to the poor prince requesting the return of her portrait, all letters, and any mementos.

Charlotte then requested that the prince break the news to her father. Not surprisingly, he refused, and so she was forced to pick up her pen. "I must wholly throw myself upon your mercy," she wrote to the regent, "in allowing me to explain, what must otherwise appear in your eyes, and to my own feelings, the most flagrant act of neglectful disrespect to you." It was all the Prince of Orange's fault: She had told him that she wished to live in England, and he had replied that "he could not go on with it."

The regent was seized with wrath and began planning Charlotte's punishment. He wrote expressing his anger but made no hint about how he would discipline her. Left to imagine the most awful retribution, Charlotte grew terrified. "Plagues you must expect," boomed the Duke of Sussex, and "if you are firm, they are for a limited time," but "should you yield, the decisive event may last as long as you live." He thought she should appear strong: "If you show *yourself afraid* the *game is clearly up.*" He believed she had a good chance of ultimate success: "At this moment *the public opinion* is with you."

Lady Jersey and the Duke of Sussex passed on shocking gossip that the princess would be seized from Warwick House and locked up. Genuinely afraid, Charlotte wrote to her father offering to justify her conduct but not promising to marry the prince. Two days later, the regent called Miss Knight and Charlotte to Carlton House and embarked on a furious rant about how Charlotte had received Prince August, as well as other princes, including the hard-drinking Paul of Württemberg. Charlotte had not realized that he knew, but little could be hidden from the regent's spies. Aware of the truth of the maxim that anticipation is always worse than the actual event, the regent worked hard to keep his daughter in suspense. He told her to return the following day.

Once she was back home, Charlotte began to fret that the prince meant to spring a trap at Carlton House, keeping her there and not allowing her to return. She was sure that he planned to send her away. "Tomorrow may probably be my last day, God knows, in this house." She had a pain in her knee, and she was very afraid. "I dread everything & I know not why I fancy horrors in every one and thing around me."

As she became more worried, her knee grew more agonizing. Declaring that she could hardly think, she begged her father to come and see her. Miss Elphinstone was summoned to give moral support. Finally, at six in the evening, the regent lumbered in, accompanied by the bishop of Salisbury. After an hour with him, Charlotte emerged in hysterics, wailing that she was to be taken for five days to Carlton House and then to Cranbourne Lodge in the depths of Windsor Forest, where she would have no visitors but her grandmother once a week. All her staff, including Miss Knight, would be dismissed. "God Almighty grant me patience," cried the princess, dropping to the ground.

Charlotte's mind was filled with horrific images of imprisonment and restraint. Hurrying to her room, all pain in her knee forgotten, she asked her maid for her bonnet and shawl. Then she slipped down the back stairs, out the door, and through the courtyard, toward Charing Cross.

13

ꔛ

"The Soldiers Will Be Ordered Out"

For the first time in her life, Charlotte was out on the street without attendants. Luckily, a Mr. Collins, who was admiring the view from his room above his uncle's print shop, saw a young lady unaccompanied and gallantly dashed down the stairs to offer his assistance. Charlotte begged him to hail a hackney cab, desperate to leave before her father came after her. When the cab arrived, she clambered in and offered the driver a guinea to head toward Oxford Street. The driver, Mr. Higgins, somewhat nonplussed by his breathless, glamorous customer, set off. Charlotte then told him to head for Bayswater.

The first and perhaps the last major member of the royal family to use public transport independently, Charlotte settled back into the carriage as it rattled westward, panting with relief. Gradually, though, she began to feel the first twinges of nerves. She had committed the most rebellious act of her life. At Connaught Place, she told the cab to stop and scrambled out, thrusting a very generous three guineas at the driver. Mr. Higgins declared later that he had thought her a fine lady's maid, traveling to socialize with the servants at Connaught House.

Charlotte entered the house expecting to be reunited with her mother, but the place was deserted. Princess Caroline had gone to Blackheath. Charlotte could think of nothing to do but pitch herself in a chair and order dinner. She was a true Hanoverian: If in doubt, eat.

Waiting to be served, she began to reflect on her impetuous act. She realized that she would need some supporters, so she summoned Henry Brougham and her uncle Sussex. The Princess of Wales finally returned home at nine, but she was rather cool when Charlotte threw herself into her arms and begged her protection. As much as she liked to use her daughter to aggravate her husband, she prized her freedom, and having the heir to the throne in her home would cramp her style. Charlotte, however, hardly understood that her mother was not entirely delighted to see her. When Brougham appeared, all three sat down to a jolly dinner, with the princess buoyantly convinced that she would soon be free of her father's tyranny. She flitted about like, in Brougham's words, "a bird set loose from its cage."

Back at Warwick House, the regent dismissed Miss Knight and tried to force her to leave the house immediately. Unable to believe that she was being turned out onto the street like a common kitchen maid, she implored him to remember her loyal service, but the regent would not be swayed. She departed in a state of shock, only to be greeted by the news that Charlotte had run away. Trembling, she was forced to return to tell the prince the news. He cheerfully declared that now all Europe would know how disobedient and wild Charlotte was. No one would want to marry her. Miss Elphinstone burst into tears. Desperate to help, she said she had heard Princess Charlotte announce that she would go to her mother's, and she and the bishop of Salisbury offered to collect her from Connaught House. The regent gave his assent, but he was unwilling to allow them to hurry off alone. He called for the Lord Chief Justice, the Lord Chancellor, the chancellor of the Duchy of Cornwall, and Mr. Leach, his personal adviser, to speed to Connaught House. The Duke of York was alerted to the situation and also set off—bearing a warrant that would allow him, if necessary, to take Charlotte by force.

Miss Knight decided that she, too, should go to Connaught House. By the time she arrived, Charlotte was in the drawing room with Brougham, Miss Elphinstone, and her mother. The bishop was kept to the dining room. Miss Knight demanded to see Charlotte alone, declaring she had a private letter to give her. Charlotte told her that she had written to her father offering to live at the lodge if she was allowed to keep Miss Knight and her other favorite lady, Louisa Louis, and receive visits from Miss Elphinstone.

Outside, the heavy carriages of dignitaries began to rumble into the courtyard, but the Princess of Wales told everybody to wait outside. She could not turn away the Duke of York, so he joined the bishop of Salisbury in the dining room. After a while, the Lord Chancellor and the Lord Chief Justice gave up and drove away. Then, finally, the Duke of York was allowed out of the dining room. Diplomatically, he kept his warrant hidden and listened to the debate. He could see that everyone was trying to encourage Charlotte to return home. "Supposing the Prince Regent, acting in the name and behalf of His Majesty," Sussex put to Brougham, "were to send a sufficient force to break down the doors of this house and carry away the Princess, would any resistance in this case be lawful?"

Brougham had to say that it would not be.

The duke turned to Charlotte. "Then my dear. You hear what the law is. I can only advise you to return with as much speed and as little noise as possible."

Charlotte drew Brougham aside and tried to make him understand how cruelly she had been treated and how terrified she was of her father. Brougham reassured her that the regent could not force her into marriage, but she would have none of it. "They may wear me out with ill treatment," she said, "and may represent that I have changed my mind & consented." But Brougham was uncompromising. "Return to Warwick House or Carlton House," he told her, "and on no account pass a night out of your own house." Charlotte started to cry, and sobbed even harder when her mother, Miss Elphinstone, and the Duke of Sussex told her that they agreed with Brougham.

The night was almost over, and everybody was exhausted. Brougham racked his brain for some way of persuading the princess. Cleverly, he decided to appeal to her love of melodrama. He guided her to the window, where the sun was rising. Puffing out his chest, he asserted, "In a few hours, all the streets and the park, now empty, will be crowded with tens of thousands. . . . [I have only to] show you to the multitude, and tell them your grievances, and they will all rise on your behalf." He conjured a picture of bloody fighting and rioting: "Carlton House will be attacked—perhaps pulled down; the soldiers will be ordered out; and if your Royal Highness were to live a hundred years, it would never be forgotten that your running away from your father's house was the cause of the mischief: and you may depend upon it, such is the English people's horror of bloodshed, you would never get over it."

Convinced of her popularity with the people, Charlotte was eager to believe Brougham's dramatic vision. Her head filled with images of anarchy, she agreed to return to Warwick House, although, she declared, only if a royal carriage was dispatched from Carlton House to take her home. But she requested that Brougham write down that she would never marry the Prince of Orange, and that if the marriage was ever announced, "it must be understood to be without her consent and against her will." Six copies were made, signed, and distributed to those present, and Charlotte said that the documents should be made public if her father insisted upon the marriage going ahead. When the time came for her to wish goodbye to Miss Elphinstone, she began weeping once more. Later she recalled the dreadful moment: "I pressed you to my burning lips, half distracted, desperate, broken hearted, at being forced from you absolutely that I could not utter one single word because you could not."

Charlotte jolted back over the uneven streets that had seemed to promise such freedom hours earlier. There were few girls in England who did not cherish a romanticized notion of her. They could dream of being a princess in a lovely dress, driving around in a sumptuous carriage, without the slightest idea that Charlotte herself had less freedom than the daughter of a whelk-seller.

When Charlotte arrived at Carlton House, she was obliged to wait for half an hour in the courtyard. Her father was not there to receive her. But the regent had been busy. He had already recruited an entirely new staff. The new ladies, Lady Ilchester and Lady Rosslyn, along with Charlotte's old governess, Mrs. Campbell, were assembled to meet her in the hall when she was finally allowed inside.

The heir to the throne found herself in the most beautiful house in

England, which she had not lived in since she was a child. The fine paintings and exquisite decorations proved to be scant consolation. Spies reported on her movements, and she was followed everywhere, never alone for a second. Forbidden to write, she was not allowed pen, ink, or paper. She sat through her somber meals, desperate for human contact and longing for word from August. When Mrs. Louis went to collect some of her items from Warwick House, Lady Ilchester followed her there and prevented her from talking to the servants or collecting any letters. Finally Charlotte managed to obtain a pen, perhaps by bribing a servant. "You have no idea of my situation," she scrawled to Miss Elphinstone. "Oh God, it ought to be remedied indeed, for it is wretched and enough to send anyone wild. I am a complete prisoner, not a letter or thing could get to me except by some merciful private hand." She felt very guilty. "Dearly am I afraid of the precipitate steps I took," she lamented, "but my anguish and self upbraidings are for having drawn you in." She poured out her heart: "My life, my everything has long been at your disposal, but how doubly, after the dreadful scene you went thro' for me. It is I who by my mad conduct brought all this upon you."

London was on fire with prints and gossip about the princess. *The Morning Chronicle* of July 14 contained a long and detailed account, presumably leaked by one of Charlotte's supporters. One caricaturist, amused by Charlotte's flight from her home, produced "Plebeian Spirit or Coachee and the Heir Presumptive," showing a rather dour but beautifully dressed Charlotte grasping a confused peasant cabman and demanding his protection, while Britannia stands weeping beside her and a footman throws up his hands.

The regent was convinced he had allowed his daughter too much freedom, and he was set on a remorseless course. On July 18, the princess was taken to Cranbourne Lodge in Windsor. Although a large house, it was isolated; unsurprisingly, some of its previous occupants had wished to stay hidden. When the thirty-one-year-old Maria, Lady Waldegrave, became the secret wife of George III's brother, the twenty-three-year-old Duke of Gloucester, in 1766, she and her daughters moved with the duke into Cranbourne Lodge. Now it was the home of the future queen of England.

The prince had put a male governor in charge of the household, the seventy-year-old General Garth, an odd choice given that he was attempting to instill a high moral tone: Garth had once been lover to the Princess Sophia. Fortunately, Charlotte found the general friendly and sympathetic, although a touch "vulgar in conversation." Her ladies remained truly loathsome, particularly Lady Rosslyn, who was "as detestable an old lump of bones as ever was . . . & [was] always listening to what [was] going on." The princess had no privacy. Even at night she had to sleep with her door open to the lady who slept in the next room. She was desperate for Prince August to propose and rescue her.

The following day, the Duke of Sussex rose in the House of Lords and questioned Lord Liverpool. Intending to embarrass the prince, in the hope that the newspapers would print every word, he demanded to know if Charlotte was allowed to write and receive letters and whether she would be permitted to visit the seaside, which he understood doctors had prescribed as necessary for her health. His point was that as she was over the age of eighteen, she should be allowed freedom of movement. Lord Liverpool refused to answer, and the Lord Chancellor admonished the duke for his presumptuous questions. Undeterred, Sussex launched into a passionate declaration that "retirement, coercion and seclusion were not the means calculated to instruct and give Princess Charlotte of Wales the most favourable idea of the beauty and advantages of the glorious constitution of this country, over which she was one day, please God, to rule."

The regent pretended to ignore his brother, but he did relent a little. Charlotte was allowed to receive her mother and to ride out in the park, accompanied by General Garth. She began to hope. Perhaps her father might soften or, as was more likely, simply grow bored with keeping her under such strict surveillance.

Then, at the end of July, she received devastating news. The Princess of Wales gleefully told her that she planned to take a boat abroad in ten days' time to live on the Continent. She had decided that she needed a new life, and she had no particular plans to return.

Charlotte fretted that public opposition to divorce might decline once the princess was away. Then her father might remarry, produce a male heir, and displace her from succession. But Caroline was too excited about escaping to worry about her needy daughter or to listen to advisers who told her that she could be damaging Charlotte's position. "I must say," Charlotte grieved, after her final visit to Connaught House, "what goes most to my heart . . . is the indifferent manner of taking leave of me . . . I feel so hurt at *that* being a *leave taking* (for God knows how long, or *what events* may occur before we meet again, or if ever she will return)".

On August 9, Caroline set off to Worthing, along with a gaggle of ladies-in-waiting, gentlemen, a doctor, servants, and Willy Austin, still sickly looking at fourteen. So many people arrived to watch her leave that she had to drive to Lancing to catch her barge. "She decidedly deserts me," wailed Charlotte. The regent, however, was delighted. The night before his wife's departure, he raised a glass and called for a toast: "To the Princess of Wales's damnation, and may she never return to England."

14

A Little Turquoise Heart

The Princess of Wales thought of her daughter as a future queen. "Great and powerful as she may be," she remarked, she hoped Charlotte "will not tyrannize over anyone because they have not the good fortune to please her." The prince regent, however, hardly able to confront the possibility that he might one day die, continued to treat Charlotte as a minor royal, almost as if she was of lower rank than his sisters. His family agreed: Charlotte should not be trained up as a politically engaged, socially adept future queen, but used as a marriage pawn.

"I see no chance for you of comfort," Princess Mary told her niece, "without you marrying." Mary was eager to see her settled and told her: "All your family should be glad if there was anything that would do." Charlotte mentioned Prince Leopold of Saxe-Coburg. Blushing deeply, her aunt gabbled that she thought him good-looking and gentlemanlike. Charlotte, immediately suspicious, told her that she did not like him "for he did not suit her taste," and she was surprised to see relief spreading over Princess Mary's face. The family beauty, thirty-seven-year-old Mary was eager to be married herself, and even though she was so much older, Charlotte always suspected that she was her rival for the attention of the opposite sex—she had boiled with jealousy when Mary had opened her ball in 1813. Now, it seemed, her aunt had her eye on Leopold, who was nearly thirteen years her junior, for herself. "I suspect there is *something there* with her," Charlotte wrote crossly to Miss Elphinstone. "If there is any tendresse, it is all her side certainly." Charlotte was like her father, in that jealousy and competition always excited her. Her aunt's suspicious interest in Prince Leopold had made him suddenly more attractive to her. She began to correspond with him via the Duke of Kent, who acted as a secret courier. As Leopold later admitted, without the duke's help "it would have been impossible as she really was treated as a sort of prisoner."

Meanwhile, *The Morning Chronicle* was still demanding that the princess be allowed a summer holiday for the sake of her health. But the summer dragged on, and the regent refused to let her leave Windsor. Finally, when August was nearly spent, he appeared at Cranbourne and blustered that Charlotte was to proceed to Weymouth that day. Charlotte had wanted to visit Brighton, but the regent wished to keep the fashionable district to himself. Intransigent as ever, he refused to listen to complaints that Gloucester Lodge, the royal residence in Weymouth, was not prepared to receive her. He wanted to send his daughter off in secret, intent that the public should have no chance to line the route and shout their support for her. Only after the queen intervened was Charlotte allowed a few days of preparation before departure.

The prince's petty tyranny continued unabated. When the party was about to leave, Charlotte discovered that not one member of her household had any money to pay the expenses. As she had not received her allowance, she could not assist. She was also deep in debt, owing more than £14,000, an astonishing sum, of which at least £2,000 was for jewels. Like a true Hanoverian, Charlotte had indulged in bouts of shopping to comfort herself.

The queen supplied the necessary funds. When she heard about her granddaughter's debts, she was utterly scandalized at Charlotte's spending and the regent's refusal to give her sufficient money. She informed her son that she would no longer mediate between him and Charlotte. "Then I shall be plagued morning, noon and night with letters and questions," the prince moaned.

Charlotte was a bundle of nerves before the carriage set off. At last, on

September 9, she was free. Every time the party stopped to change horses, she was wildly cheered by crowds, who pressed closer, hungry for a glance of their beloved princess, who had been locked away for so long. When spending the night at Sarum, she stared out at the packed streets, amazed. The road was "*lined* on both sides with people with lights of all kinds to see me & *one* acclamation the whole way. I could hardly get out of the carriage, the multitude pressed so, & when I got upstairs . . . they called for me to appear at the window, which I did, with a candle held behind that they might see me."

Next day, General Garth suggested she lunch at his rambling manor house, in Puddletown, near Dorset. She agreed, relieved to be free from the stares of the crowd for a few hours. No sooner had she arrived, however, than a teenage boy poked his head around the door, looked at her briefly, and hurtled off. Garth then made an eloquent plea for her to approach Tom. "[The] young gentleman here who you may have heard of," Garth told her, "would be much mortified if you took no notice of him." Any "abominable stories" she might have heard were all mistaken.

As Garth talked on about how the thought of sending Tom back to Harrow broke his heart, Charlotte began to realize the awful truth: that the boy must be the result of Garth's liaison with Princess Sophia. She was right. Tommy Garth had been born in the summer of 1800 in secret at Weymouth, adopted by a local couple, and housed at Garth's house from the age of three. By 1804, Sophia's affair with Garth was at an end, but, eager for a position for Tommy, his father showed him off whenever he could. If the royal family came to Weymouth, he made a habit of parading his young son in front of them. Now that Charlotte was a captive audience, he seized his chance to do so again.

Garth later brought the boy up to the drawing room door to bow to her and wish her goodbye. He then told her that he would leave her in Weymouth the following day to visit his home once more. The Weymouth trip gave him the chance to spend some time with his son. By bringing Charlotte to his house, he had coerced her into approving the frequent absences he planned. Charlotte clambered back into her carriage, moved by the General's sadness but angry because he had betrayed her trust. He controlled her household, and so, since she was not in a position to chastise him, she had to swallow her anger.

By the time she reached Weymouth, Charlotte was exhausted, but she managed to summon her most gracious smiles. The people had been waiting all day to see their princess, and they overwhelmed her with their reception. A regimental band played "God Save the King" under her window as she greeted the cheering audience below. It was a relief to finally retire into her room and admire the pretty view toward the sea. Then, taking out her secret ring from Prince August, her heart sank. "Think only of my misery & horror at the *little turquoise heart dropping out* of the setting," she wailed to Miss Elphinstone. She searched everywhere, but to no avail. "All your kind persuasions & consolation will be required to relieve my mind & foreboding spirits of their present weight," she fretted, terrified that the loss portended badly for the relationship. "You know *what a treasure* it is to me, what an *inestimable* value I set on it." If she did find it, there was a practical worry: How could she take it to a jeweler to be refitted? Word would spread that the princess had a secret ring. But she was unhappily convinced that the turquoise heart was lost forever and worried that it meant August would not write to propose. "My whole heart, soul & mind are much too much interested & bent upon it not for me to be sencible I should sink under anything that was adverse." She was simply overwhelmed. "I am tired, worn out in mind & body, & going to throw myself on my bed, & try if I can & forget the miseries of my mind & heart in a happy temporary forgetfulness of all around me."

Charlotte awoke the next day very disinclined to show herself to her faithful crowd. Soon, however, she recovered her spirits and took a walk on the sands and went for a drive with her ladies. On the Monday following their arrival, "Hail Princess Charlotte, Europe's Hope and Britain's Glory" was spelled out in lights near the beach. She visited Portland and Chesil Beach and Corfe Castle, and enjoyed evening entertainments. There were many eager to meet her. Aristocrats, journalists, and notables flocked to Weymouth, even though it was officially out of season. Hoteliers wasted no time in putting up their prices. "The visit of Princess Charlotte renders this place a continued scene of splendour and gaiety," gushed *The Salisbury and Winchester Chronicle*. "The sands are every day crowded with rank, beauty, and fashion."

General Garth was proving incorrigibly bold. He talked constantly of Tom and asked leave to spend days with him back at Puddletown. Still worse, he invited his son to Weymouth and paraded him in front of Charlotte. She despaired. "I cannot tell you how it wounds me & how severely hurt I am at this most outrageous behaviour." Young Tom Garth had started to behave like a minor royal. "He rides up & down the sands, passes my carriage daily in company with a parcel of officers who all look at him as well as my servants, who look at him & then talk to one another. I saw him in my courtyard playing with the horses & patting them." She was angry that he was attracting too much attention. "I know perfectly well that all Weymouth went to see the boy when he was at his hairdresser's," she wrote furiously. Charlotte rightly suspected that Garth was exploiting her presence as a way of getting his son noticed, and she hated how he was implying that he had her approval to do so.

Charlotte was convinced that Garth aimed at a "sort of diabolical *revenge*" on Princess Sophia. "Not being able to torment *her now* any longer with the sight," she wrote, "he will continue it upon the relative in the world she loves best besides the D. of York." Charlotte was also worried that Garth might have an even more subtle aim in sight. "I am quite clear it is done for some purpose, some motive, & to create some interest or other in my mind, as he always talks of him when we are alone." Just like the Duke of Clarence and the Duke of Sussex before him, doting father Garth hoped that Charlotte might take a fancy to his illegitimate son. Infuriated by his behavior, she hated the very sight of the boy, but complaining to the queen would only upset Princess Sophia and would probably ensure that Charlotte was never allowed to go on holiday again. If there was one thing she had learned over her dealings with her family, it was never to confide in them. Finally, on September 17, Tom departed to start a very late term at Harrow, much to her relief.

Charlotte began her warm sea bathing on September 26, when the baths became the social hub of the town, and soon felt well enough to sail out on the boat allocated to her, HMS *Zephyr.* The weather was dipping and the gentry should have departed, but the resort remained crammed with visitors hoping for a glimpse of the princess. This was an age before waterproof shoes or umbrellas. When it rained, one simply got wet, but visitors to Weymouth happily braved bad weather to see her. Invitations to the princess's evening entertainments were frenziedly sought after. On the night of King George's jubilee, she threw a grand party, with elaborate fireworks completed by an illuminated portrait of the king. She was probably borrowing money again, with Garth as her agent.

"I am told that the eyes of the country are now fixed entirely upon me," Charlotte wrote triumphantly to Miss Elphinstone, "that I am not aware what an effect my keeping thus quietly has already produced, & that the language even in London of the best of tradespeople is such *as some* would have *good reason* to tremble at." She had high hopes that public sympathy for her would encourage her father to give her more liberty. She wanted the chance to choose her own suitor, and pick her beloved Prince August.

August, however, had not written asking for her hand. Perhaps, she pondered, he was taking a cautious approach, waiting until relations improved between her and her family. She was busily imagining how her relatives might receive the proposal. "I think & think about how it will be, & how it will all turn out, till my head gets bewildered & turns." In her mind, at least, she was as good as engaged. But still no letter came. To add to her gloom, she heard in October that Lieutenant Hesse had joined Princess Caroline on the continent. She began to worry that the letters she had not retrieved from him would fall into the hands of her mother, who might then use them in the war against her husband.

Miss Elphinstone was pressing her to forget about Prince August, passing on tales that he was secretly married or was about to take up a post as governor of Saxony, which would mean he would be unable to live in England. Charlotte protested that she would love him "long, long after he may have ceased to think [of] or to regard her," but she was allowing doubt to enter her mind. "However sanguine I am tempted at times to allow myself to feel, yet there are others when I *doubt that* his *ambition* (for he has his share) will lead him to think of me, or that he *ever thinks* me a *prize*." She could not contemplate how much it would hurt if he finally ended things, but she wrote: "Tho great as the struggle will be, yet struggle up against being wretched I am resolved I will, by instantly entering into another engagement, which. . . . will *occupy my* time (tho' not my thoughts perhaps)."

If she could not marry August, who else was there? There was talk of the Prince of Württemberg, the Princess Royal's stepson. But he had been divorced from his first wife due to differences of personality, and Charlotte believed that marrying him might be seen as condoning divorce. And then there was Prince Leopold, military hero and favorite of Miss Elphinstone, with whom Charlotte had carried on a desultory correspondence. With Miss Elphinstone pressing, she began to think favorably of him, a dependable young man whom she would be able to dominate and who would certainly think her a prize. Always eager to imagine herself at the center of a drama, Charlotte began to visualize him courting her, and then agonized over what to do if she refused him and Prince August declined to propose. She had pressed Miss Knight to write to August for an answer, making it clear to him that "it ought not to go on much longer . . . for it was not right by either party, & was not creditable to him. She wrote: "A decided answer of some kind would be a blessing really to me, when this uncertainty preyed on my health & spirits." If August abandoned her, she wrote bitterly, she would "overlook everything such as liking & so forth . . . & take the next best thing, which was a good tempered man with good sence, with whom I could have a reasonable hope of being *less unhappy* & *comfortless* than I have been in a single state. That man is the P of S-C." It was hardly a ringing endorsement.

As no word came from August, Charlotte grew dejected. She told a friend, Lady Ashbrook, that she was too "out of spirits" to write much of a letter, for she had been "very uneasy & unhappy upon certain subjects." There was worse to come. On December 14, she wrote that "My heart has had a very sudden & great shock." She and her party returned from Weymouth to Windsor. There, Charlotte found a letter from Miss Elphinstone with the awful news that her beloved Prince August was engaged to be married to another woman—a Miss Rumbolt.

15

The Black Sheep

Charlotte's feelings were "too deep . . . to allow of anything else but grief." She could hardly believe the news. "If the *plain & damning* proofs are brought to me, such as must, however unwillingly, convince me of the faithlessness of the most beloved of human beings, the struggle, the effort, however painful, must be made." She could not bear the fact that she had to "give up all hope for the future."

Determined to dissuade her friend, Miss Elphinstone sent letters full of gossip about Prince August's faithlessness, which, the poor princess admitted, gave her "no consolation." Charlotte struggled to give up on her prince. "I cannot allow my feelings or my hopes to get the better of my reason," she wrote in her last letter of the year, "or to build at all upon your news that no marriage has yet taken place or been announced. I begin to think he is dead for ever to me."

Charlotte's family were eager to help her fall out of love. The Duke of Kent comforted her that August was his family's "black sheep" and had made advances to every pretty girl in Germany. The Duchess of York declared that August had two mistresses and that nobody liked him but his mother. Also, he had terrible halitosis. "Handsome as he was, there was no going near him or bearing his approaching, for that it was worse than anything ever was, & at the opera she was obliged really to get one of her brothers to change places with her for fear of being sick."

Not long after, an *"easy, cool,* familiar, friendly" letter arrived from the prince, conveyed through Miss Knight. August returned Charlotte's ring and picture and broke off the correspondence, vowing that the portrait would only increase his regret at not being able to express the sentiments that she had inspired in him. "If anything was wanted further to *decide* the affair, this does it," Charlotte wrote.

The prince regent was still obsessed with finding proof of Princess Caroline's adultery. He wanted to surprise his daughter into telling all she knew about the child Willy Austin. On Christmas Day, he brought up the subject of Captain Hesse, adopting a kindly and sympathetic tone. Won over by his compassion and relieved at being able to tell her father all and enlist his help in retrieving the letters, Charlotte began to blurt out the truth, explaining that Hesse had ridden out beside her. Then she made the most shocking confession of all: that when his regiment had moved away from Windsor, she had met him at Kensington Palace. She told him how her mother let her suitor in through an open door and locked them into her bedroom, crying, "Amusez vous."

"God knows what would have become of me if he had not behaved with so much respect to me," Charlotte hurried to say.

"My dear child," the prince mumbled, struggling for words, "it is Providence alone that has saved you."

Seeing her father's rolling eyes, Charlotte said that she thought her mother had set her up with Captain Hesse in order to disgrace her and bring William Austin forward. She declared she "had witnessed many things in her mother's room that she could not repeat," and talked of the many lovers who visited. She also told her father that she believed Captain Manby to be the father of Willikin, and even said that a girl in the entourage, Edwardina Kent, was Caroline's child by Sidney Smith. Even more bizarrely, she pronounced that her mother flirted with Hesse, making her wonder "whether Captain Hesse was her lover or her mother's."

Charlotte had been won over by her father's confidential manner. The

regent could be wonderfully charming when he wished to be, and she had
been seduced. As she chattered on, condemning herself with every word,
her aunt Mary scribbled down the details of the conversation, her eyes popping with disbelief.

The prince left in some shock but pleased with what he had learned.
Charlotte had told him everything, and he had valuable ammunition
against his wife. He wrote to his daughter the next day, describing his "extreme satisfaction and happiness . . . at the candid communication you
made me yesterday . . . agonizing as my feelings as a parent were during
your recital." Charlotte was feeling much less content. "I live in a state of
dread in my own mind for fear of any fresh discoveries or interrogations
that might lead to them," she flurried. She suspected that the prince might
use the Hesse confession as a way of pushing her into marrying the Prince
of Orange, "a nasty insignificant thing that is *not worth thinking of once more,
much less twice.*" She was also regretting having sent a letter to her mother
full of reproaches about taking Hesse into her entourage. As the prince regent had pointed out, it could be easily read as if Charlotte *"was jealous of
her."** She had realized that if the letter was exposed, she would be revealed
as having had a lover, and her mother's reputation would also be compromised, giving the regent possible grounds for a divorce.

The regent appointed Lord Keith to interview Hesse and demand the return of the letters. He was concerned that if the story got out, society
would suspect that the Prince of Orange had rejected Charlotte after hearing about her affair with the officer. Fretting about his daughter's reputation,
he told Miss Elphinstone that he thought Charlotte should marry the Prince
of Orange as soon as possible. She disagreed, declaring it unnecessary to
marry one man in order to apologize for writing love letters to another, and
told the prince that Charlotte had confided in her that she would rather continue to suffer restraint and privations than marry the Prince of Orange.

Charlotte was growing eager to free herself from the emotional turmoil of
loving men such as Hesse and August who turned out to be faithless, and she
dreaded a renewal of all the Orange business. "What do I care for amusement
and society," she declared melodramatically. "I am hurt & disappointed with

*Hesse stayed a lothario until the end. He later became the lover of the queen of
Naples, and was finally killed in a duel by a natural son of Napoleon.

many things & unhappy & miserable at the life I spend, wh. is *dulness visible.*"
Miss Elphinstone encouraged her to think of Leopold. She soon came to the
conclusion that when Leopold had written to her father excusing himself for
visiting in 1814, he had actually asked for her hand, "when common sence &
prudence ought to have told him that he or any man that tried would be rejected." She thought, however: "He continues in favour with the PR, [so] it is
not impossible he may still succeed." She pressed Miss Elphinstone to encourage him to visit. "The Leo, as I said before, has my perfect consent to come over
directly or not. I really believe I have made in my own mind a wise choice."

Unfortunately, the prince regent was still pressing her to marry the Prince
of Orange. Railing against the "false and wicked persons" who had raised
doubts in her mind about the prince, he cruelly reminded her of her "melancholy and frightful disclosures" on Christmas Day and threatened that Princess Caroline only had "to make known the documents so unfortunately in
her possession" to kill Charlotte's chances of marriage with any prince at all.

Charlotte was devastated, but she was resolved: *"No arguments, no threats,
shall ever bend* me to marry this detested Dutchman." She had won over her
grandmother and aunts to her cause. The queen wrote grandly to her
son that "both myself and mine choose to keep quite out of it, as we will
never press what will, we know, make Charlotte miserable." Charlotte even
declared, rather implausibly, that her staid grandmother burst into tears
and "implored me on her knees not to marry *ever* a man I did not like, that
it would be endless misery." She told her father that marriage to the
prince was "quite impossible," hitting back at his attempt to blackmail her.
"My reputation is as dear to me as any woman's," she wrote, "but when I
know . . . that I am now going to be placed under your more immediate
care and attention I feel no longer any anxiety on that score." She declared,
too confidently: "Were the whole known to the world very little blame
could attach to me considering how very young I was."

As the queen was traveling to host the finest nobility at a court Drawing
Room during early 1815, the crowd stopped her chair, screaming insults
and demanding to know the whereabouts of Princess Charlotte. They
were so suspicious of her father that they could not believe she was staying
in Windsor and were sure that she had been imprisoned once more.

Charlotte was staying away from town, afraid of the riots over the unpopular Corn Laws, which limited imports of corn into the country. The

legislation pleased landowners, for it kept the price of wheat high, but infuriated the ordinary people. In the early 1790s, before the French wars, wheat had cost between 48 and 58 shillings for a quarter of a ton, but by 1800 it was 113 shillings for the same amount. This was an unbelievable increase of 135 percent, and wages had not kept pace. The people began to protest, and serious food riots began.

For the hungry, angry Britons, the Corn Laws, passed in 1815, were the final insult. Londoners were terrified, and the queen canceled her Drawing Room. "It *is said*," Charlotte wrote, "that the Queen's rooms could not be finished in time, but I believe the fact is they are *afraid of riots* &c on this Corn Bill, as London & all the country are in a flame." She begged Miss Elphinstone not to venture outside. Furious workers were screaming in the streets. A loaf of bread spattered with blood was placed on the parapet of Carlton House.

Then—fortunately for the regent—the French terror reared its head once more, and anti-monarchy sentiment was drowned by fear of invasion. The Congress of Vienna sputtered to a halt when Napoleon escaped from Elba and landed in France on March 1. "All at the Castle, are full of the affair on the Continent," wrote Charlotte. The queen was trying to "talk off danger" and the regent was "quite struck down." On March 17, the Bourbons fled Paris for Belgium. Within three days, Napoleon had entered Paris. On March 22, Wellington announced his plans to fight. "If we do not all unite to the extermination of this monster, we shall all be involved in one common ruin," Charlotte scribbled excitedly. With war afoot, however, Prince Leopold was distracted from the question of marriage, and Charlotte was feeling neglected. "The more I really wish & think of this marriage for me, the more I begin to be in despair & out of heart about it—and if I am disappointed in this too, I shall be quite broken hearted & broken spirited." She was briefly unnerved by gossip that Leopold was due to marry an extraordinarily rich Hungarian countess, but then found that it was actually his brother who was affianced.

Charlotte returned to Warwick House to wait for her prince to appear. While she had been away, her father had made adjustments of his own. The only way to enter her home now was through the Carlton House courtyard. The regent wished to check whoever entered or exited Warwick House, and he was determined to prevent his daughter ever again leaving without his consent.

16

⸙

"Everything I Could Wish & Desire
Collected in One"

Princess Caroline was threatening to return to England, and the regent was attempting to ensure that she could not do so. In May, he demanded that Charlotte sever all contact with her mother. She agreed, pledging "upon my honour never to write from this moment directly or indirectly to her, that all kind of communication shall cease & that I wil abstain from seeing her when she comes to England." She begged her father to inform the princess of her decision and wrote: "In giving up what I do now I have done my utmost." Charlotte only broke her silence to write a letter of condolence on the death of Caroline's brother, the Duke of Brunswick.

Since she had been so obedient on the question of her mother, Charlotte hoped that her father might sanction Leopold as a suitor. But the regent told Lord Liverpool that the marriage "was a subject he could not now enter upon," so preoccupied was he by political crises. Charlotte trailed off to Weymouth for the summer, pining for her poverty-stricken Saxe-Coburg. She was vexed to hear reports that he was enjoying regimental balls and dinners in Paris. If he had time to socialize at suppers, surely he could come and visit? "It is so near & it is but a run of a few hours. I quite languish for his arrival." She had one good piece of news, though: The Prince of Orange was to be married to the younger sister of the tsar, Grand Duchess Anna Pavlovna. She wrote crossly that she hoped that he might be *"made sufficiently* uneasy by his Grand Duchess."

At last the great letter arrived from Miss Elphinstone: Leopold had written complimenting Charlotte and suggesting that he might visit. She confessed herself "delighted, not to say charmed & flattered" by his words, but afraid that her father would try to put Leopold off by gossiping about Hesse, "telling tales" about her and "thus throwing difficulties & obstacles in the way." She begged her friend to ensure that Leopold knew that she had no feelings for August, so that he would be "well prepared & armed against all the lies & different things that will be told him."

Charlotte was buzzing with plans, but Leopold failed to write again, or show. "His silence to you is now what surprises & occupies me the most," she fretted to Miss Elphinstone. "My own opinion is that he will not come at all." She had done everything to convince her beloved of the "propriety & necessity" of his visit, to no avail, and she was impatient with his reluctance to give a clear date. "A time will come when I hope he will know *how* he has *danced us ladies* up & down for him." Still, she did not lose her dry humor. When she heard that two Austrian archdukes and the Prince of Hesse-Homburg—all single—had arrived in London, she joked: "I think the best thing I can do to make *all easy & equally pleased is to marry them all at once in the lump."*

One day, she looked out of the window and had a shock. On the street was a man who was the spitting image of Charles Hesse. She whipped up her telescope and gazed at the figure. Not only did he look like her old lover, but his arm was in a sling, and she had heard that Hesse's arm had been injured in battle. Charlotte was terrified that her father might hear and accuse her of falling for him again, or even suspect her of setting up a clandestine meeting. Quickly she sent General Garth out to speak to him. The general found Hesse on a bench, plumped himself down next to him, and told him that if the regent found out about his visit to Weymouth, there would be terrible consequences. Hesse assured him that he was simply passing through on his way to see friends farther along the coast. He said that he'd had no idea that Charlotte was in Weymouth, which was surely a lie since every newspaper listed her comings and goings. Garth pressed on until Hesse agreed to depart on the midday coach the following day. When she heard the news, Charlotte was overwhelmed with relief, but she watched at her window to ensure that he did indeed go for the coach. The sight of him filled her with disgust and shame.

Charlotte had other problems. Apparently the Princess of Wales was having an affair with Bartolomeo Pergami, her Italian servant. "Surely, surely, my dear Marguerite," Charlotte wrote despairingly to Miss Elphinstone, "there can be *nothing there,* a *low common servant,* a servant too!" Reports suggested that Caroline's life was growing increasingly bizarre. She recruited Germans, Italians, Arabs, French, and Turks, only to fire them quite quickly afterward. Handsome young Pergami was her chamberlain and her trusted confidant. His daughter called the princess "Mama" and had slept in her room. The prince regent dispatched Baron von Ompteda, Hanoverian minister to the Holy See, to investigate. The inquiry into the princess's adultery with Pergami was eventually abandoned because there were no witnesses seen as sufficiently reliable. But still, many were convinced that the story was true. Charlotte had to hear spiteful gossip about her mother's antics and was later sent the defamatory anonymous pamphlet *Journal of an English Traveller; or Remarkable Events and Anecdotes of the Princess of Wales.* Once more, she worried that her father would be able to divorce her mother.

In Brussels, the redoubtable Duchess of Richmond had planned to throw a ball on the evening of Thursday, June 15. She asked the Duke of Wellington whether she should proceed, and he was quite reassuring. He himself was planning to host a ball on June 21. His spies were telling him that the French planned to invade on the twenty-fifth, so there was still time to socialize. On the evening of June 15, two hundred Brussels aristocrats and officers descended on the duchess's house. As the ball started, the news began to circulate that Napoleon was advancing toward Brussels. The soldiers would have to fight the following day. As one guest reported, some men dashed away that instant; others "remained at the ball, and actually had not had time to change their clothes, but fought in evening costume." Lord Uxbridge rounded up the stragglers. "You gentlemen who have engaged partners had better finish your dance and get to your quarters as soon as you can." The Duchess of Richmond stood at the door, helplessly begging her guests to stay for supper. Only a few ladies remained in the ballroom as the men hurried away and gun carriages clattered through the streets. At dawn, the infantry regiments assembled in the Place Royale, ready to march. By seven o'clock the town was quiet. The Bruxellois had lived with British soldiers for over a year; now they had simply disappeared. "The army were gone and Brussels seemed a perfect desert," wrote one man. "The mourners were shut up in their solitary chambers, and the faces of the few who were wandering the streets were marked with the deepest anxiety."

The Battle of Waterloo finally took place on June 18 on farmland covered in summer crops. The allied army of about 73,200, under the Duke of Wellington and the Prussian general von Blücher, faced Napoleon's 77,500 men. The fighting began at 11:30. All around Wellington, soldiers fell. "The finger of Providence was upon me and I escaped unhurt," he said. By the end of the battle, thousands had died. "The *whole* field from right to left was a mass of dead bodies," recalled one spectator, "literally piled upon one another; many soldiers not wounded lying under their horses; others, fearfully wounded, occasionally with their horses struggling on their wounded bodies. The sight was sickening." Brussels became a hospital.

The regent was attending a party hosted by one Mrs. Boehm in St. James's Square when Major the Honorable Henry Percy arrived at the door, his uniform still bloodstained. He laid the eagles of the French army at the feet of the regent and handed his dispatch to Lord Liverpool. The prince was delighted but contemplative. "It is a glorious victory," he said, "and we must rejoice at it, but the loss of life has been fearful, and *I* have lost many friends." Soon he had to address the question of where to house Napoleon. The great man himself had expressed a wish to live in England, but as Lord Liverpool suggested, "he would become an object of curiosity immediately, and possibly of compassion in the course of a few months." Napoleon's request was turned down, but his flattering letter had a marvelous effect on the regent. "Upon my word," he announced, "a very proper letter: much more so, I must say, than anything I ever received from Louis XVIII."

A panic-stricken Charlotte wrote to the secretary for war for an account of the battle. She need not have worried. Leopold and his men had not arrived in Brussels in time to fight at Waterloo.

＊　＊　＊

The regent invited Charlotte to Brighton for her twentieth birthday. The town planned a great celebration when they heard that the lovely princess was due to visit. As *The Morning Post* declared, the "day was ushered in by the ringing of bells, & preparations were making in the early part of the day for a general illumination in the evening, in compliment to the Princess . . . but a desire was expressed that this mark of respect and loyalty from the town might be dispensed with." The regent, presumably, did not wish the arrival of his popular daughter to be so enthusiastically observed. The prince called his daughter to him to discuss her marriage. She assured him that Leopold was her chosen suitor, and said: "No one will be more steady or consistent in this their present & last engagement than myself."

The Earl of Lauderdale, with whom Leopold had been staying, told the regent that the young prince was polite and calm and had little interest in politics. "He had a mania for England and English manners." Lauderdale thought him fond of Charlotte but noted: "He does not shut his eyes, or at least he did not, to her character." The regent was agreeable, eager for any suitor to wed Charlotte before she disgraced herself again. He was, as many thought, "quite nervous with impatience to get Princess Charlotte married, as otherwise the Opposition might clamour for her being treated as heir apparent, and want more than . . . it would be proper to give."

On a wet, chilly morning in February, Charlotte dashed from Cranbourne Lodge to see her aunts at Windsor Castle, letter in hand. The Prince of Wales had accepted that there was no chance of the Orange marriage (partly because the tsar had offered the Dutch prince his youngest sister) and had finally agreed to Leopold as a suitor for his daughter. "Everybody talks of this marriage," wrote Cornelia Knight, now banished to the sidelines. Charlotte wrote to her "very happy in the thoughts of approaching freedom, and saying that she should send for me to visit her as soon as she was mistress of her own house." When the engagement was announced, Leopold received money from the tsar and the Lordship of Holzkirchen from the emperor of Austria—a reward for a job well done, perhaps.

Finally, on February 21, 1816, Leopold arrived. The Prince of Wales had reserved him a fine suite at the Clarendon, Bond Street, and Leopold collapsed there, faint from a punishing migraine. He had time, however, to scribble a note to his princess, noting, as she slyly reported, that he was waiting to see her to "cure *that* & all other ailments." Once the prince was recovered, he drove down to Brighton. Five days later, the princess followed, accompanied by her grandmother and aunts.

In the garish, overheated Royal Pavilion, Charlotte and Leopold met at last. "I find him charming & I go to bed happier than I have ever done yet in my life," Charlotte sighed. She had enjoyed "long conversations on different subjects" that were interesting to their "future plans of life." Unlike her miserable father and aunts, she had, as far as she saw it, chosen her own partner, and chosen well. "A Princess, never, I believe, set out in life (or married) with such prospects of happiness, real domestic ones like other people." She was entranced: "I think him very much talented, with a 1000 resources—musick, singing, drawing, agriculture, farming & botany— besides all he is a capital Italian scholar," she gushed. "I have everything I could *wish & desire collected in one.*" Even better, when she confessed all about Hesse, Leopold, she wrote, "took it uncommonly well and was v. kind" as he saw her "so distressed." He only vented his anger at her mother for encouraging the love affair; he thought Caroline did not deserve her daughter's passionate loyalty. "We did not say much of my mother," Charlotte wrote, "as he told me honestly her conduct was so notorious and so much talked of abroad that he was as well informed as everyone else about her."

Charlotte's high spirits infected her relations. Even the queen was content. "I never saw her so happy or so gracious as she is, delighted at my marriage, & with him." Her grumpy governess, Lady Ilchester, cooed: "Imagination cannot picture a countenance more justifiable of love at first sight. There is a particularly soft and gentle expression blended with positive manliness of cast." She judged Leopold "like an Englishman in all but the ease, elegance and deference of manner." Charlotte was buoyant and convinced that Leopold loved her, not the English throne. "I am quite satisfied," she wrote a few days later, "*he is really,* truly & sincerely attached to *me.*"

The prince regent did not wish Charlotte to talk too much to Leopold. He was keen that the lovers encounter each other only at dinner, and he or the queen escorted them when they did meet. He did not want to risk their discovering too much about each other or engaging in any scandalous behavior à la Hesse. One broken engagement was quite sufficient.

Leopold's kindly expression and gentle manner concealed an iron personality. Although the penniless child of a minor family, he was determined that he would not be the inferior member of the partnership. "I have had a good lecture upon economy & extravagance already," Charlotte worried. He had told her that he thought it unfit for ladies to ride, and so she had given up to him her horses, grooms, and riding master for him to use. He was also trying to encourage her to distance herself from Miss Elphinstone, an act of great ingratitude since she had supported the marriage. As Charlotte thought, the regent had been "putting him on his guard, & putting into his head about female friends" and of her "having more confidence in & being more guided by them than by him."

The thirty-year-old Comte de Flahault, once an aide-de-camp to Napoleon and probably the natural son of Prince Talleyrand, was living in London and courting Miss Elphinstone. Lord Keith and Miss Elphinstone's friends disapproved violently of the *comte,* and Leopold hated him. Secretly, he was jealous, for after he had left Paris, Flahault took over as lover to Napoleon's stepdaughter, Hortense de Beauharnais. Convinced that her fiancé's every utterance was right, Charlotte wrote a deeply tactless letter to Miss Elphinstone. She announced that Leopold "disapproves highly of him & thinks his acquaintance is likely to do you no good." When Miss Elphinstone received the letter, she was furious.

Charlotte quickly realized she had offended her dear friend. "For God's sake do not fancy I ever was or am in the least angry with your intimacy with Flahaud [*sic*]," she scrawled. "You know how much I love you, & that I can ill bear anything like an interruption to an intimacy that has constituted so many years of my happiness." She even sent Margaret copies of Leopold's letters, writing: "Never let it be known or suspected I ever showed you." But she did not retract her words about Flahault, and the damage was done.

Charlotte bubbled with passion for Leopold, but he was a little more withdrawn. The princess was a great contrast to the elegant Hortense. One of his friends wrote, "[She] surprises everybody who has not been told before of her ways." Although she was fresh and lively, she had the "features of a man in her conversation, intelligence, knowledge and wit; for the rest unrestrained merriment, disingenuousness, even a bluntness" that he described as astonishing. "She seems to have a good disposition, but is self-willed and quite indifferent to the knowledge that is required of a woman of distinction." Prince Leopold was a little bewildered by his fiancée and overwhelmed by a family so focused on one child. Trying to please the gouty, fat regent, the demanding queen, and the spinster sisters was all rather exhausting. He retired to his bed with headaches. Happily, although the regent found his future son-in-law rather pedantic, dubbing him *"le Marquis peu à peu,"* he warmed to his amiable character and liked his seeming lack of interest in politics. Still, it was something of a relief for Leopold when Charlotte was sent off to Windsor. He remained with the regent in Brighton, improving his shaky English.

Leopold was mistrusted by many of his future wife's subjects. There had been sly gossip about his sexual habits. George Cruikshank's "A Brighton Hot Bath, or Preparations for the Wedding!!" shows the groom being forcibly scrubbed with soap and water, as well as being given mercury to rid him of venereal disease. The regent leans over him, remembering his own grimy bride and declaring, "I recollect that I was served this way myself twenty years ago." The print is replete with phallic symbols—a sausage on the floor pokes toward a hole in a boot and is denoted as "a German sausage for my intended wife newly dress'd & cook'd up in the best manner." Sex manuals such as *Aristotle's Masterpiece* lie scattered over the floor. In "A German Present," the caricaturist Williams shows penniless Leopold offering Charlotte a large sausage. Charlotte leans toward it, declaring, "Oh dear me, 'tis the longest and thickest I ever saw, do let me taste it." Her father advises her not to take too much of it at a time. "You'll find it very hot."

The regent procrastinated about setting the date of the wedding, then finally settled on May 2. Charlotte had imagined a grand ceremony, with herself in a fine dress, drawing up in a luxurious carriage. Alas, her father was intent that Charlotte should receive as little press attention as possible, and so he arranged for her to be married quietly at Carlton House. She sulked and complained that her father wished to give her "a smuggled wedding" and marry her off like the simple daughter of the Princess of Wales, not the future queen of England, but he was intransigent. She could have a fine dress and diamonds, but she could not invite hosts of guests. Finally, nervous that her father might postpone the wedding again, Charlotte capitulated. Pleased with her obedience, the regent offered a bribe: She would be fitted for her wedding dress and a trousseau of thirty dresses. It would make up for the fact that she was finally forced to sell the jewels bought with the Prince of Orange's £15,000, although she hoped that she might find a way to buy back some of the pearls.

Once the wedding was confirmed, Parliament began discussing the couple's future home. As money was short, they were offered Camelford House, a poky residence on the corner of Park Lane and Oxford Street. Charlotte complained that it was far too small, since it had only one staircase and two floors. The regent, however, was pleased that his daughter would have no chance to entertain. To ensure that she would be equally restricted in the country, he suggested that their country residence should be his daughter's detested Windsor home, Cranbourne Lodge. Charlotte refused. For once, her stubbornness paid off. Instead she was offered Claremont, a large house near Esher, with two hundred acres of land. The princess clapped her hands with delight. "It is such a fine thing," she exclaimed.

Lords Liverpool and Castlereagh, the foreign secretary, suggested the young couple should receive £50,000 a year, with an additional £10,000 for Princess Charlotte alone to cover her maids and clothes, as well as £60,000 for jewels, plate, and furniture. It was a generous sum, but not enough for Charlotte, who had always fallen into debt. Moreover, the couple would be entirely dependent on her money. The regent wished his daughter to live in style (if the state was paying), and he decreed that she should have armies of servants. Attempting to please her prudent, almost miserly fiancé, Charlotte resisted, declaring that she needed no more than six footmen. Still, she could not abandon her Hanoverian addiction to luxury overnight. She chose a gorgeous style of state livery, so the footmen that she did appoint were to be splendidly arrayed in dark green coats edged with gold lace. She also arranged to retain Mrs. Campbell and Mrs. Louis in her household, although she did not call for Cornelia Knight. The queen ordered her wedding dress and a fabulous trousseau of grand dresses: two of Brussels point lace, two of British blond lace, gowns of Indian muslin intricately embroidered and trimmed with lace, and gowns of net over satin, covered with astonishing gold and silver embroidery, along with more ordinary satin gowns, as well as hats and capes.

On April 22, Prince Leopold came from Brighton to Windsor and three days later met Charlotte at a party for Princess Mary's fortieth birthday. Four days afterward, the prince and his entourage piled into two of the regent's carriages and drove to dine at the house of the famed naturalist Sir Joseph Banks, Smallberry Green, near Hounslow. There, Leopold transferred to one of the regent's dress carriages, drawn by six horses with coachmen, outriders, and footmen splendid in crimson livery. Along the route to Kensington, people jostled for a glimpse of the man who would be marrying their future queen. Crowds also surrounded Carlton House, where Charlotte arrived at half past one. When the prince clattered into Clarence House two hours later, he was wildly applauded, and people shouted until he came onto the balcony to wave.

17

※

Mr. and Mrs. Coburg

On May 2, 1816, crowds had been gathering since the early morning, determined to spot the happy couple. There was not a section of road from Charing Cross to Carlton House or all along the Mall that was not crammed with shouting, waving spectators, many clutching commemorative portraits of the pair. The country was eager for a respite from the depression that had descended after the euphoric end of the war. *The Augustan Review* hoped the marriage might "counteract the despondency which some luckless politicians would fain spread around them."

Charlotte, sitting for a sculpture at home and dining with her aunts, was left relatively untroubled. London was in the grip of Leopold fever. At two o'clock, the groom drove out to visit her, and the crowds screamed wildly. On his return, there were so many spectators that he could not get out of the curricle. Fifty constables failed to hold back the surging crowds, and a footman opening the door of the carriage was nearly crushed. Women and children toppled through the doors of Clarence House. Once the hysteria had died down, Leopold came out to wave to his admirers from the balcony.

That evening, Charlotte dined with the queen. As soon as dinner was over, she went upstairs to put on her wedding dress, and she and the queen, along with her aunts Augusta and Elizabeth, took an open carriage from Buckingham House to Carlton House, waving at the crowds as they went. As Leopold arrived, people even tried to unhitch his horses and drag the carriage. Handsome in the embroidered uniform of a British general—with a glittering gold sword and belt, a gift from the queen—he was greeted by his future father-in-law, equally fine in his scarlet field marshal's uniform and looking much healthier than he had in years. The prospect of finally seeing Charlotte married had done wonders for the regent's gout.

The Grand Crimson Room had been decorated with drapes; and candles, prayer books, and all the accoutrements of religion had been brought over from the Chapel Royal. There were many guests Charlotte would have preferred not to see, including the detestable Lord Eldon, and Lady Hertford, her husband, and their son, Lord Yarmouth, as well as Dr. Fisher. Viscount Keith was present, as well as Charlotte's beloved uncles York, Clarence, and Kent. The Duke of Gloucester did not attend. Miss Elphinstone, apparently, was ill.

Charlotte arrived, slightly bowed under the weight of her thick white and silver dress and silk net overgown, which featured shells and bouquets embroidered in silver lamé. Brussels lace adorned the sleeves and neckline, and she had a six-foot-long train of white and silver, also embroidered. The dress had cost £10,000. Around her head she wore a wreath of diamond roses; she also glittered with a diamond necklace and large earrings from her father and a diamond bracelet, a gift from Prince Leopold (who had either received money from his father or borrowed the cash), as well as pearls—perhaps those bought with the money of the Prince of Orange. She was flanked by her grandmother and aunts and five bridesmaids. This time, the archbishop had no cause to stop and stare ominously at the couple. Charlotte answered boldly and loudly, but Leopold, less confident of his English, was quieter. When he promised to endow her with all his worldly goods, Charlotte gave a quick snort of laughter. Within twenty-five minutes, it was all over. Toasts were drunk and everybody embraced. Charlotte congratulated herself on her ladylike behavior. As she wrote to Miss Elphinstone, "I promised you to behave well . . . and everyone complimented me on the composure & dignity of my manner."

Charlotte retired to change into a rich white traveling dress trimmed with ermine and a white satin hat. She then slipped down the back stairs to accompany her husband to their carriage for the journey to the Duke of York's country residence, Oatlands, near Weybridge. The queen suddenly decided that it would be thought indecent if the pair traveled together so late and instructed Charlotte's lady-in-waiting, Mrs. Campbell, to accompany them. To the young couple's delight, she refused, and they were sent off in the warm, dark carriage, alone for the first time.

"I cannot say I feel much at my ease or quite comfortable in his society," reflected Charlotte, "but it will wear away, I dare say, this sort of awkwardness." Although she thought her husband had the "perfection of a lover," she was feeling slightly overwhelmed. Oatlands had its drawbacks. Two days after her arrival, Charlotte complained to Margaret that the air was quite unwholesome, as it was "so infected & impregnated with the smell & breath of dogs, birds and all sorts of animals." A further annoyance was that hardly one of her trousseau of thirty dresses fitted. A woman from the village was brought in to alter the dazzling stacks of expensive fabric and embroidery.

Charlotte was worried that she had lost Miss Elphinstone's friendship. She wrote to promise her fervent affection, avowing that her last words were to beg the Princess Lieven, wife of the Russian ambassador to London and acute political observer, to give Margaret "a faithful account." She wrote: "[I asked] my maid just as I drove off to go & tell you how I looked & was." But Miss Elphinstone was planning to marry Flahault, and she could not forgive Charlotte her harsh words about him.

During the honeymoon, Charlotte encountered her husband's doctor and dearest friend, twenty-eight-year-old Christian Friedrich Stockmar. A shrewd, bustling little doctor, he had been sent over from Coburg when Leopold had arrived in England suffering from migraines, and had so impressed Leopold that he asked him to remain as his private secretary. Charlotte rather liked Stockmar, but he was dubious about her boisterous clumsiness. Although he admitted she was "handsomer" than he expected and considered she had good taste in dress, he found her manners "most peculiar." He was quite nonplussed by her habit of standing with her hands behind her back and her stomach pushed out, constantly bouncing about, stamping her foot to emphasize her points, and laughing and talking incessantly.

The young couple had two days alone (with the dogs) before the Prince of Wales arrived to pay a "very *unexpected* and *undesired*" call on his daughter, prattling inanely for more than two hours about regimental uniforms. Charlotte complained, but she found her father's self-centered chatter soothing, and it was a break from trying to think of something to say to her husband. Stressed by their new experiences, both Leopold and Charlotte were feeling unwell. Prince August still returned to her mind in low moments, but she tried not to think about him. She decided the foundation of her marriage was "very *reasonable.*" She wrote: "Therefore there is less chance of its ever being otherwise than with most others; indeed, on the contrary, I am more inclined to think that it will improve. I do not see how it can fail to go on well, tho' sometimes I believe it is best not to analyse one's feelings too much or probe them too deeply."

After eight days, Charlotte and Leopold moved to their London home, Camelford House. They began paying and receiving calls, as was customary for a newly married couple. On May 16, the queen hosted a Nuptial Drawing Room for the pair, attended by two thousand people, including all those of English nobility who were able, as well as distinguished foreign visitors, ministers, judges, and the higher clergy. Crowds flooded the streets and scrambled up the trees around Buckingham House in the hope of seeing their future queen. "We have not the space to list the illustrious persons present at the Drawing Room," sniffed *The Times.* "Our readers will have to be content with a few." When they swept in late to the theater, all eyes swiveled from the stage to the young couple, demanding that they move to the front of their box. Audiences around London began to sing a new version of "God Save the King":

> *Long may the Noble Line,*
> *When she descended, shine*
> *In Charlotte the Bride!*
> *Grant it perpetuate*
> *And ever make it great;*

On Leopold's blessings wait
And Charlotte his Bride.

On June 20, Parliament passed a bill to purchase Claremont and its grounds as a present for the young couple. Swept up in the general mood of adulation, ministers splurged £69,000 on the house.

After the slightly unpropitious honeymoon, Charlotte and Leopold settled into a happy relationship. They enjoyed each other's society, and they began to fall deeply in love: Leopold became a passionate admirer of Charlotte's beauty and her kind, sincere heart, while she began to depend on him absolutely. He was the kindly father figure she had never had, in the body of a handsome twenty-six-year-old. Charlotte could not have found someone more different from the often drunken, angry, spendthrift regent. Leopold never flew into jealous rages or threw tantrums, or blew hot and cold. He sulked rather than shouted, and he was often exasperatingly placid. When Charlotte raged or screamed with laughter, he admonished her gently, *"Doucement, chérie."*

Both husband and wife believed in a modern notion of marriage based on happy mutual understanding and respect. Leopold wrote that their rule was "never to permit one single day to pass over *ein missverständniss,* however trifling"—although discussions about the prince regent and Queen Charlotte usually ended in argument.

Charlotte was no longer a child ruled by the regent, but the queen of England in waiting. She had not been well prepared for her future role. Her education had been neglected, and her knowledge of history and politics was culled from the newspapers. She had met many statesmen, but they had been more interested in either catching her out or flattering her than explaining matters of domestic or foreign policy. She had seen no more of the country she was destined to rule than Weymouth, St. James's, and a few spots of Surrey. She thought of her subjects as those in the crowds who waved to her as she drove past, and she had scant notion of the poverty, inequality, and despair that plagued much of her country, particularly in the rural north, Wales, and the southwest. The people thought that Charlotte would be the queen to renew the monarchy after the parade of troubled, debauched, and spendthrift kings. But although she took a keen interest in current affairs, she had little idea about how government functioned.

As a married woman, Charlotte would be exposed to the public gaze as she had never been under the regent's strict regime. She would need more than simple youth and enthusiasm. Her father was detested not only because he was self-obsessed and hedonistic, but also because he had failed to enact any reforms. Charlotte was popular because she was believed (thanks in great part to her friendship with Earl Grey and the Duke of Devonshire) to be more liberal in outlook.

In June, Charlotte had to cancel her appearance at a performance of *Macbeth*, forgoing the chance to see Mrs. Siddons, in her greatest role, as Lady Macbeth. A month later, she was taken ill at the opera and retired to bed. She was unable to attend the wedding of her aunt Mary to the Duke of Gloucester. Finally, it was announced that she had suffered a miscarriage. Fortunately, she was soon sufficiently recovered to host a party at Camelford House.

On August 23, wagons were piled high with furniture and plate, and the servants were bundled into stagecoaches bound for Claremont. The young couple followed behind and arrived in the early evening. Standing on the steps, with the bells of Esher church ringing behind her, Charlotte announced, "Thank Heaven I am here at last!"

Claremont was a perfect Palladian villa in cream brick, complete with portico, Ionic pillars, and friezes. Perched on the top of a rolling hill, with a flight of twenty-two steps, it was graceful, spacious, and very grand. The playwright and architect Sir John Vanbrugh had built the first house on the estate in 1708. The builders were slow, and in 1714, Vanbrugh sold the house to his friend Thomas Pelham, Earl of Clare, who later became the Duke of Newcastle. Pelham was particularly concerned about improving the grounds, planting trees, and creating a ha-ha. When Newcastle died in 1768, Lord Clive of India bought the house from his widow. Clive found the house damp, demolished it, and asked Lancelot Brown, commonly known as Capability, to oversee the building of another house on higher ground.

Capability directed the rearrangement of the lands and grounds, and built the house that Charlotte came to love. The most surprising feature was a large marble bath sunk into the floor of the basement, in a specially appointed room decorated with stucco medallions, installed at a cost of over £310. After Clive's death in 1774, the house passed through various hands, and the last owner, a Charles Rose Ellis, sold it after his wife died giving birth to her third child.

After years in the most ramshackle royal houses, Charlotte was charmed by Claremont. She altered some lines by the great poet James Thomson and inscribed them on a snuffbox:

> *To Claremont's terraced heights and Esher's groves,*
> *Where in the sweetest solitude embraced*
> *By the soft winding of the silent Mole,*
> *From courts and cities Charlotte finds repose.*

The young couple resolved to live a virtuous but full life, in complete contrast to Charlotte's bitter aunts and debauched father. "Except when I went out to shoot, we were together always and we could be together, we did not tire," recalled Leopold. Stockmar gushed that their relationship had "everything that can promote domestic happiness," and that Charlotte bore Leopold "an amount of love, the greatness of which can only be compared with the English national debt." Charlotte was trying hard to please by playing the worthy new wife, sitting quietly and corresponding decorously with her husband's sister, Victoire, the Dowager Princess of Leiningen. Leopold declared that the house should be run according to careful economy, proposing that the staff sleep away from Claremont and return only when required. To the delight of the local shopkeepers, Charlotte vowed to buy household provisions from them and to settle her bills promptly, a novel experience for a Hanoverian. On one occasion, Miss Knight came to call and waited in a doorway, afraid of disturbing the couple, who seemed deep in papers. "Come in, come in!" cried Charlotte. " 'Tis only Mr. and Mrs. Coburg settling their accounts."

When Princess Mary visited in September, she was surprised that the couple's passionate mutual adoration had not dulled. "We went to see two people completely engrossed in each other, but anxious to be *kind* and do all they could to make it go off comfortably. I doubt that the sort of life they are leading can *last*, but I wish it may with all my heart." Charlotte grew jealous of any woman who caught her husband's eye, including Lady Maryborough, the Duke of Wellington's sister-in-law, even though, as Leopold pointed out, the lady was fifteen years his senior. She was so wrapped up in her beloved that she was unruffled when her aunt Mary married the Duke of Gloucester, whom Charlotte had once thought of as a beau. "He is much in love, & tells me he is the happiest creature on earth. I won't say she does as much, but being her own mistress, having her own house, & being able to walk in the streets all delights her in their several ways." Many were baffled as to why Mary had accepted the stolid Duke; Charlotte was sure she had simply wanted to escape Windsor. "He is certainly all attention to her," she wrote, "but I cannot say she looks the picture of happiness or as if she was much delighted with him." However far from ecstasy, Mary's situation was better than that of the Princesses Elizabeth and Sophia, still marooned in the castle.

Charlotte was the partner in the relationship who had to try the harder. As Leopold confessed years later, in his early married life he had been "sometimes inclined to be sulky and silently displeased." He was keen to increase his influence over Charlotte's family and assist his own siblings. The Duke of Kent, Charlotte's favorite uncle, was casting about for a wife in the hope that Parliament might pay off his disastrous debts. Leopold politely began to press the cause of his sister Victoire, a lively thirty-year-old widow with two young children. After listening to hours of praise, the duke made plans to visit her at her residence of Amorbach, near Darmstadt, and Princess Charlotte gave him a letter of recommendation. But Victoire was unwilling to leave her home, for fear of endangering her son's claim to the principality of Leiningen. When the duke proposed in 1816, she turned him down.

Charlotte had been repeatedly betrayed by her parents, who had both tried to wheedle her into revealing confidences that might hurt the other. But she was sweetly trusting of Leopold. She accepted absolutely that his every suggestion was for the best and seemed to rather enjoy conforming to his desires. He even managed to discourage Charlotte from her love of adoring crowds. When they went to the local church, sightseers in their finest outfits scuttled down from London and from miles around to admire the young couple and sit by them if they could. Local residents were disgruntled at seeing their humble church packed with fashionable ladies. After Leopold made gentle suggestions, Charlotte agreed to pay her devotions at Claremont's private chapel.

Charlotte might have been saving money on potatoes and greens, but she was not holding back on dress or entertainment. She adored the consequences of being a married woman, able to receive her relations on her own terms. The Duke and Duchess of York, conveniently situated at nearby Oatlands, became particular favorites. Of her aunt's Christmas fair for the local families, Charlotte wrote, it was "the gayest and prettiest sight I ever saw I think, the numbers of children, their parents, and all the happy merry faces, the noises they make with their toys and things." Although she and her husband had been offered the spectacular Marlborough House in St. James's as an alternative London residence to Camelford House, they preferred Claremont. Charlotte decided not to attend a grand ball thrown by the prince regent in Brighton on January 7, 1817, to celebrate her twenty-first birthday. She remained at home to admire Claremont and the village of Esher illuminated and hung with streamers.

"We are doing a great deal to improve the place, which employs a vast many poor labouring people who could otherwise be quite out of work and probably starving for want of it," she gloated. The starving people elsewhere in England were not so fortunate. The harvest of 1816 had been very poor, and inflation, impossibility of export, and expenditure on the war had left the country poor. The euphoria of the war was followed by mass unemployment as thousands of young men returned from fighting to look for work and industries that had been fed by the war machine began to lay off workers. Charlotte Bury wrote:

> The people cherished hopes that peace would pour forth its cornucopia of plenty into the lap of the nation, and they were naturally disappointed and attributed the calamities which they suffered to something wrong in the administration of the government. A general paralysis affected industry. The loom stood silent, the merchants were

perplexed with bankruptcies . . . the few who considered the alliance
between cause and effect, saw that the war had given employment to
many whom the peace necessarily deprived of their occupation.

At the beginning of 1817, the regent was driving to open Parliament when his carriage was stoned, and some even declared that shots were fired. In response, he led a campaign to buy British, and Charlotte and Leopold followed suit by purchasing £1,000 worth of Spitalfields silk to decorate their home, as well as buying English china. For once, the regent and Charlotte were in agreement: The way to improve the situation of the poor was to encourage the rich to spend.

On May 2, 1817, Charlotte and Leopold held a party to celebrate their wedding anniversary. Miss Elphinstone was invited, but Charlotte was less concerned to renew their friendship than to encourage her old confidante to return all her letters. Two days later, Prince Leopold wrote to tell the regent that Margaret had resolved to keep the correspondence, despite Charlotte's pleas. Still, the young couple had some happy news. On April 30, Prince Leopold announced to his father-in-law that Charlotte was pregnant once more. It would be the first legitimate birth in the royal family since her own, twenty-one years before.

18

"Some Strange, Awkward Symptoms"

Wild bets were made on the sex of Charlotte's baby. Economists calcu-lated that a princess would raise the stock market 2½ percent, while a prince would inflate it by 6 percent. At Claremont, Charlotte's days fol-lowed the same tranquil round. After breakfast at eleven, she sat for a por-trait by Sir Thomas Lawrence, and then drove slowly out around the grounds, with Leopold walking by her side. After another sitting, the cou-ple dined, and then passed the evening playing the piano and playing cards with their company. The young mother-to-be seemed to be blooming, but others were concerned. "Princess Charlotte is going on in her *grosseuse*, but there are some strange, awkward symptoms," Lady Holland reported. Characteristically, the princess was taking very little exercise, however much Leopold pressed her to walk with him. She had no female compan-ion. When Lady Ashbrook wrote to offer her company, Charlotte replied that she had refused the queen, so could not accept anyone else.

As the pregnancy wore on, Charlotte's health began to deteriorate. She started to feel more and more exhausted, and to suffer from low spirits and depression. Leopold later said to Queen Victoria that his wife had not exercised enough in pregnancy and this had contributed to her death, but it also seemed as if she was simply sick with fatigue. At the beginning of November, she took communion and told the chaplain, "I have not now a wish ungratified. Any change must be for the worst."

Sir Richard Croft, the leading obstetrician of the day, was brought in to assist Charlotte's regular physician, Dr. Matthew Baillie (whose wife was also sister to Sir Richard), as well as another obstetrician, Dr. John Sims. Jealous of his distinguished patient, Sir Richard declared he wished to treat Charlotte independently. He judged that she was eating too much and growing too heavy, and decided that the best way to prepare a young and nervous first-time mother for the birth of what seemed to be a very large baby was to put her on a stringent diet, as well as bleeding her regularly. His hope was to reduce the weight of the baby; instead, he simply weakened his young patient.

Charlotte's date was estimated for the middle of October. Mrs. Griffiths, a nurse with thirty years' experience of midwifery, moved into the house, and Sir Richard was always present. The press reported on October 9 that the baby was due within nine or ten days. But by the twenty-first, there was still no sign of a child. The following day, Charlotte's physicians decided to bleed her. On November 1, the queen—although she later declared, "Charlotte's figure was so immense (to me not natural) that I could not help being uneasy to a considerable degree"—left to take the waters at Bath.

Charlotte was growing weary of being large, and she was missing her mother. After hearing from a friend that the doctor Henry Holland was in attendance on Caroline, she expressed her appreciation of those who trailed with the Princess around Europe. "I have it not in my power at present to repay any services to the Princess of Wales, but if ever I have, those who remain steadfast to her shall not be forgotten by me," she remarked. "I refrain from making professions of gratitude, but I do not feel them the less towards all those who show her kindness. I have not heard from my mother in a long time. If you can give me any intelligence of her I shall be obliged to you to do so." It was one of the last letters she ever wrote.

On the evening of Monday, November 3, Charlotte came in from a stroll with Prince Leopold and was just removing her cloak when the pains began. She took to her bed, feeling brave and energetic. "I will neither bawl nor shriek," she told Mrs. Griffiths. Sir Richard, confident that he could direct the labor alone, encouraged her to walk but would not allow her to eat. He declared that the birth would be in the early morning, and so dignitaries including the archbishop of Canterbury and bishop of London, Lord Sidmouth, the Home Secretary, Lord Eldon, the Lord Chancellor, and even Earl Bathurst, the secretary for war, were summoned from London. Journalists and sightseers flocked to the village. But by early evening of November 4 there was still no sign of a baby. Rather than worrying that the labor pains were too weak, Croft declared to the dignitaries that the birth was proceeding well since Charlotte was not crying out in pain. "Nothing can be going on better," he blustered. She had emitted "not a murmur or complaint."

As it became clear that Charlotte was unable to expel the child, Croft and Baillie began to ponder the use of "artificial assistance" and finally summoned Dr. Sims. When Sims arrived, Sir Richard decided that the labor must be nearly over, so there would be no need of forceps. They were very afraid of intervening too much and damaging the baby, for in the days before sterilization, forceps could kill. Moreover, it was not a case of attending a royal wife, who could simply be replaced if she died—Charlotte was the one and only heir to the throne. Croft reported to the dignitaries that his patient had "made a considerable, though gradual progress throughout the night" and so he and his fellow doctors hoped therefore that the child would be born "without artificial assistance."

There was no queen or regent to take charge, and Leopold was too inexperienced to be of use. Charlotte struggled on. She had been without sleep for thirty-six hours. She had had no food for twenty-four, and she was weakened from months of bleeding and a starvation diet. She had not the energy to give birth. By Wednesday afternoon, she was dozing. It was only at midday on November 5 that she began to experience greater pain. Nine hours later, she gave birth to a boy, large, handsome, and stillborn.

Frantically, the doctors and Mrs. Griffiths plunged the baby into warm water, pumped his chest and rubbed him with salt and mustard, but to no avail. The child could not be saved. Charlotte herself was so weak that she could hardly absorb the news, repeating only to Mrs. Griffiths that it was the will of God. The nurse still had to carry the corpse to the dignitaries for inspection. They judged it a noble-looking child and hurriedly, unhappily mounted their carriages to return to London.

Leopold retired to write to the regent that after more than forty-eight hours of pain, the princess had given birth to *"un enfant, mâle, mort."* He had been awake for most of the time, powerless to help.

Charlotte was still bleeding, and her uterus was swollen. The doctors decided to remove the placenta by hand, rather than wait for it to emerge naturally. After they had extracted it, Charlotte was finally given the food she so craved: chicken broth and toast with a little barley water, along with some camphor julep to stimulate her heart, for the beat was sluggish. Much to the doctors' relief, she seemed to bear her loss bravely and even attempted to cheer her despairing husband.

Finally, at eleven o'clock, the exhausted, devastated household retired for the night, leaving Charlotte in the care of Mrs. Griffiths. Leopold took an opiate and collapsed into bed. Just after midnight, Charlotte began vomiting violently, unable to keep down the camphor julep or the broth. For a few minutes she was quieter, and then she clutched her stomach, crying, "Oh, what a pain! It is all here!" Mrs. Griffiths hurried for Sir Richard. He found that the princess was cold and struggling to breathe. She was also bleeding heavily, and her pulse was racing. Dr. Baillie was summoned. Croft put hot-water bottles on her and a hot flannel on her stomach, and Baillie plied her with wine and brandy, but their efforts were hopeless. The future queen of England was mortally ill.

Croft told Stockmar to rouse Leopold. The grieving father, however, was under the influence of the opiate and unable to move. As Stockmar tugged at him, he received a message from Baillie begging him to return to the princess. He dashed back to find Charlotte in "a state of great suffering," hardly able to breathe, delirious, and tossing in pain. Baillie was desperately trying to ply her with wine. After a life surrounded by her family to an almost suffocating degree, the princess was dying virtually alone.

When Baillie told her, "Here comes an old friend of yours," she stretched out her hand to grasp Stockmar's. "They have made me tipsy," she uttered, and fell into convulsions. Then, he wrote, "the rattle in the throat began. I had just left the room [to fetch Leopold] when she called out loudly 'Stocky! Stocky!' I went back; she was quieter, but the rattle continued. She turned more than once over on her face, drew her legs up, and her hands grew cold." Princess Charlotte's time of death was recorded as half past two. By the time Leopold arrived, it was too late. He sat by the body for a while and then left the room. "I am now quite desolate," he said to Stockmar. "Promise to stay with me always."

The future queen of England was dead.

"It really was as though every household throughout Great Britain had lost a favourite child," wrote Brougham. The country went into immediate mourning, and there was a run on black cloth. Public buildings were draped in black, and even the poorest beggars wore black bands. The theaters were shut down, along with the docks, the Royal Exchange, and the law courts. Shops that had been displaying portraits of Charlotte and Leopold for those excited about the royal birth hurriedly began selling souvenirs showing Charlotte ascending to heaven with the angels. The public bought memorial cards, plates, cups, pitchers, and entire tea services, snapped up memorial rings and bracelets, and contributed in their droves to a fund that had been set up by the Duchess of York to pay for a marble memorial. "We never recall so strong and general an expression and indication of sorrow," mourned *The Times*.

The shops closed for a fortnight. Every place of worship planned a special service. Even the gambling houses shut down on the day of the funeral. The wax makers quickly re-dressed their models of Charlotte in black and began parading her around the country. "One met in the streets people of all class in tears, the churches full at all hours," wrote the commentator and wife of the Russian ambassador, Princess Lieven, "and everyone, from the highest to the lowest, in a state of despair, which it is impossible to describe." Grief was so severe, indeed, that manufacturers of silk, ribbons, and other fancy items of dress petitioned the government to reduce the period of mourning. England's great hope was gone.

"Her death is one of the most serious misfortunes the country has ever met with," considered the Duke of Wellington. When Lord Byron heard the news while in Italy, he threw open the windows of his apartment and bellowed so loudly that he could be heard all the way down the Grand Canal. He later wrote in *Childe Harold's Pilgrimage*:

> *Fond hope of many nations, art thou dead?*
> *Could not the grave forget thee, and lay low*

Some less majestic, less beloved head? . . .
. . . in the dust
The fair-hair'd Daughter of the Isles is laid,
The love of millions!

The prince regent had been staying with his mistress, Lady Hertford, at her estate at Sudbourne, in Suffolk, when he was told that his daughter had gone into labor. He hurried to Carlton House, arriving at three o'clock on Thursday morning. On learning that the child was dead, he went to bed. The Duke of York woke him later to tell him that Charlotte had also died. He fled to Brighton, consumed by grief. The queen said to console him: "[You] had it in your power to make your child completely happy by granting her to marry the man she liked and wished to be united to." She pointed out that, as well, he had given her a home she loved, but her words could not alleviate his grief. He hid in his room in shock, being bled by the doctors, until he had to emerge to plan the funeral. He left to Leopold the task of informing the Princess of Wales, but the bereaved husband procrastinated, and the princess heard the awful news by chance, from a courier destined for the Pope. She fainted in shock. "England, that great country, has lost everything in losing my ever beloved daughter," she mourned. The Duchess of York tried to pay a call on Leopold but collapsed in the hall of Claremont. The Prince of Orange burst into tears when he heard the news, and his wife ordered all the ladies of his court to wear mourning dress.

"It is true that I loved her for her physical beauty, but I can vow that what I loved more and more and came to appreciate more every day was her noble heart," Leopold wrote. He had lost not only his beloved wife and his son but also everything that he had hoped for, not least his future as possible joint ruler of England. Wandering around Claremont in despair, he demanded that nothing be moved from his wife's room. Even her boots, left on the floor after her last walk, were to remain. "November saw the ruin of this happy home, and the destruction at one blow of every hope and happiness of Prince Leopold," wrote Stockmar. "He never recovered the feeling of happiness which had blessed his short married life."

The day after Charlotte's death, the doctors came to carry out a postmortem on the bodies. Sir Everard Home, sergeant surgeon to the king, removed their guts and embalmed them. Once the postmortem was over, the undertakers swathed the baby in linen and laid him in an open coffin. His heart, which had been removed, was placed in a separate urn. Charlotte was also covered in linen, and lowered into a coffin draped with blue velvet. "It was grief to look at him," wrote Mrs. Griffiths of Leopold as he watched his wife and child being laid out. "He seemed so heartbroken."

On the evening of November 18, 1817, the ornate mahogany coffins of Charlotte and her son were taken from Claremont to Windsor in a quiet procession, the separate hearses each drawn by eight black horses. The infant was taken directly to St. George's Chapel and not given any service, according to the principle that stillborn children had no soul and thus needed no prayers. The following day, Charlotte lay in state at Lower Lodge, in Windsor. The crowds were so eager to enter that a detachment of Royal Horse Guards had to restrain them. That evening, she was taken to St. George's Chapel in a procession lit by thousands of torches. Leopold, flanked by the dukes, walked behind the black-velvet-draped coffin. The prince regent, the queen, and her daughters were absent, but all the cabinet ministers were in attendance, along with the bishops, the courtiers of all the royal households, Stockmar, and the doctors Croft, Baillie, and Sims. In a short service, the princess's body was lowered into the royal vault. There her coffin still sits, stacked up with all the other royal coffins, on the left-hand side of the middle row, with the Duke of Kent shelved above her. Her stillborn son, in his coffin studded with silver nails, was placed at her feet.

The press immediately churned out descriptions of the funeral for an eager public. Charlotte's death was later commemorated by the great marble memorial that was bought with the donations to the fund set up by the Duchess of York. The donations from the public had totaled £12,346, so there was great outrage when the monument was not placed in a public park such as Kensington Gardens or Hyde Park but in the private chapel of the king, St. George's Chapel at Windsor. George IV ignored their protests. Created in the grand neoclassical style, the sculpture reflects the many memorial pictures of the princess in apotheosis. Her body lies covered with a shroud, with only her hand just visible. Two female mourners draped in sheets weep on either side of her. Above the body, however, is a sculpture of the princess ascending to heaven, in full beauty, her face upturned

toward the light, flanked by angels. One angel carries her infant son, who
also looks up toward the sky. For the poet Shelley, there was too much concentration on the dead princess and not on the social imbalances of the nation. In *An Address to the People on the Death of the Princess Charlotte*, he
complained that she was memorialized, when three men executed the day
after she died for demonstrating against the government had been forgotten.

On December 16, Sir Thomas Lawrence came to Claremont to deliver the
portrait of Charlotte that he had painted during her pregnancy. The whole
household wept bitterly when it was unveiled. "Two generations gone.
Gone in a moment," declared Prince Leopold. "My Charlotte is gone from
this country."

The postmortem was inconclusive. The regent personally exonerated
Sir Richard Croft, but many criticized him for his reluctance to act during
the labor, and certainly for leaving the princess alone after she had under-
gone such an ordeal. Sir Richard never recovered from the shame. Three
months later, while attending a woman who was also struggling to give
birth, he snatched up a gun from the wall and shot himself.

Leopold remained at Claremont with Stockmar, who was always at his
side. A sympathetic Parliament lavished honors on the bereaved husband.
The regent awarded him the title of Royal Highness and also made him a
field marshal and a privy councillor. Parliament voted to continue his
£50,000 allowance and gave him Claremont for life. Mr. Wilberforce declared in Parliament that the "Princess Charlotte and the excellent man of
her choice were so much endeared by the nation" because theirs had been
a "marriage of the heart." But Lord Liverpool worried, "The great and general question which everyone asked himself and asked his neighbour was
how will this event operate on the succession to the Crown." The king was
wailing in madness at Windsor, and the prince regent was estranged from
his wife. Unless the prince or one of his siblings had a child, the Hanoverian line would be at an end. It has been calculated that George III had an
astonishing fifty-six grandchildren. He did not have one legitimate heir.

The vision of Charlotte had sustained the people through the direst
years of the regency. Without her, all hope seemed gone.

INTERLUDE

1817–20

Drunken Dukes

19

"The Dregs of Their Dull Race"

On a chill morning in late November 1817, the Duke of Kent was enjoying a leisurely breakfast at his Brussels home with his lovely mistress of nearly thirty years, Julie de St. Laurent. The house was borrowed from a friend, and the lovers were heavily in debt, but they were content, and Mme de St. Laurent expected to live with the duke until he died. Before the duke began opening his letters, he briefly scanned *The Morning Chronicle*, just arrived from London, then tossed it over to his mistress. Within seconds, he recalled, "My attention was called to an extraordinary noise and a strong convulsive movement in Madame St. Laurent's throat." She seemed to be having some kind of fit, and he hurried to her side, terrified that she might be suffering a heart attack. At last she recovered, and he begged her for the cause of her sudden spasm. With one weak finger she pointed to an article in the *Chronicle*. The writer proposed that the royal brothers should marry, and mentioned that the Duke of Kent had been pondering "one of the sisters of Prince Leopold." Kent promised Julie that he would never desert her, but he was lying. His thoughts had already turned to finding a wife.

While the nation mourned Princess Charlotte, her uncles were gal-
vanized into action. Of the prince regent's six brothers, only the fifty-
four-year-old Duke of York was legally married. The princesses were all
childless and over forty. The Duke of York's childless union was a sham: He
indulged himself with mistresses while his Prussian wife of twenty-six
years, Frederica, lived at his home in Oatlands Park, near Weybridge, with
her squawking parrots and packs of dogs, very few of which were house-
trained. The five remaining royal dukes—Clarence, Kent, Cumberland,
Sussex, and Cambridge—all had morganatic wives or mistresses and illegitimate children, but no legitimate offspring. The brothers had been coasting
into middle age, enjoying their lovers, accruing huge debts, convinced that
Parliament would eventually help them out. Dubbed by the Duke of
Wellington "the damndest millstone about the necks of any Government
that can be imagined," the dukes had refused George III's attempts to
marry them off. Revolted at the thought of arranged alliances, they preferred to spoil themselves with London's pretty courtesans rather than be
tormented by pop-eyed German princesses.

The public found them repulsive. Shelley wrote fiercely:

> *Princes, the dregs of their dull race, who flow*
> *Through public scorn—mud from a muddy spring*
> *Rulers who neither see nor feel nor know,*
> *But leech-like to their fainting country cling.*

In contrast, the self-indulgent dukes still considered themselves superb
catches, even though they were fat and unhealthy, with "plum pudding
faces," in the words of the Princess of Wales. Eager to be seen as the sav-
iors of England, they quickly embarked on what one writer dubbed
"Hymen's War terrific."

First out of the blocks was the Duke of Cambridge. At forty-three, the
youngest of the brothers, he was the most attractive proposition, even
though, as seventh son, any offspring of his would be behind those of the
Dukes of York, Clarence, Kent, Cumberland, and Sussex, and, of course,
the prince regent. Cambridge was a reasonably handsome man, despite his
fondness for puffy blond wigs. His debts were small, and he had no long-
term mistress. Less than ten days after Charlotte's death, he wrote to

Augusta, Princess of Hesse-Cassel, asking for her hand in marriage. Augusta accepted. His success at catching a princess so quickly raised the stakes, and his brothers began dashing off letters to Europe's single royal ladies.

Ever since he had been retired from the navy at the ripe old age of twenty-four, William, Duke of Clarence, had been feeling sorry for himself. Mired in inactivity, he had never managed to achieve much. By all accounts a difficult and uncouth man, the duke had lived with the celebrated comic actress Mrs. Dora Jordan for twenty comfortable years, relying on her earnings and doting on their illegitimate children, five boys and five girls. By 1811, the duke was starting to find his lover considerably less appealing. Furthermore, he needed money to buy his sons army commissions and give his daughters dowries. When he met Catherine Tylney-Long, a scatty heiress possessed of over £40,000 a year, he came to a decision. Soon afterward, Mrs. Jordan was handed a letter before she was due to go on stage. The duke proposed a separation. He callously demanded that she give up all rights to see her sons, and her daughters soon severed links with her as well. Poor Mrs. Jordan, heartbroken and deserted, fell into debt and died alone in France in July 1816.

Although he had abandoned Mrs. Jordan, the duke still wished to be compensated if he married. He wrote crossly to the queen, a piqued fifty-two-year-old child: "[If the] Cabinet consider the measure of my marrying one of consequence, they ought to state to me what they can and will propose for my establishment." He had debts (over £50,000 worth) that needed to be paid and ten children dependent on him. More estimably, he declared that he would not marry unless he was allowed to see his daughters by Mrs. Jordan whenever he wished.

Miss Tylney-Long wisely chose another suitor, so the duke pursued various unsuspecting aristocratic ladies. Charlotte's friend Margaret Mercer Elphinstone, Lady Charlotte Lindsay, lady-in-waiting to the Princess of Wales, the Dowager Lady Downshire, and Lady Berkeley all refused him. The Duke of Gloucester's sister, Princess Sophia, was similarly unenthusiastic, as was Princess Anne of Denmark, and he had no chance at all with the tsar's ambitious, fashionable sister, the Grand Duchess of Oldenburg. The eldest Princess of Hesse considered him for a moment, but her father blocked the marriage.

Clarence then met a Miss Wyckham, a wealthy young heiress from Oxfordshire, who had inherited an estate worth £16,000 a year. Loud and loquacious, she reminded him of the dramatic Mrs. Jordan, and he thought her marvelous. Unfortunately for him, the regent and the government disapproved of the marriage because she was not a royal. The duke was obliged to accept that he must, like his brothers, find a Protestant princess to be mother to the heir to the throne, which meant scouring Germany for a wife. He finally alighted on the twenty-five-year-old Princess Amelia Adelaide of the tiny toy-state of Saxe-Meiningen. To the surprise of many, she consented.

The duke fretted that he was making an alliance with a woman less than half his age. "She is doomed, poor, dear, innocent young creature to be my wife," he pondered to twenty-four-year-old George FitzClarence, his eldest son, who had once admired Princess Charlotte. "I cannot, I will not, I must not ill use her . . . what time may produce in my heart I can not tell, but at present I think and exist only for Miss Wyckham." Dowdy, dumpy Adelaide had none of Miss Wyckham's gay vibrancy, and she was afflicted with a nasty skin complaint: Cold sores blistered around her mouth, and red blotches spattered her face. Nevertheless, she was kindhearted and intelligent, and she was brave enough to agree to act as stepmother to Clarence's ten illegitimate children, the eldest of whom was only a year younger than she.

Princess Adelaide arrived on July 4, 1818, and met her future husband for the first time. The pair were married in a quiet ceremony in the drawing room at Kew Palace nine days later, alongside the Duke of Kent and his new wife. Despite weak health, the queen sat through the ceremony, but she did not attend the celebratory dinner.

The marriage between young Adelaide and the duke succeeded, if only through low expectations on both sides. The duke learned to appreciate her patience, forbearance, and kindness, and he was delighted to see that she settled quickly at home in Bushey. She was kind to his children, and the younger ones, still in their early teens, grew very fond of her. Her restrained manner had a great effect on the duke, who began to drink less and behave less rambunctiously. Finally, in November, the happy event occurred. The Duke of Kent shrugged to George FitzClarence: "The Duchess of Clarence certainly is, I believe, in the family way."

"She was a young lady of more than ordinary personal attractions; her features were regular, and her complexion fair, with the rich bloom of youthful beauty." Princess Charlotte was tall and, like all Hanoverians, prone to plumpness.

Caroline, Princess of Wales, and Princess Charlotte by Sir Thomas Lawrence. Little Charlotte was a charming child, but grew up sadly affected by the divisions between her parents.

George IV by Sir Thomas Lawrence, 1822. "He will either be the most polished gentleman or the most accomplished blackguard in Europe, possibly an admixture of both," declared a tutor of George, Prince of Wales, when he was fifteen.

The R—t Kicking Up a Row, or Warwick House in an Uproar showed the prince regent attempting to beat Charlotte's ladies, as his daughter runs away down the stairs and toward her mother.

Playing on the popular prejudice that Germans never washed, *A Brighton Hot Bath, or Preparations for the Wedding!!* shows Prince Leopold being scrubbed, as well as dosed with mercury to rid him of venereal disease. Engraving by George Cruikshank.

Princess Charlotte's beautiful lace wedding dress was said to have cost ten thousand pounds.

Prince Leopold of Saxe-Coburg: brave, charming—and penniless.

"Thank Heaven I am here at last!" Charlotte adored Claremont, her country home in Surrey, and grasped every excuse to spend time there.

An engraving after the last portrait of Princess Charlotte, by Sir Thomas Lawrence. She never saw the finished painting.

The elaborate memorial monument to Princess Charlotte, funded by public subscription and installed in St. George's Chapel, Windsor Castle.

"I am nothing more than a soldier, 50 years old . . . not very fitted to captivate the heart of a young and charming Princess." The Duke of Kent was fat, indebted, and pompous—but he had a kindly soul.

Handsome, commanding, and devious, John Conroy quickly became the Duchess of Kent's absolute confidant—and the bane of little Victoria's life.

Victoria's first surviving letter reads, "My dear Mamma I love you Victoria."
But relations between the Duchess of Kent and her daughter were soon riven
with arguments.

Princess Victoria with her beloved spaniel, Dash, by Sir George Hayter.

Kensington Palace, which Victoria thought *"dreadfully* dull, dark and gloomy."

"She is the *most affectionate, devoted, attached* and *disinterested* friend I have." Isolated and lonely, Victoria saw Baroness Lehzen, her governess, as her only friend.

The princess was a keen collector of dolls and spent many happy hours dressing them in fine outfits.

Victoria adored her "dearest sister Feodora" and missed her greatly when she left to be married.

The earliest dress of Queen Victoria's known to survive, probably worn when she was about twelve.

At sixty-five, King William IV was the oldest individual ever to ascend to the throne.

"I never was happy until I was eighteen." Queen Victoria acceded to the throne in June 1837. One of her first acts was to move her bed from her mother's room.

"I shall ever remember this day as the *proudest* of my life," Queen Victoria wrote of her coronation.

"She not merely filled her chair, she filled the room." The new queen at her first Privy Council, on June 20.

"It was with some emotion that I beheld Albert— who is *beautiful*," Victoria enthused in her diary.

The Queen refused to wear her royal robes for the wedding ceremony and instead designed her own dress, adorned with exquisite Devonshire lace.

Prince Albert's favorite portrait of Queen Victoria, painted when she was twenty-four by Franz Xaver Winterhalter.

Victoria reached Windsor Castle, where the bridal couple was to spend the honeymoon, quite deaf from the cheers of the crowds who lined the route.

"I think, dearest Uncle, you cannot *really* wish me to be the 'Mamma d'une *nombreuse famille.*'" But the queen had nine children, and she and Albert became the model of the ideal royal family.

Seven months into the pregnancy, the duchess caught a chest infection, which turned into pleurisy. She was repeatedly bled, but a combination of the illness and panic caused her to give birth prematurely. The child was named Charlotte Augusta after her dead cousin. But the little princess lived only a few hours and was buried next to the body of George I in the palace crypt.

The wily, mustachioed Ernest, Duke of Cumberland, had in 1814 met and fallen in love with Frederica, daughter of the queen's brother, Charles, Duke of Mecklenburg-Strelitz. A glamorous widow with two children by her second husband, Prince Louis of Prussia, the thirty-seven-year-old Princess Frederica was more than a match for her devious cousin. Unfortunately, she had initially been betrothed to Ernest's younger brother, Adolphus, the Duke of Cambridge, before hurriedly jilting him for the Prince of Solms-Braunfels, who then divorced her on the grounds of "loose behaviour." As a consequence, when Cumberland married her, the queen refused to receive her daughter-in-law (who was also her niece) and compelled her daughters to follow her lead. Parliament gave the couple no money. Frederica had given birth to a stillborn daughter in 1817, and there had been no further sign of a child for the unhappy, much disliked pair.

Augustus, Duke of Sussex, was better esteemed. He hardly ever said anything to offend and was more liberal in his views than most of his brothers. He had married Lady Augusta Murray in 1793, but the king refused to sanction the union, so their two children—including the persistent Mr. D'Este, who had once winked at Charlotte from behind a pillar at Kensington Palace in an effort to seduce her—were deemed illegitimate. The relationship ended in 1806, and the duke promised to send Lady Augusta £4,000 a year. Returning to live at Kensington Palace, he soon took up with Lady Cecilia Buggin, daughter of the Earl of Arran, and refused to marry another princess.

Edward, Duke of Kent, the king's fourth son, declared that he was performing a great act of unselfishness by considering a wife. "Altho' I trust I shall be at all times ready to obey any call my country may make on me," he trumpeted, "God only knows the sacrifice it will be to make, whenever I shall think it my duty to become a married man." He expected the same settlement as the Duke of York, £25,000 a year, magnanimously offering to refrain from "making any demands grounded upon the difference of the value of money in 1792," when York married, and the present time. As for the payment of my debts, I don't call them great. The nation, on the contrary, is greatly my debtor."

The priggish Kent was tall and heavyset, more or less bald, with a plump, florid face, and a stiff, erect bearing. The Duke considered himself a soldier and had acquired a reputation for excessive harshness in his army days, although he had been equally strict with himself, shunning drink and late nights, rising early, and eating sparingly. Dubbing himself "the strongest of the strong," he often boasted that he would outlive his brothers. He was intelligent, music loving, open to liberal ideas, and punctilious where his brothers were slapdash. He also took a genuine interest in the details of government and maintained three private secretaries for correspondence. His "name was never uttered without a sigh by the functionaries of every public office." Kent was also loyal and kindhearted, supporting no fewer than fifty-three charitable ventures. He kept up a long correspondence with Mrs. Fitzherbert, the prince regent's abandoned morganatic wife. Princess Charlotte had also been very fond of him, and it was he who had carried her secret love letters to Prince Leopold.

In 1791, the duke had fallen in love with Julie de St. Laurent, a young woman hired to entertain him at one of his evening functions.

Mme de St. Laurent, the Besançon-born daughter of a civil engineer, had been mistress to two French aristocrats. Beautiful, patient, and forbearing, she went to live with the duke in Gibraltar, and they enjoyed a happy domestic existence. In 1803, he was forced to leave the army after his decision to close the cheap wine shops in Gibraltar sparked a terrible mutiny. Called back to England, he spent £50,000 on a substantial estate in Ealing and bought a home for Mme de St. Laurent in Knightsbridge, as well as undertaking extravagant renovations of his apartments at Kensington Palace. He had a generous income of £27,000, but he simply could not live within it. By 1816, he owed over £200,000, and he had no choice but to attempt to live inexpensively abroad. He and Mme de St. Laurent set off for Brussels, famed for its cheap prices, after he had signed over more than half his yearly income to his creditors and agreed to live on £10,000 a year.

The duke had been considering marriage even before Charlotte's death, aware that there was no other way to settle his debts. In early 1816, the forty-nine-year-old duke proposed to Princess Katherine Amelia of Baden, sister of the tsarina of Russia. He borrowed money from the tsar to visit her and set off in September, while Mme de St. Laurent was away visiting her sister in Paris. But the subterfuge was wasted. The duke was not expecting a dreary spinster of forty-one. He wanted a younger, prettier woman, and Leopold began to encourage him to pay court to his elder sister, Princess Victoire, the Dowager Princess of Leiningen. Victoire, at thirty, shared her brother's darkly handsome looks, although her tall, elegant exterior belied a character prone to nervous terror. She had been married at seventeen to a dour widower twenty-three years her senior, who had made a great show of avowing enduring love for his first wife. Two years after the marriage, her husband succeeded to the principality of Leiningen, but Napoleon had taken much of the territory, and there was little more to rule than the minuscule realm of Amorbach, near Darmstadt, in lower Franconia, with only fifteen thousand inhabitants. He spent most of his time at his hunting lodge, leaving his young wife to while away her days at his tumbledown palace with her lady-in-waiting, Baroness Späth. She behaved to her cantankerous husband as an obedient niece rather than a wife, and his death in 1814 was a blessing. Victoire welcomed her independence, content to be the mother and guardian of the heir, ten-year-old Prince Charles, as well as his sister, Princess Feodora, age seven.

Leopold praised his sister's beauty and gentle character until the duke was absolutely convinced that he should try to win her. Equipped with a letter of recommendation from Charlotte, and pretending to Mme de St. Laurent that he was traveling abroad to arrange their move to Brussels, he set off from Ealing to visit Victoire. After two days staying at her ramshackle palace in Amorbach, the duke was so charmed by the plump, gentle princess and her two pretty children that he proposed. Alas, she refused. Not only was she a contented widow, with no desire to marry another elderly man, but she did not speak any English, and the Duke of Kent was hardly an appealing prospect. He was far from the throne; he was portly, pedantic, and without occupation; and his debts were huge. She had begun to lean heavily on Captain Schindler, master of her household, to such a degree that some declared he was essentially co-regent with her. Schindler argued forcefully against the marriage, pointing out that she would lose her position and her allowance of £5,000 a year, just to marry a man twenty years her senior. She also still suspected that if she left the country, she might lose her guardianship of her adored son, Charles, heir to the principality.

After Charlotte's death, Leopold became more determined to see the pair married. If his sister became the wife of the duke, he had a chance of regaining some power over the succession. He encouraged Kent to renew his proposal and pressed his sister to reconsider. Polyxene von Tubeuf, wife of a Leiningen courtier and the duchess's favorite female friend, lectured her that she should embrace a "connection to the first of all Royal Courts." Charlotte's death meant that any children they might have would be closer to the throne, and there was the possibility that Victoire might even become queen of England. It certainly seemed as if she would be welcome: The edition of *The Morning Chronicle* that so upset Mme de St. Laurent declared that Kent's marriage to a sister of Leopold would be greeted by the English with "rapturous delight."

At the beginning of January 1818, the duke wrote to Victoire requesting an answer to his proposal. The prince regent pledged that the princess would remain guardian of her children, under his protection. The duke had also agreed to spend part of every year in Germany. On January 25, Victoire accepted, writing, "I am leaving an agreeable, independent position in the hope that your affection will be my reward."

The duke was overjoyed. "I want you to know, my very dear Princess, that I am nothing more than a soldier, 50 years old and after 32 years of service not very fitted to captivate the heart of a young and charming Princess, who is 19 years younger." He promised her tender care and affection, and hoped she might be able to forget the age difference. He also applied himself to severing all links with Mme de St. Laurent, hoping that the government would fund her, lying that she was "of very great family and has never been an actress, and I am the first and only person who has ever lived with her."

The engagement was greeted with universal pleasure. "The lady, in the Duke of Kent's eye, is not ill-chosen for popular effect," mused John Wilson Croker, politician and commentator. "She is the sister of Prince Leopold." The fortune-hunting Coburgs had succeeded again. "We can wish the Duke no higher felicity than the possession of a woman who may prove herself akin in virtue to her excellent and illustrious brother," declared *The Times*. The duke borrowed £3,000 to set himself up and buy Victoire wedding presents and a magnificent dress, and demanded money from Parliament. On April 15, the Foreign Secretary suggested to Parliament a grant of £25,000 for Clarence and £12,000 for the other dukes. The opposition began chivying against it, and many government members were unenthusiastic. The Duke of Wellington felt sympathetic to the rebels. "They [the dukes] have insulted—personally insulted—two thirds of the gentlemen of England [that is, MPs] and how can it be wondered that they take their revenge upon them when they get them in the House of Commons?" After a fiery debate, Parliament agreed on £6,000 each for Clarence, Kent, and Cambridge, but nothing for Cumberland. The Duke of Kent was dismayed. The sum would hardly cover the interest on his huge debts, and he had already spent thousands on his fiancée, showering her with jewelry, two saddle horses, a riding habit, his miniature, a pianoforte, perfume, lace, and elaborate feathered hats.

In 1818, the middle-aged Princess Elizabeth married the fat and ugly Prince of Hesse-Homburg. A caricature—"John Bull supporting the Nuptial Bed!!!"—shows the country, symbolized by the beleaguered figure of Bull in his blue coat, struggling under the weight of the prince and his new wife, while the rest of the royal family around the bed make crude innuendoes about penetrating hair and heirs. Another caricature, "Old Snuffy inquiring after her daughter Betty," depicts the queen paying a visit to the couple, with the princess leaning out of bed to tell her mother that her husband has not "found it out" and so there is no likelihood of an heir. At forty-eight, she was too old to produce a baby.

The prince regent was encouraged to redouble his efforts to divorce his wife, on the basis that she had committed adultery in Italy with her handsome courtier, Bartolomeo Pergami. Although Baron von Ompteda had been unable in 1814 to gather any hard evidence about the suspected adultery, the regent persuaded the government to fund three English gentlemen to carry out another investigation. William Cooke, a barrister, John Powell, a solicitor, and Major James Browne, an Italian-speaking diplomat from the British Embassy in Vienna, formed the Milan Commission, named after the city in which it originated. They set about finding the crucial evidence that would allow George to divorce his wife.

20

ᴥ

"As Plump as a Partridge"

The Duke, though a man of the world, was at first rather embarrassed at bursting like a bomb into the midst of our large family circle," wrote Victoire's mother, the Dowager Duchess of Saxe-Coburg. The Duke of Kent had arrived at Coburg on May 26, ahead of schedule and in splendid form, much to the consternation of the ladies. He soon settled in, chattering away in French and charming the little Princess Feodora.

Three days later, at half past eight at night, the Duke of Kent and Princess Victoire were married in the Ehrenburg Palace in Coburg, with the bride looking lovely in a white dress, orange blossom in her hands. The wedding was solemnized on July 13 at Kew by the archbishop of Canterbury, in a ceremony lasting three quarters of an hour, alongside that of William, Duke of Clarence, and Adelaide of Saxe-Meiningen. The regent gave away both brides, and Victoire was the more splendid, in an opulent dress of satin trimmed with Brussels lace and a gold tissue gown over the top. The Kents retired to a sumptuous state banquet and later drove with Leopold to Claremont for their honeymoon. The Dowager Duchess, Victoire's mother, expressed her hopes that her daughter would "find in this second marriage a happiness she never found in the first." However, the new bride was nervous about living in a large and unfamiliar country with a famously complicated and refined court life. She was also failing to understand English. The duke, though, was happy and proud. He had captured a lovely younger wife, managed to associate himself with Leopold, the nation's favorite widower, and in his view had even behaved well by his mistress.

Mme de St. Laurent retired to live on a modest pension in a Paris hotel, where she was known as the Comtesse de Montgenet, a title granted by Louis XVIII. There, she lived quietly, dreading that she would read yet another report of the duke's marital felicity. The duke wrote to ask his friend Baron de Mallet to visit his ex-mistress. "Her nerves are *still* in a *very critical* state," the duke lamented. "[Although] an intimacy now of eight months with the Duchess has attached me *sincerely to her,*" he mused, "we must *never* lose sight that our unexpected separation arose from the imperative duty I owed to obey the call of my family and my Country to marry, and *not* from the least diminution in an attachment which had stood the test of 28 years and which, but for *that* circumstance, would unquestionably have kept up the connexion, until it became the lot of one or other of us to be removed from this world." Such sentiments were small comfort to the comtesse.

The Kents quickly settled into domestic comfort. Victoire liked to have a man to rely on, and he was happy to pet her and give her avuncular advice. Unlike his older brothers, he was neither vulgar nor boastful, and he was patient with her poor English. The only blight on their happiness was money, for the duke's debts were mounting once more. Unable to help, the queen suggested that life overseas would be cheaper.

The seventy-three-year-old queen had been ailing ever since the death of Princess Charlotte. Swollen with dropsy and fighting to breathe, she confined herself to her room at Kew Palace and wrote her will. Soon, even the slightest movement was excruciating. "I wish to God I could see your brothers," she wept to Princess Augusta, racked by pain. "I wish I was near the dear King." On November 17, 1818, the queen died sitting up in her chair, clasping the hand of the Prince Regent.

The king was too ill to understand that his wife was dead. Deaf, blind, and quite deranged, he veered wildly between hysterical laughter and violent bouts of tears. He lived in terror of a great flood and chattered incessantly to armies of imaginary friends. There seemed little hope of recovery. The regent was now the sole holder of power in the royal family.

In September, barely two months after their wedding, the Kents left Kensington Palace for Amorbach. The palace there was cold and unmodernized and fifty miles from the nearest town, but the duchess was happier in Germany, and Kent was eager to please her. The pair enjoyed a happy domestic existence, along with Victoire's daughter, Feodora (Prince Charles was at school), her faithful lady Baroness Späth, and Sir John Conroy, a tough, ambitious thirty-two-year-old Irishman whom the duke had taken on as military equerry in 1817. Kent attacked his rambling new home with all the enthusiasm for interior design that he had brought to Kensington Palace. Teams of workmen were soon building stables and installing a new heating system. He had the workmen tear out the main staircase and embarked on elaborate alterations to the gardens, erecting a temple on an island in the canal and even creating a landscaped walk to the house.

Soon the Kents had one piece of excellent news—Victoire was pregnant.

Unfortunately for the Kents, the Duchesses of Clarence, Cumberland, and Cambridge were also with child. Convinced that his offspring had a good chance of inheriting the throne, the Duke of Kent decided that he should bring his wife to give birth in England, so that key dignitaries could confirm his child's legitimacy in the normal way. He wrote to the regent requesting a yacht for the journey, £1,200 for travel expenses, rooms in Kensington Palace, and a house by the sea after the baby was born, his only attempt to suggest economy. The regent refused. The Duchesses of Cambridge and Clarence were both to have their children in Hanover (the Clarences had moved to save money, and Cambridge had been appointed governor general of Hanover). The prince regent was keen that the Kents should also stay away.

The duke's friends devoted themselves to raising money for his journey, redoubling their efforts when the Duchess of Clarence's child died within a few hours of her premature birth in November 1818. On New Year's Eve in Amorbach, the duke wrote an affectionate letter to his wife.

This evening will put an end, dear beloved Victoire, to the year 1818, which saw the birth of my happiness by giving you to me as my guardian angel . . . all my efforts are directed to one end, the preservation of your dear health and the birth of a child who will resemble you, and if Heaven will give me these two blessings I shall be consoled for all my misfortunes and disappointments, with which my life has been marked.

By March, the Duke of Kent had accumulated the astonishing sum of £15,000 through loans, bonds, and gifts. He wrote to the prince regent to send the royal yacht to Calais for him and his wife. Dreading criticism from the papers for ill-treating his brother, the prince reluctantly agreed.

Victoire was nearly eight months pregnant when she and the duke set off for England on March 28. It was a difficult and uncomfortable journey of nearly 430 miles over appalling roads. The duke drove the duchess himself in a cheap cane phaeton, so that he would not have to pay a coachman. Apart from Prince Charles, who was at school in Switzerland, the entire household was transported to London, including the duchess's precious pet birds and dogs. Trailing behind the duke's carriage came coaches containing their belongings, along with Princess Feodora and her maids, the duchess's lady-in-waiting, Baroness Späth, English maids, two cooks, and various other staff, including Dr. Wilson, an ex-naval surgeon, and a distinguished high-society female obstetrician, Frau Charlotte Siebold, in case the jolting of the carriage sparked premature labor.

While in Frankfurt, the duke dashed off a letter to the Baron de Mallet asking for his opinion of the Comtesse de Montgenet's state of health. "I fear what she recently read in the papers, has had again a very sensible effect on her nerves, which I gather, from the contents of her last letter, written, although with her usual affection, evidently under great agitation."

The party reached Calais on April 18, then drummed their heels for a week before the weather became sufficiently clement to sail. The duchess breathed deeply and waited, while the duke fretted about his ex-mistress. On the twenty-fourth, they embarked for England. After less than three hours of quite rough seas, the party landed and set off for Kensington Palace.

Kensington then was a country village, and the palace looked out onto trees and rolling lawns. The couple's apartment had been empty since the Princess of Wales had left to cavort across the Continent in 1814. It was grand, with large reception rooms and a private garden, but shabby, as all the fittings and furniture had been removed in an attempt to dissuade the Princess of Wales from returning. The rooms were also dusty, damp, and plagued by dry rot. The duke quickly found that he could not even store meat in his larder as the ceiling was constantly dripping. He began buying new furniture and drapes, including white curtains, cambric for the four-poster bed, a mahogany crib, red curtains and carpet for the dining room, as well as bookcases and a desk for his library, spending over £2,000. He also applied himself to improving the room where the duchess would give birth, installing luxuriant curtains and carpets. The room received its final touches on May 22, and next day, at ten thirty in the evening, the duchess's labor began.

After only six hours of labor, at quarter past four on May 24, 1819, the duchess gave birth to a "pretty little Princess, as plump as a partridge." The duke had been beside her throughout. Waiting outside were various dignitaries, including the Duke of Wellington; the archbishop of Canterbury; the bishop of London; the marquess of Landsdowne; the future prime minister, George Canning; Nicholas Vansittart, chancellor of the exchequer; and the Duke of Sussex—all ready to assert that the princess was indeed the daughter of the Duke of Kent. Everything had proceeded according to plan. "Thank God the dear mother and child are doing marvelously well," wrote the duke to his mother-in-law. He praised Frau Siebold effusively: "It is not possible to show more activity, more zeal and more knowledge than she has done." He was not disappointed by the sex of the child. "I have no choice between Boy and Girl," he wrote to Baron de Mallet," and I shall always feel grateful for whichever of the two is bestowed upon us, so long as the Mother's health is preserved."

"Again a Charlotte," wrote Victoire's mother, the Duchess Augusta, from Coburg. "The English like Queens," she proclaimed, "and the niece of the ever lamented beloved Charlotte will be most dear to them." Adolphus, Duke of Cambridge, had produced a healthy son, George, in March. But the little girl was the closest to the throne, and everybody doubted the ability of her older uncles to produce children. Frances Burney, the writer and previously lady-in-waiting to the queen, named the baby the "Queen presumptive."

The duke was overjoyed. The little princess was, he decided proudly, "truly a model of strength and beauty combined," although he later admitted she was more of a "pocket Hercules, than a pocket Venus." The Duchess of Kent was full of vigor, elated by her achievement, and eager to feed the child herself. "I would have been desparate [*sic*] to see my little darling on someone else's breast," she confessed. Charmed by every aspect of being a family man, the duke watched in fascination. The duchess's rare decision to feed her child herself had an important impact on history, for had she not done so, she could have fallen pregnant again quickly, perhaps with a son who would have displaced her daughter.

A few weeks after delivering the little princess, Frau Siebold returned to Germany. She had another eminent mother to assist. The nineteen-year-old Princess Louise, Duchess of Saxe-Coburg, sister-in-law to Leopold and the Duchess of Kent, was pregnant with her second child. On August 26, pretty Louise gave birth to Francis Charles Augustus Albert Emmanuel, whom everybody called Albert.

Leopold was abroad, still moping after Charlotte (as well as keeping mistresses and purchasing a castle near Coburg), when he heard that his sister was about to give birth. He set off for England, arriving nearly ten days after the happy event. "The appearance of His Royal Highness is much improved since his departure," declared *The Times* on his arrival, "yet he still looks very pale and much dejected." Initially, Leopold struggled to look at his niece, for she reminded him too bitterly of what he had lost. She had a chance to become queen and possess the power that he had once believed would surely be his.

Hopelessly fat and ill, dosed with laudanum to dull the pain of his swollen legs, widely reviled, and chained to a wife he detested, his child and grandchild dead at a stroke, the regent was sickened by his brother's triumphant declarations that he had produced the heir to the throne. On June 21, he wrote to Kent informing him that the child would be christened three days later, in a small private ceremony in the Cupola Room at Kensington Palace. No sparkly dress uniforms or evening wear should be worn, and no foreign dignitaries would be invited. Only eight guests would be permitted: himself, the Yorks, the Gloucesters, Princess Augusta, Princess Sophia, and melancholy Prince Leopold. Much to the annoyance of the prince regent, the inordinately powerful Tsar Alexander of Russia had asked the Russian Embassy to express to the Kents his wish to sponsor the child, and he could hardly be refused, however much the regent detested him. The other sponsors were Charlotte, previously the Princess Royal, queen of Württemberg; the Duchess of Kent's mother, Augusta, the Dowager Duchess of Saxe-Coburg; and a very unenthusiastic prince regent. It would be a ceremony suitable for a very minor child.

The Kents had planned to name the child Victoire Georgiana Alexandrina Charlotte Augusta, after her mother and then her four sponsors. Even though his brother had flattered him by putting the feminized version of his name first after Victoire, the regent was dissatisfied. The night before the christening, he wrote to say that he could not allow his name to precede the tsar's, and he did not wish it to follow. He declared that he would inform the parents of the child's names at the christening the following day. All the gossip about a future queen had rattled him. He had already asked Leopold to ensure that she was not called Charlotte.

On June 24, at three o'clock, the nameless child who would inherit the throne of England after her uncles the prince regent, York, and Clarence, and her father, was dressed up in a fine christening robe and carried to the Cupola Room, which had been swathed in velvet for the occasion. At the critical moment, the archbishop of Canterbury held the baby over the elaborate silver font and waited to be given a name. The regent decided against the typically royal names of Augusta and Charlotte, and after some deliberation finally declared that she should be called Alexandrina. The Duke of Kent requested another name, and suggested Elizabeth. The regent refused and glared crossly at the duchess, who burst into tears, and spat, "Give her the mother's name also then, but it cannot precede that of the Emperor." The child was duly christened Alexandrina Victoria.

Wrecking the christening might have satisfied the regent temporarily, but his jealousy of his brother was corrosive. Intent on pushing the couple to live overseas, he took every opportunity to snub the Kents and made a point of refusing them money. But the duke was determined to stay. The Duchess of Clarence had miscarried at Calais on the way to England, and no other wife was pregnant. "My brothers are not so strong as I am," the duke declared. "I have led a regular life, I shall outlive them all; the crown will come to me and my children."

꙳

Alexandrina Victoria

E ngland barely noticed the birth of the little princess. After the upsurge
of jubilation at the end of the Napoleonic Wars, the country had sunk
into severe depression. War-torn Europe could not buy as much from
Britain as it once had, and there was competition from countries that had
previously been restricted by Napoleon's blockades. By 1816, Britain's overseas trade was only two thirds what it had been in 1814. Still worse, three
hundred thousand men who had been soldiers and sailors were thrown
onto an already strained job market. Wage levels were pushed down, and
parishes struggled under the strain of giving relief to so many unemployed
men. Then exports of grain and a poor harvest in 1816 pushed up the
price of wheat from 77 shillings 4 pence in August to over 100 shillings in
December—an economic event of the same significance as the rise of the
price of oil to $140 a barrel today. Many could not afford bread, and riots
over food broke out across the country. In July, gangs of unemployed col-
liers from the Midlands dragged carts of coal around the countryside in an
attempt to attract support for their appalling situation. They were only prevented from reaching London by the arrival of the guard at the outskirts.

"We must expect a trying winter," declared the Home Secretary, Lord Sidmouth, "and it will be fortunate if the Military establishment which was pronounced to be too large for the constitution of this country shall be sufficient to preserve its internal tranquillity."

Matters worsened. A wave of protest against low wages in factories swept the country. At one point, in Manchester, twenty thousand workers were on strike. On August 16, 1819, groups of discontented workers and their families gathered at St. Peter's Fields, Manchester, to hear the radical speaker Henry Hunt. By late morning, more than sixty thousand men, women, and children had assembled, and the demonstration had taken on something of a holiday air. People held up banners declaring "Unity and Strength" and "Liberty and Fraternity," cheerily expecting Hunt's talk. The Manchester authorities, however, were terrified of a riot and executed a warrant for his arrest. Soon after he arrived at one o'clock, forty yeomen cavalry broke into the heaving crowd, striking out with their sabres to get to Hunt. He was hurried away, but the hussars were then called to dispel the crowd. Thousands of people attempted to flee, and many were trampled or suffocated, while others were beaten down by swords or sabres. Within fifteen minutes, eleven people had been killed and four hundred wounded. At least 140 had sabre cuts. The atrocity was quickly dubbed the "Peterloo Massacre." There was a national outcry that thousands of unarmed citizens had been so brutally attacked. Manchester was patrolled by troops, and there were riots in Macclesfield. Across the country, meetings were called to condemn the actions of the authorities. Afraid of further reprisals, the government introduced harsh legislation banning trade unions and meetings of more than fifty people. They also increased the stamp tax on cheap pamphlets and newspapers, so that the poor would be unable to read articles attacking the government and the royals. The Home Secretary set up an elaborate network of spies to keep an eye out for possible rebellion.

Privately, government ministers rued the actions of the Manchester authorities, but their public line was conservative. The prince regent conveyed his thanks to the authorities for "prompt, decisive and efficient measures for the preservation of public peace." But many moderate members of the middle classes turned to the Whigs, convinced that reform was necessary.

With the country simmering with insurrection, the government could not make a public award to the impecunious Kents even if they had wished to do so. Prince Leopold invited the little family to stay for a short while but suggested that they return soon to Germany. He was fully preoccupied with furnishing and organizing the London residence he would have occupied with Princess Charlotte, the grand Marlborough House next to St. James's Palace, spending excessively on improving the building, repainting, laying down luxuriant carpets, and buying exquisite new furniture.

The Duke of Kent decided he had no choice but to take an inexpensive house by the sea. In Sidmouth, in Devon, he alighted on the pretty Woolbrook Cottage, a low house surrounded by trees with lovely views toward the sea. The family were confident that the move would not harm Victoria. Little Vickelchen, as her mother called her, was growing stronger by the day. She had been vaccinated for smallpox on August 2, and there were no side effects (she would be vaccinated again in 1827 and 1835). Her first portrait, painted in August, depicts a sturdy, chubby little girl. At seven months old, she looked like a child of one. She was weaned in December, then probably fed with a spoon on the standard infant diet of a bread-and-water slop sweetened with sugar.

The Duke of Kent did not scrimp on his household. He had decided that twelve-year-old Feodora should have her own governess. After inquiries with Dr. Kuper, the reader at the German Lutheran chapel at St. James's Palace, he selected Louise Lehzen, the capable, clever, middle-aged daughter of a Lutheran clergyman, who had gained excellent references after working for the aristocratic von Marenholtz family. Fräulein Lehzen arrived in December and proclaimed Feodora "very prepossessing" and Victoria a "splendid baby."

On November 2, the Kents threw a party for the duke's fifty-second birthday. Princess Feodora sang, Prince Charles sent a congratulatory letter from his school in Geneva, and little Victoria was dressed up in a pretty frock for Papa. But the gift Kent needed most of all—relief from his debts—was not forthcoming. Throughout the winter, he struggled to raise money, hoping, against the odds, that the family would be able to stay in London. By December, he had realized that no money would appear. On the twenty-first, the Kents, along with Feodora, baby Victoria, and Fräulein Lehzen, as well as Baroness Späth, John Conroy, a physician, Dr. Wilson, and assorted gentlemen and servants, traveled to Salisbury, where they remained a few nights, and then continued to Devon. They arrived at their new home in the afternoon of Christmas Day, in the middle of a snowstorm.

The winter of 1819 was freezing, and the nights were perishing. Woolbrook Cottage is now a cozy hotel with a swimming pool, an easy walk from the Sidmouth promenade. Then, it was a badly insulated semi-farmhouse, and the entire party, used to living in palaces, were acutely aware of the discomfort. The duchess passed the time by practicing her English, walking along the sea front with Feodora, and taking salt baths. But she too was lonely and unhappy, and the debts were soaring. The family decided to return to Amorbach in the spring.

The duke caught a heavy cold. Convinced that he was much more resilient than his languid, debauched older brothers, he decided not to submit to his illness. Soldier like, he stomped out on long sea walks, often returning soaked to the bone, and devoted his time to planning the return to Amorbach. On Thursday January 6, he wrote to Admiral Donelly, a friend of his in Brussels, asking him to acquire some horses for him since he would be sending four carriages to Amorbach in the spring. It was the last letter he ever wrote. Next day, his cold had worsened. By Sunday, he was very sick, but still attempting to conquer his illness by ignoring it. He refused to allow his wife to cancel a dinner party scheduled for that evening. That same night he fell into a deep fever, and the next morning was unable to get out of bed.

By Wednesday, January 12, the duke was delirious, vomiting frequently, and suffering from severe pains in his chest. He had to be propped up to breathe properly. Dr. Wilson had him bled, then again on Thursday, but his condition only worsened. Terrified, the duchess called for the royal physician, Sir David Dundas, but he was fully occupied caring for the king, who had fallen into a sharp decline. "I am nursing my beloved one to the best of my abilities," the duchess sighed. Marooned in a freezing house with a severely ill husband and a baby who had also fallen sick, she felt helpless. She struggled to understand Dr. Wilson, and she was suspicious of his eagerness to apply leeches to her husband's chest.

After a week with no discernible improvement, Dr. Wilson decided to take the severe resort of cupping his patient. He made cuts all over the duke's body, covering each with a hot cup. The vacuum created in the cup drew out the blood, causing agonizing pain. The duchess winced, hardly able to watch, and later wrote: "For four hours they must have tormented him." When the cupping seemed to have no effect, they began to bleed him again, and even cut and cupped his head. The following day, a carriage arrived from London bearing William Maton, previously physician to Queen Charlotte.

Dr. Maton was a passionate believer in bleeding and immediately decreed that the patient should be cupped again, even though the duke had already been bled of six pints. "My poor dear Edward has had already to endure so much," the duchess lamented. "I cannot think it can be good for the patient to lose so much blood, when he is already so weak." She was soon beside herself, watching him being "tormented with this dreadful cupping." The duke was feverish and struggling to breathe; when Dr. Maton commanded yet more bleeding, he burst into tears at the prospect.

Next day, the duke was bled for the sixth time. "It is too dreadful," the duchess agonized. "There is hardly a spot on his dear body which has not been touched by cupping, blisters or bleeding. He was terribly exhausted yesterday after all that had been done to him by those cruel doctors." On Friday, Dr. Maton declared that the royal family should be informed that he lay in grave danger. The prince regent sent a concerned note, but Leopold, forgetting his earlier melancholy about the baby princess, came to the fore in the crisis, hurrying down to his sister.

Accompanied by his beloved Stockmar, Leopold arrived on January 22. The duchess was deeply relieved to see Stockmar, a doctor with whom she could finally communicate. She took him to examine her husband and begged his opinion. At about five o'clock in the afternoon, Stockmar took the duke's pulse and had to tell the duchess the truth: "Human help could no longer avail."

Still sentient, the duke managed to summon the strength to ask for his will to be drawn up, appointing the duchess sole guardian of their child and leaving his property to his executors in trust for his wife and daughter. His property was little more than a mountain of debt, but the will was an important document nonetheless. At a time when men usually left their property to their sons or brothers, allowing their female relations only interest on a sum, the duke bequeathed everything to his wife. He was too shrewd to leave his estate to the regent. He struggled to hold the pen and was worried that his signature might not be legible.

Next morning, at ten o'clock, the fifty-two-year-old duke died, holding the duchess's hand. Only a month before, he had been bouncing with health. His wife was devastated. "I am hopelessly lost without my dearest Edward, who thought of everything and always shielded me," she grieved. "Whatever shall I do without his strong support?" She had not changed her dress for five days. Hardly able to speak English, she was stranded in a country she did not know, without even the money to leave Woolbrook Cottage, detested by her in-laws, and very reliant on her brother. She had a sick baby and a distressed and fractious twelve-year-old daughter. Only thirty-two, she had been widowed twice over. "She kills all her husbands," sniped Princess Lieven.

The public were shocked that of all the brothers, the Duke of Kent should have died. "He was the strongest of the strong. Never before ill in his life and now to die of a cold when half the kingdom have colds with impunity," marveled John Wilson Croker. "It was," he remarked, with some understatement, "very bad luck indeed."

The day after the duke's death, the undertakers arrived and the planning for his funeral commenced. Surgeons invaded Woolbrook Cottage and instigated the postmortem, which had to be completed before the embalmers could begin work. The duke had an enormous coffin. More than seven feet long and weighing a ton, it was decorated with plumes of feathers and covered in velvet.

Leopold persuaded his sister to return to London, and on January 23, as the undertakers busied themselves with the arrangements, the duchess and her children, along with Captain Conroy, set off for the capital, a journey paid for by Leopold. It was a matter of some urgency that the regent allow the duchess to live at Kensington Palace, for servants at Claremont had been struck down by the measles and the house was in quarantine. After Leopold begged her to help, Princess Mary wrote to her brother to solicit his assistance. "In every respect her situation is most melancholy for Edward had nothing in the world but debts & now there are all his old servants without a penny piece to provide for them." On the brink of becoming king, the prince was in a benevolent mood, and he knew that refusing to give the duchess and her child a home before the funeral would be unpopular. He sent a letter inviting her to Kensington. She would, however, have to buy every item she needed for the apartments herself. Unfortunately, as the duchess soon found, she had not "a spoon or napkin of her own, as everything belonged to the creditors." She soon renounced all interest in her husband's estate and left it to be administered by the executors.

The duke's death caused many to reflect on their own health. "That Hercules of a man is no more, while I—a slip of a creature—am still alive and well, from which I deduce that the weak will go further than the strong," declared Princess Lieven. After his endless requests for money, she thought: "No-one in England will mourn the Duke." But England's opportunity to mourn him—or not—was brief. At Windsor, King George lay dying.

The eighty-one-year-old king had been severely ill for the past ten years. Ever since Amelia's death, he had been confined to his apartments and sometimes to a straitjacket, chattering to his crowds of imaginary attendants, weeping hysterically, and insulting his physicians and nurses. In December of 1819, he suffered a terrible seizure and talked hysterically nonstop for almost sixty hours. Throughout Christmas and the New Year, he was hardly able to eat or drink. The Duke of York worried over the "degree of weakness and languor in his looks and the emaciation of his face." Just after half past eight on the evening of January 29, the king finally died.

The whole nation went into mourning: Shops closed their doors, and even the poorest wore black ribbons or armbands to show their sympathy. Thirty thousand people came to Windsor for his funeral in St. George's Chapel on February 16. Dozens of mourners in black paraded with the coffin from the castle, along a walkway that had been specially built and covered in black cloth. "The chanting, & indeed the whole service, was most impressive and affecting," marveled Mrs. Arbuthnot, diarist, political hostess, and intimate friend of the Duke of Wellington. Tributes to the king filled the pages of the newspapers, and the people snapped up pious prints praising his virtues. He had lost America and sired a clutch of useless children, but his plain speaking pleased his people, and his long struggle with illness had won their sympathies. They grieved for him and dreaded the regent becoming king.

The fifty-seven-year-old prince regent finally possessed what he had desired for so long—ultimate power. One of his first acts was to exclude the name of his wife from the prayers for the royal family in church.

The Duchess of Kent arrived at Kensington Palace on the same day that the king died. The remaining dukes had lost both parents and also their brother, and they had scant time for his widow. Their brother's death had shocked them, particularly because he had lived so abstemiously, and they dreaded the duchess begging for money. Moreover, they were slightly nervous of her power. Now that her father and grandfather had both died, baby Victoria was third in line to the throne.

The duchess wished to see the new king, but George IV had fallen seriously ill with pleurisy soon after the death of his father. Ministers fretted that his might be the shortest reign in history, and panicked doctors submitted poor George to aggressive bleeding. He recovered slowly, but the duchess remained low on his list of priorities. Not long after he returned to health, he heard that Caroline was planning to return to England to take up her rightful position as queen by his side. The prime minister offered her £50,000 (£5 million in today's money) to stay abroad and renounce her claim. But Caroline refused and set off on her triumphal progress back to England.

There was no grand funeral for the Duke of Kent. He was buried on the night of February 12 in the family vault at Windsor, while the duchess sat alone in the palace, as she wrote, "in my solitude here, eating my heart out." Prince Leopold paid the funeral expenses.

The new George IV hoped that the duchess would quickly leave for Amorbach. "Sick at heart and very lonely" in the chill, shabby rooms of Kensington Palace, the duke's widow was eager to return home. After all, she had married the duke only on condition that she could spend part of the year in Germany. There she could speak the language, Feodora would be happy, she would have the money to bring up Victoria, and she would not feel so terribly unwanted. She was hopelessly in debt, she dreaded the new king's ire, and she blamed him for her husband's death, since it was he who had abandoned the family in that freezing cottage. She was equally angry with her brothers-in-law, who had given her no assistance, financial or otherwise. Only the Irish equerry John Conroy seemed eager to help. Under the strain of events, she was beginning to rely on him absolutely, praising Edward's "dear devoted friend" and declaring: "[He] does not desert his [the duke's] widow, doing all he can by dealing with my affairs."

Leopold was determined that his elder sister and Victoria should stay in England. Not only was his position greatly enhanced by his influence over his sister and niece, but Vickelchen was the heir to the throne after her two uncles York and Clarence. As he reminded the duchess, she had little choice but to stay in England: The palace at Amorbach was entirely uninhabitable, as the duke's renovations had been abandoned half finished, the bills unpaid. The palace servants were owed money, and Captain Conroy was also pressing the duchess to stay. Reluctantly, she agreed. She borrowed £6,000 for the apartments, relinquished the regency of Leiningen, and began to run every decision past the beguiling Irishman whose opinion she so valued. "I don't know what I should do without him," she sighed.

George IV refused to give the duchess a penny, arguing that Leopold should care for her (strictly speaking, a widow was the responsibility of her family, not of her husband's relations). The king hated having to pay so much to his former son-in-law, and Leopold's profligate spending did not win Parliament over to his sister's cause. Leopold offered a measly £3,000 a year from his annual £50,000. Victoire would have to manage on that and the £6,000 a year that had been the duke's. She was soon seething with bitterness about her priggish younger brother. Just short of thirty, he lived in splendid luxury at Marlborough House, surrounded by beautiful paintings, and frequently traveled abroad, while she was mired in dreary Kensington Palace, forced to bring up two daughters on a pittance.

The Duchess of Kent was thirty-three, twice married, and the ex-regent of Leiningen. She was a mature woman, and yet everything was dependent on her retaining influence over her daughter. As "the little mouse" had already shown signs of a stubborn Hanoverian spirit, mother and daughter were set on a rocky road.

PART TWO

1820-37

Little Victoria

22

꒰꒱

An Idol in Kensington Palace

Until the age of five, Princess Victoria was, as she later admitted, "very much indulged by everyone and set pretty well *all* at defiance." For "Baroness Spaith, the devoted Lady of my Mother, my nurse, Mrs. Brock, dear old Mrs. Louis—all worshipped the poor little fatherless child." Drina, as she was known in her earliest years, was nearly eight months old when she, her mother, and their servants moved to Kensington Palace. In the drafty ground-floor apartments, Victoria enjoyed the customary upbringing of a high-society infant, except that she had no young siblings and received much more attention than a typical upper-class girl. Her mother anxiously watched her every move, and the servants adored her. As she later admitted, she had been "too much an Idol in the House."

The modest red brick mansion of Kensington Palace did not have the cachet as a residence that it does today. When William and Mary came to the throne in 1689, they began searching for a new royal residence, convinced that the damp location of Whitehall Palace next to the Thames would exacerbate William's chronic asthma. They quickly alighted on Nottingham House, a Jacobean mansion built in 1605, situated in the quiet rural village of Kensington. After extensive improvements, Kensington became the key court, and more than six hundred courtiers, staff members, and servants were soon in residence. The palace remained vital under the reigns of Queen Anne, George I, and George II. George III, however, preferred Windsor Castle and Buckingham House, and he ignored Kensington until he decided to use it to house some of his demanding band of offspring. The Duke of Sussex, another chronic asthma sufferer, took the former housekeeper's apartments and lived there quietly with his morganatic wife, the Duchess of Inverness (previously Lady Cecilia Buggin), along with his beloved collection of clocks and fifty thousand books. Princess Caroline, the estranged wife of the then prince regent, had been given a set of fine rooms, and the Duke of Kent had two floors of the southeastern corner of the palace, which once had been the apartments of George II. Kent embarked on a prohibitively expensive series of repairs, creating a new porch, a fabulous double staircase, and handsome public rooms. The bills soon mounted up, until he and Mme de St. Laurent fled from his creditors to Brussels in 1816.

By 1820, Kensington was a pleasant, expensive residential area with lovely villas set in large gardens and a cluster of smaller houses and shops around St. Mary Abbots church. Mother and daughter returned to live in the most splendid villa of all, on the same two floors that the Duke of Kent had occupied, as well as the further rooms allocated to them that had previously belonged to Princess Caroline. The duchess expected to be treated properly as mother of the heir to the throne, and so she was piqued that she was not to be given the State Apartments on the second floor. Victoria felt similarly disgruntled by the *"dreadfully* dull, dark and gloomy" rooms, later complaining that she "never had a sofa, nor an easy chair, and there was not a single carpet that was not threadbare." Even in the spring, the wind wailed around the chimneys and set the clock chains swinging. When the Duchess of Clarence once asked the little girl what she would like for her birthday, Victoria replied that she would like to have the windows cleaned. Black beetles—"our Kensington friends"—as she called them clambered over the damp carpets. The dreaded beetles infested houses and, as one housekeeping manual warned severely, could "multiply till the kitchen floor at night palpitates with a living carpet, and in time the family cockroach [would] make raids on the upper rooms travelling along the lines of hot water pipes." Beetles would clutch each other and hang in corners, like bees, even in palaces. Not surprisingly, little Victoria fell in love with her uncle Leopold's lavishly furnished Claremont.

The duchess had been celebrated for her fashionable gowns, but now she and her daughter were deep in mourning. A widow was expected to wear a black dress of a dull sheen such as crêpe (silk was considered far too luxurious for mourning dress, and any woman wearing it would be socially reviled) for at least twelve months. She was also obliged to remain indoors for the same period, only receiving visits from family and close friends. All letters were written on black-edged mourning paper. The second period of mourning began a year and a day after the death (although most widows waited a few extra months, so as not to seem precipitous); during this she could wear a black dress in any fabric or a black and white outfit. Once two years had elapsed, she could wear half-mourning, which meant purple, gray, lilac, or gray and black. All the while, she was supposed to refrain from social contact. The duchess, however, could not follow such strict rules. She had to move home, set up a new establishment, and attempt to deal with the legal issues ensuing from the duke's death.

Little Alexandrina Victoria grew into a plump toddler with pink and white skin and big blue eyes. But her angelic looks hid a fiery temper. She was not sly or prone to nursing grudges but flared up easily, shouting, crying, stamping her feet, and even throwing things in fits of rage. From very early on, the little girl had pronounced likes and dislikes. She positively refused to do anything that she did not wish to do. After placid Princess Feodora and her brother, Charles, the duchess was sorely tried by her third child's behavior. "She drives me at times into real desperation," she wailed. "Today the little mouse . . . was so unmanageable that I nearly cried." Early on, the "pocket Hercules" was compared to men rather than women. Lady Granville dubbed the chubby baby the image of her grandfather, "*le roi Georges* in petticoats."

Victoria recalled that her first memory was of crawling on a yellow carpet in Kensington Palace and being warned that if she cried, her uncle Sussex, who lived next door, would come and punish her. Not so easily cowed, Victoria took to screaming loudly every time the Duke of Sussex walked past.

When in a good mood, Victoria was an engaging and friendly child, deeply affectionate, and quick to apologize. But she was always demanding and manipulative. Her grandmother, the Dowager Duchess of Saxe-Coburg, recalled:

> *In the morning, she sometimes does not want to get out of bed, pre-ferring to tell all sorts of tales. Lehzen takes her gently from her bed, and sits her down on the thick carpet, where she has to put on her stockings.*
>
> *One has to contain oneself not to burst out laughing, when she says in a tragic tone of voice, "Poor Vicky! She is an unhappy child! She just doesn't know which is the right stocking and which is the left! I am an unhappy child!"*

It was an age when children, even small infants, were beaten as a matter of course, trained to be "seen and not heard." Victoria was indulged more like a modern-day infant, petted and stimulated, the focus of the household. She was punished by being put out on the landing with her hands tied behind her back, which would not have been viewed as a particularly harsh form of chastisement. A typical nineteenth-century girl would have seen her parents only when beautifully dressed before a meal, and been quickly taught that she was the inferior in the household, subservient in particular to her brothers. Victoria enjoyed constant attention, was introduced to adult visitors to the household, and was never expected to fetch, carry, or serve her half-brother, Prince Charles of Leiningen. She grew accustomed to receiving curtsies and bows, flattery and applause, and to great men call-ing her "Your Royal Highness," much to the jealousy of Princess Feodora. "With you," Feodora later wrote to her half-sister about Baroness Späth, "it was a sort of idolatory, when she used to go on her knees before you when you were a child."

The little girl was treated like a queen from the very beginning. A foot-man in splendid livery accompanied her wherever she went, and servants bowed subserviently when she trotted along the corridor. "You must not touch those, they are mine," she once told a young visitor, Lady Jane Ellice, who wanted to play with her toys. "And I may call you Jane but you must not call me Victoria." The little princess was already imperious.

"I have grown up all alone," Victoria later said, referring to her childhood as "rather melancholy." She was kept apart from her cousins, Princes George of Cambridge and George of Cumberland. Their very names were snubs to the duchess; the regent had refused her child the name of Georgina. Victoria became "accustomed to the society of adults (and never younger people)," for although children were mainly excluded, curious and distinguished adult visitors flocked to see the little princess with such a strong claim to the throne. Abolitionist, philanthropist, and Yorkshire MP William Wilberforce, invited over by the duchess, reported that she was "with her fine, animated child on the floor by her side with its playthings, of *which I soon* became one." Conroy's relation by marriage, John Fisher, bishop of Salisbury, previously Charlotte's detested tutor, knelt down beside Victoria and let her play with the shiny badge he wore as chancellor of the Order of the Garter. Unsurprisingly, given that Victoria received the keen attention of so many adults, her grandmother later declared: "She talks to everybody and thinks a lot about what is being said."

A little butterball with popping eyes, Victoria was not a pretty child, but she was the pet of her family. Uncle York was devoted to his little niece, and Victoria remembered him as "very kind but extremely shy" and someone who always gave her "beautiful presents." He also arranged a Punch and Judy show for her at a friend's home in Brompton and gave her a donkey, Dickey. Dickey was a great favorite, and she happily paraded for all to see around Kensington Gardens on her patient new friend. The Duke and Duchess of Clarence were equally fond. "My children are dead," wrote mournful Adelaide to the Duchess of Kent, "but your child lives and she is mine too." The Clarences wrote to the little girl on her third birthday that they were "very sorry to be absent on that day, and not to see their *dear, dear* Victoria," as they were sure she would be "very good and obedient to dear Mamma on that day, and on many, many others." George IV, growing increasingly reclusive in his elaborate, heavily renovated Cumberland Lodge in Windsor, complete with turrets, menagerie, an elephant, and his mistress, Lady Conyngham, did not visit.

The duchess dreaded the attention of her husband's family. She was consumed by fears that the king or his brothers would take Victoria to be brought up at court. George IV certainly wished to have the little princess close, and the Duke of Wellington claimed that only his intervention prevented the king from taking the child. The young widow still felt "friend-less and alone," struggling to improve her English and accustom herself to a new country. She also missed her son, Prince Charles, who was at school in Geneva. Aware that, as a foreigner, she was viewed with some suspicion, she was desperate for someone to trust. Leopold, bored by her neediness, neglected her demands. She began to depend more and more on John Conroy for practical assistance and emotional support.

Six feet tall, with black hair and gray eyes, Conroy was a handsome man with a vulpine nose and a sensual mouth. Although of Irish background, he had been born in Wales in 1786, and at the age of seventeen entered the army, where he did not achieve the success he had sought, serving neither in the Peninsular War nor the Waterloo campaign. His great skill was for charming women as a means of gaining the promotions he desired, begin-ning by marrying the daughter of his general. Like so many soldiers, he was desperate for employment after the wars. When the duke was intro-duced to Conroy, he made every effort to help him and took him into his household.

Vain, determined, quick-tempered, ambitious, and quite unscrupulous, Conroy told anyone who would listen that the duke had entrusted Victoria and the duchess to him on his deathbed. He paid the duchess unqualified attention, listening to her complaints, discussing her concerns, and taking control of the confusing issues of business. He groaned about "the immen-sity of his *service* and *sacrifice*" and encouraged her to think that she could not do without him. "What you said so often and what hurt me," the duchess confessed to Conroy, "unhappily is true, I am not fit for my place, no, I am not—I am just an old stupid goose." Naturally submissive, she apologized profusely for her shortcomings, as she had done with Captain Schindler in Amorbach. Reassured to have a man to give her orders, and entranced by Conroy's decisive confidence, she soon appointed him comptroller of her household.

Conroy retained a position in the army until 1822 and later worked for the Colonial Audit Office, but his energies were devoted to the duchess. Not long after he arrived in the palace, he began to befriend Princess Sophia when she drove over from her home in Connaught Place. Dizzy, easily muddled Princess Sophia, mourning her fading looks and nine years his senior, swiftly fell under Conroy's spell, and was soon regularly dining with the duchess and Victoria. Jealous, and annoyed by her sister-in-law's unworldliness, the duchess could not stand her, but Conroy argued that she would make a useful ally against George IV. In fact, he saw great advantage in the spinster princess for himself, realizing that he could win her gratitude by handling the aggressive demands of her illegitimate son, Tom Garth, failed soldier, gambler, and womanizer. Sophia soon moved into apartments adjoining the Duchess of Kent's and also handed Conroy control of her accounts. She bought her *"cher ami"* a large house in Kensington, on Campden Hill, for his wife and children for £4,000, as well as a country home in Reading and an estate in Wales with extensive lands and mines worth £18,000 (he later improved the estate by £10,000, thanks to her money). In 1823, Conroy's credit with Coutts Bank was just over £100. By 1825 his account contained an astonishing £22,000.

For Conroy, Princess Sophia was a fund of cash and the Duchess of Kent a source of potential power. Victoire might have been feeble, nervous, and impecunious, but she was the mother of a future queen and thus a conduit to unlimited riches. Many wondered why she relied so on him. The gossipy diarist Charles Greville and the Duke of Wellington came to the conclusion that the couple were having sexual relations. Indeed, it has even been suggested that Conroy was Victoria's father. But the duchess and Conroy were probably not lovers, and if they ever had an affair, it was of short duration. Conroy was sufficiently clever to know that he would have a greater influence over the duchess if sex was not involved. He preferred to keep her in a state of nervous erotic subordination. A sexual relationship could have altered the power balance in her favor; but while he maintained his authority as her chief adviser, she remained the dependant, ever anxious that he might leave her.

An early-nineteenth-century woman was forced to rely on a man to run her household. Men of business and money, let alone government ministers, would not negotiate with a woman. Without a husband, the duchess needed a male agent to act for her. She was an attractive young widow and mother to the potential queen of England. Any would-be suitors were discouraged by the aggressive Irishman always at her side.

Whether or not the duchess and Conroy were lovers, they were as wholeheartedly engaged on one mission as any husband and wife. They were intent on becoming regent to the little Princess Victoria.

23

※

"The Nation's Hope"

From 1825, Your Royal Highness conceived and acted on a System, that was to make the Princess 'The Nation's Hope.'" Conroy enthused to the duchess, "It would take volumes to narrate, your difficulties—your anxiety." Fat, bewigged George IV struggled to walk, while the portly, puffing Dukes of York and Clarence seemed unlikely to survive their sixties or produce heirs. The duchess was sure that her daughter would ascend the throne before she was eighteen. Then she would be able to take revenge for all the petty humiliations she had suffered at the hands of George IV and his courtiers. She would be the de facto queen, rich, powerful, and highly respected. In her view, she deserved to be regent, for she had almost been the wife of a king. Victoria later wrote that, according to her mother, "If my Father had not died, *she* would be in *my place.*"

Nowadays, we might imagine that the duchess would become regent as a matter of course. But this was an age when custody of a child was automatically awarded to the father if the parents separated. Women were not thought to have the stature, legal or otherwise, to care for a child. It was not until 1886 that married women were given the right to become a child's guardian after the death of a husband, and only in 1925 were women awarded equal rights over their children. Many people would have expected to see one of the royal dukes appointed as regent to Victoria. Fortunately for the duchess, the next in line for the throne after her daughter was Ernest, Duke of Cumberland, the most detested of all the royals, dogged by scandalous gossip that made the other dukes look almost upstanding. Parliament hated him, for he was an archconservative, entirely unsuited to wield any power in a country where the desire to broaden the electorate was strong. "Your immediate successor, with the mustaches," wrote Leopold to Victoria, "is enough to frighten them into the most violent affection for you." Augustus, the liberal Duke of Sussex, was more esteemed by Parliament and people alike, but it would be difficult to appoint him as regent if Cumberland was still alive.

The ambitious Conroy had a frail wife and six children (two sons later died) to support. The Duchess of Kent's complete dependence encouraged him to believe that he could achieve much more than simply managing her affairs. Scoffing that she "lived in a mist," he intended to be her absolute controller when she was regent, achieving power, a peerage, riches, and stability for life, as well as ensuring that his own children were appointed to plum positions at court. But although he knew that the duchess trusted him utterly, he was not so sure about her stubborn little daughter.

The duchess and Conroy attempted to bend Victoria to their will, in a plan that became known as the "Kensington System." According to Prince Charles of Leiningen, "the basis of all actions, of the whole system followed at Kensington for many years" was to ensure that the duchess had such influence over her daughter that "the nation should have to assign her the Regency." The pair aimed to keep the little princess's education entirely in the duchess's hands and to ensure that "*nothing* and *no one* should be able to tear the daughter away from her," so that the king could never take her to live at court. They also wished to acquire a wide following for the duchess, ensuring she was always associated in the minds of the public with Victoria. A secondary aim was to "give the Princess Victoria an upbringing which would enable her in the future to be equal to her high position" and also to "win her so high a place in the hearts of her future subjects, even before her accession, that she would assume the sceptre with a popularity never yet attained and rule with *commensurate* power."

Conroy and the duchess planned to detach the child as far as possible from the king and the royal dukes, as well as from Leopold, who also had his eye on the role of regent. To this end they cultivated influential Whig politicians and supporters, in conspicuous opposition to the extreme Tory-ism of the Duke of Cumberland, as well as the reactionary bent of George IV and the Duke of Clarence. The Duke of Kent had been of liberal sym-pathies, and Conroy and the duchess were convinced that the Whigs were an untapped source of support. Indeed, after the horrors of the Peterloo Massacre and the fiasco of the king's attempts to divorce his wife, even the most conservative citizens were warming to the idea of reform. Robert Peel wrote to John Wilson Croker:

> Do you not think that the tone of England—of that great compound
> of folly, weakness, prejudice, wrong feeling, right feeling, obstinacy,
> and newspaper paragraphs, which is called public opinion—is more
> liberal—to use an odious but intelligible phrase—than the policy of
> Government? Do you not think that there is a feeling, becoming daily
> more general and more confirmed . . . in favour of some undefined
> change in the mode of governing the country?

The scheming couple ignored Leopold's concerns about backing a par-ticular political faction. As he remarked, a row between parties "generally ends with the abolition of something or other which might have proved useful for the carrying on of Government." Indeed, the duchess and Con-roy were espousing a cause that would eventually deprive Victoria of power as queen. Courting the Whigs would afford them influence and as-sist their endeavors to alter government, much to the horror of William IV. Since the Whig principle of expansion of the electorate meant that govern-ment was less dependent on the whims of the monarch, the duchess and Conroy were essentially supporting the process that would ensure the diminution of Victoria's power to that of constitutional monarch, able to approve legislation but not to initiate.

The royal family had always been Tory. Conroy and the duchess wished to present Victoria as completely new and fresh, a reborn ruler with no link to her drunken, wastrel uncles, "those of the English Royal Family, against whom so many public accusations of misconduct persisted." They planned that the child would never be seen with her uncles or their offspring. The public had to believe that mother and daughter were quite inseparable.

The Kensington System also involved constant surveillance of *"every-thing* down to the smallest and most insignificant detail" about Victoria. Every cough, every piece of bread and butter consumed, every stamp of the tiny foot was all reported to Sir John. The little girl was forbidden to see any child or adult without a third person—usually her governess or the duchess—present, and she was never allowed to be alone. Although there were plenty of rooms at Kensington, Victoria slept in her mother's chamber, and Fräulein Lehzen sat with her until the duchess came to bed.

Victoria was also watched in case she became too reliant on any of her servants. She was continually surrounded by Conroy's own brood. "We were one family," blithely declared Conroy's son Edward. He and his siblings were always at the palace, or else Victoria was taken to visit them at their Kensington home. Victoire, Conroy's second daughter, a dull child of Victoria's own age, was thrust upon her as a constant playmate. The little princess was keenly resentful at being obliged to spend time with a girl she considered her social inferior. Furthermore, she suspected that Victoire spied on her and reported any conversations back to her father.

Victoria detested Conroy. His practice of controlling women with threats followed by fulsome promises of devotion worked wonderfully with the easily led duchess, as well as with Princess Sophia. But the way to influence the little princess, very much like her dead aunt Princess Charlotte, was by expressing loyalty and affection, by letting her have her own way in small matters, and by treating her consistently. This the vain, mercurial Conroy could not do. His temper tantrums and coarse outbursts distressed Victoria, and she hated her mother's fascination with him. The duchess later admitted, "The passions of those who stood between us estranged my beloved child from me."

Victoria blamed the Kensington System for her unhappiness as a child. She yearned to visit her uncles York and Clarence, and to enjoy court life. There was little fun to be had at Kensington Palace. Although her restrained childhood meant that she was comparatively unschooled in the practical complexities of politics when she came to the throne, the Kensington System was crucial in creating her popularity and her reputation. As Sir Sidney Lee, who published a biography of the queen in 1902,

avowed, the throne had been occupied successively by an "imbecile, a profligate and a buffoon." Victoria, in contrast, became a beacon of optimism
for the English people.

The British public fell in love with their little Victoria from her infancy,
their passion only amplified by the fact that she was seen so infrequently.
Mrs. Brock had to repeatedly tell her to acknowledge those who gathered
to stare at her while she was driving out or riding Dickey. Her fair hair and
sturdy figure led many to declare that she resembled the "late beloved
Princess Charlotte." Whenever she was playing in Kensington Gardens, an
audience gathered outside the railings to watch, and she would immediately perform for the crowd, curtsying and kissing her hand, even running
up to greet them. When Mrs. Brock tried to bundle her away, little Vickelchen would wriggle free, returning "again and again . . . to renew the
mutual greetings between herself and her future subjects."

24

Imperial Robes

On July 19, 1821, London hosted the most opulent royal ceremony England had ever witnessed. Tightly laced to reduce his incredible girth, the new George IV lumbered, sweating and red faced, up the aisle of Westminster Abbey. Flapping behind him was a twenty-seven-foot-long train of crimson velvet adorned with golden stars, which had cost over £24,000. At the altar, he received the crown of King Charles II, glittering with over twelve thousand diamonds. Music resonated through the abbey, and the choir sang sweetly. The king was satisfied, confident that his lavish ceremony had outshone even Napoleon's grandiose coronation. He had spent over £250,000 and had apparently sent an envoy to Paris to acquire the pattern of Napoleon's robes—for £700.

Outside, the people were shouting for their new king. George, however, was having trouble concentrating and had to be revived with sal volatile. He was somewhat distracted. As Mrs. Arbuthnot noted:

> *The king behaved very indecently; he was continually nodding &*
> *winking at Ly Conynham [sic] & sighing & making eyes at her.*

At one time in the abbey he took a diamond brooch from his breast,
& looking at her, kissed it, on which she took off her glove & kissed a
ring she had on!! Any body who could have seen his disgusting figure,
with a wig the curls of which hung down his back, & quite bending
beneath the weight of his robes & his 60 years wd have been quite
sick.

The licentious king lumbered back down the aisle, past his bowing subjects, and finally appeared at the door of Westminster Abbey. The assembled crowd burst into applause, awed by all the pomp and circumstance
into welcoming a man they had previously hated. As George III had been
an invalid recluse for years, it was a long time since any of them had seen
a king.

On a raised walkway so that the public could see him properly, the new
king and his guests progressed to Westminster Hall for the banquet.
George was preceded by some of the prettiest young aristocrats of the day,
walking backward in their elaborate outfits and throwing rose petals in his
path. The king and his new ministers seated themselves in their extraordinary costumes and tucked into salvers of fish, mutton, and veal with nearly
five hundred boats of gravy, along with a thousand bottles of wine and a
hundred gallons of cold punch. The most spectacular moment came when
the King's Champion, a symbolic appointee, entered with the Duke of
Wellington and the Earl Marshal, Lord Howard, all three on horseback.
The Champion handed the king a silver cup, witnessed him drink, and the
three then had to back their horses out of the hall.

Replete after his gargantuan meal, the king waved as he stepped into his
grand carriage for the triumphal journey to Carlton House. Then disaster
struck: Overturned vehicles were blocking the road, probably simply because too many people had tried to drive near to the abbey and there had
been scuffles, although it is possible that the prince's enemies had overturned coaches to sabotage his journey. The obstruction forced the exquisite procession to take an alternative route and wend its way through the
less salubrious streets of Westminster, passing seedy brothels, gin palaces,
counterfeiters' hideouts, and slums that teemed with London poor.

★　★　★

To his chagrin, the king remained a married man. On July 13, 1819, the Milan commissioners reported that, after interviewing eighty witnesses, they were satisfied that the princess and Pergami had enjoyed a sexual relationship. The cabinet did not consider the evidence sufficiently strong to convict the princess of adultery but conceded that they would allow proceedings for a divorce if she returned to England and attempted to become queen. On the afternoon of June 5, 1820, the King's nightmare came true. As *The Times* reported:

> *Neither at the landing of William the Conqueror, nor at that of the Earl of Richmond, nor of William III were the people's bosoms of this metropolis so much agitated as they were last night, when it was known that Her Majesty, Queen of England, had once again— bravely, we will say—set her foot on British ground. The most important Parliamentary questions were adjourned, the King's Ministers fled to the council-chamber, the streets were crowded, everyone was inquiring, "When did she land? Where will she sleep? Where will she reside? How will she enter London?"*

An odd, dumpy figure in an outlandish black wig, her florid face daubed with rouge, Caroline was determined to take London by storm. Crowds cheered as she rode in, and a mob kept up a steady cry of "Long live the queen" outside the house where she slept, pelting anyone who did not remove his hat as she passed. A battalion of the guards mutinied, and crowds catcalled outside Carlton House until the king fled to Windsor. One baffled onlooker reported:

> *Often riding to Windsor have I been detained by an army of working men, with bands and banners, and placards, headed by deputations of their several committees with wands of office—all terribly in earnest—all perfectly convinced of the Queen's immaculate purity— all resolved that repression should not triumph.*

Unfortunately for the king, radical MPs and ordinary Englishmen and women had taken up Caroline's cause, outraged that he was accusing his wife of adultery when he himself had kept mistresses and married Mrs.

Fitzherbert. They were also shocked by gossip that he was attempting to find evidence through blackmail and bribery. The American ambassador was astounded by the "boundless rage of the Press," and the caricaturists scribbled into the night, lampooning George's foolishness and portraying Caroline as a long-suffering victim. "I shall support her as long as I can, because she is a Woman, and because I hate her Husband," declared Jane Austen, speaking for many. "I am resolved at least to think that she would have been respectable, if the Prince had behaved tolerably by her at first."

On July 5, 1820, a bill was introduced to deprive Caroline of the right to be queen and to dissolve the marriage on the basis that she had committed adultery with Pergami. On July 17, lolling in her chair and occasionally shouting at the witnesses, the queen was put on trial in front of the House of Lords. Henry Brougham opened with a dazzling critique of the hypocrisy of the proceeding, lambasting an attempt to "punish an offence in the weaker sex which has been passed over in the stronger." He drew attention to the king's own adultery, as well as noting the Duke of York's sorry affair with Mary Ann Clarke.

The familiar accusations of adultery were trotted out again. Witnesses answered questions in lurid detail, and the public pored over the reports in the newspapers. Even though many ministers believed that the queen might have committed adultery, they were dubious about the prudence of bringing a case against her. On November 6, the bill was voted through on the narrowest of margins, and so had to be abandoned. Caroline was determined to taunt the king with her triumph. "I do indeed feel thankful at having put my enemies to confusion, and received the justice my conduct and character deserved," she gloated. "Her who would have rejoiced with me at her moder's triumph is lost to me; but she is in a much better world than the present, and we shall meet soon, I trust."

The capital rejoiced. Anne Cobbett, writer and daughter of radical leader William Cobbett, declared that within half an hour of the decision, "guns were firing, bells ringing, and illuminations in every street and suburb." She marveled at "all the ships in the river lighted to the mastheads, processions marching with bands of music carrying busts of the Queen with the crown on her head covered with laurel, playing God Save the Queen and bearing torches."

In desperation, the king proposed to publish Charlotte's memorandum of 1814, in which she described how her mother had encouraged her toward Captain Hesse. Ministers refused, aware that the public would be shocked at such cruel exposure of the dead princess, whom they still adored. The king had to accept it. He would not obtain his divorce.

Caroline had been machinating to be crowned alongside her husband, even though the Privy Council had decreed that she could not be if it was contrary to the wishes of the king. As George planned his robes and discussed his jewels, she and her ladies visited a dressmaker to be fitted for splendid gowns. On the morning of the coronation, she arrived at Westminster Abbey, accompanied by two ladies-in-waiting and three gentlemen—Lord Hood, Willy Austin, and Captain Hesse—and demanded to be admitted. At each entrance, guards turned her away. Finally she arrived at the entry to Westminster Hall and begged, "Let me pass; I am your Queen, I am Queen of Britain." As one onlooker reported, the deputy to the Lord High Chamberlain shouted, " 'Do your duty, shut the Hall door,' and the red pages immediately slapped it in her face!" The queen fled home, angry and humiliated.

On the night of the coronation, according to Lady Anne Hamilton, Caroline's lady-in-waiting, "her Majesty put on the semblance of unusual gaiety, but the friends who were around her observed that though she laboured hard to deceive them, she only deceived herself, for while she laughed, the tears rolled down her face." Her spirit broken, her health began to decline. On July 30, the uncrowned queen of England decided to attend a theatrical reenactment of the coronation at Drury Lane Theatre. On her return, she collapsed in bed with an agonizing stomachache. "Do you think I am poisoned?" she begged her physician. Within two days the doctors had decided that she was dying and began to subject her to a course of severe bleeding. When she had the energy, she devoted her time to burning her papers, letters, and memoirs. On August 7, Caroline suffered excruciating pain from four in the morning until ten at night. At twenty-five minutes past ten, her doctor felt her pulse and "at last closed her Majesty's eyes and declared, 'All is over.' "

George IV received the news of his wife's death on August 11 while traveling to Ireland on a steam packet. Although he retired below deck when he heard, he was said to be "gayer than it might be proper to tell." When Napoleon had died on May 5, a few months earlier, the king had been told, "Sir, your bitterest enemy is dead." "Is she, by God!" he cried. Now he decreed that there would be no general mourning for Caroline; he arrived in Ireland blind drunk.

Caroline's many supporters were roused to fury by her death. The body of the queen was to be sent to Brunswick for burial, but the government, nervous of any violent demonstrations, decided that her procession should not go through the city on its way to the port of Harwich. On the morning of August 14, a large crowd of supporters stopped the hearse and its ten black mourning coaches from proceeding by overturning carriages in front of it, forcing it to go through the city. The Life Guards were summoned to provide an escort. At Hyde Park Corner, the crowd became so desperate to prevent the hearse's exit from the park that they hurtled toward it, heaving bricks at the guard, who shot back in response. In the panic, two men were killed and many were wounded. Finally, at Tottenham Court Road, the authorities admitted defeat, and the procession was finally directed through the city, before making its way to Essex.

In her will, Caroline had begged that a plate should be nailed to her coffin reading, "Here lies Caroline of Brunswick, the injured Queen of England." The government refused permission and attached a plate with a Latin inscription. As the body lay overnight at Colchester, someone unscrewed the plate and replaced it with one bearing Caroline's desired wording. A few hours later, the government representative removed it and reaffixed the original. Caroline was refused the last word.

The king did not wear black. His spirits were buoyant. "His mind is clearly made up to have another wife, and all his family are of that opinion," declared Thomas Creevey. "He goes straight to Vienna after his Irish trip, so probably he will pick up something before his return at Christmas." But the fight with his wife had kept the fifty-nine-year-old king young. Now that she was dead, life lost some of its spice, and his health rapidly declined. Hardly able to walk, short of breath, and tormented by gout, the man was a wreck. "He looks ghastly; he is plunged into gloom, he talks about nothing but dying. I have never seen him so wretched," observed Princess Lieven.

George IV was not enjoying his reign. Terrified of ridicule in the press, he retired to Windsor. "It is a rather melancholy thing to see a king playing at hide and seek in this way," judged Anne Cobbett. His interests went little further than dispatching officers to bribe caricaturists to stop vilifying him so grotesquely. Otherwise, he retreated into the bosom of his Lady Conyngham, a fifty-one-year-old mother of five, no great beauty, and, according to Princess Lieven, "nothing but a hand to accept pearls and diamonds, and an enormous balcony to wear them on." To the relief of the duchess and Conroy, George IV seemed to show no interest in other women. The king wanted motherly comfort, not glamour.

Frederica, the Duke of York's childless wife, died in August 1820 after a six-month illness. Before she was in her grave, the elector of Hesse sent word that he had an eligible daughter. But the fifty-seven-year-old duke was resolved not to remarry. He felt he had done his duty, and like his older brother, he had little interest in respectable young ladies. He was also infatuated with the Duchess of Rutland, who already had a husband. Still, as the Duchess of Kent worried, there was no guarantee that he might not change his mind and take a second, younger wife.

In the summer of 1820, the friendship between the duchess and Adelaide, Duchess of Clarence, cooled when Adelaide confirmed that she was pregnant. After one child lost in babyhood and a miscarriage a few months later, the delighted Duchess of Clarence gave birth on December 10 to a girl who, although six weeks premature, seemed healthy. "She will be a worthy Queen if she does not have a brother," gloated Princess Elizabeth, jubilant at frustrating the hopes of Leopold and the Duchess of Kent. The Clarences would have preferred to call their daughter Georgina, but the regent insisted on the very royal Elizabeth. Elizabeth Georgina, he was suggesting, was a true heir. "We are all at the kick and go," reported John Conroy. "Our little woman's nose has been put out of joint."

Princess Elizabeth seemed sturdy and well, but the very cold winter affected her, and she fell ill in early March. Within two days she was dead of an inflammation of the bowels. The duchess offered her condolences, but she was filled with relief. Still, Adelaide was only twenty-seven, and more children were quite possible. There were, however, no more children. Adelaide became pregnant again, with twins, in 1822, but miscarried in April. "I want words to express my feelings at these repeated misfortunes to this beloved and superior woman," wrote the anguished duke. "I am quite brokenhearted."

For Victoria's fourth birthday in 1825, the king sent her a miniature portrait of himself set in diamonds. Soon afterward, he invited her to a state party. Immaculate in a plain white dress with the miniature ornamenting her sleeve, Victoria conducted herself beautifully, and the king "expressed himself greatly delighted with his little niece." The other guests were "much gratified with the opportunity thus afforded of seeing the royal child, whom they could not but look upon with the deepest interest as their probable future sovereign."

Otherwise, Victoria's life continued quietly in dusty Kensington. Her health was a natural concern for her mother. "I must confess that I am over anxious in a childish way with the little one, as if she were my first child," the duchess said. Even as late as 1899, after death rates had dropped exponentially, 16 percent of children died before their first birthday. Not only were they at risk from smallpox, measles, scarlet fever, whooping cough, typhus, and diphtheria (more than three-quarters of children had suffered one of these diseases by the age of five), even teething could kill. If Victoria was to die, the whole household would have to move. She was their sole reason for living in the palace. Luckily, despite an extended bout of dysentery in 1825, Victoria grew up a strong and healthy child.

25

❧

Living in a
Very Simple Manner

Little Victoria could not be the imperious monarch of the nursery forever. When she was just short of four, the princess had her first tutor. The kindly Rev. George Davys, vicar of Willoughby-on-Thames, Leicestershire, and a fellow of Christ's College, Cambridge, was a young man of liberal sympathies and patient character.* Victoria had been resistant to learning to read, but he decided on the innovative idea of teaching her by writing words on cards and hiding them about the room—a charming game that she adored. He also worked hard to obliterate the Germanic ring of her English, correcting her habit of confusing her *v*'s and *w*'s and training her to produce the "ch" sound. As she grew older, he began to teach her to write on a slate and complete simple arithmetic. He was impressed by the princess's quickness, although her powers of concentration did not equal her obduracy. "She seems to have a will of her own," he wrote wearily in his journal.

---

* Davys went to live at the palace in 1827, was appointed dean of Chester in 1831, and was made bishop of Peterborough in 1839.

Finally, when Victoria was five, her adoring nurse, Mrs. Brock, "dear Boppy," departed. The duchess dreaded outside influences, and any Englishwoman with the rank necessary to be governess to the princess would inevitably have a political connection and prominent friends. She finally decided to ask Louise Lehzen, forty-year-old governess to Princess Feodora, to assume the role. According to Charles, Prince of Leiningen, Conroy and the duchess thought that "the governess being *entirely dependent* upon the Duchess of Kent would also conform in all matters entirely with the latter's will." Lehzen knew that she had been chosen because she seemed dependent, and she was determined not to be treated as a servant. She pronounced herself more than aware of the "great difficulties" of educating a possible heir to the throne, but she had one favor to ask: If the Duchess received visitors and required the presence of the princess, Lehzen should also attend. She declared that she herself would receive "no one but those the Duchess chose to send, *never* my own acquaintance." She would give up her friends and contacts, if the duchess admitted her as an equal. The duchess allowed her to join the company, much to the chagrin of some of her guests. On one occasion, the queen of Württemberg shrieked at dinner that she would not "sit down to table with a maid servant."

A dark-haired, attractive woman despite her beaky nose and rather sharp manner, Lehzen was a hypochondriac, prone to stress headaches, always picking at her food and gnawing caraway seeds to cure indigestion. She had great resolve. Certain that Victoria had been indulged too long by her nurses and Baroness Späth, she refused to be moved by tantrums or pretty pleadings. The little princess would learn to obey, to practice what she did not wish to practice, and to finish what she had started. Victoria rebelled in horror at such discipline, screaming, shouting herself hoarse, and once even throwing a pair of scissors at her governess. "You used to torment Lehzen and myself during my French lessons when we were at Ramsgate," remembered Feodora. "Do you recollect, dearest Sister."

Lehzen later remarked that she had never known a child as naughty as Victoria, but she always treated her with kindness and patience, offering absolute loyalty. "She never for the 13 years she was governess to Pss. Victoria, once left her," wrote Queen Victoria, years later, "and knew how to amuse and play with the Princess so as to gain her warmest affections. The Princess was her only object and her only thought. She was very strict and the Pss. had great respect and even awe of her, but with that the greatest affection." Lehzen rewarded Victoria when she was obedient and devoted every minute to the child, supervising lessons and piano practice, driving around the park, and watching the little girl play. She read her charge stories while she was being dressed to ensure she did not get into the habit of gossiping to the servants. On free afternoons, the governess, Princess Feodora, and the little princess went out walking and driving. Even when the household holidayed in Ramsgate or Tunbridge Wells, Lehzen was always on hand, and Victoria had her lessons in her governess's room.

Victoria had collected small ceramic dolls from an early age. Before the era of plastic, children's dolls had much in common with the china fashion dolls created to sell dresses to women in the seventeenth and eighteenth centuries. They were delicate toys and often beautifully dressed. Victoria had little interest in fashion, but she adored to see her dolls in exquisite silk and velvet gowns, with matching feathered hats. Each doll, she decided, was a fine lady, with her own refined, beautiful house. Lehzen expressed genuine interest in Victoria's dolls, and she was soon busily cutting out and styling little outfits with the princess. The two passed many happy afternoons cutting up pieces of ribbon and silk to adorn the dolls. Lehzen attempted to train the little girl in the rudiments of sewing, needlework, and knitting, but the princess was an impatient needlewoman. Even when she was making dresses for her dolls, she preferred to direct Lehzen with ideas for styles.

On the whole, life with Lehzen was disciplined and quiet. "We lived in a very simple manner," the queen wrote later. "Breakfast was at half past eight, luncheon at half past one, dinner at seven—to which I came generally (when there was no regular large dinner party)—eating my bread and milk out of a large silver basin. Tea was only allowed as a great treat in later years." Like many children across England, she was raised according to a strict timetable and fed plain foods. Parents forbade rich fare, especially for girls, in case their passions became aroused: Fresh bread was risky, and "hot rolls, swimming in melted butter" were out of the question. Day-old bread was to be preferred, without butter. Jam was considered a luxury and marmalade a concoction that single ladies should not consume, on account of its strength. Little Victoria, a Hanoverian to the core, yearned for richer foods and vowed to consume mutton every day when she was grown up.

Unlike many nineteenth-century children, Victoria was allowed to meet her mother's visitors and sup with the adults, including Princess Sophia. Such treats did not occur often enough, for the princess loved gay company and parties. "I led a very unhappy life as a child," she recalled, "had no scope for my very violent feelings of affection—had no brothers and sisters to live with—never had a father—was not on a comfortable or at all intimate or confidential footing with my mother . . . and did not know what a happy domestic life was!" Visits to Uncle Leopold were "the brightest epoch" of her "otherwise rather melancholy childhood." The brief holidays to Ramsgate or Tunbridge Wells were also sources of pleasure and some freedom.

In the summer of 1825, the Kensington household traveled to Claremont for a family party. Escorted by the twenty-one-year-old Prince Charles of Leiningen, a handsome if slightly vacant young man, the sixty-seven-year-old Dowager Duchess Augusta of Saxe-Coburg had come to see her granddaughter, to whom she was also godmother. Victoria met her half-brother and grandmother for the first time—and was rather fonder of the latter. The dowager duchess was soon besotted by the little princess, declaring her "big and strong as good health itself," graceful and poised and "so vivacious and so friendly." She was not so entranced, however, as to be blind to the little girl's propensity for willfulness. "I shall never forget her coming into the room when I had been crying and naughty at my lessons and scolding me severely, which had a very salutary effect," wrote Queen Victoria many years later. A determined sightseer, the duchess dragged her reluctant granddaughter on long carriage rides around the Surrey countryside, and then around London when the party moved to Kensington. On August 17, Victoire celebrated her thirty-ninth birthday. Feodora woke her mother with an enthusiastic song, and the six-year-old Victoria dressed up her dolls in their robes of state. "The Little One is nothing less than a beauty, yet a darling clown," praised the dowager duchess, sad to leave her new favorite to return home in September. "She is incredibly precocious for her age and very comical, I have never seen a more alert and forthcoming child."

To mark Victoria's seventh birthday, on May 24, 1826, Leopold threw a grand party at Claremont, and the little girl was showered with presents.

The Marchioness of Huntley sent her a tiny pair of Shetland ponies, and the duchess and Leopold gave her a matching small phaeton. Just wide enough to hold her and Lehzen, it was a young girl's dream: a little postilion, in a livery of green and gold, with a black velvet cap, was mounted on one of the ponies, and the whole equipage preceded by a little outrider. Thrilled by her fairy-tale gift, the princess rode around the park or into the Claremont countryside every day throughout the summer.

Leopold considered himself to be a perfect regent, even though he paid little practical attention to Victoria's upbringing. He was reveling in spending his huge grant of £50,000 a year on London's loveliest women. Deftly avoiding the endless stream of fond mothers thrusting their eligible daughters at him, he indulged himself with various mistresses, including Countess Ficquelmont and Lady Ellenborough. In 1826, on a visit to Prussia, he visited the theater in Berlin where Stockmar's twenty-year-old niece happened to be on stage. In the leading role in the musical comedy *The Hottentot,* Caroline Bauer was a vision in a tiny red dress trimmed with coral trinkets and tiger fur, her hair adorned with black and white feathers. Leopold was struck with love at first sight. Next day, he came again in a hired carriage and begged Caroline to live with him. "At the very first glance my heart was drawn to her," he told Caroline's mother, "because she looks so wondrously like my departed Charlotte," even though the princess had preferred long white gowns to short scarlet costumes. He was delighted to discover that Caroline came from respectable stock: Her father had been an officer in the Light Dragoons. It seems very likely that Stockmar encouraged the relationship, praised his niece to Leopold, and suggested that she behave vivaciously, to recall Charlotte.

The lady herself was reluctant. "It is very hard for me to give up my career as an actress," she wrote to Leopold, "but my heart asks me to make this sad, afflicted man happy again." She had clearly remained ignorant of Leopold's recent amorous adventures, writing mournfully that she should "join him in his loneliness in England." Finally, however, Leopold's money and seeming need for her won the day. She and her mother set off to London. Leopold installed her in a giant, blushing pink cake of a house in Regent's Park, covered in thick rose drapes and filled with caged birds.

Caroline had anticipated a life of wealth and glitter as the mistress of a man with two fine houses and £50,000 a year, the uncle of England's future queen. But there was no one to meet her at the house, and when Leopold did arrive, his opening remarks were hardly encouraging: "Oh," he cried, "how the spring sun has burnt your cheeks."

Leopold knew that the public would hate the idea of his taking a mistress and that it would provoke further outcry about the money he received, so he kept Caroline hidden. He refused to take her out in public and, when at Claremont, packed her off to a very dark and chilly cottage with brown carpets, on the edge of the grounds. It was an awful contrast to her feted life back in Germany, and Caroline soon sank into a profound gloom. She spoke no English, she could not make friends, and worst of all, Leopold was a crashing bore. Pretending to be the beloved dead wife of a grieving widower was no fun at all. She had expected lively evenings in the wealthiest city in Europe. Instead, Leopold expected her to stay in and wait for him to arrive and gaze at her. He would demand that she read him a moral tale while he played with his latest passion—a "drizzling" machine.

Drizzling had first caught on at the court of Marie Antoinette. The drizzler put old epaulettes, tassels, and bullion lace into the machine, turned the handle, and gold and silver threads appeared from the bottom; these could then be sold. Always fond of vowing that he was saving money, Leopold thought the machine quite superb and drizzled enthusiastically in Caroline's presence. Indeed, he turned the handle so conscientiously that he produced and sold enough thread to buy his niece a silver soup tureen. Caroline was stunned by her poor fortune. She had left the applause of the stage in the hope of being a famous beauty, and she had become a neglected mistress, tormented by her tedious lover and the dreaded drizzling machine. She excoriated Leopold in her memoirs, mocking his black wig and his habit of putting gold clamps in his mouth to stop him from grinding away his tooth enamel at night. He, however, was blissfully content.

When the Duke of Cumberland heard that the Duke of Wellington, the new prime minister, was to offer political concessions to Catholics, he decided to hurry back from Berlin to London. He arrived in England in January 1829, ready to lead the hard-core Protestant opposition and eager to goad his brother the king into a rage against Catholics. A rumor began that Cumberland would lead twenty thousand Protestants to Windsor. At the end of February, an alarmed Wellington announced that he would resign if Cumberland did not leave England. The king resisted but finally changed his mind, consenting to the Catholic Relief Bill in April.

Thwarted, Cumberland now turned his attention to Victoria, the child who stood between him and the throne. He loathed the Duchess of Kent. Indeed, whenever he met her, he would harangue her, declaring that the duke had promised him that he would never marry, and maliciously step on her toes. Conroy and the duchess were soon convinced that he was employing agents to drug, then kidnap and kill, her. The anxious duchess commanded that her daughter should not even walk downstairs without someone holding her hand. She should be watched at all times, and her food should be tasted. Boisterous, robust little Victoria was treated like the most delicate doll.

Conroy blamed Cumberland for reports in the newspapers that Victoria was a sickly child with warped feet and legs that were too feeble to hold her weight. To counter such derogatory suggestions, Conroy and the duchess made sure that the princess was seen out as often as possible, walking in the most public parts of Kensington Gardens, the epitome of a healthy little girl. Lord Albemarle—once George Keppel, Princess Charlotte's playmate, now attending the Duke of Sussex—remembered: "One of my occupations of a morning, while waiting for the Duke, was to watch from the window the movements of a bright pretty little girl, seven years of age. It was amusing to see how impartially she divided the contents of the watering pot between the flowers and her own little feet." The public were soon ambling to the palace grounds, eager to catch a glimpse of the princess. Leigh Hunt reported that he saw the princess in Kensington Gardens holding the hand of another little girl and followed by a footman who looked like a "gigantic fairy" behind the tiny pair. In spite of her highly restrictive regime, Victoria still desired her mother's approval. In her earliest extant letter, dated 1825, the six-year-old sent her mother a flower and wrote, "My dear Mamma I love you Victoria."

Victoria was not the only one to suffer. At the Leiningen court, Princess Feodora had been a princess, sister of the future ruler, but at Kensington, uprooted from her home at the age of ten and separated from her brother, she was little more than a poor relation, with only a governess and a small child for company, forced to converse in English, a language she did not like. "When I look back upon those years which ought to have been the happiest in my life," she lamented to Victoria years later, "I cannot help pitying myself. Not to have enjoyed the pleasures of youth is nothing, but to have been deprived of all intercourse and not one cheerful thought in that dismal existence of ours, was very hard. My only happy time was going or driving out with you and Lehzen; then I could speak or look as I liked." Both girls felt watched. Victoria was "always on pins and needles, with the whole family hardly on speaking terms," she later confessed. "I (a mere child) between the two fires—trying to be civil and then scolded at home! Oh! it was dreadful."

26

❧

"I Was Greatly Pleased"

In the summer of 1826, young Princess Victoria arrived with her mother and Feodora at the elaborate faux-Gothic Royal Lodge at Windsor to see the reclusive king. A rouged and perfumed mountain of a man popped up, roaring, "Give me your little paw." Plump Lady Conyngham, whose husband and grown-up children lived at the lodge, pinned a miniature of the king set in diamonds on the little girl's dress, and she was set on his knee to kiss him. The princess did as she was told, despite flinching at the heavy layer of grease covering the face of His Majesty.

The king deputed Lady Maria Conyngham, daughter of his mistress, to entertain the little princess by taking her to see the royal menagerie of "wapitis, gazelles and chamois" (the celebrated elephant had presumably died). The next day, while driving around Virginia Water, they were overtaken by the king's carriage. "Pop her in!" roared George IV, and the little girl was whipped into his elegant phaeton, squeezed between himself and the Duchess of Gloucester, previously Princess Mary, who clung tightly to her little charge. Victoria recorded her delight at the escapade. "I was greatly pleased," she wrote, "and remember that I looked with great respect at the scarlet liveries etc." Her mother stared grimly after her, fearing that her little girl would never be returned.

The King and his niece spent the afternoon on a barge in Virginia Water to hear a band play and to parade in front of fervent crowds. At a pause in the proceedings, the king inquired what his niece wished to hear the band play next. "Oh Uncle King," she cried out, "I should like them to play 'God Save the King.'" Victoria's life in Kensington Palace had taught her how to please adults, and she charmed her uncle.

Afterward, the king asked her what she had most enjoyed. "The drive with you," the clever little princess replied. The king promptly sent her a gift of two diamond bracelets.

George was almost as charmed by pretty Feodora as he was by his niece. Victoria reported that the king "paid great attention to my Sister, and some people fancied he might marry her!" Feodora was lovely, well mannered, and, as a Protestant princess, a suitable (if impecunious) choice for the wife of an English king. The duchess and Conroy were horrified by such a possibility. If Feodora married the king, she would surely produce a child. They began hunting for possible husbands who would take her far away from the excitable George IV. Conroy also wished to get rid of Feodora because he thought she encouraged Victoria to complain. He told the duchess that she should "marry soon." He declared, "It is necessary for yours and the Pss. Victoria's interest that it should take place—the interest you ought to have over her [Victoria] will be endangered if she sees an older sister not so alive to it as she should be—and recollect, once your authority is lost over the Princess V you will never regain it."

The prospect of Feodora marrying set many men boiling with jealousy. One Stephen, an Irish furrier, trotted after her whenever she drove around St. James's Park, so convinced he had made a good impression that he wrote to the king, every member of the royal family, and each of the cabinet ministers, telling them that the princess loved him. Robert Peel's strongmen were sent to arrest the importunate lover at an inn. "Reasoning was of no avail," Peel wrote. "I propose therefore to try the effect of prison discipline for a day or two & then I hope he will be effectively undeceived." Alas, Stephen's passion was not so easily dampened: He was soon writing to the Duchess of Kent, demanding an inquiry in the Houses of Parliament as to why his proposals had been ignored. The hypochondriac Augustus D'Este, son of the Duke of Sussex, neighbor at Kensington Palace, who had once vied for Princess Charlotte, had also fallen for Princess Feodora. "I need not tell you that I am as legitimate a Prince as any to be named in either of our houses," he boasted, as he began sending surreptitious letters along the Kensington corridors. He even persuaded the duchess's lady-in-waiting, Baroness Späth, to slip Feodora a gold ring. When the duchess heard about the secret proposals, she angrily told her brother-in-law to restrain his son.

Meanwhile, the indefatigable Conroy sought real suitors for the twenty-year-old princess. The Prince of Schönburg, the Austrian minister, was mooted but abandoned, because their union would mean Feodora would remain in London, when Conroy wanted her out of the country, unable to influence Victoria. The Duke of Nassau was rejected because he was too rich and powerful. Finally, Conroy plumped for the thirty-two-year-old Prince of Hohenlohe-Langenburg, an impoverished scion of a family almost ruined by the Napoleonic Wars. As a woman's status was entirely dependent on that of her husband, Feodora would be without influence and too poor to visit her half-sister. Conroy wrote: "I think the Princess would find that character, that dignity of conduct which would tend to preserve her own happiness." Fortunately, though, her "life would be unmarked by anything very splendid." Princess Feodora herself was eager to leave home and was prepared to do almost anything. "I escaped some years of imprisonment which you, my poor dear Sister, had to endure after I was married," she later wrote to Victoria. "Often have I praised God that he sent my dear Ernest for I might have married I don't know whom—merely to get away."

Conroy rubbed his hands with glee as the engagement progressed. Beautiful, clever Feodora, the half-sister of the future queen, was to be packed off cheaply to a penny-pinching life in the threadbare Schloss Langengburg, on an income of £600 a year. Only Leopold had the power to change matters. But he was too preoccupied with drizzling and his mistress Caroline. Even though the exasperated Caroline fled back to Germany in 1827, vowing never to see another drizzling machine again, it was too late.*

---

* Caroline returned to the stage to great acclaim and later married a Polish count.

Feodora's fate was sealed. At the end of the same year, her official engagement was announced. Feodora admired Prince Ernest of Hohenlohe-Langenburg, who was kind, handsome, and relatively young, but she could have made a much more magnificent marriage.

George IV decreed that he would give the bride away but demanded that the marriage take place in private. Four days before the ceremony, however, he was unable to walk, after a particularly painful attack of gout, and was forced to withdraw. On February 18, 1828, in the Cupola Room where Victoria had been baptized, twenty-one-year-old Feodora became the Princess of Hohenlohe-Langenburg. Victoria was her bridesmaid. "I always see you, dearest, little girl," wrote Feodora, "as you were, dressed in white—which precious lace dress I possess now—going round with the basket presenting favours." At three o'clock the party went to the Grand Hall to await the king, but he never appeared.

After a honeymoon at Claremont, the Prince and Princess of Hohenlohe-Langenburg left for Germany on February 26. Victoria missed her sister dreadfully and sent letters pouring out her feelings and sending news of her dolls, even writing notes purporting to be from the "babies" themselves. "I was delighted to see a little letter from you directed to me from your darling hands," Feodora wrote in April. "How often I should like to kiss them and your whole little person." The new Princess of Hohenlohe-Langenburg wrote about once a fortnight with news of her husband's pets, and sent painted paper dolls, dried flowers, and little presents of drawings and books. "If I had wings and could fly like a bird," she wrote on Victoria's tenth birthday, "I should fly in at your window like the little robin today, and wish you many very happy returns of the 24th, and tell you how I love you, dearest sister, and how often I think of you and long to see you." But she had to admit, Ernest would miss her, and he was "rather tall and heavy for flying." Victoria longed for more news. But Feodora, in her chilly schloss, was busy and happy with her husband, and soon a family of six children.

The Duke of York had been suffering from gout and dropsy for some time. In the summer of 1826 he fell seriously ill, and on January 5, 1827, he died at the age of sixty-three. The Duke of Clarence was now heir presumptive, much to the chagrin of the king, who had preferred York. "Look at that idiot!" he had sneered to the Princess Lieven. "They will remember me, if ever he is in my place." Conroy and the duchess certainly shed few tears at the death of the duke. Now there was only one brother left between Victoria and the throne.

The Duke of Clarence was elated. "He did not act the part of Chief Mourner very decorously," commented Peel. "I heard him enquire from Lord Hertford how many head of game he had killed at Sudburn." The king and the government created him Lord High Admiral, essentially commander in chief of Britain's naval forces, but before long he had riled the Admiralty board with his excessive spending and his impatience with what he saw as tedious matters of bureaucracy. On one occasion, the duke and a squadron of ships were at sea but nobody knew exactly where he had gone. Exasperated, the government informed the king that if his brother did not step down, they would resign. The king acquiesced, reassuring the Duke of Wellington that he would "leave him the example of what the duty of a King of this country really is"—hardly a statement to inspire much confidence. The duke resigned and promptly took to his bed for a week to recover. Still, he had some consolation. The government awarded him and Adelaide an increase in income of £9,000, and many who had snubbed him for years were suddenly keen to praise his wit and excellent taste. He was besieged with invitations and tokens of esteem from the highest in the land. The only blight in his life was his failure to produce an heir.

Now that Victoria was second in line to the throne, Conroy pressed his devoted Princess Sophia to suggest to her brother the king that he and Lehzen should receive titles because a princess possessed of such great position should not be served by commoners. George IV agreed, and since he was king of Hanover, he made Lehzen a Hanoverian baroness and Conroy a knight commander of the Hanoverian Order. The humble Irish soldier became the elevated Sir John Conroy. Everything was falling into place.

27

Educating a Princess

"A woman on the throne of so great a country, how ridiculous!" puffed Prince George, son of the Duke of Cambridge, reeling at the realization that his cousin preceded him in the succession. As time had progressed, the English had become less forgiving of women in power. The queens regnant of England, such as Anne and Mary Tudor, were widely seen as failures, and Elizabeth I was considered by many as cruel. The Duchess of Kent and Conroy knew it was vital that Victoria be seen by all as the perfect choice for the throne.

The Duchess of Kent decided that she should be treated with great pomp, as the mother of the heir, and started spending heavily to aggrandize herself. Like Leopold, the duchess had a taste for the finer things in life. She wanted expensive dresses of deep velvet to set off her still lustrous chestnut hair and handsome dark eyes, and fine hats with trailing ostrich feathers. She was also keen to stage fabulous entertainments. Rooms were quickly dressed and decorated as nobles, ambassadors, politicians, and dignitaries came for lavish dinners. She borrowed huge sums to hire chefs, singers, wine waiters, and top-class cooks for the most spectacular patisserie.

Victoria's wardrobe was also supplemented extravagantly with stiff layers of velvet and lace, puffy organdy dresses, thick sashes, and lacy pantalets. She was invited to sup her child's meal with her mother's distinguished guests before entertaining the company with a tune on the piano or by reciting a poem. Visitors were charmed by her manners and her speaking voice but unimpressed by her appearance. No amount of silk and petticoats could transform Victoria into a beauty, thanks to her resemblance to her stodgy-faced father. She was bright and sturdy, but she was plain, and her singing, playing, and recitals were unexceptional. Compared with other, violently eccentric adult royals, however, the robust little princess seemed the epitome of good English common sense, and the guests always admired her dignified bearing. Her mother's insistence that she keep her head straight by tying holly under her chin had paid off.

In 1825 the duchess had refused the government's offer of £4,000 a year for Victoria's maintenance. Six thousand had been offered for the support of Prince George, son of the Duke of Cumberland, and she was irritated by the implication that Victoria was in any way inferior. When Parliament capitulated and offered £6,000, the duchess was satisfied. She had debts of £9,000 and was quite unable to run her household, which was hardly surprising when she was spending so riotously and Conroy, her rock, was siphoning off money for the upkeep of his properties and his unwieldy family.

The duchess appointed further tutors for her daughter. Thomas Steward, writing master of Westminster, was chosen to instruct Victoria in writing, geography, and arithmetic; and M. Grandineau came to teach French. The patient Rev. Davys taught history. There was a riding master as well as a French dancing mistress, for it would not have been proper for a man to teach a young lady to dance. Mr. Richard Westall, a respected Royal Academician, became the drawing master, and Mr. Sale, the organist at St. Margaret's, Westminster, taught Victoria singing and music. His was not the easiest job. On one occasion, when told that if she wished to succeed in music she must practice like everybody else, she slammed shut the lid of her piano and shouted, "There! there is no must about it."

Lessons were from nine thirty to eleven thirty, then there was play or walking, with an hour for lunch at one. The second half of the school day lasted from three until five, after which Victoria learned English, French, and German poetry by heart for an hour. On Wednesday afternoons Rev. Davys gave her religious instruction. On Thursdays she had a dancing lesson and on Fridays, music. On Saturdays she read over her lessons until eleven, learned German at three, wrote letters from four until five, and then practiced French for an hour. She was always accompanied in the lessons by her mother or Lehzen, and later also by the Duchess of Northumberland and sometimes visiting aristocrats and dignitaries. Her rigorous education and upbringing were turning Victoria into a very modern monarch. Previous kings had spent their time hunting, drinking, or dallying idly with the court. The principle of the duchess was that, as Feodora wrote, young ladies should never be allowed to "be unoccupied, for at first it must be habit, and afterwards it becomes necessary to one's happiness to be occupied." Victoria was trained to be disciplined and hardworking, and she grew up absolutely accustomed to being watched and on show.

The rigid organization of Victoria's day was typical for a girl of her time, but the academic quality of her education was unusual. Many girls were still taught at home by their mothers. A narrator of one of Mrs. Gaskell's novels recalled, "We helped her [their mother] in her household cares during part of the morning: then came an old-fashioned routine of lessons, such as she herself had learnt when a girl—Goldsmith's 'History of England,' Rollin's 'Ancient History,' Lindley Murray's 'Grammar,' and plenty of sewing and stitching." Education was little better in the girls' schools proliferating across the country, in which rote learning, sewing, and copying, particularly of music, prevailed. The idea was for young women to be prepared for the role of submissive wife, with just enough qualities to make them appealing. Victoria, however, was being conspicuously educated to be heir to the throne.

Education of the Tudor queens had involved study of the classics, the sciences, and esoteric branches of mathematics. Victoria's school day was not so academic. She was taught drawing, dancing, and singing, but sewing and embroidery were neglected in favor of arithmetic, a subject usually offered by girls' schools as an "extra," for which parents paid. It also seems as if she was spared continual declarations that femininity inhered in obedience, duty, and looking pretty. Many girls her age were encouraged to read improving texts in which they were advised to hide their learning or refrain from arguing, as Hannah More had proposed. Victoria was encouraged to read history and consider the behavior of kings and queens, and she appears never to have been taught that she should be submissive to men.

Victoria had a particular aptitude for drawing, she was a graceful dancer and a strong rider, and her singing voice was good. She was enthusiastic about history, but her attainment in other lessons left something to be desired. She found German grammar and French tricky, even though she had spoken German as a child.* In her free time, she did her homework, sketched, walked with Lehzen, and looked forward to any escape from the palace. She also played make-believe with her "babies." As she grew older, she dressed them after characters from her favorite plays and operas, keeping a list of all 132 dolls and which character each represented. Like most children, she conceived sudden passions for collecting. "You asked me if I was still looking for shells?" she wrote to Feodora from a holiday in Broadstairs. "I am very fond of having them, but it makes my back ache so to look for them myself." When Feodora made Victoria godmother to her daughter Eliza in 1830, she occupied herself making little presents for her godchild. Busyness was one of her most enduring and, indeed, most Victorian characteristics. "I love to be employed," she wrote in her diary. "I hate to be idle."

Despite her governess's attempts to discipline her, Victoria still had problems controlling her temper. "I hope never any more to hear Mamma say 'I am shocked,'" she wrote in 1829, hoping to become a "good and obedient child" and "to hear her say 'I am pleased.'" In 1830, the princess and Lehzen began to keep "Good Behaviour Books," which detailed Victoria's frequent outbursts. She often confessed tantrums three days in a row, declaring she had been, for example, "very ill behaved and impertinent to Lehzen."

Victoria's behavior was endlessly scrutinized, but it appears that little

---

* The queen later wrote that she "never spoke German until 1839, not allowed to"— meaning that she was not allowed to use it outside of lesson time. The Dowager Duchess of Saxe-Coburg, however, declared that the little girl was "adorable" when she spoke German.

attention was paid to her looks. She had the Hanoverian recessed chin, prominent nose, and slightly goggling eyes. Her blond hair darkened early, and she was naturally plump, with a tendency to leave her mouth hanging open. In a fit of jealous pique, Prince George of Cambridge declared her a "fat, ugly, wilful and stupid child." Most people who met her were struck by her diminutive stature, and indeed at full height she would be only four feet eleven inches. At a juvenile ball given by the king for Donna Maria II, the ten-year-old queen of Portugal, an unimpressed Charles Greville described Victoria as a "short, vulgar looking child and not near so good-looking as the Portuguese." Unfortunately, however, the little queen had a nasty fall and left in tears, while Victoria danced all night.

As Victoria moved into her teens, her appearance improved. She grew more slender, and people began to admire her flawlessly fair skin and pretty blue eyes. She was particularly proud of her long, abundant hair and had her maid dress it in the latest styles every morning. Thanks to interminable exercises, she never lost her graceful deportment. Even as late as 1885 one admirer declared, "She moves with grace, ease and lightness." She was also blessed with good health and plenty of energy, which was more than her uncles possessed. Perhaps most engagingly, she was unruffled by her appearance. On one occasion she wrote to Feodora, "[I was] very happy to hear that the portrait of my ugly face pleased you, and that you find it like; had it not been for your dear sake, I would not have spent so many tedious hours for Collin [the portrait painter Henry Collen]."

Still afraid that the Clarences and the king might snatch Victoria from her, the duchess wrote to the bishops of London and Lincoln asking them to set examinations for her daughter, and so conclude whether "the course hitherto pursued in her education" had been the best, and if not, where it had "been erroneous." The duchess was keen that they should appreciate her self-sacrifice. "I became deeply impressed," she wrote, "with the absolute necessity of bringing her up absolutely in this country, that every feeling should be that of her native land and proving thereby my devotion to duty by rejecting all those feelings of home and kindred that divided my heart."

The bishops arrived to examine Victoria in the first week of March. Used to performing for visitors, Victoria demonstrated a good knowledge of scripture, history, and the precepts of the Church of England. She was equally adept at geography, arithmetic, Latin grammar, and finding countries on her globes, and her English and Latin pronunciation were also good. The examiners endorsed her grasp of modern languages and decided her drawings were "executed with the freedom and correctness of an older child." They had only one recommendation: the princess should know her "future position in this country."

The following day, an event occurred that has passed into myth. Lehzen declared that she put a "chronological table" into the princess's history book. When the princess saw it, she whispered, "I see I am nearer to the Throne than I thought." She continued, "There is much splendour, but there is more responsibility," then said, "I will be good." The words are stilted and lack the spontaneity we associate with Victoria. It also seems improbable that she had no idea how close she was in line to the throne. Even as a child, she had demanded of her nurse why men lifted their hats to her but not to Feodora. It is more likely that it was Lehzen who chose to give her remarks such emphasis. Victoria herself remembered the incident quite differently. "I cried much on learning it and ever deplored this contingency." She was told that her aunt Adelaide might produce an heir, and if so, she would not be queen. "I always hoped she would have children," Victoria wrote.

The archbishop of Canterbury came to interview the reluctant future queen in May and emerged quite satisfied. According to him, when questioned on the character of the English sovereigns, the young princess "appeared to have thought for herself, and for a young person of her age to have formed a just estimate."

Victoria's views on her predecessors were quite conventional. On Elizabeth I, she later wrote, "Elizabeth was a great *Queen,* but a *bad woman,* and even in her royal capacity, she erred sometimes; she had a very great idea of her prerogative and was more arbitrary even than her tyrannical father." At the age of eleven, the princess was treading a tricky path between finding models for queenship and expressing the sort of virtuous opinion considered appropriate for a young woman. "The harshness of her character (which she inherited from her father Henry the 8th of England) made her delight at having a rival in her power though every kind heart would pity a poor exiled Queen like Mary." She felt deeply sorry for Mary, Queen of Scots, so often portrayed in the literature of the time as gentle and feminine in comparison to her more masculine rival. Lehzen, however, proposed Elizabeth I as a "model of perfection." She could "pardon wickedness in a Queen, but not weakness." Victoria was greatly influenced by Lehzen's insistence on the importance of remaining resolute.

Victoria was always more sure about the excellence of girls than boys. She wrote and illustrated a little story for Lehzen, "Sophia and Adolphus: in the style of Miss Edgworth's Harry and Lucy." "Harry and Lucy" is a pedagogical tale in which the children ask their parents searching questions. Like them, Sophia and Adolphus are siblings in the bosom of a happy family. Victoria opens the tale with a picture of the family sitting together in the evening, chatting, while a dog pulls cheekily on the father's coattails, a scene quite different from that at Kensington. Instead of being concerned with politics and influence, her ideal little family engage with simpler questions of domestic virtue. On one occasion, Sophia wishes to be friends with the two Miss Smiths, particularly Miss Maria, who can sing, dance, and speak French. She is less keen on the vicar's daughters. Her mother chastises her that Maria might be talented, but she is frivolous. "She never reads good books she always reads novels which cannot impress upon her mind any good knowledge of geography and history." The mother also warns against "fashionable and affected acquaintances." It is interesting that Victoria calls the young lady who needs to be reformed Sophia, after her aunt, for whom she had no particular fondness. Sophia was also the name of her illegitimate FitzClarence cousin. In the tale, Victoria allowed her love of melodrama free rein. When Adolphus considers an ice-skating trip, all hell breaks loose. "'Oh! Adolphus' said Sophia as she threw her snowy white arms about her brother's neck, 'don't go, you will be drowned, you will be drowned!'" He is indeed injured after falling through the ice. In Victoria's imaginary world, girls were always right.

Even though they had charmed the bishops, the duchess and Conroy were still anxious that the king might take Victoria to live with him in order to boost his declining popularity. John Conroy suspected Baroness Späth, who had criticized his methods with Victoria, of spying for the king. Soon the duchess was equally convinced that her loyal lady-in-waiting of twenty-five years was a traitor, and she banned the baroness from spending time alone with Victoria or joining her for walks. But Conroy had conceived a profound dislike for Späth, and so, at the end of 1830, the duchess fired her.

The household was shocked. Mr. Paget, one of the gentlemen-in-waiting, burst into tears. "How cruel after so many years of faithful service," he wept.

Conroy complained to anyone who would listen that Späth talked too much, that she spoiled the princess, and that she was simply not right to serve the duchess. Few believed him. The Duke of Wellington told Greville that Princess Victoria had "witnessed some familiarities" between the duchess and Conroy. "What She had seen She repeated to Baroness Späth, and Späth not only did not hold her tongue, but (he [the Duke] thinks) remonstrated with the Duchess herself on this subject. The consequence was that they got rid of Späth, and they would have got rid of Lehzen too if they had been able." Lehzen never forgave Conroy for treating her friend with such casual cruelty.

The source of Wellington's evidence about what Victoria might have witnessed was most probably one of the royal family, such as the Clarences. Did sheltered ten-year-old Victoria see her mother in a compromising position? It is more likely that she saw Conroy angrily bullying the duchess (which might suggest to many adults that they were lovers). Victoria later confided in Baron Stockmar that she resented Conroy's "impudent and insulting conduct" and that she had been angry to see him abuse the duchess in her presence.

Princess Feodora kindly found Baroness Späth a place in her household, where she whiled away her days in the cold and shabby schloss of Hohenlohe-Langenburg. Victoria was devastated to lose her kindly friend and began to fret that her mother was also trying to send Lehzen away. She could not bear the idea of a future without her beloved ally, and she feared that with no one to shield her from Conroy, she would be dogged wherever she went by him and his family. Even worse, her uncle Leopold was also making plans to go abroad. Greece had been declared independent from Turkey in 1829, and he had been lobbying for the throne. Victoria felt isolated and alone. The "babies," she wrote to Feodora, were "pensioners, not because they are broken, but because I am tired of playing with them."

The royal family was deeply concerned about Conroy. "In the family it is noticed that you are cutting yourself off more and more from them with your child," wrote the Duchess of Clarence to her sister-in-law. It was, she declared, "the general wish" that she should not allow Conroy "too much influence . . . but keep him in his place." She painted a humiliating picture of Victoire as hopelessly manipulated by her adviser. "They believe he tries to remove everything that might obstruct his influence, so that he may exercise his power alone, and alone, too, one day reap the fruits of his influence." Conroy was not devoted to the duchess but was "cherishing dreams of future greatness and wanting to achieve a brilliant position for his family," and everyone recognized "these aspirations, towards which his every action" was directed. The Duchess of Clarence was firm: "He must not be allowed to forbid access to you to all but his family, who in any case are not of so high a rank that they alone should be the entourage and the companion of the future Queen of England."

The letter turned the duchess against the Clarences forever. As she saw it, her husband's family had left her stranded after his death, without money, organizational support, or advice. Conroy had stepped in to help, despite the fact that she could pay him little. It seemed to her that the Clarences wanted to see her return to her old position of vulnerability, so they could make use of Victoria's appeal as a royal icon or even take her for themselves. Bitterly indignant, she was more convinced than ever that her daughter should separate from her uncles as much as possible and spend time only with her Coburg relations. She succeeded: Victoria later wrote to Leopold, "The word *Uncle, alone,* meant no other but you."

28

※

Sickly Uncle King

At sixty-eight, George IV was in failing health, hidden away in splendid isolation in Brighton. He had lost the sight in one eye, his legs were horrifically swollen, and he had also contracted an excruciating bladder infection.* Dosing himself constantly with laudanum to relieve the pain, he was often too insensate to receive visitors or look over official documents. Lady Conyngham drummed her fingers, bored by her role as nurse to such a pathetic, self-indulgent wreck. Conroy and the Duchess of Kent "held themselves very high," noted Princess Lieven, "as if the throne was to be theirs tomorrow."

In the last year of his life, the king's weight shot up from seventeen to twenty-two stone (that is, 238 to 308 pounds—hardly a gargantuan weight by twenty-first-century standards, but quite shocking to eighteenth-century observers). His stomach reached his knees; his body was, according to the Duke of Gloucester, "like a feather bed." By the spring of 1830,

---

* The king's last appearance in London was at the 1829 juvenile ball held for Victoria and the Infanta of Portugal.

he had to sleep sitting up because he could not breathe lying down. He made himself more unwell by continuing to overindulge. Wellington reeled to see him consume before bed: "two glasses of hot ale and toast, three glasses of claret, some strawberries!! and a glass of brandy." Breakfast might be two pigeons and three beefsteaks, "three parts of a bottle of Mozelle, a Glass of Dry Champagne, two Glasses of Port, and a Glass of Brandy."

By April, the king was in agony. His legs had become hard and had to be drained regularly, sometimes of "several quarts of water," and he was often unconscious. At half past eleven on June 25, 1830, he retired to bed, with one of his doctors, Wathen Waller, sitting beside him. He woke at two o'clock, drank some clove tea, and asked for the windows to be opened. Then he gripped Waller's hand, looked him in the face, and declared, "with an eager eye": "My dear boy! This is death." He drew his last breath at quarter past three on the morning of June 26. Around his neck was a diamond locket containing a miniature of Mrs. Fitzherbert.

William, Duke of Clarence, was called down in his dressing gown and informed that he was king. He declared that he wished to return to his chamber, for he had "never yet been to bed with a Queen."

"No monarch will be less generally mourned," decreed *The Times*. "What eye has wept for him? What heart has heaved one throb of unmercenary sorrow." The paper did not spare its criticism. "An inveterate voluptuary, especially if he be an artificial person, is of all known beings the most selfish." The postmortem showed that the king's heart was coated in fat and he had a tumor the size of an orange on his bladder. The immediate cause of death had been the rupture of a blood vessel in his stomach.

At nine o'clock in the evening of July 15, George IV's colossal coffin was carried by dukes and sons of dukes to St. George's Chapel. Escorted by lines of Grenadier Guardsmen, the procession was led by trumpeters, drummers, and fifers of the guards, peers bearing banners, the Duke of Wellington with the Sword of State, and the new king, William IV, in a sweeping purple cloak. Inside the chapel, all dignity was lost as the crowds jostled for places. According to *The Times*, "servants of the household, the friends of the carpenters and upholsterers, the petty tradesmen of the town" pushed the official guests out of the way. "We never saw so motley, so rude, so ill-managed a body of persons," despaired the journalists.

"They who first entered not only seized the best places, but prevented others from taking any." In the middle of a hymn, a piece of the carved wood hanging over the stalls crashed onto the head of Sir Astley Cooper, the king's surgeon. Manfully, Sir Astley stayed in place, clasping a handkerchief to his injury.

Not one person in the congregation (except perhaps Sir Astley) seemed distressed. William IV bounced up the aisle, beaming with happiness, grasping the hands of friends, and babbling inconsequentially, even when he sat at the head of the coffin. In London on the day of the funeral, the shops were shut and church bells tolled, but people refused to stay indoors. In Windsor, there were so many street parties and impromptu dances that gangs of pickpockets roamed, grasping the purses of the drunken revelers. Mrs. Fitzherbert, however, mourned her husband sincerely. William IV ordered her to wear a widow's mourning dress, bestowing on her, finally, the recognition she had craved.

At sixty-five, the Duke of Clarence was the oldest individual ever to ascend the English throne (although our current Prince Charles may yet win the title from him). He was so excited by his succession that he could hardly contain himself. On the morning after George IV's death, the new King William IV rode up from Bushey to be sworn in, bursting with energy and waving enthusiastically at his subjects. He signed his name in front of the assembled privy councillors, barking loudly at the clerk, "This is a damn'd bad pen you have given me." "What can you expect," shrugged Greville, "from a man with a head like a pineapple."

The new king, according to one spectator, was a "little old red-nosed, weather-beaten, jolly-looking person, with an ungraceful air and carriage." He looked ludicrous in his kingly robes, but he always wore a big smile on his perpetually flushed face. As Princess Lieven judged, he was a *"bon enfant,"* the epitome of the expression, "Happy as a King."

The *"bon enfant"* was hot tempered, selfish, and often silly. His time in the navy had nourished his tendency toward outspokenness and aggressive behavior. He was, however, engagingly cheerful, loyal to those he esteemed, and less selective in whom he favored than his brother George had been. Since he had lived away from court for nearly forty years, his subjects knew little more about him than his ignominious performance in the navy, his long affair with Mrs. Jordan, and his undignified scramble for a wife.

The new king was eager to rid himself of his brother's taint of debauchery and extravagance. He ordered the cavalry to shave off their mustaches and fired the French cooks from the palaces. He demolished Royal Lodge, the overblown house in Windsor Great Park where George had lived with Lady Conyngham, sold three yachts and many of the royal racehorses, donated trinkets and the entire royal menagerie of 150 birds and animals to the nation, and pruned the staff from the royal residences—including a German band that had cost £18,000 a year.

Unlike his brother, William quickly settled into a routine. He rose on the dot of ten minutes to eight every day, took an hour and a half to dress, and breakfasted with the queen and her ladies at half past nine. During breakfast, he read *The Times* and *The Morning Post*, intermittently bellowing, "That's a damn'd lie!" After breakfast, he worked on papers with Sir Herbert Taylor, his private secretary, lunched at two on cutlets and sherry, then drove out until it was time for the evening meal. He ate a moderate dinner, washed down with a bottle of sherry, and went to bed at eleven. He was in need of strict working habits: There were nearly fifty thousand state papers that George had been too incapacitated to sign. Like many, the new king wished to reward those he felt had been loyal to him. He pushed ministers to award a peerage to his beloved Miss Wyckham. Finally, in 1834, ministers capitulated, and the lady became Baroness Wenham.*

On July 26, 1830, Victoria had a taste of the kind of pomp that she would one day enjoy if her uncle remained childless. A month after the death of George IV, dressed in mourning and wearing a veil that reached the ground, she walked behind Queen Adelaide at a chapter of the Order of the Garter at St. James's Palace, patiently enduring the dull ceremony. When William IV opened Parliament for the first time, Queen Adelaide watched from the garden with Princess Victoria. As the crowd began to shout, "The Queen! The Queen!" Adelaide picked up the little princess and perched her on the wall beside her. "God Save both Queens!" came the cry.

---

* Baroness Wenham never married and lived at Thame Park, near Oxford, dying in 1870.

The Duchess of Kent was most unhappy at the queen's actions. She wished Victoria only to appear in public by her side.

The day after George IV's death, the duchess sent a letter, written by Conroy and signed by her, to the prime minister, the Duke of Wellington. She demanded that the office of regent be vested fully in herself, asked for Victoria to be given an official governess, a lady of rank to accompany her on formal occasions, and also requested that her daughter receive twice-yearly examinations from the archbishop of Canterbury, the Lord President of His Majesty's Privy Council, the bishops of London and Lincoln, and the Lord Chief Justice of the King's Bench. Most importantly, she wished to be given the position and precedence of Dowager Princess of Wales, to receive an appropriate income, and to have all her debts paid. No direct grant should be made to the princess. The duchess was making it brutally clear that she did not imagine Queen Adelaide would have another child and was essentially suggesting that she should set up her own court.

The Duke of Wellington replied quickly: "I earnestly advise and entreat your Royal Highness to allow me to consider it as a Private and Confidential Communication; or rather as never having been written." The duchess did not give up easily: "Irksome as it must ever be to my feelings, to be Regent . . . I feel I *owe it in my conscience, to Her.*" Wellington simply ignored her demands. When the regency was debated, there was some suggestion that Cumberland should assume the role. No final decision was made.

The duchess had been a little nervous of George IV, but she had no fear of King William. When the Whig Lord Grey succeeded the Duke of Wellington as prime minister in July, she besieged the king with demands for money and new rooms, much to his anger and Grey's frustration. "She is the most restless persevering troublesome devil possible," opined the politician Thomas Creevey. "Through Conroy, she expresses the most violent indignation against the King and Grey considers and states that as Mother of the Princess Victoria she is entitled as *matter of right* to every thing she asks." The duchess demanded the more ornate state apartments on the second floor of Kensington Palace, high-ceilinged rooms better suited to the type of grand entertainments she desired to host. They were, she declared to Grey, "unoccupied and used only for old pictures." She asked Sir Jeffry Wyatville, who had renovated Windsor Castle for George

IV, to remodel the staircase, create fine rooms for entertaining, and improve the drive. But King William was so infuriated at the duchess's request that he refused to see Sir Jeffry.

Mortified at being denied the money and the accommodations she desired, the duchess began to behave in a very grand fashion. When Adelaide came to visit her niece at Kensington Palace, she was instructed to wait. Even the queen would have to be announced into the presence of the eleven-year-old heir to the throne. The duchess also behaved more haughtily toward the king's FitzClarence children, who were always at court, along with their extended families. The illegitimate brood were forever hurtling about the drafty corridors and begging sweets from the queen. The duchess made a point of leaving the room when one of the FitzClarences walked in, even when she was the king's guest at Windsor. "Did I not keep this line," she declared, "how would it be possible to teach Victoria the difference between Vice and Virtue."

The FitzClarence boys were permanently dissatisfied, agitating for titles and money, threatening suicide and desertion in an attempt to force their father to keep them in the way that they believed they should live. As Greville put it, they expected to "relive the days of Charles II." Despite their relentless demands, the king adored his family, and the duchess's insulting treatment of them caused him great grief.

To William's fury, the duchess began to augment her power base with Whig supporters, including John Lambton, the future Lord Durham, and Lord Dover, who would later assist in the founding of London's National Gallery. The king hated the duchess's presumption in offering such patronage to Whig families, for she was suggesting implicitly that they would have the ear of the next monarch. England was clamoring for Whig reforms, and the duchess's actions sent her popularity soaring.

The duchess, in fact, had greater plans than simply inviting supporters to dinner. Together, she and Conroy planned a spectacular tour of England, aiming not only to gather genteel supporters to the cause and remind thousands of ordinary people that Victoria was heir to the throne, but also to promote the mother of the future queen.

Centuries earlier, Elizabeth I had made spectacular progresses around the great houses of England, delighting the ordinary people and securing the eternal loyalty of the noblemen she visited, even though her huge entourage wrecked grounds and furniture bought in their honor and gobbled thousands of pounds' worth of food. The early Hanoverians, in contrast, had been far more familiar with their tiny German home state than the country they came to rule. Then, George III had visited Weymouth to bathe, George IV entertained at Carlton House or skulked in Brighton, and William IV lived contentedly with his family of illegitimate children at St. James's. The last spectacular tour had been when Lord Nelson and his mistress Emma Hamilton flaunted their fame across the Midlands and Wales in 1802, to the delight of their public and to effusive reports in the newspapers. Perennially disgruntled that government was so focused on London, the populace was desperate to experience the magic of royalty, but many people were never able to leave their hometowns. When news of the duchess's planned tour leaked out, the country was whipped into excited anticipation.

After months of planning and poring over maps, the duchess and Victoria, along with Conroy and his daughter Victoire, drove to Stratford, Kenilworth, Warwick, and Birmingham, then to visit the Duke and Duchess of Marlborough at Blenheim Palace, and call on Earl Beauchamp at Madresfield Court, Malvern. The duchess was in her element, treated with great deference wherever she went, met by waving crowds and flattered by local dignitaries.

The princess hated traveling. She had grown up in comparative isolation, but now she was required to charm and receive dignitaries and wave patiently at crowds. The little girl missed her pets at Kensington and often found herself pushed to one side while the duchess, statuesque in her stylish hats, took the limelight. She was feeling so isolated that she even warmed a little to Conroy's daughter. In Malvern, she noted happily, she "had the permission to keep Victoire the whole day," and she threw a joint tea party for her "big doll as well as two of Victoire's." On the return journey to Kensington, the party visited Badminton House, owned by the Duke of Beaufort, waved at crowds at Hereford, Worcester, Gloucester, and Stonehenge, and visited Bath, where the princess opened the Royal Victoria Park.

Back at St. James's, the king was furious as he read all about Victoria's joyful reception. He was incensed by the duchess's behavior, as well as by songs such as "Victoria—Pride of our Land" written in celebration of the monarch-to-be. Conroy and the duchess returned from the tour quite satisfied. Their plan to rally Whig support had been most successful.

In November, Parliament reassembled. The Lord Chancellor declared in the House of Lords: "The manner in which her Royal Highness the Duchess of Kent has hitherto discharged her duty in the education of her illustrious offspring—and I speak upon this subject not from vague report, but from accurate information—gives us the best ground to hope most favourably of her Royal Highness's future conduct." The duchess's campaign to charm Whig grandees, her sedulous courting of the bishops, and most of all, the tour, had won her the great prize. She was appointed sole regent. Conroy had also achieved his ambition: He was the closest adviser to the Regent and, he hoped, the future queen.

29

Charlotte the Queen?

Now that she was heir, the eleven-year-old Victoria became the subject of close scrutiny. Tales were spread about whom she might marry, her uncle's sympathies for Catholicism, and her mother's political leanings. Gossip about her weak health persisted. Victoria kept a clipping from a copy of *The Times* in 1831, which published a letter refuting the report that she was so frail that she was unable to stand, another suggestion said to have come from the Duke of Cumberland. Mostly, however, people were exercised about her name.

The government had finally accepted that the plump little princess would be queen. But how could a queen of England bear a preposterous foreign name like Victoria? No one had ever been called such a ludicrous invented name, let alone the monarch. At the end of December, the prime minister offered the duchess an extra £6,000 per annum and suggested that a peeress should fulfill the role of official governess to Victoria, as the duchess had desired. Having softened her up, he dropped the bombshell. He told the duchess that the king wished Victoria's name to be changed to

Elizabeth or Charlotte, typically royal names and those he had chosen for his dead daughters.

It seems peculiar now to consider Victoria as a foreign name, which, as the duchess wrote, the princess alone used. But the king complained [it is] "a name which is not English, had never been known heretofore as a Christian name in this country, not even German but of French origin."

For the first time in her dealings with William IV, the duchess adopted an emollient position, declaring she was "ready to do that which is most suitable to Her Station and the feelings of her Country." Aware that the English hated the suggestion of foreignness in her daughter's background, she proposed that the Russian-sounding Alexandrina be dropped and Charlotte put in its place. Victoria would remain as a middle name, not to be used but to "gratify all the feelings my child and I share from bearing alike that same name." Lord Grey and the king agreed, relieved to have the matter settled so swiftly.

Everyone thought the solution excellent. It was, after all, an age when a new baby was often named after a sibling who had died. Ministers calculated that calling the little girl Charlotte, after the young woman who had died before she could be queen, should give her inordinate popularity.

The duchess, however, began to doubt her decision. Some of her powerful friends advised that the little girl should be called Elizabeth, not Charlotte; others told her not to give in at all. She soon concluded that she should refuse to change the name, deciding that the government meant to push her out of her daughter's life. She wrote to Lord Grey, "It will be *quite contrary* to the Princess's and my feelings, if the King persists in changing Her name—and I trust his Majesty may be advised to abandon the intention." She was adamant. The king had to be told that there was nothing he could do to force her.

When she was seventeen, Victoria wrote to her uncle Leopold:

About a year after the accession of the present King there was a desire to change my favourite and dear name Victoria to that of Charlotte, also most dear, to which the King willingly consented. On its being told me, I said nothing, though I felt grieved beyond measure at the thought of any change. Not long after this, Lord Grey, and also the Archbishop of Canterbury, acquainted Mamma that the country,

*having been accustomed to hear me called Victoria, had become used
to it, enfin, liked it, and therefore, to my great delight, the idea of a
change was given up.*

The duchess's refusal to concede over the name was the last straw for
the king. The two courts were now at war.

On February 24, 1831, Princess Victoria donned a dress of English lace
draped over white satin, and a row of pearls, and attended her first Drawing Room, to celebrate the queen's birthday and see ladies being presented
to the queen (always by married ladies who had themselves been presented). According to one magazine, Victoria "was the object of interest
and admiration on the part of all assembled, as she stood on the left of Her
Majesty on the throne. The scene was one of the most splendid ever remembered and the future Queen of England contemplated all that passed
with much dignity, but with evident interest." King William was less impressed, complaining that Victoria looked at him coldly.

The Duchess of Northumberland was appointed Victoria's state governess. The Duchess of Kent and Conroy had expected her to simply accompany Victoria on public and ceremonial outings. To their dismay, she
began visiting Kensington frequently and insisted on involving herself in
her charge's life. She wanted to sit in on lessons so that she could report
back to the king about Victoria's education, and she made sure to impart
her own opinions about the princess's exercise and reading matter.

The Duchess of Kent tried to secure the support of the governess by
flattering her, once telling her "how particularly anxious I was, to give
Victoria a dignified sense of her great station: And that she could be of
great use to me, and assist me, by her advice." She tried to seem confidential. "I made also the remark that I like secrecy in all who are about
me." But the Duchess of Northumberland would not compromise on
her belief that her first loyalty was to the king, and then Victoria, with
the Duchess of Kent coming very far down. Increasingly, Conroy and
the Duchess of Kent found themselves ranged against the Duchess of
Northumberland and Baroness Lehzen—with Victoria tending to side
with her governesses.

*   *   *

Across Europe, monarchy was in crisis. "The position of what is generally called great people has of late been extremely difficult," fretted Leopold. "They are more attacked and calumniated, and judged with less indulgence than private individuals. . . . Ever since the revolution of 1790 they are much less secure than they used to be." In France, King Charles X, who had come to the throne in 1824 on the death of his brother Louis XVIII, had censored the press, disbanded the Chamber of Deputies, and appointed a reactionary cabinet of politicians who were very unpopular. Parisians began demonstrating in the streets and were soon attacking the garrison and burning buildings in what became known as the July Revolution. The panicked king fled to Scotland, and his distant relative the Duke of Orleans became King Louis-Philippe.

In 1826, there had been a crisis of succession in Portugal. King John VI had left two sons: Peter, who had become emperor of Brazil, and Michael, who was in exile. The country had no desire to see the thrones of Brazil and Portugal united, so Peter declared that his seven-year-old daughter, Donna Maria, should be queen. Michael had promptly deposed her, and ruled Portugal harshly. Leopold thought England should assist. "I am very ready to furnish some troops, but we have not means of transporting them that must come from England, and that great country is particularly fond of doing nothing." Victoria was unsure. "I feel for her," she remarked, "her education was one of the worst it could be." Donna Maria was finally restored to the throne by her father in 1834.

In 1815, the country known as the Southern Netherlands had been incorporated into the United Kingdom of the Netherlands by the Treaty of Vienna, and William I, previously the Prince of Orange, father of Charlotte's jilted fiancé, had been made king. He enacted repressive measures toward the French-speaking Roman Catholics, imposing heavy taxes and refusing to give them equal representation in the upper house of Parliament. In the summer of 1830, a performance of Daniel Auber's opera about repression in Naples, *La Muette de Portici,* was the catalyst for riots in Brussels, which soon spread to southern Belgium. King William found he could not defend himself. He begged the Russians, the Prussians, and the Austrians to send men, but they could not help, and England ignored his pleas. The Belgians declared their independence on October 4, 1830—and then they had to look for a king. In April 1831, they offered the throne of the newly created country to Leopold.

Leopold was keen to assume a position of power, and now that the duchess was confirmed as the future regent, there was little role for him in England. Moreover, he was gratified to be offered a kingdom that the father of his old rival for Charlotte, the Prince of Orange, had lost. He accepted and, to Conroy's delight, departed for Belgium on July 16, 1831. Nearly fifteen years after Charlotte's death, Leopold relinquished some of his £50,000 annual sum, but still took £20,000 a year to make donations to English charities and maintain his home and servants. The twelve-year-old Victoria was sad to lose her dear uncle, but was careful not to reveal her full feelings.

"I often think, when our children—yours and mine—are grown up," wrote Feodora to Victoria later, "and think back upon their happy childhood, how different their feelings will be from what ours are when we think back. We both have not enjoyed a father's love; and . . . how they are surrounded with affection and care." Although the duchess treated Victoria in a way that she found cruel and restrictive, her efforts with her daughter did bring some genuine benefits. The little girl's popularity had been increased by separating her from her corrupt uncles. The duchess's plan to show the child while she walked in Kensington Gardens, rather than in pompous carriages or at gilded court dinners, was equally well judged. As the century wore on, the depraved dukes seemed like relics from a permissive and extravagant era, whereas Victoria appeared different: a virtuous child of simple tastes, good sense, and regular habits.

Royalists hoped that Victoria would quell all protests against the power of the monarchy, and even republicanism. One visitor, Lady Wharncliffe, thought the princess "the most perfect mixture of childishness and civility I ever saw. She is born a Princess without the *least appearance* of art or affectation." Entranced by Victoria's graceful, feminine ways, she suggested that they had the power to quell republican sentiment. "She is really very accomplished by taste, being very fond both of music and drawing, but fondest of all of her *dolls*. In short I look to her to save us from Democracy."

30

"The Queen Does Nothing but Embroider Flowers"

On September 8, 1831, King William IV, with his blotchy-faced Queen Adelaide, was to be crowned at Westminster Abbey. The king was reluctant to undergo a coronation, declaring it a "useless and ill-timed expense," and agreed only on the condition that it would cost as little as possible. He decreed that there would be no grand ceremonial banquet in Westminster Hall with dishes borne aloft by officers of state on horseback. Participants were told to order their own liveries, and the queen made her own crown, taking jewels from her collection and paying for the setting herself. Scandalized at the proposed lack of pomp, the Tories threatened not to attend, but the king refused to be deflected from his plans, shrugging that there would be "more room and less heat" without them. Thanks to his parsimony and the do-it-yourself crown, the cost was £30,000, compared to £250,000 for the coronation of George IV. Some wits dubbed it the "half-crownation."

The king commanded that Princess Victoria must follow behind his brothers as he walked up the aisle. Bridling against what she saw as a deliberate slight on her daughter's position, the duchess declared that she and the princess would not be present, making the excuse that the long ceremony would strain Victoria's health. *The Times* reported that the duchess "had refused to attend, yes refused to attend," judging her decision "indecent and offensive." The editor made it patently clear who should be blamed: "We should be glad to know who are the advisors of this misguided lady?"

Victoria was devastated to be denied the pleasure of seeing her uncle crowned king. Skulking miserably around Norris Castle on the Isle of Wight, where her mother had whisked the household, she wept bitterly on her dear Lehzen's bony bosom. "Nothing could console me," she lamented, "not even my dolls." Back in London, drawing rooms reverberated with gossip about the duchess's awful snub to the king. A few days after the coronation, Greville dined with the Duke of Wellington and dug for information. The duke blamed John Conroy. "I concluded he was her lover," Greville recalled, "and he said he 'supposed so.'"

King William IV proceeded to cause havoc in the court by overturning points of etiquette imposed by his father and his sedulously polite elder brother. Fat, red-faced, and fidgety, he was impatient with formality and did just as he pleased. He refused to sit facing his gentlemen-in-waiting when he drove out, much to their consternation. Ladies at court received smacking kisses on both cheeks or one, depending on their beauty rather than their rank. George IV had hoped to create a court of fine arts and elevated etiquette that would be envied across Europe. His brother summoned old naval chums to dinner at Brighton, blustering, "Come along directly, do not bother about clothes. The Queen does nothing but embroider flowers after dinner." Princess Lieven complained, "In the evening we all sit at the round table. The King snoozes, the Queen does needle-work, talks a good deal and with much amiability but never a word of politics." Unlike George IV, King William was painfully bored by the arts, snored his way through the opera, and had no interest in erecting new buildings, happily for the much-depleted royal coffers.

The new king also had an unfortunate habit of haranguing. On one occasion he threatened the president of the Royal Academy, bellowing in front of the whole company, "If the Queen was not here, sir, I would kick you downstairs." Wellington sighed over the king's habit of "wiping his nose with the back of his forefinger" rather than with a handkerchief. At a

New Year's dance at Brighton Pavilion in 1832, he seized the hand of an elderly admiral and whirled him around the floor, while the rest of the party stared in astonishment. A few days after becoming king, he sauntered into St. James's Street alone, to enthusiastic cheers and vigorous attempts to shake his hand. A courtesan grasped him and kissed him on the cheek, prompting panicked members of the nearby White's club to come hurtling out to rescue him. "Oh never mind all this," he shrugged, after being bundled safely back to the palace. "When I have walked about a few times they will get used to it."

The public were delighted to see a new king on the throne, but their euphoria soon waned. William IV was resolutely opposed to Whig measures to broaden the electorate, for he was well aware that such measures would reduce his power. The country, however, was eager for reform. Particularly hated were the "rotten boroughs," which contained a few voters under the sway of a great landlord and were thus often available for purchase with bribes of honors, land, or money. After refusing to pursue the cause of reform, the Tory prime minister the Duke of Wellington fell in November 1830, and the Whig Charles, Earl Grey, once defender of Charlotte, became prime minister. He proposed a radical reform bill demanding the end of sixty boroughs with populations of fewer than two thousand and the partial disenfranchisement of another forty-seven with fewer than four thousand. At a stroke, 168 seats would be abolished. Only those voted for by a wider section of the population would survive. The Tories reviled the Bill, the bishops declared against it, and the king refused to assist its passage.

The bill was rejected in the Lords on October 8, 1831, and terrible riots soon followed. In Bristol, the mob went on the rampage for three days, setting fire to jails, the town hall, and the bishop's palace, and attacking the mayor's mansion. After looting houses, the rioters sat down to a large feast of stolen food and drink in the middle of Queen Square, popping a cap of liberty on the head of the nearby statue of William III. The damage was estimated at over £30,000. Twelve people were killed and ninety-four wounded in the riots. Elsewhere, Nottingham Castle was burned down and Derby jail was stormed. According to Greville, Lord Melbourne had been "frightened to death" by the bloody chaos in Bristol and had authorized reprisals against any rioters in London. Four hundred Greenwich pensioners and 629 marines were called up, 7,490 special constables were enrolled, and 2,000 police mobilized. They waited on tenterhooks for violent demonstrations, as angry meetings took place across town and placards appeared in London and all over the country promoting a run on the banks: "To stop the Duke, Go for Gold."

Since 1780, England had been undergoing an accelerated transition from an agrarian and local economy to an industrialized, more centralized state organization. A severe postwar depression coupled with the growing industrialization of the countryside had left many without work. In the countryside, the old system of "common land" for every villager to work was dying. The writer John Cowper claimed in 1732 that he knew of "no Set of Men that toil and labour so hard as the smaller Farmers and Freeholders, none who are more industrious to encrease the Product of the Earth; none who are more serviceable to the Commonwealth; and consequently none who better deserve Encouragement." The later eighteenth century had no time for such sentiment. A flurry of enclosure bills appeared in the House of Commons in the 1760s and 1770s, directed at turning common land into fenced pastureland, and the practice was validated by the Enclosure Act of 1801. As one critic remarked, twenty farmers were impoverished to enrich one. Increased rents and prices followed, and those who had worked their own land were now "tools" for landlords, who could be complacent, lazy, and tyrannical. The more comfortably off left for the burgeoning towns, leaving the poor "fenced out of their livelihood," unable even to gather turf for their fires. Parliament itself was occupied by those who derived their income from land (and condemned those who worked common land as indolent). As a result, repeated Enclosure acts were passed between 1800 and 1814.

A dire harvest in 1828 was followed by a worse one in 1829, and in 1830, the countryside erupted into anger. Furious at the introduction of threshing machines and also the employment of cheaper Irish labor, mobs of workers began to attack the machines and set fire to farm buildings, under, it was said, the leadership of the mysterious Captain Swing. Farmers received letters from Swing warning them that they would suffer if they did not alter their ways. Within a few months, workers were rampaging across the country, and their cause was joined by those of the artisan classes, such as carpenters and smiths. Fires struck sixteen counties, and farmers across the country were soon guarding their buildings with guns. Special constables were brought in to stem the riots. During the reprisals that followed, 1,406 rioters were tried, nine hanged, 657 imprisoned, and 464 transported.

The city panicked. "London is like the capital of a country desolated by cruel war or foreign invasion, and we are always looking for reports of battles, burnings or other disorders," reported Charles Greville. After seeing Charles X summarily deposed and replaced by Louis-Philippe, the royals were deeply concerned about the power of the mob. Queen Adelaide hoped that although she would not make a very pretty Marie Antoinette, "please God, she would prove a courageous one."

In March 1832, the Reform Bill was voted through in the House of Commons. On May 7, a clause of the bill was defeated by a committee in the House of Lords—after the House had passed the entire bill with a tiny majority in the previous month—and it all had to be abandoned. Grey asked the king to create at least fifty peers sympathetic to reform, to ensure the bill's safe passage through the House of Lords. The king grudgingly agreed to limited measures, promoting Scottish and Irish peers to peerages of the United Kingdom and calling up eldest sons to already existing peerages. It was not enough. The bill was defeated, and Grey and his government resigned.

The public flew into a rage. "The King, the Queen, and Royal Family are libelled, caricatured, lampooned and balladed," wrote the politician John Wilson Croker. "They are constantly compared to Charles [I] and Henrietta, and to Louis and Antoinette, and menaced with their fate. . . . Depend upon it, our Revolution is in a sure, and not slow progress." When the king drove from Windsor to London under heavy guard, crowds along the way heckled him and threw mud balls at his carriage. Under fire, the king discovered he was unable to form a new government. The Tory Duke of Wellington found it impossible to gain the support he needed. The king had no choice but to give in, send for Grey, and agree to creating peers, although in the end Wellington and a hundred Tory peers left their seats to allow the bill to pass. On June 7, 1832, the Reform Act became law, to the joy of the people. The worst of the rotten boroughs had been lost, and one out of every seven men now had the vote (not until 1867 was one in three men enfranchised). William IV had been thoroughly humiliated by the success of a bill he loathed. As Greville declared, "the regal authority had been wrecked."

In the wake of the Reform Act, slavery was abolished in 1833 (the trade in slaves had already been outlawed in 1807), with the slave owners compensated for their loss with a payoff of £20 million. A less admirable innovation was the cruel Poor Law, passed by the government of Lord Melbourne in 1834, which imposed stringent conditions on the impoverished who required parish assistance. The postwar economic slump had pushed down wages and sent hundreds of destitute men onto the job market, while rural economies were degraded by poor harvests, enclosure, and the effects of the Corn Laws. As a consequence, there had been a steep rise in the numbers claiming poor relief, and it has been estimated that by 1830, over 10 percent of the population of southern and eastern England were receiving support. Government worried that the parishes could not cope with such demands, and there was a widely held notion that the able-bodied were indolently living on handouts. A law was passed decreeing that all those seeking relief should be sent to the workhouses, cold, sparse, and often diseased institutions in which men and women were separated. The system of workhouses had already existed, but the Poor Law centralized and formalized matters to ensure that there was no escape. The most vulnerable members of society were penalized: Families were torn apart, children were impoverished and cruelly treated, and the old, blind, and sick died without dignity. As Charles Dickens wrote sardonically in *Oliver Twist*, published in 1839, the workhouse boards:

> established the rule, that all poor people should have the alternative
> (for they would compel nobody, not they), of being starved by a grad-
> ual process in the house, or by a quick one out of it. . . . They made a
> great many wise and humane regulations, having reference to the
> ladies . . . kindly undertook to divorce poor married people . . . and,

instead of compelling a man to support his family, as they had theretofore done, took his family away from him and made him a bachelor!

Still, there was some acceptance that the lower orders were not simply there to be exploited by those above them. Campaigners began to petition against the cruel use of children to clean chimneys. Small children between the ages of five and ten, usually sold by their parents as indentured labor to the sweeps, were sent scaling up chimneys, some as narrow as seven inches, with sticks. Lit straw was sometimes poked up at their feet to hurry them along. Those few who survived falls and suffocation were cast out of employment when they grew too large, often useless for further work as their spines and ankles had become twisted. The failure of the law to protect them enraged campaigners and inspired William Blake to write his angry "The Chimney Sweeper" (1794), depicting a "little black thing among the snow, crying weep, weep in notes of woe," too young to actually shout "sweep, sweep," sold into essential slavery by his parents and forgotten by a complacent Church and the king. Finally, an act was passed in 1834 forbidding any child under the age of fourteen to perform the job. Unfortunately, the penalties were so small that the exploitation did not end. Although new machinery had been created that would clean chimneys, little boys were cheaper. It was not until 1864, when Lord Shaftesbury brought in an act with punitive measures, that the practice of using children began to cease.

On the evening of Thursday, October 16, 1834, the old, ramshackle rabbit warren of the Houses of Parliament burst into flames after a court official had turned his back on a stove used to burn the old wooden "tallies" of the medieval exchequer. The conflagration began on the west side. Within ten minutes, the roof was on fire, and in a matter of hours the whole building was flaming. The fire could not be stayed until a floating fire engine was sent along the Thames at one o'clock in the morning. Thousands gathered to watch the buildings burn and collapse into rubble.

King William decided that Buckingham Palace, which he hated, would be the ideal home for Parliament. "I mean Buckingham Palace as a permanent gift!" he crowed. "Mind that!" he added, eager to rid himself of the trouble of paying for the palace. He declared it the royal prerogative to decree the place where Parliament should meet. Melbourne, horrified at the thought of occupying such a large and unwieldy building, let alone one so stamped with the authority of the monarch, had to use all his powers of tact to dissuade the king. The palace, he told him, was simply too large—and "Lord Melbourne need not recall to your Majesty's mind the fatal effects which large galleries filled with the multitude have had upon the deliberations of public assemblies." Instead, a competition was begun to design the new houses.

On May 24, 1832, Victoria entered her teens. "Time flies," wrote Leopold in his birthday letter. "It is now thirteen years that you came into the world of trouble; I therefore can hardly venture to call you any longer a little Princess." He instructed his niece: "Give your attention more and more to graver matters" and promised her: "You will always find in your Uncle that faithful friend which he had proved to you from your earliest infancy." The duchess's birthday letter was characteristically self-congratulatory. "I wish my beloved Victoria to become a *Pattern* to Others:—you possess every means for doing so, you receive the most suitable education." Both she and her brother made a principle of emphasizing to the little girl how much she owed them. Leopold later puffed, "I should like to know what harm the Coburg family has done to England." In his view, he had "done everything to see England prosperous and powerful," but received only "scurrilous abuse." Not only had he been a perfect husband, he had been an ideal uncle. "I did a great deal for my own sister and the dear little daughter, when the King and Country did not think it fit to give you *both a sixpence more* than the pittance of the Royal widow." Many would have judged £3,000 out of his yearly £50,000 rather less than a "great deal," particularly since, strictly speaking, a widow in this period was the financial responsibility of her own family, not of her dead husband's. One wonders if the Coburg success at marrying above their station was partly due to their ability to proclaim their great sacrifices, as well as their equine good looks. Leopold had zealously claimed to Charlotte that he had sacrificed all for her, and tried to do so to his niece; the little princess, however, proved willing to admire but dismayingly resistant to emotional blackmail.

Unnerved that Victoria was on the brink of adulthood, the duchess had devised a new way to check and control her. On July 31, 1832, the princess opened her book and inscribed, "This Book Mamma gave me that I might write the journal of my journey to Wales in it. Victoria." The duchess had bought Victoria a diary and declared that she and Lehzen would read her entries.

The duchess and Conroy were planning a tour to Wales, eager to show Victoria off to the country, with her loving mother at her side. The king was infuriated by the news. He knew that the duchess would be presenting herself as the Whig heroine, implicitly casting him as the Tory villain. To add to England's woes, the cholera epidemic that had swept across Europe entered Britain. The disease hit the large cities hard, and the people blamed the authorities. As the duchess and Conroy planned the trip to Wales, thousands were dying across the country (more than thirty-two thousand would die in the next two years). Victoria was never in any particular danger, for cholera mainly killed the poor, but the decision to travel was courageous. Wild tales were circulated that the government was spreading the disease because it wished to kill off the burdensome poor.

On August 1, Princess Victoria, the duchess, and the Conroys, the servants, and even Victoria's horses and grooms, set off for Wales. Conroy had been profligate with the duchess's money to create a grand procession. The carriage was drawn by gray horses, and, as Victoria gloated, the post boys had "pink silk jackets, with black hats" and the horses had "pink silk reins with bunches of artificial flowers." Festooned in flowers and ribbons, the magnificent carriage wound its way to Wales, past exultant and often baffled crowds.

"The men, women, children, country and houses are all black . . . the grass is quite blasted and black," Victoria wrote, shocked by the mining areas. "The country is very desolate . . . engines flaming, coals, in abundance, everywhere, smoking and burning coal heaps, intermingled with wretched huts and carts and little ragged children." It was her first introduction to the industrialized England that created the wealth she enjoyed, and she was dismayed by what she saw. She much preferred Welshpool, where the houses were decked with ribbons, flags, and flowers, and people waved and cheered from the roadside. As her carriage arrived, a cannon fired and bands struck up. At Caernarfon, children walked ahead of their royal visitors throwing flowers, and arches of flowers decorated the steps to the castle. Unfortunately, their plans to stay at an inn at Beaumaris were cut short by an outbreak of cholera, and Lord Anglesey offered his home, Plas Newydd, on the isle of Anglesey. There, Victoria reveled in sailing and riding fast over the neighboring fields, exulting how her horse, Rosa, "literally *flew.*"

Victoria loathed traveling. She suffered from severe nausea, stomach upsets, and backache; the heat bothered her; and she missed her pets in Kensington. She could not bear her close proximity to the Conroys, and she wearied of the long days and early starts, sometimes at five in the morning. She threw tantrums. On the afternoon of September 24, 1832, she took up her Good Behaviour Book and confessed that she had been "VERY VERY VERY VERY HORRIBLY NAUGHTY!!!!," underlining each word four times.

On the return journey, they enjoyed the hospitality of Lord Grosvenor at Eaton Hall in Cheshire, the Whig Duke of Devonshire at Chatsworth, and Lord Shrewsbury at Alton Towers. Victoria was charmed by the gaudy stained glass and gilt decoration at Eaton Hall, but bored by its inhabitants, dubbing Lady Robert Grosvenor's newborn daughter "a great fright . . . so red and shapeless." At Hardwick Hall, she was entranced by a spectacular display of fireworks, "blue lights, red lights, and rockets, &c. &c." She wrote: "But towards the end Mamma was taken unwell & was obliged to leave the room, when the prettiest part began. I stayed on and saw a temple & my name in stars & a crown." It was a joy to have a little time without Mamma. Otherwise, the ever-present reminder that she would be queen was a little overwhelming. "She hardly ever sleeps," wrote Lady Grosvenor to her mother, "occasioned, I believe, by her constant anxiety as to the future."

Oxford was delighted to see the future queen, greeting her "WARMLY and ENTHUSIASTICALLY." One local poet flourished:

> VICTORIA *comes—our Britain's hope,*
> *To view the ancient Towers*
> *And Sylvan walks that vainly boast*
> *Of equal blooming flowers.*

At the Sheldonian Theatre, Victoria watched Conroy receive an honorary degree of civil law. She then had to listen to the regius professor of civil law effuse about Sir John's "singular prudence" and "industry." He declared: "Can you wonder that he who had gained the esteem of the Husband, should also have pleased his surviving Consort." Some in the audience would have raised an eyebrow at the word "pleased." Sir John swelled with pride. He had been confirmed in front of the University of Oxford as indispensable to the duchess and as the remarkable author of Princess Victoria's success.

On Friday, November 9, after more than three grueling months of traveling, the party returned home. The duchess was perfectly satisfied. She had shown herself off as the future regent, Victoria had been ecstatically received, and King William was fuming about her majestic reception by the country. In the battle of the two courts, the duchess had won, and she was in a generous mood. At Christmas, Victoria had her own little tree hung with lights and sugar ornaments, and piled around with presents. She was then taken up to her bedroom, with "all the Ladies," she wrote. "There was my new toilet table with a white muslin cover over pink, and all my silver things standing on it with a fine new looking glass." She was a young lady at last.

31

⁂

"How Very Old"

I am today fourteen years old! How *very old*," the Princess wrote in her journal on May 24, 1833. Her mother gave her a "lovely hyacinth brooch and a china pen tray" as well as dresses, books, prints, handkerchiefs, jewelry, and a bag she had embroidered herself. King Leopold and Princess Feodora sent kind letters, and dear Lehzen gave a china figure and a basket. The dean of Chester, her tutor, offered some books, while Prince Charles, in the style of many older brothers, promised to give her a present later. At half past ten, the Conroy family arrived, and Sir John gave her a "very pretty picture" of her new pet dog, Dash, while his wife and children gave jewelry and trinkets. After lunch, the king and queen, as well as Princess Augusta, Princess Sophia, the Duke and Duchess of Cumberland, and the Duke of Gloucester, arrived with gifts, mainly jewels. In the evening, the king celebrated her birthday with a juvenile ball at St. James's Palace. Victoria opened the ball by dancing with her cousin, Prince George of Cambridge. In contrast to her poor aunt Charlotte's juvenile balls, there were many young men whom she knew, and she danced with the Earl of March, the Earl of Athlone, Lord Fitzroy Lennox, and Lord Emlyn. Fizzing with energy, the birthday girl was delighted with all the attention and much gratified by her place at dinner between the king and queen. "We came home at ½ past 12," she wrote in her journal. "I was VERY much amused."

At fourteen, Victoria had fine brown hair, attractive eyes, and a vivacious manner, but she was very small for her age, and she was still plump. By the end of the year, she wrote crossly that her medical examination had deemed she was "unhappily very fat." Leopold thought he knew why, since he had heard that "a certain little princess . . . eats a little too much, and almost always a little *too fast*." He was perplexed about her diminutive stature, since he and his sister were statuesque and the Duke of Kent had also been far from short. In March, he wrote to her that he had "not been able to ascertain that you really have grown taller lately—I must recommend it."

Even though he was now king of the Belgians, Leopold wanted to ensure that Victoria saw him as her chief adviser. He requested reports from Lehzen about her welfare and the politics at Kensington Palace, and bombarded his niece with priggish instruction on everything from politics to exercise and the importance of chewing food properly. He sent her books and extracts describing the errors made by other monarchs, and lectured her on how to be queen, instructing her to avoid frivolous amusements, think on serious matters, and consider her actions carefully. His letters were ponderous but always framed by his dearest love and little stories he thought might amuse her. In one, he noted that his dog was "looking generally into the fire and thinking about the affairs of Europe."

Victoria felt she needed no instruction to be serious: Life was solemn enough. Now that she was older, she was bored of riding out and downcast that there was simply nothing to do in the "gloomy" and "stupid" palace. All her visitors were adults, and even staying up until late for the grand dinners thrown by her mother began to pall. She took solace in her beloved caged birds and her favorite, "darling Dash," a black King Charles spaniel that Conroy had given to the Duchess of Kent in January 1833. Within a few months, Victoria had essentially adopted the dog, enthusiastically bathing him, teaching him tricks, and dressing him up in little outfits. When George Hayter painted her portrait in oils in early 1833, he portrayed Dash at her feet, stealing a glove. "Little Dash is perfection," she sighed.

Victoria was working diligently at her lessons. An 1834 exam, taken at

Tunbridge Wells, showed she was strong in history, by which her examiners meant her ability to remember the dates of battles, sovereigns, and political events. As she declared to her uncle Leopold, "I am very fond of making tables of the Kings and Queens as I go on, and I have lately finished one of the English Sovereigns and their consorts as, of course, the history of my own country is one of my first duties." The heir to the throne had a naturally precise mind that reveled in cataloging, whether it was lists of birthday presents, dresses worn by her dolls, guests at a ball, or the kings of England. As with her childhood interest in shells, which she gave up after she decided it made her back ache to look for them herself, she conceived a brief zeal for collecting autographs, which largely meant asking Uncle Leopold which signatures he could acquire for her. Although he found her the signature of Louis XIV, her interest in autographs soon waned.

Victoria's consuming passion was the opera, and she conceived a devotion to the lovely Giulia Grisi. "She is a most beautiful singer and actress," she wrote, "and likewise very young and pretty." The princess became the ardent admirer of the petite star, recording every dress and change of hairstyle in her journal, even noting whether her idol had gained or lost weight and if she looked tired. When she turned sixteen, she had the great pleasure of meeting the lady herself in York. "She is a fascinating little creature," Victoria decided, "extremely handsome, nearby," even though she wore "an ugly dingy foulard dress" and "a frightful little pink bonnet." When the lovely Giulia began to sing, Victoria was in raptures. "Never did I hear anything so beautiful. It was a complete triumph! and was quite electrifying!"

In the summer of 1833, Victoria endured yet another tour, this time to Plymouth, Portsmouth, Torquay, Exeter, Weymouth, and Dorset, as well as the Isle of Wight. On July 1, the party set off, arriving at Portsmouth in the late afternoon, and afterward traveling to Cowes. Both the princess and her mother found the Isle of Wight delightful. They stayed at Norris Castle, while John Conroy and his family were accommodated at Osborne Lodge, later the site of the queen's beloved Osborne House.

Once more, the princess suffered on the road, complaining of nausea, colds, and severe headaches, as well as sore eyes and backache. It seems as if she was suffering from a recurrent condition, possibly related to the bowels, which took hold when she was tired or low-spirited. She listed her illnesses in her journal for her mother to see, but the duchess was intent on the tour. The progress continued, unrelenting. Even when a pier that the duchess was due to open at Southampton was wrecked by furious boatmen protesting low wages, she was undeterred. She and Victoria descended from the royal yacht to stand on the dais beside the wrecked pier while twenty-five thousand spectators stood in the rain. On July 18, the princess visited the great *Victory* at Portsmouth, pondered the "spot where Nelson fell" and tasted some beef, potatoes, and grog, as an example of sailors' rations. On August 22, the duchess threw a splendid party for the local gentry, and on September 16, she and Victoria paid a visit to the fourteen-year-old queen of Portugal and her twenty-one-year-old stepmother, the Duchess of Braganza, who were staying in Portsmouth. Victoria was enchanted by the rapturous reception she received. "The whole way from the dock-yard to the Admiral's house, where their Majesties reside, was lined with troops and various bands were placed at different distances," she related.

The king was sadly "disgusted at the Duchess of Kent's progresses with her daughter through the kingdom . . . with her sailings at the Isle of Wight, and the continual popping in the shape of gun salutes to Her Royal Highness!" He promptly ordered that the duchess should not be saluted by any naval ship. As Duke of Clarence, the king and his wife had been on friendly terms with the duchess. Now they had become bitter enemies.

In spring 1834, Lord Grey resigned and was succeeded by fellow Whig Lord Melbourne. The new prime minister suggested that Lord John Russell should be leader of the House of Commons. "I cannot bear Lord John Russell," thundered the king and promptly dismissed the government. The Tories, called to form a government unexpectedly, were stunned, particularly as Robert Peel, who would be prime minister, was holidaying in Rome. Once he had struggled back home, Peel found he had little support, and when his government was defeated in 1835, the king was forced to accept the Whigs back in power. Lord John Russell became leader of the House of Commons. "I will have no more of these sudden changes," the humiliated King wailed. "The country shan't be disturbed in this way, to make my reign tumble about, like a topsail sheet-block in the breeze." As the King's authority diminished, so the Duchess of Kent and Princess Victoria moved into the ascendant in the hearts and minds of the public.

★ ★ ★

In 1834, the laborers in Tolpuddle, an impoverished parish in Dorset, approached their masters for an increase in their wages to 10 shillings a week—the wage that most other laborers in the district were paid. The masters refused, and when the workers protested, their wages were cut to 6 shillings a week. One laborer, George Loveless, proposed setting up a trade union. As a consequence, the local grandees put up posters threatening any man who joined the union with seven years' transportation. A few days later, in the early morning of February 24, Loveless was arrested, along with several other laborers, and marched to Dorchester jail, where all were clapped in irons. The governing class feared trade unions, suspecting them of sedition and fostering revolutionary sentiments, and the harmless laborers of Tolpuddle were considered threats to the established order. They were sentenced to seven years' transportation and quickly sent overseas.

The news of the fate of the laborers caused outrage across the country. A petition was signed by two hundred and fifty thousand people, and a thirty-thousand-strong procession strode along Whitehall to deliver it to Downing Street. Lord Melbourne, who was Home Secretary, refused to accept the petition. Lord John Russell was more sympathetic, and eventually the men were given free passage home and awarded land to work. The affair of the Tolpuddle Martyrs fueled the growing hatred of the king. The gentry already resented his refusal of reform, and the poor blamed him for spiraling prices and the misery of those such as the martyrs. The English cherished the idea of young Victoria, the dutiful little princess who toured her regions and seemed so sympathetic to reform.

32

"When Nobody Wishes to Change and Nobody Wants to Give In"

As Victoria neared fifteen, her mother saw her chances of becoming regent crumbling. William IV was keen to advertise his good health, making it clear that he felt able to live for another three years. The duchess and Conroy decided to present Victoria as too childish to govern herself, let alone the country. "Until you are at the age of either eighteen or twenty-one years, according to circumstances," the duchess pronounced to her daughter, "you are still confided to the guidance of your affectionate mother and friend."

Conroy and the duchess began to insinuate to every dignitary they met that the princess was weak-minded, frivolous, and foolish, a spoiled and immature child governed by whims and indulged by Lehzen. They even suggested that Victoria herself desired for a regency past the age of eighteen. At the same time, they stepped up their efforts to bully her, telling her that she was a mere child, dismissing her concerns, and laughing off her illnesses. They appointed one of their allies, Sir James Clark, as her physician, and he toed their line that she was never ill when she complained of being so, but simply malingering. They taunted her that she was as penny-pinching as her dreary grandmother Queen Charlotte and ugly like the goggle-eyed Duke of Gloucester. Miserable, isolated Victoria believed that Lehzen was her only friend.

The duchess and Sir John mishandled the princess. Had they employed more sweetness, they might have had better luck. A show of deference, respect, and lashings of flattery always melted Victoria. As Disraeli said of her later, "Everyone likes flattery; and when it comes to royalty, you should lay it on with a trowel." With her, he admitted, he laid it on "rather thick." Victoria was persuadable if she felt she was regarded as the most important person in the room.

Baron Stockmar suggested that the duchess treat Victoria as a "grown up daughter and friend," advising that the princess should appoint her own ladies-in-waiting. Like George IV, who had tried to keep Charlotte a child by denying her an establishment, the duchess refused. Instead, she took into her household twenty-eight-year-old Lady Flora Hastings, the clever, rather masculine daughter of the Marquess of Hastings, to be her ally. Intent that her daughter should not be alone with her governess, the duchess forbade Victoria from driving out with Lehzen without Lady Flora.

Lady Flora soon seemed as enthralled by Conroy's charisma as the duchess and Princess Sophia. "What an amazing scape of a man he must have been to have kept three ladies at once in good humour," pronounced Lord Melbourne. Victoria branded her a "Spie of J.C." and despised her, for she supported Conroy's endeavor to bully the princess into obedience and took every opportunity to be cruel to Lehzen.

There was worse to come: Jane and Victoire Conroy were appointed as Victoria's companions. Instead of her own ladies, she was accompanied by Lady Flora and the low-ranking daughters of her enemy. She knew that Conroy intended that she should award his daughters great positions when she came to power, and she was angered by his repeated declarations that "his daughters were as high as" her. She found them intrusive. One morning, she was feeling ill when, as she complained, "At 8, Mama, Lady Flora, Lady Conroy, Jane and Victoire came into my room. Lehzen of course being with me." She soon lost all warmth for the Conroy girls and began to refer to her childhood playmate in her diary not as "Victoire" but "Miss V. Conroy."

Exasperated by Victoria's refusal to appoint Conroy as her adviser, the duchess begged Stockmar to come to Kensington Palace and convince her. He declined to do so and suggested to the duchess that her attempt to change her daughter's mind would fail. The princess, he observed, had become "resentful of what must have looked to her as an exercise of undue control over herself." Wherever she went, "she encountered Sir John as the sole regulator of the whole machine." And indeed, he noted, "Your Royal Highness yourself has agreed with me that Sir John's personal behaviour towards the Princess has been apt only too often to worsen this state of affairs." He thought the ex-equerry seemed "an excellent business man and absolutely devoted to your Royal Highness. But how can I overlook that he is vain, ambitious, most sensitive and most hot tempered?" He wished that the man could "find the way back to the place which he never should have left." Victoria, he believed, was as stubbornly determined as her mother. "How can my words help when nobody wishes to change and nobody wants to give in?"

Stockmar was quite right about Conroy's qualities. Even if Victoria had adored him, he would have been a bad adviser. He was passionate and resolute, but he was inexperienced in politics and had no idea how to exercise the kind of diplomacy or restraint required to deal with courtiers and ministers. He saw people as either with him or against him, strongly took against those who disagreed with him, and had made a number of enemies. But the duchess would not be persuaded of his unsuitability, even by Stockmar. She blamed Lehzen for Victoria's intractability and began to attack and undermine her, while sniping at the Duchess of Northumberland.

Through unhappy days, Victoria dreamed of the impending visit of her half-sister. Finally, on June 5, her prayers were answered with the arrival of "My DEAREST sister Feodora whom I had not seen for 6 years." Victoria was enchanted by her "sweet, good tempered" little nephew Charles, age four and a half, and three-year-old Eliza, a *"perfect* little beauty." She wrote, "[They are] dear sweet children, not at all shy, and so good, they never hurt or spoil anything." Other girls her age were surrounded by little brothers and sisters, as well as cousins, and were used to playing nursemaid to younger siblings. Victoria, the only child in a house of adults, had little experience of small children, and it is perhaps unsurprising that she found it difficult to sympathize with babies.

The two sisters went out driving in a phaeton, played with the children in Feodora's rooms at Kensington Palace, and talked incessantly. "I could enter into all your opinions," wrote Feodora, "your little whims and faults, in which I have often found my own of former days." Victoria relished having someone to confide in. The whole party stayed at Windsor Castle and also visited the races at Ascot, where crowds waved enthusiastically. She placed a bet with King William and won a pretty little chestnut mare, which she named Taglioni, after her favorite ballet dancer, Marie Taglioni.

At the end of July, Princess Feodora and her family departed for their shabby schloss. "I clasped her in my *arms,* and *kissed* her and *cried* as if my *heart* would break, so did she *dearest* Sister," wrote Victoria. "We then tore ourselves from each other in the *deepest grief.* . . . When I came home I was in such a state of grief that I knew not what to do with myself. I sobbed and cried most violently the whole morning." Travel was so expensive and difficult that she knew she would not see her sister for another ten years.

The duchess and Conroy were relieved to see Feodora depart. They did not like Victoria having such a close confidante.

Leopold often took the opportunity to remind his niece that there was more to life than pleasure. In his ponderous, schoolmasterly fashion, he was instructing her to read history, so that she might learn how to behave when queen. "If you do not prepare yourself for your position, you may become the victim of wicked and designing people, particularly at a period when party spirit runs so high." He thought she should pay particular attention to the period before the accession of Henry IV to the French throne. "*Intrigues* and *favouritism* were the chief features of that period, and Madame de Maintenon's immense influence was very nearly the cause of the destruction of France." Victoria, who believed herself immune to the temptation of choosing favorites, replied that she was already reading plenty of history with her tutor, the dean of Chester, and that she liked to sample "different authors, of different opinions, by which means I learn not to lean on one particular side." Weary of her uncle's lectures, she wrote impatiently: "I am much obliged to you, dear Uncle, for the extract about Queen Anne, but must beg you to show what a Queen *ought not to be,* that you will send me what a Queen *ought to be.*" Leopold complimented her on her "clever, sharp little letter," replying in the self-satisfied, cautious way that had so infuriated George IV that he would indeed tell her what she should be: "This task I will very conscientiously take upon myself on the very first occasion which may offer itself for a confidential communication." He did sometimes accept that he was behaving pompously. Once, after a long letter recommending humility, he signed off, "your sincerely devoted camp preacher and uncle."

Leopold's advice tended to be vague. When pondering how monarchs had lost their thrones, he advised his niece to ensure that she was not "intoxicated by greatness and success, nor cast down by misfortune." In Leopold's view, the continuation of the monarchy was directly related to the capacity of the ruler to withstand depression or egotism. Good behavior was sufficient to soothe the people's demands for reform or liberty. Leopold's very personalized view of ruling had a great influence over Victoria, who focused on improving her heart, rather than devoting attention to political movements.

The king of the Belgians hoped to use his niece to increase his standing on the world stage and also to advance the standing of the Coburg family. He wrote repeatedly about great wars and revolutions and the characters and actions of the kings and queens of Europe. Lehzen, too, was more interested in international politics, and so the young princess came to be better informed about foreign wars than domestic travails. When she toured, she largely saw her country to advantage: smiling, happy people waving flags, and spruced-up towns that seemed to glow with prosperity. The other England, where miners and laborers toiled for a pittance and children were deformed from early work in factories, was mostly hidden from her. Although she had been shocked by the coal-blackened mining areas she visited on her first tour, she had little idea of the severe poverty that oppressed so many of her countrymen.

"Today is my 16th birthday!" breathed Victoria on Sunday, May 24, 1835. "How very old that sounds; but I feel that the two years to come till I attain my 18th are the most important of any." Her mother gave her an enamel bracelet containing a lock of her hair, a pair of china vases, a shawl, and some English and Italian books; Lehzen gave her a leather pencil case and a print of Marie Taglioni; and there was an ivory basket of barley sugar and chocolate from Dash. The king gave her sapphire and diamond earrings and a prayer book. A few days earlier, the duchess had arranged a private birthday concert, in which one of the performers was Victoria's idolized Giulia Grisi. "No one can be *more enchanted* than *I* was," she bubbled. "I shall never forget it."

Victoire was deeply discontented, for she was no nearer to securing the appointment of Sir John as the royal adviser or forcing Victoria to accept a regency until twenty-one. In an anxious New Year's letter at the beginning of 1835, the duchess had written that only she could be trusted. She pleaded for Victoria's obedience. "This letter, I dare say you will often read:—perhaps very often,—when the hand that wrote it may be motionless,—and the heart that dictated it, has ceased to beat. Your own heart can now lead you to value it:—And at the later time your happiness will be encreased if you have followed it." Over and over, Victoria was reminded that the only way to be happy was to obey her mother.

The duchess was determined to surround Victoria with her allies. Lehzen was protected by the king, and it was impossible to oust her, so she concentrated on attempting to expel the Duchess of Northumberland. When the king sent a message to her about Victoria's forthcoming confirmation, via the Duchess of Northumberland, Victoire gave her reply to the archbishop of Canterbury to be passed to the king. Furious at his sister-in-law's act of great disrespect to the Duchess of Northumberland, the king wrote in his own hand to forbid the bishop of London to allow Princess Victoria to be confirmed in any of the Chapels Royal. The Duchess of Kent had to surrender and accept that the Duchess of Northumberland would stay.

The king then suggested that they celebrate the confirmation with a dinner at Kew, and that Victoria and her mother should visit Greenwich Hospital with the king and queen on the following Saturday. In retaliation for his letter to the bishop of London, the duchess refused. Her behavior was the last straw for the king. "Nothing could be worse than the terms on which their Courts are together," marveled Lady Holland. Windsor and Kensington Palace could not be reconciled, and the king and queen grew very suspicious of Victoria. As Leopold later instructed her, "she would want all her natural caution with them." Spies were all around. "Never permit yourself to be induced to tell them any opinion or sentiment which is beyond the *sphere of common conversation* and its ordinary topics. Bad use would be made of it against yourself."

On July 30, 1835, Princess Victoria gave the duchess a pin and a drawing, and Lehzen a ring, then at half past eleven set off for the Chapel Royal, St. James's. There, the sixteen-year-old princess, dressed in a white lace gown and a white bonnet wreathed with white roses, walked in on the arm of the king. She was confirmed by the archbishop of Canterbury, assisted by the bishop of London, in front of the queen, other royals, the Duchess of Kent, the dean of Chester, Baroness Lehzen, Lady Flora Hastings, and the Duchess of Northumberland. Conroy tried to enter the chapel, but the king ordered him to leave. Shaken by her mother's anger and the king's evident fury, Victoria was on edge, tearful and "frightened to death" by a tirade from the archbishop of Canterbury on the great importance of her responsibilities to the country. "I felt the whole very *very deeply,*" she wrote. After the ceremony, they retired to the king's closet, where Victoria received a set of emeralds from the King and a matching headpiece from the queen.

Within an hour of the confirmation, the Duchess of Kent gave her daughter a letter expounding upon her great sacrifices. She told her that she had informed Lehzen that her services would no longer be needed, and instructed Victoria to do the same. The princess refused to obey. She considered her confirmation to be an acknowledgment of her adult status, and it fortified her against her mother's demands. "I felt that my confirmation was one of the most solemn and important events and acts in my life," she wrote in her diary. "I went with the firm determination to become a true Christian, to try and comfort my dear Mamma in all her griefs, trials and anxieties, and to become a dutiful and affectionate daughter to her. Also to be obedient to *dear* Lehzen who has done so much for me." She underlined "dear" for Lehzen, but not for Mamma.

33

Victoria on Tour

At the beginning of August 1835, Victoria, her mother, the Conroys, Lehzen, and their entourage holidayed at Tunbridge Wells, spending two nights with Lord Liverpool in his house at Buxted Park on the way. Unhappy and suffering from backache, Victoria lay on a couch listening to Lehzen read and dwelling on the horror that awaited: a great tour to the Midlands, the North, and Norfolk. She was dreading the rush of traveling, and she was sure she would be ill.

The king was incensed to hear about the tour. He was particularly vexed that the princess would attend the musical festival at York, for he felt that she would be exposed to different political factions and "would necessarily become the object of party jealousy," and so he forbade the duchess to travel. Predictably, she dug in her heels. "It requires but one step more to assign the Princess and myself, a limit as to residence to be prisoners at large," she objected to Lord Melbourne. Confident that she could command the nation's sympathy, she declared that if she was prevented, all possible "odium would fall back on that Person," the king. Quaking at the thought of the duchess mounting a public campaign, Melbourne tried to discourage the king from protesting, but he was not to be deterred. He wrote directly to Victoria: "I hope the newspapers will not inform me of your travelling this year—I cannot and therefore do not approve of your flying about the Kingdom as you have done the last three years, and which if attempted I must and shall prevent in future. It is your real good and permanent happiness I have really at heart." Both the king and the duchess were claiming to the princess that they were only trying to do what was best for her.

The king's letter full of lies and emotional blackmail succeeded. On the day before the proposed departure, Victoria refused to go, pleading with her mother that she could not bear the journey or the fatigue. The duchess responded with a rambling, repetitive letter in defense of the tours. "If the King was another man,—and if he *really* loved you," she declared, he would "not only approve of them, but even press one to them." If Victoria did not go, she would "fall in the estimation of the People of this Country." Her presence was of the utmost importance: "Nothing can be more critical than these present times;—much will depend, on your character, for the future." She declared, "You will not see that it is the greatest consequence that you should be seen,—that you should know your Country,—and be acquainted with, and be known by all Classes." The letter droned on:

> I can have no object, but your welfare:—in a short time, as it flies, I shall be a Spectator;—could I bear to see, my fondest hopes, not realized:—can you be dead, to the Calls, your position demands:—Impossible!—reflect,—before it is too late.—Whatever is sown, of that you will reap.—Let the country see you anxious to meet it,—open and cordial in your manners,—shew a promise of character, let the People hope for something, worth having,—free from the faults of former reigns.—Turn your thoughts and views to your future Station—its duties,—and the claims that exist on you.

The phrase "let the People hope for something, worth having" showed her astute recognition of the importance of the image of royalty. Although the Prince of Leiningen exaggerated when he later blustered to his half-sister that Conroy had "worked hard" to create her enormous popularity, Victoria did owe him a debt of gratitude for organizing such long and complicated tours.

Victoria capitulated to her mother, and the carriages rumbled north from Kensington Palace as planned on September 3, 1835. Crowds tugged the princess's carriage through the streets, bands played, houses were festooned in colorful banners, and local gentry hosted evening receptions and balls in her honor. Conroy ensured that he was the center of all the processions and celebrations, even going so far as to answer for the duchess when the Marquess of Exeter read a public address to her. The party stayed with the archbishop of York and attended the York musical festival, where the princess was thrilled to hear her favorite bass, Luigi Lablache, sing, as well as Giulia Grisi. For an evening fancy dress ball, she reported that she wore "a wreath of white roses" round her head like Grisi . . . in the *Puritani*."

The carriages plowed on to Doncaster, Leeds, Wakefield, and Barnsley. Victoria was exhausted by the relentless pace. As she protested, when "one arrives at a nobleman's seat, one must instantly dress for dinner and consequently one could never rest properly." After opening a ball for three hundred distinguished guests at Burghley House, partnered by the Marquess of Exeter, she declared she was suffering from a headache and retired to bed after the first dance. At Holkham Hall, home of the Earl and Countess of Leicester, she nearly fell asleep during dinner. She could hardly eat, was "well nigh dead by the heat and fatigue" and suffered frequent headaches and backaches, as well as stomachache and bilious fever. Tired and fractious, she thought Cambridgeshire all "ugly barren fields, & the whole country as flat as a table." When they stopped at King's Lynn in Norfolk:

> *The people, of whom there were a dense mass, insisted upon dragging us through the town & in spite of every effort which was tried to prevent them from so doing, they obstinately persisted in their wish & would dragg us through the town. Not only through it, did they dragg us but round it, so, that we were detained exactly* 1 hour & a ¼ *in Lynn! I could see nothing of the town; I only saw one living, dense, mass of human beings!*

Victoria was petulant and decidedly out of sorts. She noted briefly that they had run over a "poor man" just as they stopped. "But he is not materially hurt, I hear."

The princess and her party finally arrived back at Kensington Palace on

September 25. "It is an end to our journey, I am happy to say," she wrote. "Though I liked some of the places very well, I was much tired by the long journey & the great crowds we had to encounter. We cannot travel like other people, quietly and pleasantly." She was hoping that her mother would take the hint.

Three days later, the party set off to bathe at Ramsgate. Concerned about the battles over the regency, King Leopold had decided that it was time to see his niece away from Kensington Palace. He was coming to the resort, accompanied by his twenty-three-year-old wife, Louise, and her twenty-one-year-old brother, the Duc de Nemours. Since Victoria had last seen her uncle, four years ago, he had married Princess Louise, daughter of King Louis-Philippe of France. Although the princess was pretty and ac-complished, Leopold was middle-aged and tired of women, and his feel-ings for her were muted. He enumerated his wife's charms as if she were a horse for sale, declaring her an "example for all young ladies, being Princesses or not" but fretting over her laziness about music. Leopold's marriage had mollified the pro-French among his people but angered the English, who whispered that he had become a Catholic like his wife and so did not deserve to retain his grant from the state.

On the day of Leopold's arrival, Princess Victoria and Lehzen, "with beating hearts and longing eyes," watched from a window of the Albion Hotel, along with the ubiquitous Lady Flora and Lady Conroy. Crowds in the streets waved and shouted, and guns fired from the pier as Leopold's steamer chugged into the harbor. "What a happiness it was for me to throw myself in the arms of that *dearest* of Uncles," Victoria wrote, "who has al-ways been to me like a father, and whom I love so *very dearly!*" She was im-mediately charmed by young Queen Louise, only seven years her senior, who gently took her arm and whispered, "You must consider me like a sort of elder sister."

Queen Louise proceeded to treat her niece with the deference she craved. She visited Victoria in her room, played draughts with her, admired her drawings, and discussed fashion. After a childhood with dowdy Princess Sophia and the now Queen Adelaide, sallow Lady Conroy, and beaky Lehzen, Victoria was entranced by her stylish new aunt, reveling in her splendid Parisian dresses and hats. Louise sent her hairdresser to dress Victoria's hair in imitation of her own, with curls by the ears. She also gave her little gifts—cravats, ribbon, a tippet, and a cap. Captivated by her uncle's pretty, loving wife, Victoria paid little attention to the charismatic Duc de Nemours in her journal, even though many believed he had been invited in the hope that he might catch the princess's eye. She found him "timid" and "good looking, but not so much as his brother, the Duke of Orleans."

Leopold wanted to spend time with his niece alone. On the Sunday after he arrived, he visited her for three-quarters of an hour and gave her "valuable advice" on "many important and serious matters," no doubt on how to withstand attempts to make her extend the regency or appoint Conroy as an adviser. "I look up to him as a Father, with complete confidence, love and affection," Victoria continued. "He is the best and kindest adviser I have. He had always treated me as his child and I love him dearly for it." It was a pointed snub to her mother. But there was a disappointing aspect to his *"very good and valuable advice."* Leopold, who always liked to sit on the fence and avoid confrontation, would not save her, as she had hoped, from the misery at Kensington Palace. Unable to tell her mother to desist or inform other dignitaries of what was occurring behind the closed doors, he could only encourage her to stay resilient.

Victoria was soon ill once more, suffering from sickness and excruciating pain in her back. Exasperated by his sister's lack of sympathy, King Leopold insisted that Dr. Clark should be called in.* Clark lectured Conroy on his tyrannical behavior and told the duchess that her daughter's health would be improved by more exercise. He also recommended that she attempt to minimize tension at the palace. The duchess refused to listen. She was convinced that Victoria was shamming illness to gain attention.

The princess felt almost too ill to bid farewell to her uncle and aunt. But she gathered her strength and managed to climb on to the carriage to Dover to see them off. On her return to Ramsgate, however, she burst into tears, lamenting that life was "terribly *fade* & dull without them."

---

* Dr. James Clark had been Leopold's physician, and in 1834, at his recommendation, he was appointed doctor to the Duchess of Kent. He was put in charge of the princess's health in April 1835.

34

※

Victoria's Whims

Sick and feverish, Victoria begged to see Dr. Clark. Two days later, Clark arrived from London, but declared that he did not consider the princess's illness to be serious. He departed, promising to return on the following Tuesday, four days later. "Dr. Clark says that if all you report were true," the angry duchess admonished Lehzen, "they would be the most alarming symptoms, but I know it to be nothing but Victoria's whims and your imagination."

Victoria's illness did not pass. She had a high temperature, and her pulse rate increased. By Sunday, she begged her mother to summon Dr. Clark from town. The exasperated duchess demurred. "How can you think I should do such a thing?" she snapped at Lehzen. "What a noise that would make in town; in short we differ so much about this indisposition that we had better not speak of it at all."

On Tuesday, Dr. Clark did not come as he had promised, writing laconically that he assumed the princess was recovered since he had not heard otherwise. Presumably, he had been encouraged by Conroy to think that the best way to jolt the princess out of her malingering ways was to ignore her. But Victoria was growing sicker, struggling to eat or drink, and she could not sleep. On Wednesday the duchess sent an urgent message to Dr. Clark, begging him to come to Ramsgate immediately. He sent word that he would not be able to arrive until late. Around six in the evening on Wednesday, Victoria became delirious and the household began to panic. As Lehzen reported, "even *he* [Conroy] was visibly upset." The duchess called in a local doctor, but he was too intimidated to suggest any form of treatment. Victoria was terrified, fearing that she was dying. Next morning, Clark appeared and immediately understood the gravity of her illness, prescribing treatment and, in Lehzen's words, "restoring to her the necessary *peace of mind.*" He diagnosed a bilious fever. In fact, the princess was suffering from typhoid, a newly discovered disease that was hardly understood in England. What Victoria later called her "dangerous illness at Ramsgate during the months of October and November" was probably contracted through drinking infected water or milk. Clark paid the princess every attention. But if Victoria thought that a diagnosis of illness would ease matters, she was wrong. For the duchess and Conroy, illness was an opportunity.

While the princess was tossing in bed with sickness, her mother seized the chance to ask her to sign a document confirming Conroy as her private secretary. When Victoria refused, the duchess began to rail at her. Then she sent Conroy to attack her daughter with threats. He thrust the paper under her nose and commanded her to sign. The Conroy girls begged while Lady Flora taunted. Only much later could Victoria write of it: "All I underwent; their (Ma's and JC) attempt (when I was still very ill) to make me promise before hand, which I resisted in spite of my illness, and their harshness,— my beloved Lehzen supporting me alone." Conroy pushed a pen into her hand and tried to force her to sign, but she still refused.

Victoria's already fragile constitution failed under the strain. She lost her hair, her weight plummeted, and she was delirious. Later, in 1871, when the queen fell so ill with a throat abscess that her doctor judged she had only twenty-four hours to live and she had to be "fed like a baby," was the next time she felt so unwell. "Never, since a girl, when I had typhoid fever at Ramsgate in '35 have I felt so ill," she wrote.

The local press began to inquire into why she had not appeared publicly, but were deflected by Sir John's claims that she was merely slightly indisposed with a cold.

Victoria was confined to her room for five weeks, but in early November she began to improve. She was able to manage a little soup and meat, and although she still could not walk, she could begin to write once more. "I am much better and getting stronger, but am still confined to my room," she told her uncle on November 3. "Dr. Clark says I shall grow quite tall after this. I should be glad if it was the case, if it was only to please you, dear Uncle." Two days later, she resumed her journal, enthusing that Lehzen had been "so unceasing in her attentions to me that I shall never be able to repay her sufficiently for it but by my love and gratitude. . . . She is the *most affectionate, devoted, attached* and *disinterested* friend I have and I love her most *dearly.*" The experience in Ramsgate had convinced her that she could not live without her governess, who had, as she later wrote, "at the risk of her health if not of her life preserved the Queen from this *horrible man.*"

Victoria had resisted the bullying of both her mother and Conroy. She emerged from her terrible ordeal resolved henceforth to rely on herself.

It took some time for the princess to recover her health. For many weeks, her hair continued to fall out, her weight remained low, and her circulation was poor. Her feet were so cold that Lehzen had to rub them for an hour every day. Not even a gift from Queen Louise of bonnets and three sumptuous dresses made by Mlle Palmyre, "the first dress-maker in Paris," could console her. Louise had also sent a box full of hairpins, so that Victoria could pin up her curls, but the poor princess had lost a lot of hair during her illness and feared it would not return. She was "literally going bald," she complained.

Dr. Clark decreed that the princess should have a whole new routine, with plenty of fresh air and exercise. Instead of spending hours sitting at a desk, which was thought to squash the organs, she should be encouraged to enjoy the open air as much as possible. She should walk often, even inside the house, and exercise with weights to improve her figure and circulation, and even write at a standing desk. She should also take a warm bath every four or five days and chew her food slowly. The windows in her apartments should be kept open, and Clark advised that it would be a good idea if the entire household moved from the ground floor in Kensington Palace to the first.

At last the duchess had an excuse to move into the upper floor of rooms, officially laid aside for the king. Victoria's health required it. She sent word to the architect Sir Jeffry Wyatville to push ahead with his original designs, but not to alter the drive to the palace. The King's Bedchamber would become her own bedroom, and the King's Gallery would be divided into three, the easternmost room to become the princess's sitting room. The entire party remained at Ramsgate over Christmas to give Victoria a chance to recover fully and to allow the builders time to create the grand apartments that the duchess desired.

The duchess and Victoria arrived in their new home on January 13, 1836. Victoria was quite enchanted. "We instantly went upstairs, that is to say, up two staircases, to our new sleeping and sitting apartments, which are very lofty and handsome." Unaware that the new rooms had been obtained without the king's permission, she was delighted at how the old gallery had been partitioned into "3 large, lofty, fine and cheerful rooms" to be her sitting room, her study, and anteroom. The former was "very prettily furnished indeed." She began carrying her precious dolls, ornaments, and books to her new rooms. Lehzen was occupying Victoria's old bedroom downstairs.

Although she was allowed much more free time for exercise and even driven up with Dash to Hampstead Heath—still a rather wild area on the outskirts of London—for a long walk three or four times a week, Victoria was always accompanied by the two Miss Conroys and Lady Flora Hastings, as well as Lehzen. Sir John, Lady Conroy, and their daughters, along with Princess Sophia, dined most evenings at Kensington. Victoria treated them all coolly, even her confused, nearly blind aunt. She reported drily that Sophia could not come to dinner on one occasion because she had set her cap and dress on fire and "came to her servants all in a blaze; most fortunately they instantly put it out, and she was not much burnt."

After the crisis at Ramsgate, Conroy had temporarily ceased pressing Victoria to make him regent, and now that the duchess had her grand apartments, she was more content. Victoria was soon exploring London and visiting the zoological gardens, newly opened in 1828 and well stocked with the animals George IV had collected. Victoria fell quite in love with the gentle-looking giraffes. She was also impressed by an orphanage in Chiswick that transformed "poor vagrant girls" into good, obedient servants, mostly to be sent to the Cape of Good Hope, and listed some of the stories of the girls in her journal. "I was very much pleased indeed with all I saw," she wrote.

Eager as always to show herself off to an audience, the duchess took her daughter to the theater and opera. Victoria was particularly impressed by the young actor Charles Matthews, whom she saw in a "burletta of *One Hour* or *The Carnival Ball.*" She sketched him and reported that he had given up studying to be an architect for the stage, commenting: "We see how it has succeeded—*most perfectly!*"

Victoria was a true romantic. She loved the works of Sir Walter Scott, particularly his *Bride of Lammermoor.* "Oh! Walter Scott is my *beau idéal* of a Poet," she rhapsodized. "I do so admire him both in Poetry and Prose!" Her greatest passion was for Italian opera, and she loved taking singing lessons with the Irish-Neapolitan singer Luigi Lablache after begging her mother to appoint him. Said to be the best Leporello in musical history, his performances in London attracted huge crowds. With the princess, however, he was less exacting than he was with himself. Their sessions were not so much lessons, for he did not set the princess exercises, but instead the pair would sing together. He tended not to criticize her. She noted, "He is too indulgent." Lablache loved Mozart, but she wrote: "I must say I prefer Bellini, Rossini, Donizetti, etc., to anything else; but Lablache who *understands* music *thoroughly* said, '*C'est le Papa de tous.*' " Victoria liked music full of high passion and drama. "I am a terribly modern person," she decided.

"I liked my lessons extremely," the princess wrote in her diary. "I only wish I had one every *day* instead of one every *week*"—a hint her mother ignored. She was inspired by Lablache to dream of Italy. "Oh! could I once behold bella Napoli, with its sunny blue sky and turquoise bay dotted with islands," she enthused. She knew only too well that the only traveling she could look forward to would be to the provincial parts of England. "But these are all vain thoughts, all air castles! of *my ever* seeing Naples, or any part of Italy, *sono senza speranza.*"

Victoria's life was never as colorless as she liked to claim. She attended her mother's formal dinners and parties, packed with Whig supporters and grandees, and pasted newspaper accounts of the evenings into her journal. She also enjoyed the occasional royal Drawing Room at St. James's Palace. Not everyone would have found her weeks so dull, but Victoria loved gaiety, music, bustle, and company, and she felt that a future queen should enjoy a much more scintillating social life. As she complained to her uncle Leopold, "*pleasure* does more good than a hundred walks and rides." Still, she was allowed to avoid embroidery, the dull prison of many nineteenth-century girls. "I am charmed to hear," she wrote cheerfully to Feodora, "that Eliza is such a clever arithmetician and reader. In work, she begins to resemble her worthy Aunt in England who never works at all."

Now that Victoria was growing up, the dean recommended that there should be more depth in her studies. It was agreed that she would drop the Saturday oral examination for written monthly questions, to which she would write answers in her own time. The dean wished for more Latin, but the duchess refused, arguing that the princess was so well educated that she was "quite prepared to enter on a course more fitting to the character of a Prince than a Princess." Instead, Victoria began to study anatomy, Blackstone's *Commentaries* on English law, and political history. She read French and English authors aloud with Lehzen, as well as reading the English newspapers. She was so seldom at the court of William IV that she had to rely on the newspapers for information about government and politics. As she wrote to King Leopold, "It is extremely necessary for me to follow the 'events of the day,' and to do so impartially."

35

Crowds of Princes

We have had a crowd of Princes here," grumbled John Conroy, "and until that matter is settled, of course every season, will bring Them over." In 1828, *The Watchman* had anounced that it was "rumoured and confidently believed in the highest circles that Prince George, Son of His Royal Highness, the Duke of Cumberland," would be "speedily betrothed to his royal Cousin, the Princess Victoria." Both children were ten at the time. French journalists claimed that she had been betrothed to King Leopold before he married, while others plumped for the Duke of Brunswick, the Duke of Orleans, the future king of Denmark, and Prince Adelbert of Prussia. As Victoria grew up, newspapers across the world filled spare pages by speculating about her marriage. There were few eligible princes (and indeed, half-bred, mad, cross-eyed ones) who were not touted as potential suitors.

Many at court thought the Cumberland marriage an excellent plan, for it would ensure that England and Hanover remained united.* Victoria, un-

---

*As a woman, Victoria would be unable to rule Hanover. Britain and Hanover had been joined since George I.

fortunately, had only friendly feelings toward Prince George, and the duchess hated the idea of being further united to the brother-in-law she most detested. The king and queen were fond of Prince George of Cambridge, but Victoria and he were not greatly enamored of each other. As the king realized that Victoria showed little interest in her English cousins, he began to propose the sons of the Prince of Orange, the ugly, frog-faced prince whom Princess Charlotte had jilted. The king was resolved to prevent the duchess and Leopold from strengthening their hold over Victoria by marrying her to one of their relations. It was a good dynastic match because the Oranges were stalwartly Protestant, unlike the Coburgs. The Prince of Orange was eager to have Victoria as a daughter-in-law, and he was more than pleased to have the chance of frustrating Leopold, the man who had "taken both my wife and my Kingdom," or Charlotte and Belgium respectively.

The duchess was determined to see her daughter marry one of her German relations, and she intended to use her grand apartments to entertain them. In June 1833, the household welcomed Prince Alexander and Prince Ernest Württemberg, sons of the duchess's sister Antoinette. Victoria delighted in her two tall, dashing cousins. "Alexander is very handsome and Ernest has *a very kind expression*," she burbled. "They are both *extremely amiable*."

The queen invited the Kensington household and their visitors to a ball in June, but the duchess stormed off early and demanded that her party follow, probably because she felt she was not receiving sufficient attention. Otherwise, the cousins spent happy days together, and the Württembergs accompanied the duchess and Victoria on the first stage of their tour to Portsmouth and the Isle of Wight. Victoria wrote that she was "very very sorry that they are going . . . we shall miss them at *breakfast,* at *luncheon,* at *dinner, riding, sailing, driving, walking,* in fact *everywhere.*"

In March 1836, the duchess welcomed Ferdinand and Augustus, sons of her second brother, Prince Ferdinand of Saxe-Coburg-Kohary. In a fabulous match engineered by Leopold, Ferdinand had been betrothed to the young queen of Portugal and was on his way to visit her. The king planned to welcome the brothers with dinner and dancing at Windsor Castle, and the duchess organized two lavish balls at Kensington Palace, one in fancy dress. Even though Ferdinand was engaged, the princess found him far more attractive than Augustus. "He is very good looking, I think. It is impossible to see or know him without loving him," she wrote. "I think Ferdinand handsomer than Augustus, his eyes are so beautiful, and he has such a lively, clever expression." For her, Ferdinand was "superior to Augustus in many ways." The unattainable groom-to-be was a safe target for her affections.

At the dinner before the first ball at Kensington, the princess sat between her cousins. "It was a most merry and happy dinner, the merriest we have had for a long long time." After the fancy dress ball, Victoria was even more joyous. "Oh! could they but be always with us! How happy should I be! . . . Oh! when I think *how very soon* I shall not see that *dear dear* Ferdinand any more I feel quite wretched! This is the last day we spent together! Oh! I love him so much, he is *so* excellent." Victoria had enjoyed her time with her cousin, but her passionate pleasure in Ferdinand reflected how few friends she had of her own age, apart from the awful Misses Conroy and Lady Flora. Victoria loved to laugh, and Ferdinand was "funny and childishly merry," which she delighted in. Most of all, she loved being the focus of everybody's attention. As she was coming to understand, she was a young lady whom every prince in Europe wished to marry.

Augustus and his father remained for a few days after Ferdinand had left, and when they, too, departed, Victoria felt despondent. The past days seemed like a dream of "joy, happiness and gaiety." The princess was effusing in her diary in the hope that her mother might invite more young male relations to stay. She was not disappointed. The duchess quickly invited her eldest brother, Ernest, Duke of Saxe-Coburg, and his two sons, Ernest and Albert, to Kensington.

Leopold had long planned to unite Victoria to his nephew Prince Albert of Saxe-Coburg, and the duchess was in accord, for Albert seemed modest, sensible, quiet, and sufficiently pliable to be a useful ally. Many women, however, preferred his older brother, Ernest, even though he was a rake and a womanizer. He was more charming and easy to talk to than the uptight Albert. Princess Feodora wrote to her half-sister confessing that Ernest was her favorite, even though Albert was cleverer. Unfortunately, he preferred books to women, partly because he found the latter unpredictable. Albert was so tongue-tied with women that he came across as superior and sometimes rude.

In April, the duchess and Conroy had discovered that William IV had invited the Prince of Orange and his two sons, Princes William and Alexander, to visit. The duchess wrote to her brother to come to England immediately with Ernest and Albert. The angry king blustered that "he could not allow the two young Princes to live under the same roof with Princess Victoria." The duchess protested that it was a simple family engagement and that the duke was already on his way. The king could not refuse them entry to the country, but he sent Lord Palmerston to persuade Conroy to arrange for the princes to be lodged in a hotel, rather than at Kensington Palace. His request was refused.

Leopold scribbled in a passion to his niece, raving against the king's presumption:

> *The relations of the Queen and the King, therefore, to God-knows-what-degree, are to come in shoals and rule the land, when* your relations *are to be* forbidden *the country. . . . Really and truly I never heard or saw anything like it, and I hope it will a little rouse your spirit; now that slavery is even abolished in the British Colonies, I do not comprehend* why your lot alone should be to be kept a white little slavey *in England for the pleasure of a Court, who never bought you, as I am not aware of their having gone to any expense on that head, or the king's even having* spent a sixpence for your existence. *I expect that my visits in England will also be prohibited by an Order in Council.*

The overheated harangue appeared not long after the Prince of Orange had arrived with William and Alexander in tow. On Friday, May 13, the king threw a welcome ball for the Orange party at St. James's Palace. "The boys are both very plain," Victoria wrote to her uncle. "They look heavy, dull and frightened and are not at all prepossessing. So much for the *Oranges,* dear Uncle."

Leopold devoted his energies to promoting Albert. "I talk to you at length and through you speak to Victoria," he wrote to Lehzen. "For years Victoria has unfortunately been treated as a mere subject for speculation . . . her youth, as well as her future gave ample opportunities for a thousand avaricious schemes." He declared that only he and Lehzen "cared about her for her own sake," and

> because this was so we were systematically persecuted, for it was par-
> ticularly feared that the child might grow fond of us, and find in us
> friends apart. . . . The chief plan has been, since 1828, to drive you
> away. Had I not stood firm . . . you would have followed Späth. . . .
> Had I not come to England last year, and had I not had the courage,
> in Ramsgate, to tear apart the whole web of intrigue, Clark would
> never have learned the true state of affairs, and God knows what
> would have become of the Princess; that visit was one of the most im-
> portant factors in her recovery.

Leopold was never one to hide his light under a bushel, but his declaration that he tore apart the web of intrigue, allowing the princess's illness to be properly treated, was an exaggeration even by his standards.

"The Princess's 17th birthday marks an important stage in her life: only one more year and the possibility of a Regency vanishes like an evil cloud. This is the perfect time for us, who are loyal, to take thought for the future of the dear child," vowed Leopold. He wished Lehzen to urge Victoria to a decision. "The Princess might do well, for the sake of composure and peace of mind to find a choice and firmly anchor herself to it." He praised his nephew's "pure, unspoilt nature." But Lehzen was not so easily manipulated into declaring for Albert. She wished Victoria to remain unmarried for as long as possible, so as to ensure that her position remained secure.

The Princes Albert and Ernest arrived on May 18, along with their father. Victoria was delighted by her uncle's present to her of a large colorful bird, so tame that it did not bite her when she poked her finger into its beak. She thought her new guests "very amiable, very kind and good, and extremely merry." Albert she judged "extremely good-looking," but she was to be a little disappointed by his manners.

Ernest, the elder son, was due to inherit his father's land and title and so would not be a suitable husband. Poor, stiff, shy Albert seemed unimpressive by comparison with his vivacious brother, and he did not have the same stamina for staying up late dancing and drinking. He liked to be in bed by half past nine, and he found balls, banquets, and parties a terrible strain.

Victoria was in her element, enjoying the fine balls and concerts and the chance to wear pretty clothes. Even her beloved opera she liked "twice as much with them than alone." On Friday, there was a dinner and a concert until two a.m. On the following day, there was a Drawing Room for the king's birthday, attended by nearly 3,800 people, then a dinner and a concert, at which the princess ignored the Princes of Orange. On the following Monday, the duchess threw a large dinner at Kensington. Albert went to bed at the first opportunity. The next day was Victoria's seventeenth birthday, and the king and queen hosted a state ball to celebrate the occasion. It was the last straw for Albert. He wrote to his stepmother, "You can well imagine that I had many hard battles to fight against sleepiness during these late entertainments." Victoria reported: "After being but a short while in the ball room and having only danced twice, [Albert] turned as pale as ashes; and we all feared he might faint; he therefore went home."

"I am sorry to say," she wrote to Uncle Leopold, "that we have an invalid in the house in the person of Albert." The would-be suitor had retreated to bed. It was unfortunate news. As the king of the Belgians knew, the large and busy English court saw a constant round of entertaining, and the husband of a future queen would need greater fortitude.

After a quiet weekend, Albert seemed to be sufficiently recovered to bear the duchess's grand ball at Kensington on the Monday. In the most splendid formal occasion at the palace since its great days under George II, the duchess's own rooms as well as swaths of the state apartments upstairs were sumptuously decorated and filled with orchestras and musicians. The princess danced with the Orange princes and Prince Ernest before supper, and then with Prince Albert after the meal (perhaps in the hope that some sustenance might have given him strength). Alas, after their second dance, he flopped into his chair, unable to manage more. Victoria left him mopping his brow. "We all stayed up until ½ past 3 and it was broad daylight when we left the room," she wrote in her diary. She felt "all the better for it" next morning. "All this dissipation does me a great deal of good," she informed King Leopold.

During the rest of the visit, Albert tried hard to please his cousin, even though staying up much past eleven was beyond him. He sang duets with Victoria, attended her lesson with Lablache, and accompanied her to the opera. He fitted in easily around her daily routine and made a point of petting her beloved Dash.

On June 7, Victoria wrote to Leopold and did not tease him that she preferred Ernest.

> *I must thank you, my beloved Uncle, for the prospect of great happiness you have contributed to give me, in the person of dear Albert. Allow me, then, my dearest Uncle, to tell you how delighted I am with him, and how much I like him in every way. He possesses every quality that could be desired to render me perfectly happy. He is so sensible, so kind, and so good, and so amiable too. He has, besides, the most pleasing and delightful exterior and appearance you can possibly see.*

Unfortunately for Leopold, though, she would not, as he had hoped, "find a choice and firmly anchor herself to it." She preferred conversing with various suitors to the idea of settling on one. She knew that she would have to choose her husband from a small and fairly uninspiring pool of Protestant princes. "A poor girl has not much free choice," she later wrote, "if she does not dislike the man—and if her parents like it, why if she refuses him she runs the risk of getting no husband at all. . . . For a Princess— a very sad, bad lookout." But, not yet eighteen, she was far from ready to make her choice.

Three days after she had written the letter, the visitors departed.

> *At 9 we all breakfasted for the last time together! It was our last HAPPY HAPPY breakfast with this dear Uncle and these dearest, beloved Cousins, whom I do love so VERY, VERY dearly; much more dearly than any other Cousins in the world. Dearly as I love Ferdinand and also good Augustus, I love Ernest and Albert more than them, oh yes, MUCH more. Augustus was like a good affectionate child, quite unacquainted with the world, phlegmatic, and talking but very little; but dearest Ernest and dearest Albert are so grown up in their manners.*

Victoria was careful not to single out Albert for particular praise. Still, she had agreed to write to him, and at the time, the very act of corresponding privately with a man, even a cousin, usually signaled an engagement.

Prince Albert of Saxe-Coburg was born three months after Princess Victoria, on August 26, 1819. His nineteen-year-old mother, Louise, was desperately lonely. She had married Ernest I, Duke of Saxe-Coburg, two years before, when she was seventeen and he was thirty-three. He was almost immediately unfaithful to her. The birth of their first son, Ernest, in 1817, encouraged him into the arms of his mistress, and Albert's arrival marked the beginning of the end of his relations with his wife. Duchess Louise threw her heart into her children, particularly her beloved second son. "Albert is superb, extraordinarily beautiful," she wrote, and she loved him passionately, fascinated by his slightly girlish looks. As Albert's tutor, Herr Florschütz, later reported, "She made no attempt to conceal that Prince Albert was her favourite child." The young Albert also charmed his uncle Leopold, who was always wishing to be near him and kissing him at every opportunity.

Duchess Louise doted on Albert, but she was young and rebellious, and motherhood could not fill the deep void in her heart. Her husband was trying to force her out of his household in an attempt to seize the lands that she had brought with her to the marriage, and she was miserable. In 1822, she fell passionately in love with Baron Alexander von Hanstein, an army lieutenant two years her junior. Her husband took the opportunity to expel her from his household, sending her away when Albert was just five and sick with whooping cough.

The duke divorced his wife and married his niece and Albert's cousin, Princess Mary of Württemberg. Louise was banished to Liechtenstein, and when she married, she was denied all access to her children. Albert would have been able to see his mother when he grew older, but she died of cancer of the womb in 1831, when he was eleven and she was only just in her thirties. The duke was an absent parent, and Albert grew up depending on his tutors for affection. A delicate, studious child, he took any negative evaluation of his work desperately to heart and was inclined to burst into tears whenever he was criticized. By his early teens, he was self-conscious and shy.

After betrothing one nephew to the queen of Portugal, Leopold planned that the other would rule England. Stiff, priggish, and intellectually unexceptional Albert, a poor princeling from an insignificant German state of about half a million inhabitants, was hardly ideal material for his uncle's ambition. He was a little younger than Victoria, in a period when tradition decreed that the husband should be at least five years older than his wife, and he lacked the passion for politics that he would need to be the consort of Queen Victoria. His one great quality was an ability to stick to a routine and work hard. He was a good organizer but quite unable to make large plans or see the greater picture. In reaction against the salacious gossip that followed him thanks to the behavior of his lascivious father, he was painfully upright, moralistic, and judgmental.

Leopold, assisted by Stockmar, set out on a two-pronged operation to transform pusillanimous Albert into a man whom Victoria would respect. He would first be encouraged to improve his mind at Brussels and then Bonn University, accompanied by his beloved brother, Ernest. There he would study a broad curriculum of history, philosophy, science, and law. At the same time, he would have lessons in singing and dancing. Then, in an attempt to imbue him with romantic sensibility, he would be taken to Florence and Rome and around the Italian lakes, Milan, Venice, northern Italy, and Switzerland. Leopold was aware that Victoria wished to see Italy, and he hoped that she might be impressed by her cousin's knowledge of the country.

Victoria missed her cousins greatly, even more so because she knew that there would be no more visits for the foreseeable future. It was back to the round of lessons and escaping the duchess's demands. "Everything that is pleasant, alas!" she wrote, "passes so quickly in this 'wide world of troubles.'"

36

"I Cannot Expect to Live Very Long"

The seventy-year-old king was sick, weak, suffering from gout, and plagued by bronchitis. A guest at a levee in May 1836 thought him "shrunk both in mind and body," and he was beginning to shake when he stood up after his nap. At times, it seemed as though he might be losing his mind, waving his arms and shouting, pestering his ministers with the suggestion that Britain go to war with China. "There is a very strong impression that the King is cracked," sniffed Greville. "He gets so very choleric, and is indecent in his wrath." Nevertheless, there were some matters on which his mind was clear. He was determined to stay alive until Victoria was eighteen. "I cannot expect to live very long," he told Lord Melbourne, "but I hope that my successor may be of full age when she mounts the throne."

In August 1836, the king invited the duchess and Victoria to celebrate the queen's birthday at Windsor on the thirteenth and remain there until his, on the twenty-first. The duchess announced that she intended to observe her own birthday at Claremont and wrote that she would come to Windsor on the twentieth. The king was infuriated. While she was at

Windsor, he traveled to London to prorogue Parliament and decided to visit Kensington Palace. He saw to his horror that the duchess had occupied new rooms and remodeled the upper floor, against his strict instructions. She had taken over seventeen rooms, appropriated his State Bedchamber for her boudoir, and divided the King's Gallery. Returning to Windsor in his fabulous carriage, the fat old king seethed about his sister-in-law's disobedience, and his pineapple head turned red with anger.

It is hard to believe that the king had received no intelligence about the refurbishments. He had his palace spies, and the rooms had been described in the newspaper report of the ball for Princes Albert and Ernest. Clearly, however, he had not realized the full extent of the alterations or understood the grand scale of the duchess's new rooms.

After dwelling on his rage for the entire journey to Windsor Castle, the king arrived at the Drawing Room at about ten o'clock. The court and guests were chattering politely after dinner, but the king paid them little attention. He puffed over to his niece and, clasping her hands, told her how happy he was to see her and how he wished he saw her more often. Then he turned to the Duchess of Kent, bowed curtly, and proceeded to berate her for taking the new rooms "not only without his consent, but contrary to his commands" and said that "he neither understood nor would endure conduct so disrespectful to him." The room fell silent. The duchess looked at her hands, utterly humiliated. She had been exposed in front of everybody, including many people who would report on it or note it on their diaries. She later attacked Victoria for "making up" too much to the king.

The king had not exorcised his anger. Next day, at his birthday dinner for a hundred guests, he rose to speak after his health had been drunk, and launched into a diatribe against the duchess in front of the entire court, as well as various politicians and dignitaries.

> I trust in God that my life may be spared for nine months longer, after which period, in the event of my death no regency would take place. I should then have the satisfaction of leaving the royal authority to the personal exercise of that young lady (pointing to the Princess), the heiress presumptive of the Crown, and not in the hands of a person now near me, who is surrounded by evil advisers and who is herself incompetent to act with propriety in the station in which she

would be placed. I have no hesitation in saying that I have been in-sulted—grossly and continually insulted—by that person, but I am determined to endure no longer a course of behaviour so disrespect-ful to me.

Emboldened by drink, the king poured out all the resentment he had been storing up since he came to the throne. The guests listened, elec-trified. He thundered that he had been particularly angered by how Victo-ria had "been kept away" from my court.

She has been repeatedly kept from my drawing rooms, at which she ought always to have been present, but I am fully resolved that this shall not happen again. I would have her know that I am King, and I am determined to make my authority respected, and for the future I shall insist and command that the Princess do upon all occasions appear at my Court, as is her duty to do.

Victoria was in tears before the king concluded. The duchess sat stony faced. The fine wines and foods sat untouched. When the ladies left the table, the duchess declared that she would call for her carriage. She was finally persuaded to remain until the following day, as planned, for an im-mediate departure would have created a great scandal and increased the possibility of the newspapers discovering the story.

The king was unrepentant. When his son, Lord Adolphus Fitz-Clarence—no friend of the duchess—suggested to his father that a private rebuke might have been better, the king proclaimed that he did not care where he said it or who heard, because "he had been insulted by her in a measure that was past all endurance, and he would not stand it any longer."

The king could be rude and often ungallant, but his drunken tirade had been truly shocking. Although Greville judged that nothing could be "more unaccountable . . . more reprehensible" than the duchess's uppity behavior, he thought that the King had acted in a manner "as injudicious and undignified as possible, and this last sortie was monstrous." Greville thought it a "gross and public insult," particularly with Victoria sitting be-side the duchess, "an unparalleled outrage from a man to a woman, from a Host to his guest and to the last degree unbecoming the station they both

of them fill." Guests dashed to report the news to their friends and to spec-
ulate on what other excesses might have happened behind closed doors.
One Lady Elizabeth Belgrave wrote to her mother that the king had told
the princess that "she was now quite *independent* and under *nobody's control.*" He "must have put the Duchess of Kent in a great rage!" she noted.

The hysterical arguments between her mother and her relations made
Victoria yearn for independence. But she was not necessarily thinking of
the suitor her mother proposed. On August 26, she wrote dutifully in her
journal, "Today is my dearest Albert's birthday, on which day he completed his 17th year. That every happiness that this world can bestow, may
be his portion, is my most earnest & heartfelt prayer." She expressed kindly,
cousinly wishes, little more.

A month later, King Leopold arrived at Claremont for a stay of six days.
He was without Queen Louise, who was heavily pregnant with her second
child. The gentle queen had sent Victoria some more fine clothes, again
from the atelier of the great Mlle Palmyre. "She is an Angel and I do so love
her," Victoria exclaimed in her journal. The princess was equally delighted
by Leopold, her "solo padre." "He is indeed like my real father, as I have
none!" she gushed. "I love him so very much; oh! my love for him approaches
to a sort of adoration." John Conroy, she meant to make clear, could never
occupy the position of guardian. She and her uncle Leopold were enjoying
their private chats. After he had sat with her for an hour and "talked over
many important things," she was full of gratitude. "He is *so* clever, so mild,
and so prudent; he alone can give me good advice on *every* thing." It was
not an entry to please her mother.

Leopold was surely telling her, as he had done in his letters, to be cautious of King William and to hold fast against her mother's attempts to gain
control over her, as well as pressing the credentials of Prince Albert.

King Leopold always liked to cast himself as the hero of the hour.
Nearly thirty years later, he told Victoria that he had spoken to Conroy at
Claremont, informing him that "his conduct was madness and must end in
his own ruin, and that, although late, there was still time!" But it appears as
if he only really intervened when it became apparent that Victoria would
come to the throne past the age of eighteen. Until then, he hedged his bets
by trying to please both the princess and her mother. His overt aim was to
be able to influence the English throne to defend the interests of the

Coburg family in Europe, whoever was the occupant. "My object," he wrote to the princess, "is that you should be no one's *tool*," but his ambition was to ensure that she was influenced by him alone, through Albert if necessary. Victoria, however, saw him as her true and disinterested friend. "It is dreadful how quickly this long looked for stay of dearest Uncle has come and is passed. Oh! it is dreadful . . . that one is almost always separated from those one loves dearly and is encumbered with those one dislikes."

The duchess and Conroy continued to plot to gain control of Victoria. They applied themselves to edging out anyone they did not believe was an absolute ally. Lady Catherine Jenkinson, daughter of Lord Liverpool and Lady of the Bedchamber to the duchess since 1830, was pushed to retire. She was too great a friend of Lehzen and, as Victoria wrote, "quite possessed her confidence."*

The duchess also summoned her son, Prince Charles, to come to England with his wife and family. Prince Charles, at thirty, was loyal to Conroy because he needed money. He had been out of favor with his family for marrying the penniless Marie Klebelsberg, once lady-in-waiting to Duchess Louise, the mother of Prince Albert. After living off the impecunious Princess Feodora in Langenburg, he had moved with Marie to Amorbach and commenced wildly expensive renovations, aiming to replace the old hunting lodge with a castle modeled on Windsor Castle, complete with terraces and towers. The money appears to have come from the duchess's accounts, via Conroy. To Prince Charles, a regency meant that his mother would be able to further finance his plans, and so he devoted his energies to supporting the endeavor. When Victoria realized that her half-brother was on the side of Conroy, she grew to hate him, railing against "the wickedness of the Prince of Leiningen and his friend S. J."

The duchess fretted that the king wished to award Victoria her own establishment. Leopold advised that a good compromise might be if Victoria had "something like that which Charlotte had," a separate little home

---

*Lady Catherine retired, but she had a happier future than many of those ousted from the palace, as she later married Colonel Francis Harcourt, son of the archbishop of York and equerry to the Duchess of Kent.

adjacent to her mother's, with the Duchess of Northumberland, Lehzen, and the dean of Chester, her old tutor, in attendance, as well as a few ladies-in-waiting. No other gentlemen should be permitted. "It is highly probable that any other would be put about you as a spy," he wrote to Victoria. Leopold had completely misread the situation at Kensington Palace. The duchess would not countenance the idea of her daughter living alone, and Victoria's aim was to oppose their efforts at presenting her as needing a regency past the age of eighteen.

As arguments raged around her, Victoria conjured visions of escape. "I would give millions to behold, but for a day, Brussells [sic], Paris, Germany, Italy & Spain & envy all those who do! Perhaps another who was compelled to travel would long to be bound as I am to my native soil!" In August, she begged Albert to send her a little souvenir from each place he stopped at on his journeys. When she received one of his tokens, she was quite overjoyed and wrote to him expressing envy that he had seen Naples.

Victoria had started reading the newspapers for hints about politics, and she was particularly interested by Robert Peel's speeches. She marveled at the insults traded between politicians, judging George Byng "rather strong" in calling Peel and other Tories "the cloven foot." Politics close up seemed all so vexingly childish. "I think that *great* violence and striving such a pity, on both sides, don't you, dear Uncle? They irritate one another so uselessly by calling one another fools, blockheads, liars and so forth for no purpose. I think violence so bad in everything. They should imitate you, and be calm, for you have had, God knows! enough cause for irritation from your *worthy* Dutch neighbours and others."

Christmas was spent at Claremont with the Conroys, Lady Flora, and the rest. The visit started badly when they were forced to stop at an inn. Victoria complained that she was "totally unprepared, Lehzen's and my wardrobe maid are gone on to Claremont, and I hate sleeping at an Inn." Matters did not improve. Isolated in the country, far from London, Victoria tried to ignore Conroy and keep herself busy. As she later wrote to Feodora, while in the country, she "drew sailors, french boys, Spaniards, Gypsies and illustrated tragedies," working sedulously with her pencil, holding strong to her beloved faith that any evil could be chased away by industriousness.

By February, Victoria had been away from London for too long, and she was bored. "My letter will, I fear, be short and stupid," she grumbled to Princess Feodora. "I have literally nothing of the news kind to tell you." She wrote to her uncle, "My *Operatic* and *Terpischorean* feelings are pretty strong now that the season is returning, and I have been a very good child, not even *wishing* to come to town until now." She always wanted to believe that King Leopold would weigh in on her side.

The party returned in March, and after recovering from a cold, Victoria informed Leopold that she was "as well as can be, and fit for a great deal of dissipation, which unfortunately I have not had. . . . [I am] very fond of *pleasant* society and we have been for these last three weeks immured within our old Palace, and I longed sadly for some gaiety. After being so very long in the country I was preparing to go out in right earnest, whereas I have only been twice to the play since our return." She looked forward to her singing lessons with Lablache, which would begin after Easter.

"The time is fast approaching when I had the great happiness of seeing you last year," she wrote to Albert, "and I can assure you my dear cousin, I regret more than I can say, not to have this gratification repeated this year." Visiting the opera would "recall the delightful evenings" they spent together vividly to her mind. When she did attend the opera, alas, she forgot about Albert. At one performance, she spotted Charles, the Duke of Brunswick—her cousin and the nephew of Princess Caroline of Brunswick, who was the wife of George IV—a handsome young man with a terrible reputation for rakish behavior. Victoria watched him intently across the auditorium. She reported that two ladies had judged his expression quite shocking, "dreadful, so very fierce & desperate," and their hostility convinced her that he was a great romantic hero.

When she encountered the Duke of Brunswick while walking in Kensington Gardens, Victoria was impressed. "He is, I think, very good looking, for we passed him close," she wrote. He certainly made sure to put himself in her way, sparkling in his box at a performance of *Otello*. The following day, while driving in the park, she saw the duke and a friend nearby, looking "very wild and odd." Her fascination with the duke quickly waned. Indeed, when she saw him a few months later, she decided he looked "pale and haggard," and decided "it was well felt in him not to come near."

May slipped ever closer. The newspapers were beginning to make wild predictions about Victoria's personality and her views on religion and politics. "You have been the subject of all sorts of newspaper paragraphs," remarked King Leopold. "Your good and sensible way of looking on these very creditable productions will *be of use to you.*" Victoria replied cheerfully that newspapers were "indeed a curious compound of truth and untruth. I am so used to newspaper nonsense and attacks that I do not mind it in the least."

The country was on tenterhooks, waiting for Victoria to come of age.

In May, the king's health took a turn for the worse. "It may *all be over* at any moment and yet it may last a few days," Victoria wrote. Prompted to action by his illness, he sent a letter to the princess to be seen by her alone. When Lord Conyngham, the Lord Chamberlain, set off for Kensington with the precious letter in hand, on May 19, he was met by Conroy, who demanded to see it. Conyngham repeated patiently that the king had ordered him to give the princess the letter, even as the duchess tried to seize it from his hand. Still, Victoria had to read it in the presence of her mother. To her joy, she found that the king had written that when she turned eighteen, in five days' time, he would apply to Parliament for £10,000 a year for her, to be used by her alone. She should appoint her own keeper of the privy purse and set up her own establishment, with her own ladies if she wished. She would have full independence from her mother, in her own little court.

Delighted by the proposals, Victoria declared that she wished to answer immediately, accepting and proposing her tutor, Mr. Davys, the dean of Chester, as keeper of her privy purse. The duchess forbade her to reply. She told her daughter that she could not discuss the matter with Lord Melbourne, as she wished, and moreover, she must decline the offer. The arguments were so bitter that Victoria retired upstairs and stayed in her room throughout dinner. "Felt very miserable and agitated," she wrote in her journal.

The duchess railed, and Victoria gave in. She copied out a letter written by her mamma. Pleading "youth and inexperience," she refused the king's offer. "I wish to remain as I am now, in the care of my dear Mother," she wrote, biting her lip. "Upon the subject of money, I should wish that whatever may be necessary to add, may be given to my dear Mother for my use, who always freely does everything I want on pecuniary matters." When the king received the letter, he cast it aside in disgust, crying, "Victoria has not written that letter." He was right: Conroy noted on the draft, "Written by the Duchess of Kent on Sir John Conroy's advice."

The duchess demanded of Lord Melbourne whether he sanctioned the measures. He admitted responsibility, declaring that every proposition submitted by the Crown to Parliament had to be subject to the advice of ministers. She replied angrily that she saw it as given "in a manner calculated to wound every feeling that belongs to my maternal station,—contrary also to the wishes of my child and which does not correspond with the confidence reposed in me by the country." The self-aggrandizing words came easily.

> *Passed over, wounded on every occasion that circumstances will allow, I still know what is due to my maternal duties, supported by the tears of my child; who has, of her own free will, told the King that she desires nothing but to be left as heretofore with Her Mother—conscious that every moment of my life has been devoted to my duties to her and the country . . . the Princess and myself reject the idea, that on such a subject, we could have a separate feeling.*

The prime minister wrote immediately to the king that the duchess must be prevented at all costs from publicizing her ill treatment. "It is worth while to make almost any sacrifice in order to avoid open difference and dissension in the Royal Family," he proposed. Melbourne's Tory government was shaky. He was concerned that talk of arguments within the royal family would damage his standing, and he was quite panicked about the duchess's determination to fix him "with the responsibility of what has been done," which showed that she contemplated "publicity." Other advisers were less convinced by the duchess's claims of devotion and thought she could be bribed. Lord John Russell proposed that the £10,000 should be split, according £6,000 to the duchess and £4,000 to Victoria. The duchess refused the offer, again speaking for Victoria without consulting her, and Melbourne weakly let the matter drop.

Frustrated and angry, the king retired to bed. On May 22, Victoria reported that she had heard from his doctor. "The King was in a very odd stage and decidedly had the hay fever and in such a manner as to preclude his going to bed. I trust he *may* get over it, but he is 72."

37

"It May All Be Over
at Any Moment"

Today is my 18th birthday! How old! and yet how far am I from being what I should be," mused the Princess on May 24, 1837. As she had been sleeping, palace workers had hammered a white and gold banner embroidered with her name across the front of the palace. The event that the duchess had dreaded for so long had occurred. Princess Victoria had turned eighteen, and the king was still alive.

Kensington was festooned with banners, a choir sang under the princess's window, and the shopkeepers on Kensington High Street displayed signs wishing her many happy returns of the day. In great contrast to her previous birthdays, and a world away from Charlotte's subdued eighteenth, it was a day of receptions, social events, and adulation. In the morning, the princess hosted an official reception in the palace for deputations from various towns across the country. Ladies in their fine silks and hats crowded in, impatient to see the future queen. In the afternoon, she took a drive with Lehzen for an hour and a half, merrily waving to the admiring hordes. "The demonstrations of loyalty and affection from all the people were highly gratifying. The parks and streets were thronged and everything looked like a *Gala* day." It was delightful to greet her public without her mother beside her.

In the evening, the king threw a state ball for her, although he was too ill to attend. People had been waiting all day to see Victoria drive to her celebrations. "The Courtyard and the streets were crammed when we went to the Ball, and the anxiety of the people to see poor stupid me was very great, and I must say I am quite touched by it." The ball was splendid, and the king gave her a generous present of a grand piano. Victoria enjoyed her day, even though the duchess did her best to wreck the evening, arriving in a separate carriage and flouncing off early.

There have been few mothers in history for whom their daughter's eighteenth birthday was such a disaster. A visitor to the morning reception thought the duchess looked "anxious and harassed." The princess "gave my beloved Lehzen a small brooch of my hair," but she did not say what, if anything, she presented to her mother. At the end of the day, Victoria wrote in her diary, busily resolving "to study with renewed assiduity, to keep my attention well fixed on whatever I am about, and to strive every day to become less trifling and more fit for what, if Heaven wills it, I'm some day to be!"

There was no mention of relying on Mamma.

The day after Victoria's birthday, Sir John recommenced his campaign of harassment in earnest, determined to press her into making him her private secretary or into agreeing that she would need a regency until the age of twenty-one. He had the zealous assistance of Lady Flora and Prince Charles of Leiningen. King Leopold encouraged her not to give in to the threats. "The violence which is sometimes shown is so well known to you," he wrote. "You *must keep up your usual cool spirit*, whatever may be tried in the House to teaze you out of it." He was shocked to hear about the king's offer. "You have had some battles and difficulties of which I am completely in the dark," he wrote. He read a copy of the letter Victoria had sent to the King and found it baffling. "Avoid in future to say much about your great *youth* and *inexperience*. Who made the letter? Was it yourself or came it from your Mother?" Realizing that his sister was stepping up her campaign to discredit Victoria and install Sir John as her secretary or treasurer, Leopold sent over his faithful adviser, Baron Stockmar.

Stockmar, the fat, bustling doctor-courtier who had become so preoccupied by Leopold's affairs that he hardly saw his own wife and family, was forty-nine, as sure of himself as ever, and ready for a fight. Victoria was relieved to have a new ally. Stockmar was "Uncle Leopold's greatest and most confidential attached and disinterested friend, and I hope he is the same to me, at least I feel so towards him; Lehzen being of course the *greatest* friend I have." The baron was horrified to find that the duchess had never shown Victoria the letter from Melbourne offering £6,000 for herself and £4,000 for her daughter. He was shocked that the duchess had lied to everybody that Victoria had declined the proposal.

Stockmar warned the Prince of Leiningen to desist from his bullying behavior, telling him that "treachery, lies and fraud" were not "the weapons of success," but the prince, undeterred, continued to aid Conroy in his attacks on Victoria. "Do you think the native hails your reign with unparalleled joy, calls you their hope, because you will be a Queen of eighteen years? Oh no!" he pronounced, on one occasion. "They expect that you will follow the path which your mother has gone for many years." Conroy, he judged, should be rewarded, for he had "worked hard many a year to create this enormous popularity for you." The duchess, meanwhile, stepped up her desperate efforts to beg her daughter to obey.

Soon after Stockmar arrived, Victoria dictated a memorandum to Lehzen in which she explained how the duchess had forbidden her to install the dean as the keeper of her privy purse or meet with Lord Melbourne, and had then given her a draft letter to copy to the king in which she refused the £10,000.

> I have objected on the 19th May, as well as always before to allowing Sir John Conroy any interference in my affairs. Whatever he had done, it has been done by order of my Mother, as I requested in her name, without making me responsible for any of her actions, as Sir John Conroy is Her private secretary and neither my Servant, nor Advisor, nor ever was.

Obsessed by the idea that they had sacrificed everything for the princess, Conroy and the duchess expected to be compensated. Unfortunately, their regime had failed to turn Victoria into a dependent, obedient heir. An obstinate, stubborn Hanoverian, she was convinced of her own fitness to rule.

She had a disciplined mind, a propensity for hard work, and a quick intelligence. The Kensington System had caused her great misery, but it had also ensured that she had become a serious young woman. It had compelled her to conceal her feelings and, as Stockmar noted, "live on outwardly submissive and affectionate terms with people she distrusted and disliked."

The king had managed the superhuman effort of staying alive past Victoria's birthday, and he seemed healthier than he had been for weeks. Lord Palmerston wished he would rally, for "there was no advantage in having a totally inexperienced girl of eighteen, just out of strict guardianship, to govern an empire." Quite why a teenage girl was worse than a king who was, at times, hardly sensate, Palmerston did not explain.

By June, the king was severely ill. The duchess put off the ball she had been planning for the eighth, and an opera visit was canceled. Conroy began to attack Victoria frenziedly. Stockmar reported:

> On the 10th, 11th and 12th, we in Kensington were constantly playing out some comedy or tragedy. O'Hum [Conroy] continues the system of intimidation with the genius of a madman, and the Duchess carries out all she is instructed to do with admirable docility and perseverance. . . . The Princess continues to refuse firmly to give her Mama her confidential promise that she will make O'Hum her confidential adviser. Whether she will hold out, Heaven only knows, for they plague her, every hour and every day.

As the king sickened, passions intensified. "You are still very young," the duchess wrote to Victoria. "Do not be too sanguine in your own *talents* and *understanding.*" She was remorseless. "You are untried, you are liked for your youth, your sex and the hope that is entertained, but all confidence in you comes from your mother's reputation." She told her daughter that she needed an adviser of great ability and no bias. "That person I must repeat to you again your father considered to be Sir John Conroy. I therefore solemnly and on my knees advise you to take Sir John Conroy—this advice I give you only for your own security." She even declared: "The stain will remain on you; to attempt to hurt Sir John Conroy as a daughter's first act to her parents would be a very injudicious measure." The duchess did not take her daughter to visit the king, perhaps because she dreaded him weighing into the battle and giving Victoria yet more courage to resist.

"The news of the King is so very bad that all my lessons save the Dean's are put off, including Lablache's, Mrs. Anderson's, Guazzaroni's, &c, and we see *nobody*," wrote the Princess on June 15. "I regret rather my singing-lesson, though it is only for a short period, but duty and *proper feeling* go before *all pleasures*." She returned to her journal at lunchtime: "10 minutes to 1—I just hear that the Doctors think my poor Uncle the King cannot last more than 48 hours. Poor man! he was always kind to me and he meant it well I know; I am grateful for it, and shall ever remember his kindness with gratitude. He was odd, very odd and singular, but his intentions were often ill interpreted!"

Lord Liverpool, a family friend, was summoned to Kensington and lectured by Conroy on how Victoria was mentally weak and even unstable, "younger in intellect by some years than she was in age." Hoping to appeal to the hoary old sexism he trusted was crusted around Lord Liverpool's Tory heart, he declared Victoria "light & frivolous & . . . easily caught by fashion and appearances." It was a tricky position to uphold, after having spent so long declaring Victoria's superb education and her great intelligence. Conroy suggested that Lord Liverpool recommend that the would-be queen "clear out entirely" her household, which would mean losing Lehzen. He wanted her to install his own daughters as attendants. But Lord Liverpool was not easily convinced, remembering how his own daughter, Lady Catherine, had been summarily dismissed as a lady-in-waiting for too close a friendship with Lehzen. He declared that it would not be right for Victoria to have a private secretary, as George IV and William IV had, and suggested that Conroy could only be keeper of the privy purse, with "small duties" and, as Conroy well knew, no political power.

Lord Liverpool then called on the princess, and she, as she wrote, "had a highly important conversation with him—*alone*." But although he was sympathetic to her situation, he, like Stockmar, told her that she could not set up an establishment separate from her mother, for this would be unseemly.

The duchess had tried begging, threatening, declaring her sacrifices, and crying that the public adored Conroy. All had failed. Conroy demanded that the duchess use force to compel Victoria to obey. "She is pressed by Conroy to bring matters to extremities and to force her Daughter to do her will by unkindness and severity," Stockmar wrote. Extreme measures were proposed. Conroy told the duchess: "If Princess Victoria will not listen to reason, *she must be coerced.*" There was wild talk of shutting Victoria up or exercising physical force on her, so that the duchess should "keep her under duress till she had extorted this engagement from her."

"I know that I am going but I should like to see another anniversary of Waterloo," the king whispered to his doctors. "Try if you cannot tinker me up to last over that date." He just managed to last until June 18, the day of the anniversary, bravely refusing to complain, sitting up in his chair in order to breathe. "The King dies like an old lion," declared Disraeli. "The King's state, I may fairly say, is hopeless," Victoria wrote to Leopold the following day. "I look forward to the event which it seems is likely to occur soon, with calmness and quietness. I am not alarmed at it, and yet I do not suppose myself quite equal to all; I trust, however, that with *good will, honesty,* and courage I shall not, at all events, fail."

Leopold recommended prudence. Victoria should be sure to "not be hurried into important measures, and to *gain time,*" he wrote. "A new reign is always a time of hope; everybody is disposed to see something for his own wishes and prospects. The policy of a new Sovereign must therefore be to act in such a manner as to hurt as little as possible the amour-propre of people, to let circumstances and the force of things bring about the disappointments which no human power could prevent coming sooner or later." He instructed her firmly that her first act should be "to entrust Lord Melbourne to retain the present Administration." She should also be sure to show her loyalty to the Church at all times. He declared that he would come over if she wanted him, but he thought that he should not. "People might fancy I came to enslave you," he wrote, and even that "I thought of ruling the realm for *purposes of my own.*"

By the early evening of June 19, King William was past recovery at Windsor Castle. He had finally fallen unconscious in the late afternoon, and at twenty minutes past two on the morning of June 20, 1837, he breathed his last. His final discernible word was the name of his valet.

Lord Conyngham and Dr. William Howley, the elderly archbishop of Canterbury, set off to inform Victoria. They arrived at five o'clock, but the gate was shut. Finally they reached the palace, only to be told that the princess was asleep. The duchess was not willing to see her daughter as queen just yet. At six o'clock, Victoria was awoken by her mother with the news. Lord Conyngham and the archbishop were waiting to see her.

PART THREE

1837–41

The Young Queen

38

"Just the Sort of Life I Like"

I never was happy," Victoria would later say, "until I was eighteen." The new queen of England sat in her night wear with the archbishop and the Lord Chamberlain. She heard about her uncle's last moments and asked Lord Conyngham to pass her "feelings of condolence" to Queen Adelaide. Outside the door, the duchess plotted, undeterred by the fact that she had not been asked to sit in on the meeting. She was not regent, but she was sure that great riches and power were still within her grasp.

Victoria's first act as queen was to ask for an hour alone. Then she requested that her bed be moved from her mother's room and made up in her own chamber. The duchess had been sure that she would be able to compel her daughter into giving her power. Victoria was determined to prove her wrong.

The new queen returned to her room to dress and wrote in her journal: "Since it has pleased Providence to place me in this station, I shall do my utmost to fulfil my duty towards my country; I am very young and perhaps in many, though not in all things, inexperienced, but I am sure, that very few have more real good will and more real desire to do what is fit and right than I have."

Victoria dressed in a black gown, for she was now in mourning for her uncle. The tiny dress today lies in a long drawer in Kensington Palace under layers of tissue paper in a specially humidified room. It appears to have been a colored dress that was dyed black, for it has turned a muddy yellow-brown, but the exquisite material still falls in graceful folds, over which the tiny lace-edged cuffs lie folded over the breast.

After breakfast, Victoria sat down with her pen. She wrote quickly to her "dearest, most beloved Uncle" Leopold that the king had died and she expected Lord Melbourne imminently. She then wrote to her half-sister: "Dearest Feodora, two words only to tell you that the poor King died this morning at 12 minutes past 2, that I am well, and that I remain for life your devoted attached sister, V. R." She was wise to snatch a few minutes to write to her two favorite relations, for her time was not to be her own. Soon after breakfast, a messenger brought her an urgent note. The prime minister, Lord Melbourne "presents his humble duty to your Majesty and will do himself the honour of waiting upon your Majesty a little before 9 this morning." Privy Council would be held at eleven. It would be her first great test as queen.

Victoria received Lord Melbourne, as she wrote in her journal, "of COURSE quite ALONE." He was fifty-eight, handsome, and suave, with a rakish past. Victoria had only once before met a man without a chaperone, when family friend Lord Liverpool had paid a call just before she ascended the throne. Now she was alone with the famously stylish and urbane prime minister. He was fatherly, courtly, and gallantly admiring, and she was delighted by him. She immediately told him that she planned to retain him and the other ministers in charge of affairs. Melbourne bowed to kiss her hand in thanks. There was only one man she wished to relieve of his position: John Conroy.

Lord Melbourne then read the queen his draft of her declaration to the Privy Council, an assembly of advisers appointed by the monarch, most of whom had possessed, or still held, high office. She decreed Melbourne's draft "very fine," which was fortunate, for there was no time to make alterations. The Council was due to take place in the Red Saloon of Kensington Palace later that morning.

Some 220 privy councillors hurried to the palace in response to the call, eager to be at the first council of a new queen. Among them were Victoria's uncles Cumberland and Sussex, as well as most of the highest holders of political, military, legal, and ecclesiastical office in the realm. Melbourne asked the queen if she wished to be accompanied into the room. She refused, unafraid. There was a hush as the doors were opened and the queen appeared, in her plain black dress. She bowed to the lords, sat, and then read out, in an impressively clear voice, her declaration, in which she solicited the support of divine providence and announced that she would "place my firm reliance upon the wisdom of Parliament and upon the loyalty and affection of My People." She added that she would "steadily protect the rights and promote to the utmost of my power the happiness and welfare of all classes of my subjects."

The new queen then had to swear in the crowd of privy councillors. They delighted in her conduct. Even the acerbic Charles Greville, then clerk of the council, was charmed by the way she behaved with "perfect calmness and self-possession but at the same time with a graceful modesty and propriety." Victoria made sure not to show any particular signs of favoritism to those who came to be sworn in, even to Melbourne. The captivated hoary gentlemen of the Privy Council dashed to record their heightened emotions in journals and letters. Croker rhapsodized about the modest blush on the queen's cheek, which ensured she looked "as interesting and handsome as any young lady I ever saw." The Duke of Wellington burbled that if she had been his own daughter he could not have desired to see her perform her part better. Stirred by chivalric interest, every councillor was fascinated by the little Queen's looks. "She not merely filled her chair," declared the duke, "she filled the room."

Victoria's day was spent in giving audiences to various dignitaries, while ignoring her mother. She saw Lord Melbourne four times and Baron Stockmar frequently. She dined alone, and at twenty to nine, Melbourne arrived for his final visit and stayed until ten. All day the duchess and John Conroy strained to get close to the new queen, without success. In her journal, Victoria noted all those she encountered that day, but there was no reference to her mother until the end of the day, when, as she remarked, she "went down and said good night to Mamma, etc." Finally, she could retire to her own private room and write her diary without fear of her words being read (although she still allowed her dearest Lehzen to peruse the pages). That night, for the first time in her life, Victoria slept alone.

"I am completely beaten," Conroy told Stockmar on the day Victoria came to the throne. After long years of feeling miserable and secluded at Kensington Palace, the queen had seized the chance to be independent and to make her point to her mother that she had been treated unfairly. Stockmar and her ministers had advised her to show forgiveness, but although Victoria agreed to treat her mother politely, she had not exonerated her. Throughout her first days on the throne, the duchess made repeated attempts to see her daughter. Each time Victoria told her she would have to apply for permission, and when she did so, the new queen told her she was too busy. "I had to remind her *who* I was," she declared to Lord Melbourne. "Quite right," he replied, "disagreeable but necessary."

Sir John realized that his hopes for public influence and fame were in tatters. Aiming to grasp as much money and favor as he could, as fast as possible, he demanded a pension of £3,000 a year and a peerage. He required compensation, he pronounced, because he might have joined the army or civil service, rather than serving the Duke and then the Duchess of Kent at his own expense. His demands were exorbitant, especially since he had creamed off thousands of pounds of the duchess's cash, but the new queen was desperate to rid herself of him. She agreed to the £3,000 and hoped that in return he would leave the court. When he remained, she ignored him and vowed that she would not receive him or invite him to court functions.

Her mother was furious that Victoria would not receive her beloved friend. "In marking Sir John as You have done he is branded in the eyes of the world," she wrote, begging her daughter to change her mind. Victoria refused. Conroy would not go quietly, for like any blackmailer, he always wanted more. He hoped to be paid with additional money and a peerage. "I wrote to you that a certain shocking person was finally put down, that is to say I never see him, nor does he meddle in my affairs, but he still continues to tease me by ways and underhand means," Victoria scribbled to Leopold.

The queen's correspondence file bulged with letters of congratulation. Prince Albert sent a labored effort, expressing pleasure at her accession, wishing her a long, happy, and glorious reign, and suggesting that she might think of her cousins in Bonn and "continue to them that kindness you favoured them with til now." Victoria responded warmly to his stilted lines. "I cannot tell you how happy you have made me by your kind dear letter which I have just received," she enthused. "Many, many thanks for it, my dear cousin, and for the good wishes contained in it." She could not resist a little boasting. "My new situation is not an easy one, no doubt, but I trust with good will, honesty and courage I shall not fail. I delight in the business which I have to do and which is not trifling either in matter or quantity."

The sheltered eighteen-year-old was turning herself into a businesslike queen. Following Leopold's advice, she kept regular hours, rose at eight, signed dispatches until breakfast, and saw ministers between eleven and half past one. After reclusive George IV, and William IV, who had soon wearied of hard work, her ministers were delighted. Much less to their taste was her preference for pondering over decisions, again a principle advocated by Leopold. "Whenever a question is of some importance," he asserted, "it should not be decided on the day when it is submitted to you." Even more troublesome was his suggestion that she never permit people to speak to her on subjects concerning herself and her affairs without her having "desired them to do so." She should "change the conversation and make the individual feel as if he has made a mistake."

The queen was learning about her constitutional role. Unlike George III, she no longer had the power to change governments. But she could advise about policy and make suggestions, which ministers would have to take seriously. Her life in Kensington had kept her isolated from her future role. Now, thanks to Lord Melbourne, she was discovering the scope of her powers.

After subdued, dismal months in Kensington, the queen was thriving on being occupied. Her busy days were a delightful novelty. It was as if her previous bouts of ill health had never occurred. Victoria was on fire with energy. "I must see my Ministers every day," she retorted to her uncle Leopold when he suggested she spend time at Claremont. She delighted in the "regular, hard" but to her "*delightful* work" that she was required to do. "It is to me the *greatest pleasure* to do my duty for my country and my people, and no fatigue, however great, will be burdensome to me if it is for the welfare of the nation."

The young queen loved doing "business" with adoring older men. Lord Holland reported that he had visited court and been closeted with the

"Virgin Queen." He was, he declared, "come back quite a courtier & a bit of a lover." The queen was no beauty but she was "really in person, in face & especially in eyes and complexion, a very nice girl & quite such as might tempt." The temptation continued to exert its hold over him. "Like the rest of the world I am captivated," he sighed later. Even waspish Charles Greville was smitten. After Victoria's second Privy Council, he remarked that although the queen was small and plain, the "gracefulness of her manner and the good expression of her countenance give her on the whole a very agreeable appearance, and with her youth inspire an excessive interest in all who approach her, and which I can't help feeling myself."

"Is it not sometimes to yourself like a dream," Feodora asked, "that everything is so completely changed, and so of a sudden too?" Victoria confessed that she did indeed sometimes wake afraid that her happiness was all a dream. Life was marvelous. "Everybody says that I am quite another person since I came to the throne," she decided. "I look and am so very well, I have such a pleasant life; just the sort of life I like."

Ballads, newspapers, and caricatures flooded from the presses, all idealizing their young, lovely monarch. One, "Figaro in London," showed John Bull willing to cut off his own ears if the little queen required. Monarchs are usually popular when they come to the throne, but the passion for Victoria was so intense that many compared it to a madness. There was, *The Spectator* claimed, a "Reginamania" so wild that writers were obsessed with fatuous detail, "dwelling constantly on the beauty not only of the Queen's face and features but of her feet and even of her slippers." A long-term stalker, one Captain Goode, who had followed Victoria obsessively when she had been a princess at Kensington, stepped up his campaign and had to be committed. *The Times* reported the matter fully, under titles such as "The Gross Outrage to Her Majesty." Another admirer broke into the Chapel Royal and began bowing and kissing his hand to Victoria. Yet another, Tom Flower, tried to get into the queen's box at the opera (he was finally arrested when he tried to force his way into the coronation).

On July 8, William IV was buried at Windsor in a relatively modest ceremony. The fickle public, entranced by the youthful Queen Victoria, had already forgotten their old king. The dean of Windsor stumbled through the service, and only the guardsmen managed to retain appropriately solemn expressions. Greville complained that one man stood laughing at the foot of the coffin when it was lying in state. No one, not even the king's loyal private secretary Sir Herbert Taylor, shed tears. Queen Adelaide moved out of Windsor and returned to Bushey. The FitzClarences began writing desperate letters to the queen, begging for her assistance. The era of William IV was finally over.

Ever since the time of George I, Great Britain and Hanover had been joined. But the Salic law that prevailed in Hanover forbade a female monarch. So Victoria was queen of England but not electress of Hanover, and the Duke of Cumberland inherited the title. Hanover was a poor booby prize for the man who had hoped that Victoria might die and so enable him to be king. Still, it was a kingdom, and the duke set off for his new home of Herrenhausen Palace with all possible pomp, arriving on June 28. Although nervous about reports of his tyrannical disposition, the Hanoverians welcomed their elderly king with enthusiasm. He would be the first in 123 years to live among them. The English and their queen were delighted to see the duke depart for his new home. He was, however, Victoria's heir presumptive, and so, unless she had a child, there remained the grisly possibility that he might return.

On July 13, Victoria moved from Kensington Palace to Buckingham Palace. Her childhood home was not sufficiently large or grand for the court of a queen, the state apartments had been divided up by the Duchess of Kent in 1836, and Kensington was a little too far from central London. Victoria had been told that Buckingham Palace was not yet ready for her, but she was eager to leave Kensington as soon as possible. She had, indeed, written to Leopold that she hoped to move there straight after the funeral of the king. Still, she felt a little nostalgic when the time came to say goodbye. "I have gone through painful and disagreeable scenes here, 'tis true," she wrote, "but still I am fond of the poor old Palace." She did not return to her "poor old Palace," however, for years, and she allowed it to fall into disrepair.

Victoria had only recently been a young girl living in a small suite of rooms with a governess and a few personal maids. Now she was the possessor of palaces that cost thousands to maintain, and she was surrounded by servants. At Buckingham Palace, she had a bedroom, a sitting room, and an audience room, far away from her mother, who was exiled to distant apartments. She loved the spaciousness of her new home, but she was soon fully occupied sending letters to the Lord Chamberlain demanding new fixtures and fittings. As she was beginning to realize, the palace was frustratingly chaotic and much less luxuriously comfortable than it appeared. Even at the best of times, it was drafty. When Victoria arrived, the fires could not be lit because the chimneys smoked. Both the palace and the castle were notoriously wasteful. There were too many employees: under the Lord Chamberlain were nearly 450 people, including a painter, the poet laureate, physicians and apothecaries, and even a rat killer. Two-thirds of the servants did not have to answer to an overseer who was present in the house, and so tended to begin and end their duties rather as they pleased.

The problem was that the upkeep of the palace and the administration of the servants were the responsibility of three departments. Instead of one authority in charge of all, the Lord Steward, the Lord Chamberlain and the Master of the Horse divided the duties between them, with little logic as to which task was allocated to whom. The Lord Chamberlain took responsibility for the housekeepers, pages, and housemaids, while the footmen, livery porters, and under-butlers were directed by the Master of the Horse. Kitchen staff and all the other palace servants were the lord steward's domain. Unfortunately, he and his two fellow masters were not dedicated household managers, for their offices were political and changed each time a new government was installed. Highborn aristocrats and politicians, they did not live in the palace and had little time for mundane questions of scullery maids and dusting. They delegated many tasks to lower servants, who often neglected their commands. The duties of the different departments were often altered, and there was constant dispute between them, with the predictable result that the servants would decide that the matter in question was not their responsibility.

On one occasion, the queen asked why the fire in the dining room had not been lit. She was solemnly informed by an officer from the department of the Lord Steward: "It is not our fault; for the Lord Steward lays the fire only, and the Lord Chamberlain lights it." In similar fashion, the Officer of Woods and Forests arranged the cleaning of the outer panes of glass, while the Lord Chamberlain's staff cleaned the interior. It was thus only seldom that the queen was able to admire her extensive grounds through sparkling windows.

Dinners were often served as cold as the rooms, there were rats in the kitchens, and nothing was particularly clean. Repairs took so long to organize that there were always broken shelves, cupboards, and windows throughout the palace. Then there was the problem of pilfering: Food disappeared, wine stocks were rapidly depleted, and linens went astray. New candles were placed in the rooms every day, even though many had not been lit the previous day, for it was tradition that staff could sell unused candles for their own gain (and wax candles were hugely expensive). Tradesmen were given money for supplies that never arrived, meals were paid for that were never served, endless carriages were ordered in other people's names, and among the huge staff were many paid purely as sinecures. The footmen had been taking candles, food, wine, and the rest for years to supplement their salaries; the houses had always been chilly and disorganized; and there was, surely, simply no way to run such behemoths efficiently. On the first day of her reign, the queen had decided: "My dear Lehzen will ALWAYS remain with me as my friend but will take no situation about me, and I think she is right." But she soon changed her mind and gave her beloved former governess overall responsibility for organizing her homes, as well as taking charge of her purse. Lehzen made few changes to the running of the households, and so everything creaked on as inefficiently as it had before.

At the end of 1837, a small boy crept into the gardens of Buckingham Palace and approached the house. He skirted the walls and doors before finally creeping in through a back entrance. Since the palace was overstaffed but generally unguarded, he was able to steal along the passageway and find his way around the servants' quarters. He soon discovered a wonderland: soft beds to sleep in, kitchens bursting with food, and items to pilfer, including a sword, a pair of trousers, and two glass inkstands. He even opened a sealed letter to the queen. During the day, he stowed himself in chimneys. The baffled servants would find oddly blackened sheets, half-eaten pieces of food, traces of crumbs on tables, and dirty plates and glasses lying around, but there was no sign of an intruder. Whispers began that the palace was haunted. The child was only apprehended a year later, when he was actually trying to leave the palace. There was talk of how the security of the palaces should be improved, but little was done.

* * *

"I shall never forget my feelings," wrote the Duchess of Kent in her journal, "when I saw her sit on the Throne! That young girl 18 years old being the sole sovereign of this great country." On July 17, the people had their first opportunity to see their new queen in full regalia, at the dissolution of Parliament. She donned the heavy parliamentary robe and proceeded into a crammed House of Lords. "I prorogued Parliament yesterday in person," Victoria wrote to the king of the Belgians, "was very well received, and am not at all tired today, but quite frisky." On July 19, she held a levee and delighted in having her hand kissed nearly three thousand times. She was wildly popular. Everyone, declared Mrs. Stevenson, wife of the American ambassador, was "mad with loyalty to the young Queen. . . . In all societies nothing is talked about but her beauty, her wisdom, her gentleness, and self-possession. A thousand anecdotes are related to her goodness, and the wonderful address with which she manages everybody and everything."

In mid-August, Victoria departed to spend the summer at Windsor Castle. Arriving on a rainy day, she felt cast down by the weight of the past. "I cannot help feeling as though I was not the Mistress of the House and as if I was to see the poor King and Queen. There is a sadness about the whole which I must say I feel." A visit from her beloved Uncle Leopold and Aunt Louise soon lifted her spirits. The weather improved, Lords Melbourne and Palmerston also came, and the queen began to relish the joys of roaming Windsor Great Park on horseback, flanked by thirty or so other riders. She had not ridden for two years, and she delighted in being back in the saddle, particularly on a favorite horse she called Leopold. She particularly enjoyed riding Leopold during a military review at the park while inspecting the lines of men and watching them maneuver and shoot. "The whole went off beautifully; and I felt for the first time like a man, as if I could fight myself as the head of my Troops."

The queen was reveling in being the center of attention. She was delighted when her game of chess with her aunt Queen Louise turned into a weighty battle. Lords Melbourne, Palmerston, and Conyngham, and Sir John Hobhouse, President of the Board of Control,* stood behind her and made suggestions about how to win, but all failed. Happily, the castle had

---

* The Board of Control oversaw the East India Company.

no main room where guests could lounge and assemble and talk, and so it was easier for Victoria to avoid her mother until dinner.

On October 4, the queen left Windsor to visit the Brighton Pavilion for six weeks. "I am *very sorry* indeed to go!" she reflected in her diary. "I passed such a very pleasant time here; the pleasantest summer I EVER passed in my life, and I shall never forget this first summer of my Reign."

Victoria found George IV's beloved folly bizarre. Already the Pavilion seemed like something from another age, bedecked with crazy red colors, chinoiserie, ornamental palm trees, and wild decorations: a "strange, odd Chinese looking thing, both inside and outside. I only see a little morsel of the sea from one of my sitting room windows," she complained.

She far preferred to be in London. When she traveled to the lord mayor's dinner in November, her first state visit to the city, she was quite thrilled to see how "the greatest concourse of people" she ever witnessed crowded every window, street and balcony to see her. "It is really most gratifying to have met with such a reception in the greatest capital in the world and from thousands and thousands of people. I really do not deserve all this kindness for what I have done."

In November, Parliament voted the queen an annuity of £385,000 a year, which she would receive in addition to her revenue of £27,000 from the duchies of Lancashire and Cornwall. She was not only the most powerful woman in the world, at just eighteen, but the richest. She was also about to be celebrated by one of the most flamboyant coronations in history.

"You have it in your power to make thousands happy," wrote Feodora to her half-sister. Parliament voted £200,000 in the hope of creating a truly wonderful spectacle, four times more than had been accorded to William IV. George IV had enjoyed a dazzling occasion, but the point of this coronation would not be to surround the monarch in luxury and congratulate the aristocracy but to fortify the loyalty of the ordinary people. For the first time, members of the House of Commons would be invited to the abbey, and there would be organized celebrations for the subjects. Bands would play; there would be fireworks displays and a two-day fair covering Hyde Park. Most important of all, for the first time since 1760, the queen would proceed in full state to the abbey, before returning in her robes and bearing her orb and scepter.

For such a great procession, a new crown was required. The St. Ed-ward's Crown, made for King Charles II, and the Imperial Crown, worn by Victoria's two uncles, were deemed too heavy and out of date. The jewels from the latter were combined into a new crown plump with rubies and sapphires for the bargain price of £1,000. The jewelers appointed to create it, Rundell, Bridge, & Rundell, decided to turn their great commission to their commercial advantage and put the crown on show. Crowds queued up for tickets and officers were brought in to prevent the hundreds of eager sightseers from breaking down the doors of the shop.

Then there was the question of fashion. The Duchess of Richmond was in charge of the dresses for the young girls who were to act as robe bearers, and she was determined on white and silver dresses and silver headdresses. Some objections were raised, but the duchess, as she put it, "would have no discussion with their Mammas about it."

Queen Victoria's first grand state ball was planned for May. Melbourne complained that too many people had demanded invitations. Moreover, it was to be filled with people much older than a young and excitable eighteen-year-old might wish. But Victoria was quite happy and grasped every opportunity to skip around the hall, although she had to sit out the waltzes for there was no man of sufficient stature to partner her in this most intimate of dances.

As the coronation approached, eager crowds began arriving in London. The city's population of one and a half million was swollen with four hun-dred thousand visitors, and the streets were absolutely packed. "It is as if the population had been on a sudden quintupled," complained Greville. "Not a mob here or there, but the town all mob, thronging, bustling, gap-ing, and gazing at everything, at anything, or at nothing; the Park one vast encampment, with banners floating on the tops of the tents, and still the roads are covered, the railroads loaded with arriving multitudes." Vast sums changed hands for positions and windows along the route. Thou-sands crammed into the specially erected stadiums, impatient to reserve their places, and it was said that four hundred thousand people slept in the streets the night before the ceremony.

That night, the queen could hardly sleep, tormented by "a feeling that something very awful was going to happen" the next day. Since she had never attended a coronation, she had very little idea of what to do, and she was naturally nervous of making a mistake. Lord Melbourne took a typically sanguine approach to her worries. "It's a thing that you can't give a person advice upon, it must be left to a person," judged the man who had seen both George IV and William IV crowned.

Poor, restless Victoria was woken at four by the sound of cannons firing and then found it impossible to go back to sleep "on account of the noise of the people in the streets, bands etc." By seven, she had got up to look at Green Park, which was already teeming with soldiers, bands, and crowds of admirers. It all seemed rather a lot of fuss for such a small person. Outside, the other coaches were making their way toward the abbey, packed with foreign royals and diplomats in their finest jewels. She struggled to eat some breakfast, then donned her robes of white satin and red velvet, along with a circlet of diamonds for her hair. Then she entered her gilded state coach and set off for the slow journey to Westminster Abbey, via Constitution Hill, Piccadilly, and Whitehall. "Many as there were the day I went to the City, it was nothing—nothing, to the multitudes, the millions, of my loyal subjects who were assembled in *every spot* to witness the Procession. Their good humour and excessive loyalty was beyond everything, and I really cannot say *how* proud I feel to be the Queen of *such a Nation.*"

After an hour and a half, the queen reached the abbey. She went to the robing room, where she donned a long red mantle lined with ermine. Lord Melbourne preceded her, dosed up on laudanum and brandy because he was ill with a stomach upset, and carrying the Sword of State like, according to Disraeli, "a great butcher." Followed by her eight train bearers and Lord Conyngham, she walked, dazzled, into the abbey. There, in the interior that had been newly decorated with crimson and gold hangings and tapestries, the floors covered with oriental carpets, were the assembled peers and peeresses of the realm and eminent representatives of foreign countries, including Prince Esterhazy, the Austrian minister, who was covered in diamonds. The queen herself looked charming. Lord Melbourne declared her floating on a silver cloud, a vision perhaps intensified by the quantities of laudanum he had consumed.

At the altar covered in gold plate, Victoria was received by the archbishop of Canterbury and heard him proclaim her "the undoubted Queen of this realm." The congregation returned, "God Save Queen Victoria," as she turned first to the north, then to the south and the west, before vowing to uphold the Protestant religion. The queen then withdrew into St. Edward's Chapel, where she took off her robes and diamond circlet and put on a linen shift and a golden tunic. Bareheaded, she returned to the altar and sat in St. Edward's chair. Four knights of the garter held a gold canopy over her head, as the archbishop performed the ceremony of the anointing. The Dalmatian robe of gold cloth lined with ermine was clasped around her, then she was to be given the orb, scepter, and ruby ring. Unfortunately, the Dean of Westminster, who had led the coronation services for George IV and William IV, was too ill to attend, and those replacing him had little clue about correct procedure. The bishop of Durham thrust the orb into the queen's tiny hand at the wrong time, and she, in shock, asked what she was to do with it. Even worse, the archbishop enthusiastically rammed the ring onto the wrong finger. Victoria almost cried out in pain.

After saying a short prayer, the archbishop placed the crown on her head, and Victoria was queen. The peers and peeresses donned their coronets, casting shimmering gold shadows against the walls. At "this most beautiful and impressive moment," she looked over toward Lord Melbourne, who gave her "such a kind" and "fatherly" look. Outside, guns were fired in the parks and from the tower, and drums beat. Victoria herself was "completely overcome."

The queen received homage from the archbishop, her uncles, and finally the peers, then removed her crown and took the sacrament alone. On cue, a ray of sunlight illuminated her head. The Duchess of Kent was in tears, but Victoria paid her little attention. "There was another most dear being present at this ceremony in the box immediately above the Royal Box, and who witnessed all; it was my dearly beloved Lehzen, whose eyes I caught when on the Throne, and we exchanged smiles."

Victoria saw her coronation as a state event, intended to increase patriotism, and had little recognition of its wider significance. Few of those who watched the five-hour ceremony were humbled into silence by the majesty of religion. Two of the train bearers gossiped loudly throughout. When the Lord Treasurer threw coronation medals to the lower galleries and choir, gentlemen and peers of the realm flung themselves into the fray, scrambling with "all the eagerness of children for sugar plums." Two aldermen were practically brawling on the floor, while a son of the Duke of Richmond succeeded in seizing twelve medals at once. Disraeli wrote to his sister, Sarah, that "the Queen looked very well, and performed her part with great grace and completeness, which cannot in general be said of the other performers; they were always in doubt as to what came next, and you saw the want of rehearsal." Although the queen was young and very small in stature, she was possessed of a great natural dignity and calm that made her appear more at ease than she was. "I have often seen that the *confidence of success* has been the *cause of the success itself,*" wrote Leopold, but it was good advice of which she had no need.

Then the bishop of Bath and Wells turned over two pages instead of one and declared to the queen that the service was over, so she promptly headed to leave the room. Consternation ensued—and everybody thought that the queen had fallen ill. She had to be summoned back so that she could withdraw to the chapel with proper pomp to the sound of the choir singing the "Hallelujah Chorus." In St. Edward's Chapel, sandwiches and bottles of wine festooned the altar, and beleaguered Lord Melbourne took several swigs to fortify himself for the rest of the service. Victoria then assumed the crown of state once more, took up the orb in one hand and the scepter in the other, and proceeded through the abbey to the robing room. Finally she could rest, and attempt to pull off the ring forced onto her plump little hand. She had to bathe it in cold water for about an hour, until she succeeded: "I did at last with great pain." Then she entered the state coach, weighed down by her orb, scepter, and crown, and returned to Buckingham Palace along the same winding route she had taken earlier

The queen arrived at the palace fizzing with pride. "You may depend on it," ventured an exhausted Lord Melbourne, hopefully, "that you are more tired than you think you are." Alas for him, she was buzzing with energy and rushed to give her beloved Dash a bath. After a small banquet with her family and Lord Melbourne, she stood on her mother's balcony and watched the fireworks put on for the public in Green Park. Greville commented, "The great merit of this Coronation is, that so much has been done for the people: to amuse and interest them seems to have been the principal object."

"I shall ever remember this day as the *proudest* of my life," wrote the new queen. Thousands had cheered her, every peer had paid her homage, and all this to a young girl who had once felt excluded and ignored, completely at the mercy of her tyrannical mother. She was, finally, queen.

39

❧

"He Is of the Greatest Use to Me"

He is not only a clever statesman and an honest man but a good and kind-hearted man whose aim is to do his duty for his country, and not for a party," Victoria declared of Lord Melbourne. "He is of the greatest use to me, both politically and privately." The young queen had become immediate friends with her prime minister.

Her new beloved friend, William Lamb, 2nd Viscount Melbourne, was nearing sixty and was the epitome of the Regency man: a connoisseur of wines, food, and women, a languid charmer adept at witty barbs and polite conversation. Despite his relaxed mien, he was a consummate politician, advancing his career through charm, charisma, and discretion. Now he turned his considerable energies toward pleasing Victoria.

Lamb had been born the second son into an ambitious family. A prodigious reader, he attended Eton and then studied at Trinity, Cambridge, at that time a college with scant academic renown. He later decided he had wasted his time, neither working hard nor pursuing vice with particular originality. He tried the bar and moved on to politics, but he was always distracted by the siren call of demanding, slightly histrionic women. A young man whose life had been signally devoid of passion, he admired those prone to intense, even excessive feelings, and he fell in love with Lady Caroline Ponsonby, the clever and witty daughter of the Earl of Bessborough, a woman so riven by passionate emotion that she was on the brink of suffering from nervous disease. He married her at the age of twenty-six, and even her wedding was too much for her: During the service, she tried to rip her dress, fainted, and had to be carried out of the church. Once the initial excitement had worn off, William grew weary of her behavior. He began to treat her with measured disdain, and his indifference only prompted her to further emotional excess in a bid to gain attention. Even worse, the young couple lived with William's family, who thought her ridiculous. After a miscarriage, she produced a son, Augustus, in 1807, but by the age of three he was suffering from seizures and showing signs of retarded intelligence.

Tormented by her husband's coldness and the absence of another child, in 1812 Caroline fell passionately in love with Lord Byron. To the shock of his friends, Lamb refused to chastise her or separate from her, applying his usual policy of avoiding direct action unless it was forced upon him. When Byron cooled, Lady Caroline was plunged into despair, cutting her wrists with broken glass in front of him at a ball. She soon began to lose her mind. Lamb, apparently at the behest of his parents, separated from her, but continued to care for her by accommodating her at his country home and visiting her regularly until her death in 1828. Society all agreed that he had been the perfect husband—and Victoria was entranced by his stoic loyalty. "Talked with Stockmar for some time upon various subjects, but principally about our favourite, Melbourne," she reported in her journal. "Spoke of the dreadful life his wife had led him and how very admirably he had behaved to her up to the very last."

Lamb entered Parliament in 1806 and moved up the ranks of the Whig party, becoming Foreign Secretary in 1822 and Home Secretary in 1830, after entering the House of Lords in 1829 on the death of his father. He pursued government absolutely, even if he did not always agree with it. He publicly supported Lord Grey's Reform Bill but privately dubbed it nonsense, despite his rapidly accelerating political career. In 1834, after Lord Grey was forced out of office, he became prime minister.

Until she was queen, Melbourne's interactions with Victoria had been limited, and largely driven by his customary caution. He dissuaded the king from forbidding the visit of Prince Albert and his brother, pointing out to him that it was almost impossible for him to decree Victoria's marriage. Less helpfully, he ranged himself on the Duchess of Kent's side in the dispute over Victoria's establishment, attempting to discourage the king from offering Victoria money to set up her own home, partly because he feared the duchess would embark on an offensive publicity campaign. But as soon as Victoria was on the throne, he transferred all his loyalties to her. Indeed, his life was much easier with queen than king. Instead of tactless, aggressive William IV, who badgered his ministers and tried to tell them what to do, he had a young, attractive girl who was quite open to being instructed about her rights. He encouraged her to believe that her role was to advise. In reality, she was legally entitled to do much more. As the constitutional historian Walter Bagehot put it:

> She could disband the army (by law she cannot engage more than a certain number of men, but she is not obliged to engage any men); she could dismiss all the officers, from the General's commander in chief downwards; she could dismiss all the sailors too; she could sell off all our ships at war and all our naval stores. She could make every citizen in the United Kingdom, male or female, a peer, she could make every parish in the United Kingdom a "university"; she could dismiss most of the Civil Servants; she could pardon all offenders. In a word, the Queen could, by prerogative, upset all the actions of civil government, by disbanding our forces, whether land or sea, leave us defenceless against foreign nations.

The queen's prerogatives were, in fact, not very well defined. Essentially, what mattered was what she could manage to do, without too much opprobrium, and Melbourne aimed to advise her that she could do little.

Intellectually, their characters were worlds apart: Victoria was impatient, decisive, and inflexible, whereas Melbourne was diplomatic and shied from confrontation or action. He could seem indifferent and sanguine, while the young queen was warm, emotionally involved, and devotedly loyal. They had in common great energy, a greed for experience and knowledge, and a relish for the sensual pleasures of life: food, wine, clothes, and affection. Just before Victoria came to the throne, Melbourne had been involved in a divorce case that gripped society. In 1831, he had become friendly with Caroline Sheridan, a granddaughter of the playwright, and just the type of highly demanding, vivacious woman he liked. He soon fell into the habit of calling every day on the charming young wife, who was just twenty-three years to his fifty, and whispers began that they were having an affair. In 1846, Caroline's husband, George Norton, a minor MP, brought a civil suit for damages against Melbourne, which essentially meant that the prime minister was being cited in a divorce case. Among the spectators was a young Charles Dickens, reporting on the case for *The Morning Chronicle.* Unfortunately for Mr. Norton, the witnesses could not say for sure that they had seen anything, and Lord Melbourne's letters to Caroline were merely prosaic notes on the hours he might call. Indeed, the nature of the latter were so trivial that the gallery erupted into hysteria. The case collapsed, and the friendship between Melbourne and Mrs. Norton ended soon after.

Lord Melbourne was exactly the sort of rakish Regency gentleman from whom the Duchess of Kent had attempted to separate Victoria. The young queen was, thus, very eager for his friendship, even receiving Mrs. Norton in an effort to please him. Up until her accession, Victoria had been surrounded by adults who attempted to control or undermine her: Melbourne flattered her, paid her every possible attention, and was ever willing to obey her summons to dinner or to a meeting. If she wished to complain for hours about her mother, he listened and offered comfort. "He was so kind when I spoke to him of the unhappy scene I had with poor Ma yesterday," she recorded in her journal. When she had lived at Kensington, she had perfected the art of hiding her feelings and dissembling to Conroy, but to Melbourne she could say exactly what she pleased. "I am sure none of your friends are as fond of you as I am," she informed him.

In Melbourne, Victoria had found a father figure. He tutored her patiently and feigned enthusiasm for her fascination with adolescent parlor games and jigsaws. "I have no doubt he is passionately fond of her as he might be of his daughter if he had one; and the more because he is a man with a capacity for loving without anything in the world to love," judged Greville. Melbourne's disabled son, Augustus, had died at the age of twenty-nine the year before Victoria ascended the throne, and he was, indeed, a kindly, affectionate man, utterly without wife or family (and also conveniently at Victoria's call, ready to spend hours with her at Windsor since he was a single man). Greville judged the queen's feelings for the prime minister *"sexual,* although She did not know it,"* but in fact they were more akin to a crush on a tutor. She wrote after taking communion on Christmas Day, "Lord Melbourne was there, the one I look up to as a father, and I was glad he took it with me." She had a keen desire for an older man on whose advice she could rely, and she felt very acutely her lack of knowledge about international affairs and political procedure.

Victoria was particularly delighted by the company of Lord Melbourne during her summer at Windsor. "I have seen a great deal of him, every day, these last 5 weeks and I have always found him in good humour, kind, good and most agreeable; I have seen him in my Closet for Political Affairs, I have ridden out with him (every day), I have sat near him constantly at and after dinner, and talked about all sorts of things." It was all quite beautiful. Victoria could have cozy chats with Lord Melbourne and convince herself that she was performing useful political work. As she wrote in her diary, she spent six hours a day with him, "an hour in the morning, two on horseback, one at dinner, and two in the evening." Urbane fifty-three-year-old Lord Palmerston, the Foreign Secretary, became the queen's helpmate on foreign issues. He advised her how to treat foreign kings and nobility and gave her frequent lessons in the history of international relations. But the queen felt more at home with foreign matters than domestic, and it was Melbourne upon whom she depended for the help she felt she needed with the latter.

"It is become his province to educate, instruct and form the most interesting mind and character in the world," declared Greville. Victoria could dissect her own character ad infinitum, and she knew Lord Melbourne would listen. She told him how she had trouble keeping her temper; he consoled her that a person who had a "choleric disposition" could not "help letting it out at times." She showered him with questions on everything from the treatment of servants to the behavior of cannibals, and he patiently gave his opinions. "He has such *stores* of knowledge," she enthused, "such a wonderful memory; he knows about everybody and everything; *who* they were and *what* they did; and he imparts all his knowledge in such a *kind* and agreeable manner." She was eager to know all about the

Hanoverian relations from whom she had been kept so separate, and she was constantly asking for stories about George IV, for, as she wrote, "he knew George IV *so* well" that it was "particularly curious." She analyzed herself endlessly and complained about her mother, and he indulged her, showering her with praise, sympathy—and bunches of roses. "Got a beautiful bouquet of flowers from Lord Melbourne," enthused Victoria, the recipient of expensive hothouse blooms in February 1838. "How kind of him to think of sending me flowers." The press began to venture sly hints that Melbourne and the queen might marry.

Lord Melbourne sometimes grew weary of the constant attendance and the compulsion to supply answers, but he knew that many envied his influence with the queen and were jealous of how he could visit her in Buckingham Palace or Windsor whenever he desired. The price of listening to complaints about the Duchess of Kent or spending hours playing parlor games in the drafty castle was worth it.

"Take care that Lord Melbourne is not King," the duchess wrote angrily, but she spat vitriol in vain. Melbourne had smoothly occupied the role of adviser and friend that the duchess had hoped would be the possession of John Conroy. He had also become the queen's private secretary, the only individual to be both prime minister and private secretary.

By constantly visiting the queen, Melbourne was not only guaranteeing her support but also attempting to minimize her perception that she had the right to meddle in affairs of state. William IV had been very sure of the royal prerogative, convinced he should be able to decree policy, dismiss governments, decide where Parliament sat, and regulate the marriages of his family. Victoria was told that she was able to advise, and she had been kept so isolated from William IV that he had never had the chance to suggest to her what she should claim as her rights. Through Melbourne's comforting fireside chats, the gradual transference of power from sovereign to Parliament was accelerated.

The Tories were infuriated. The politician John Wilson Croker, who thought that the prime minister piled Victoria with work so that she would be unable to cope and so would leave decisions to him, considered that "his situation is certainly the most dictatorial, the most despotic, that the world has ever seen. Wolsey and Walpole were in strait waistcoats compared to him." The queen, however, relished the work, and she took her own decisions, albeit on Melbourne's advice. For although she was stubborn and had a peremptory disposition, she was entirely persuadable with the prime minister, who won her with flattery and gentle persuasion—and there began problems.

When Victoria was appointing her ladies of the royal household, Lord Melbourne recommended women from great Whig families. The exquisitely beautiful Duchess of Sutherland became Mistress of the Robes, and eight Ladies of the Bedchamber were appointed, including two marchionesses, three countesses, and a baroness. These were positions of political influence, highly sought after, and the fact that Victoria had appointed Whigs alone angered the Tories. The women were the queen's constant companions, accompanying her on both informal drives out and public processions, and even taking important roles in ceremonies. A similar situation would be if the modern-day queen appointed her permanent personal companions entirely from the wives and relatives of cabinet ministers. The charmed inner circle of advisers, who would be privy to the queen's thoughts on politics, finance, and world affairs, and would possibly even offer advice themselves, were all Whigs.* Victoria grew passionately fond of them, particularly her beautiful Mistress of the Robes, the thirty-one-year-old Duchess of Sutherland. In her adoration of them, along with her hatred of all those in her mother's household, the seeds of a future disaster were sown.

The other problem was Melbourne's lack of interest in home affairs. He who had ignored the plight of the underpaid laborers who became known as the Tolpuddle Martyrs in 1834 wished to disregard the country's serious problem of poverty. When the queen praised Dickens's *Oliver Twist,* Melbourne complained: "It's all among Workhouses and Coffin Makers, and Pickpockets. . . . I don't like these things; I wish to avoid them; I don't like them in reality and therefore I don't wish to see them represented." Unsurprisingly, Lord Shaftesbury, then Lord Ashley, thought Lord Melbourne a bad influence on Victoria, describing his cynicism and "reckless language" as "pernicious" and a "perpetual source of poison to her mind." There was

---

*Their jobs were as companions and courtiers—Victoria had eight Maids of Honour and eight Ladies of the Bedchamber to care for her personal needs. Most were much older than she. All but two were middle aged.

growing sympathy for the poor, thanks to the novels of those such as Dickens, who depicted the miserable conditions of their lives, particularly those of the factory children whose situation so touched Ashley's heart. But Melbourne believed that eradicating poverty was useless—declaring that since such children of the underclass would "never do any good," parents should be allowed to send them out to work.

Melbourne's lack of interest in the social problems of his countrymen reflected how much he was a product of the Regency age, when the poor usually attracted little political attention. By the late 1830s, the ordinary people of England were clamoring for attention. Even a few years on from the depressions of the reform years, the laboring classes were still in crisis, casualties of the growth of industrialization and mechanization, suffering poverty, unemployment, and even severe hunger. Victoria was still riding the wild wave of popularity that had followed her accession, but it could not last forever.

"My birthday is come and gone and things are much changed," wrote the Duchess of Kent in August. She was feeling absolutely humiliated. It was clear that she was "overwhelmed with vexation and disappointment," as Greville commented. "Her daughter behaves to her with kindness and attention, but has rendered herself quite independent of the Duchess, who painfully feels her own significance."

Right from the beginning, the duchess was excluded. When Victoria moved her household to Buckingham Palace, she sent her mother to live in apartments some way from her. To add insult to injury, the queen ordered there to be a doorway made between her own room and that of Lehzen, intending to show everybody that she esteemed her old governess more highly than her mother. After consistently trying to see her daughter and being turned down, the duchess wrote to her that she should show her mother respect, or else the people would not love her. "For this reason it hurts me more for your sake than for my own, when you are not always quite attentive to me." It was simply awful that her daughter would not always attend to her while walking. "You see dear love, when you do not look after me, and if you do not stop for me, I am obliged to go with your ladies, which is not my place, as I am your mother." She demanded the rank and precedence of Queen Mother, but the queen refused. "It would do my mother no good," she pronounced. The duchess pointedly gave her ungrateful daughter a copy of *King Lear* for her nineteenth birthday.

At every possible opportunity, the duchess begged Victoria to receive John Conroy, hardly recognizing that she was making her own position worse. "I thought you would not expect me to invite Sir John Conroy after his conduct towards me for some years past, and still more so after the unaccountable manner in which he behaved to me, a short while after I came to the Throne," the queen wrote in August, indignant and angry. "I imagined you would have been amply satisfied with what I had done for Sir John Conroy, by giving him a pension of £3,000 a year, which only Ministers receive, and by making him a Baronet." Unluckily, the duchess did not agree, and harassed Victoria desperately to invite Conroy to the lord mayor's dinner in November. "The Queen should forgive what displeased the Princess," she decreed.

As well as harassing her daughter about Sir John, the duchess was demanding that her own debts be paid. Throughout the winter after Victoria received her money from the Civil List, her mother besieged her with angry letters and demands. "Saw Ma and oh what a scene did she make!" the young queen recorded in her journal. Victoria was sure that Conroy had stolen much of the duchess's money, and she had no intention of rewarding her mother for so depending on him. Melbourne oozed sympathy, telling the queen that she was unfairly "subjected to so much annoyance and importunity from a quarter in which your Majesty ought only to find assistance and affection." He agreed with her that Conroy was taking money, declaring that the duchess should have been able to manage on her income, "but not if *he* makes money by it." In March 1838, *The Times* reported that Conroy had creamed off the duchess's funds and that she owed £80,000. Years later, when the duchess finally opened her accounts, it became clear that Conroy had been neglectful and dishonest. There were no proper accounts, large sums were missing, and money that had been sent by Leopold was never credited. Much of this probably went to Prince Charles of Leiningen, who had expensive tastes.* Whatever the reason, the queen distrusted her mother and was desperate to resist.

---

*Whatever Conroy stole, he frittered the sums away, for he died poor in 1854.

Victoria took every worry about her mother to Lord Melbourne. He tried to lessen her resentment of the duchess by blaming Conroy, avowing that a woman "will do anything when she has given herself into someone's hands." He also made it clear that it would be very difficult to send the duchess away: "Spoke for some time of Ma, how much better it would be if Ma was not in the house and if she would go and visit her family; Lord Melbourne observed that that would be a great thing; for if she were to go away without going to her own family, it would be awkward and we should have to state the cause to the public; and make a cause of it."

Melbourne indulged the queen, denigrating the duchess severely as a "liar and a hypocrite" and the most "foolish" woman he had ever met, but his advice was cautious: Everything possible should be done to ensure that the public remained ignorant of the break between mother and daughter. Melbourne was entirely Victoria's ally in her effort to sideline her mother; he wished to be Victoria's sole adviser and have no interference, particularly from her family. He suggested to Victoria that she allow him to answer notes from the duchess formally, but Victoire would not be deterred. "My appeal was to *you* as my child," she replied, "not to the Queen."

The duchess and John Conroy were not the only ones infuriated by Victoria's admiring dependence on Melbourne. King Leopold had assiduously sent his niece advice, books, and letters and promoted himself as her protector, only to see himself supplanted. As soon as he heard she had come to the throne, he wrote, "Before you decide on anything important I should be glad if you would consult with me." Victoria replied carefully, writing: "How fortunate I am to have at the head of the Government a man like Lord Melbourne. . . . The more I see him, the more confidence I have in him." The queen of Great Britain was firmly telling the king of the Belgians that she planned to rule alone, in the best interests of her country.

Leopold could not believe that he had been relegated to the role of affectionate uncle, but no more. In March 1838, he demanded assistance from his niece. In 1831, Belgium had agreed to cede part of Luxembourg and Limburg to the Dutch. Seven years later, the Dutch wanted to assume possession of the territories, but Leopold, annoyed by years of hostilities, decided to refuse. He wrote to Victoria begging her to defend his decision. She consulted Melbourne and wrote firmly to Leopold that Britain would not assist him in this hostile act against the Dutch, for the treaty signed by

Belgium was binding and could not be broken, and it was his responsibility to reconcile his subjects to the inevitable. Indeed, she was rather piqued that he had even dared ask. As she agreed with Lord Melbourne, it was "rather hard" of her Uncle to appeal to her "feelings of affection for him" to conclude a political matter.

The first year of Victoria's reign had been a quite wonderful time of new experiences and ardent admiration from the public and politicians alike. But as 1838 wore on, the queen became irritable and easily vexed. She hated it when Lord Melbourne was unable to see her when she wished, because he was exhausted, or to attend her at all of her appointments. "This is most provoking and vexatious," she wrote. "I'm quite annoyed and put out when my agreeable daily visit does not take place." She was beginning to tire of the duties of queen, and she was bored of receptions and Drawing Rooms. "You lead rather an unnatural life for a young person," Lord Melbourne had told her. "It's the life of a man." She was growing tired of "living so much, if not entirely, with people so much older" than herself. The excitement had worn off, and Melbourne had to tell her that things would not change. "A queen's life is very laborious; it's a life of moments, hardly any leisure." She was worrying that she was not up to her duties. "I felt *how* unfit I was for my station," she complained at the end of the year.

With overwork and a constant round of dinners and appointments, Victoria was not taking care of her health. She shrugged off Melbourne's admonition that she should eat only when hungry, asserting, "I should be eating all day." As the poor food-loving queen wrote to her uncle less than a month after she came to the throne, "I have very pleasant large dinners every day." Heavy meals were a regular part of life at court, and Victoria's regular bouts of riding and dancing were no compensation. She was not walking enough, even though Lord Melbourne had threatened her that if she did not exercise more, she might lose the use of her legs. By the end of December, she weighed herself and to her horror found that she was nearly nine stone, or 126 pounds, "an incredible weight" for her height.

The role of queen had taken its toll on Victoria's health and had not altogether improved her character, advised as she was by indulgent Melbourne and by Lehzen, who always told her she was right, and surrounded by courtiers who praised her constantly. She had quickly acquired an imperiousness comparable to that of her Hanoverian uncles. Stockmar wrote in one of his frequent reports: "[She is] as passionate as a spoiled child, if she feels offended, she throws everything overboard without exception." "People must come to the opinion," Leopold had advised, *"It is of no use intriguing, because when her mind is once made up, and she thinks a thing is right,* no unearthly power will make her change." It was unfortunate counsel, for Victoria was as convinced of the excellence of her own decision as any Hanoverian, and she had a terrible tendency to think that those around her were compelled to dance to her whim.

40

Scandal

I have, alas! seen so much of bad hearts and dishonest and *double* minds, that I know how to value and appreciate *real worth*." So the queen claimed. But she was less objective than she thought, particularly toward those of her mother's household. Most of all, she hated thirty-two-year-old Lady Flora Hastings, the "amazing spy who would repeat everything she heard." She was ever eager to listen to gossip about Lady Flora, who she was sure was lover to Sir John Conroy.

When the court came back after the Christmas break in January 1839, the news spread that Lady Flora had shared a post chaise with Sir John on her journey from Scotland. This seemed to everybody a shocking revelation of intimacy, and indeed, it was only twenty or so years earlier that Charlotte and Leopold were almost not permitted to travel alone together at night after their wedding ceremony. To make matters worse, Lady Flora consulted Sir James Clark, the queen's doctor, suffering from a distended stomach and nausea. He prescribed a diet of rhubarb and rest.

By early February, the queen and Lehzen had reached a shocking conclusion: Lady Flora was carrying Sir John's child. "We have no doubt that she is—to use the plain words—*with child*!! Clark cannot deny the suspicion; the horrid cause of all this is the Monster and devil Incarnate whose name I forbear to mention, but which is the first word of the second line of this page." The queen's passion for drama encouraged her imagination to run riot. She so detested John Conroy that she thought it entirely in keeping that he might impregnate Lady Flora and keep her brazenly at court. Moreover, Clark did not contest her suggestion that the lady-in-waiting was pregnant, even though he had not examined her without her cumbersome corset and thick winter skirts. He had misdiagnosed the queen's own illness when she had been ill at Ramsgate, but now she had every faith in him.

The households of the queen and the duchess had long been at odds, and once the tales began, they ran unrelenting. By early February, Lady Tavistock, one of the queen's senior ladies, went to Lord Melbourne to tell him that he must take matters in hand—some of the ladies had begged her to "protect their purity." Melbourne summoned Clark, who, unfortunately, told him that he thought Lady Flora was probably pregnant but that they should wait and see how matters developed. Foolishly, Melbourne concurred with his plan, and so the vicious gossip continued, fueled in particular by Clark, who told Lady Portman, the next senior Lady of the Bedchamber after Lady Tavistock, that he believed Lady Flora was "privately married."

Lady Portman asked Clark to inform Lady Flora of their suspicions and extract the truth. Lehzen suggested he begin the interview aggressively, pronouncing, "You must be secretly married." Clark, puffed up at being the center of the household and consulted by so many great ladies, duly trotted off to bully Lady Flora. In great distress, she denied his accusations. She answered that the swelling was much reduced, but he refused to believe it. "You seem to grow larger every day—and so the ladies think." He then declared that nothing else but a full examination—that is, without her clothes—could satisfy the deep-rooted suspicions of the queen's ladies. Lady Flora remained firm. "I said, feeling perfectly innocent, I should not shrink from any examination however rigorous, but that I considered it a most undelicate and disagreeable procedure and that I would not be hurried into it." An unmarried virgin, she was naturally reluctant to undergo such an intimate examination, but Dr. Clark saw her refusal as an admission of guilt. The next day, February 17, Lady Portman visited the Duchess of Kent to describe their suspicions and to tell her that the honor of the court depended on the matter being quickly resolved. Either Lady Flora must submit to a medical examination to prove she was not pregnant, or she should resign.

Lady Flora had no choice. She requested to see James Clark and another physician, Sir Charles Clarke, who had known her since childhood. In front of her own maid and Lady Portman (who later had the delicacy to say that she had covered her eyes throughout—although the maid present claimed that she was right by the bedside, watching like a hawk), the doctors conducted their examination. They then issued a statement: "It is our opinion although there is an enlargement of the stomach, that there are no grounds for suspicion that pregnancy does exist, or ever did exist." She was, they noted, a virgin.

When the statement was released, the queen and her ladies were horrified. "The Court is plunged in shame and mortification at the exposure," Greville recorded. "[T]he palace is full of bickerings and heartburnings, while the whole proceeding is looked upon by society at large as to the last degree disgusting and disgraceful." The Duchess of Kent stepped up her attempts to make political capital out of the scandal; as Lord Holland noted, she "was very active, under cover of asking advice, in spreading the story and complaining to her friends personal or political of the cruelty practised and the plot contrived against a Lady of her household."

Greville blamed Melbourne for allowing "this disgraceful and mischievous scandal, which cannot fail to lower the court in the eyes of the world, and from a participation in which discredit the Queen's youth and inexperience can alone exempt her." He, surely, had the maturity to prevent such hysterical "tracasseries."

Ashamed of herself, the queen dispatched Lady Portman to convey her regrets and made an offer to see Lady Flora when she wished. Lady Flora told her she was too ill to receive her but agreed to a meeting one week later. When the two finally did meet, Lady Flora seemed "dreadfully agitated," the queen thought. "[She] looked very ill, but on my embracing her, taking her by the hand, and expressing great concern at what had happened—and my wish that all should be forgotten, she expressed herself exceedingly grateful to me, and said, that for Mamma's sake she would suppress every wounded feeling and would forget it etc." Lady Flora was moved by the queen's attempt to show contrition. She later wrote to her uncle, "She had endeavoured to show her regret by her civility to me, and expressed it most handsomely with tears in her eyes."

Lady Flora's family, however, were not willing to let the matter rest. When her brother received a letter from her saying her honor had "been most basely assailed," he dashed to London, determined to clear his sister's name. He went to see the prime minister and demanded of him why he had failed to keep quiet a group of chattering girls. The Duke of Wellington advised him to hush up the affair, for the sake of his sister's reputation and the Crown, but Hastings would not be told. He wanted to find the culprit. Lady Flora's mother wrote to the queen, insisting that she punish all those responsible for spreading slander about her daughter, and also requested that she dismiss Sir James Clark. Lord Melbourne replied, telling her that her suggestion was "so unprecedented and objectionable" that he could do no more than acknowledge he had read it.

The sorry story of the accusations soon leaked out. "The whole town has been engrossed for some days by a scandalous story at Court," Greville reported. Foreign newspapers began to print the details. Public opinion in London was particularly hostile to Lady Flora, partly because people could not bear to think badly of the queen. Anxious to show her as the innocent victim of a court cabal, Lady Flora's family published a letter she had sent on March 8 to her uncle by marriage, Hamilton Fitzgerald, in which she blamed Baroness Lehzen for concocting a "diabolical conspiracy" against the Duchess of Kent and herself. The letter was frank. She ended it, "I blush to send you so revolting a letter, but I wish you to know the truth, the whole truth, and nothing but the truth—and you are welcome to tell it left and right."

From that point onward, the Tory Hastings family was at war with Queen Victoria's largely Whig court. When Lady Flora's mother, infuriated that the queen would not dismiss James Clark, published her acerbic correspondence with Lord Melbourne in *The Morning Post* on April 9, matters hit a shocking high. Victoria scribbled in her journal that she "wished to have hanged the Editor and the whole Hastings Family for their infamy."

The queen no longer felt so penitent for accusing Lady Flora. Sir James Clark and Sir Charles had told Lord Melbourne that there had certainly been an enlargement in her womb and also remarked that it was possible that a woman could remain a virgin and yet be pregnant. Victoria was sure that time would prove that she had been correct. "It was too bad to have to endure this for such a nasty woman, as I said, and shall and will say, Lady Flora is."

The Tory press, eager to capitalize on the scandal, mounted attacks on Lord Melbourne, Lehzen, and the Whig ladies, as well as making snide suggestions about the queen. Victoria's reputation was in danger. Matters were also about to turn much worse.

In early May 1839, Melbourne's government managed a majority of only five on a crucial bill attempting to force the Jamaican sugar planters to accept the abolition of slavery. For Melbourne, who had long been losing the confidence of the House, the mere five votes were a humiliation. He wrote to the queen that he could not persevere with the bill with such scant chance of success, and offered his resignation. He begged her, "Meet this crisis with that firmness which belongs to your character and with that rectitude and sincerity which will carry your Majesty through all difficulties." His remonstrations were in vain: Victoria collapsed in tears. "The state of agony, grief and despair into which this placed me may be easier imagined than described! . . . That happy peaceful life destroyed, that dearest, kind Lord Melbourne no more my Minister." It took some effort to summon up the courage to see him, and when she did so, she gave in to her emotions.

> I really thought my heart would break; he was standing near the window; I took that kind, dear hand of his, and sobbed and grasped his hand in both mine and looked at him and sobbed out, "You will not forsake me"; I held his hand for a little while, unable to leave go; and he gave me such a look of kindness and affection, and could hardly utter for tears, "Oh! no," in such a touching voice.

Victoria was quite devastated. Her mother was plotting against her, she was being insulted by supporters of Lady Flora, and now her beloved Lord Melbourne was leaving. It was simply too much to take. She even lost her appetite—a rare occurrence.

Melbourne recommended she summon Lord Wellington and ask him to form a Conservative government. If he would not—for he was seventy years of age and rather deaf—then she would have to call upon Sir Robert Peel to be her prime minister. The queen found Peel dry and rude, in sad contrast to flattering, paternal Melbourne. Peel was actually shy, but he came across as distant and stiff. His father had made his fortune from the Lancashire cotton industry, educated his son at Harrow and Christchurch, and then bought him an Irish "pocket borough" to launch him in politics. Intellectually quick but always socially ill at ease, Sir Robert was uncomfortable at court, partly because he knew that people mocked him. "In all ways, his dress, his manner, he looks more like a dapper shopkeeper than a Prime Minister," compained Greville. Peel's table manners betrayed him: He gobbled, and cut "cream jellies with his knife." Unfortunately, he had made no effort to single Victoria out at court functions, and she resented him for ignoring her.

Predictably, the Duke of Wellington declared himself unable to lead, and the queen had to summon Sir Robert. "Oh!—how different, how dreadfully different, to that frank, open, natural and most kind, warm manner of Lord Melbourne." She thought Peel "such a cold, odd man," and in response, she behaved at her most grandiose. He complained that forming a government would be very difficult, since Lord Melbourne still had a majority, although small. The queen ignored his qualms and demanded to know what he proposed to do about her household. All her Ladies of the Bedchamber were from Whig families or married to important supporters of Lord Melbourne; they included the daughter of Melbourne's chancellor of the exchequer, the sister-in-law of Lord John Russell, and the Duchess of Sutherland, who was the Mistress of the Robes and sister of the Irish Secretary. Since Peel was trying to form a minority government, it was impossible for the queen's closest female associates to be the relatives of his most intent political opponents. He refused to promise that she could retain them all. Victoria was devastated. The ladies were her dear friends, and she could not imagine being without them. Moreover, of course, to appoint Tory ladies at the height of the Flora Hastings crisis would only strengthen the side of the dreadful Conroy and the Hastings family. After Peel departed, she sank into panic. "The awful incomprehensible change . . . drove me really to distraction, and with the exception of walking up and down the room and . . . writing another letter to Lord M. and my Journal I could do nothing."

Melbourne instructed the queen to make every effort to support the government. At the same time, he encouraged her to insist that she should be able to choose her own household. When Peel came to see her at one o'clock on May 9, the day after their first meeting, the queen's mind was made up. She reported to Melbourne that he "insisted on my giving up my Ladies, to which I replied that I *never* would consent, and I never saw a man so frightened." She vowed to keep all of her attendants. "The Mistress of the Robes and the Ladies of the Bedchamber?" Peel asked, incredulous. The queen was adamant: "All."

Charles Greville was not alone in thinking that the queen was harping on her ladies because she was "secretly longing to get back old ministers (if she could by any pretext or expedient)." Victoria was excessively loyal to those she loved. "The Queen of England will not submit to such trickery," she wrote to Melbourne. "Keep yourself in readiness for you may soon be wanted." It is very possible that Peel was manipulating her. He was not keen to form a government in a minority, and the queen's insistent desire to hold on to her ladies allowed him to force her to an impasse that would enable him to escape.

The queen always relished a fight, and she was determined to win. "Do not fear that I was not calm and composed," she flurried. "They wanted to deprive me of my ladies, and I suppose they would deprive me next of my dressers and my housemaids; they wished to treat me like a girl, but I will show them that I am Queen of England." Such stalwart behavior had served her well when she was being threatened by her mother at Kensington. Now she was queen, it was a disastrous approach.

Peel told the queen on the evening of May 9 that he could not form a government unless she could show him a gesture of confidence. She replied that she would give him her final answer that evening or in the morning, in accordance with Leopold's advice to always sleep on important matters. That night, Melbourne called a meeting of his cabinet, who decided that the queen should stay strong. He sent her a letter he suggested should be sent to his rival. She promptly followed his advice, telling Peel that she refused his request and could not consent to a course that was "repugnant to her feelings."

Peel replied next day, resigning, "humbly returning" into Her Majesty's hands "the important trust" she had been "graciously pleased to commit to him." Lord Melbourne, with his limping majority, returned to government, and the queen was delighted. She was quite sure she had acted in the right. At a ball on May 10 at Buckingham Palace for the visit of the eldest son of Tsar Nicholas I, Tsarevich Alexander, Hereditary Grand Duke of Russia, she was still flushed with her political triumph. "I left the Ball-room at a ¼ p.3, much pleased, as my mind felt happy."

"I acted quite alone, but I have been, and shall be, supported by my country, who are very enthusiastic about it, and loudly cheered me on going to Church on Sunday," she wrote to her uncle Leopold. He sent warm congratulations—what else could he do? Others were shocked. "She has made herself the Queen of a party," Greville complained. Even Stockmar declared it a "high trial of our institutions when the caprice of a girl of nineteen can overturn a great ministerial combination." He was quite baffled by Melbourne's indulgence. "How could they let the Queen make such mistakes, to the injury of the Monarchy?"

"This day I GO OUT OF MY TEENS," Victoria wrote three days later, on her twentieth birthday. At her birthday ball, she was charmed to finally have someone of her own age with whom she could dance. "The Grand Duke is very strong, that in running round, you must follow quickly, and after that you are whisked round like in a *Valse,* which is very pleasant." The ball ended at two o'clock, and she was quite satisfied. "I never enjoyed myself more. We were all so merry." The grand duke was handsome, dominant, exotic—and most of all, a safe flirtation, for they could never marry. Both the tsarevich and Victoria indulged themselves in fluttering their eyelashes and sitting close together. When the time came to say goodbye, he blanched and faltered out, "Words fail me to express all I feel." They kissed each other on the cheek. Victoria sighed and wrote of the "dear amiable young man, whom I really think (talking jokingly) I was a little in love with, and certainly attached to." The grand duke set quite a standard for other men, and for some time afterward she thought no one was "seen to advantage" next to him.

Meanwhile, Conroy had announced that he would leave the duchess's household and go abroad. The Duke of Wellington claimed full responsibility, averring that he had cajoled Sir John into leaving. More likely, Conroy had come to recognize that the queen would never admit her mother into her inner circle and would send her away when she married. He had no interest in being part of a dreary household in a London home, with no access to court. Since many suspected him of manipulating the Flora

Hastings affair, he had no chance of ever gaining any public sympathy. So he cut his losses, took the considerable sums he had managed to extract from Victoria and her mother, and fled, deserting the sickly Lady Flora and leaving the duchess to shift for herself.

Victoria was delighted by his departure, but still frustrated that she was unable to separate herself from her mother. She complained to Lord Melbourne "how dreadful it was to have the prospect of torment for many years" because of the duchess living with her. "He said it was dreadful, but what could be done?" As they both knew, the only way in which the duchess could be expelled without causing a scandal would be if Victoria married.

By June, Lady Flora had grown thin, weak, and very sick. She was feverish and utterly unable to eat. "Then she'll die," Lord Melbourne said. The queen was not convinced and was infuriated by her mother's tearful arguments on her lady's behalf. Victoria thought that Lady Flora was shamming illness to gain the sympathies of the newspapers and those at court.

Lord Holland worried: "Had it not been for the unlucky business of Lady Flora . . . enthusiasm in favour of the Queen . . . might have been confidently reckoned upon, but many amongst us are afraid that there will be little or no sympathy with her or her ladies." As Lady Flora's condition became known, her family began winning the support of the people. The arguments between the factions at court reignited, and the households of the duchess and the queen became even more bitterly opposed.

Lady Flora sickened in her room, vomiting repeatedly, and she was too unwell to sleep. Any court member who was severely ill would usually return to his or her family, but had Lady Flora returned home, people would have gossiped that she was pregnant after all and intent on hiding her condition. Her sister refused an invitation to come to the palace, and so Lady Flora, overheated in a room doctors thought unhealthy, lay suffering alone.

By June 26, even the queen had accepted that Lady Flora was dying, and she postponed a ball she had planned for that evening. She was told that she should make haste to call on Lady Flora if she wished to see her alive. Victoria went to visit, but it was more that she was concerned to see herself vindicated rather than out of any sympathy for a young woman on the brink of death.

I went in alone; I found poor Lady Flora stretched on a couch looking as thin as anybody can be who is still alive; literally a skeleton, but the body very much swollen like a person who is with child; a searching look in her eyes, a look rather like a person who is dying; her voice like usual and a good deal of strength in her hands; she was friendly, said she was very comfortable, and how very grateful for all I had done for her, and that she was glad to see me looking well. I said to her, I hoped to see her again when she was better upon which she grasped my hand as if to say "I shall not see you again." I then instantly went upstairs and returned to Lord Melbourne who said "You remained a very short time."

Lady Flora had expressed gratitude to the queen for all she had done for her in the hope that she might make an apology. But Victoria refused to allow regret into her heart. She was so angry that she even said to Lord Melbourne: "It was disagreeable and painful to me to think there was a dying person in the house."

On Friday, July 5, Lady Flora breathed her last. Victoria reported that "the poor thing died without a struggle and only just raised her hands and gave one gasp." She told Lord Melbourne, "[I] felt *no* remorse, I felt *I* had done nothing to kill her." Few agreed. Although there was gossip that Lady Flora died of a botched abortion, most people believed that she was innocent, denied comfort in her last days by the cruelty of the ladies-in-waiting and indeed the queen. Victoria was hissed while riding in Hyde Park and catcalled at Ascot by aristocratic ladies, Lady Sarah Ingestre and the Duchess of Montrose. Shouts of "Mrs. Melbourne" followed her. All the wonderful, effusive loyalty seemed to have disappeared in a flash.

A few days after Lady Flora's death, a postmortem was carried out. A tumor was found on her liver, and the doctors declared her womb absolutely in the "healthy virgin state." On July 10, her body was taken from Buckingham Palace to St. Catherine's Wharf, for its journey to Scotland. The procession was arranged for four o'clock in the morning, in the hope of avoiding crowds. The route was lined all the way, however, some of the spectators shouting insults and throwing stones. One man shook his fist at the coach sent by the queen and shouted, "What's the use of her gilded trumpery after she has killed her?"

The Morning Post exploited the public anger. *"The Times* may continue to treat the late deep tragedy enacted at the Palace as a farce but we may rest assured that it will be brought forward before Posterity with full effect and that Buckingham Palace will be as famous in future ages as that of Holyrood House for the cruel immolation of its victim, even in the Queen's presence, with this difference, that Mary had no hand in the tragical affair." Suddenly, everyone's favorite queen was being compared to a murderer. Lord Darnley, aggressive husband of Mary, Queen of Scots, had grown jealous that his wife was having an affair with her private secretary, David Rizzio. In 1566, he and a group of co-conspirators murdered the innocent man in front of Mary herself.

One pamphlet, "The Dangers of Evil Counsel," put the matter in the starkest terms: "The cause here advocated is that of female innocence, slandered and persecuted to death: it is the cause of the weaker party, oppressed by power." Subtitled "a voice from the grave of Lady Flora Hastings to Her most gracious Majesty the Queen," the pamphlet was more sympathetic than some to Victoria, avowing support for the "cause of our innocent young Queen herself 'surprised,' 'betrayed' by evil suggestions and evil counsel into that which she knew not." The "Warning Letter to Baroness Lehzen by a Voice Beyond the Grave" blamed the queen for ignoring her mother and paying too much attention to Lehzen. "The Palace Martyr" compared the ladies-in-waiting to a pack of hunting dogs, and concluded:

> *Strange destiny that Britain's mighty isle*
> *Should hang dependent on a school girl's smile.*

In September, *The Morning Post* printed an angry letter from the Marquess of Hastings, alongside the publication of various correspondence, including Lady Flora's statement, the letters of Lord Melbourne, and Lady Portman's statement. The marquess announced that he had been told that if he brought his case to the House of Lords, it would "be immediately silenced as an attack upon the Throne." Popular support was behind him. A large wax model of the unfortunate Lady Flora was paraded around the country, garnering huge audiences as it did so. As Greville put it, the whole Lady Flora Hastings affair had been "a horrible, disgraceful and mischievous mess."

41

A Way of Settling It

"O ur little humbug of a queen is more endurable than the rest of her race," declared George Eliot, "because she calls forth a chivalrous feeling." The country soon forgot Lady Flora, and the queen was restored to some, if not all, of her previous levels of popularity. She, however, was feeling isolated and lonely, struggling with the realization that ruling meant more than delicious rides and chats with Lord Melbourne. "Living but for your duty to your country," wrote Feodora to Victoria, "difficult as it is, will prove to you a source of happiness." But the queen was wearying of living for duty alone.

With Victoria feeling beleaguered, Uncle Leopold picked an auspicious time to suggest a visit from her Coburg cousins. Victoria had long been reluctant to invite them, for she felt that her uncle was trying to thrust her into the arms of Albert. As she wrote in the year after she became queen, she wished "to enjoy two or three years more" of her "present young girlish life" before entering upon "the duties and cares of a wife." Victoria was naturally afraid of childbirth. It was impossible not to think of the abrupt death of her cousin Charlotte. She emphasized that she did not plan to give up her single life until 1840 at the earliest. She had clear reasons: She was "not yet quite grown up" and "not strong enough in health," and she was also overwhelmed with business that "marrying now would render still more fatiguing." Albert was a few months younger than she. "It would not do, were I to marry a boy, for so I rate a man of 18 or 19." Most of all, a queen's consort should be "perfect in the English language; ought to write and speak it without fault, which is far from being the case now." She detested the idea that she was being compelled to marry, for, as she wrote, "the whole subject was an odious one" that she "hated to decide about."

Now, however, the queen was willing to consider marriage if it meant escaping her mother. As she had complained to Lord Melbourne, the duchess had asserted that "she would never leave me as long as I was unmarried." Her minister's reply was swift and teasing. "Well, then," he said with a smile. "There's *that* way of settling it." The following day, she mentioned Albert of Saxe-Coburg. "Cousins are not very good things," a doubtful Melbourne replied, noting that the Coburgs were disliked by many of the foreign royals, particularly the tsar. He was too polite to tell her that they were also unpopular in England. He had remarked to Lord Palmerston when the king was trying to prevent Albert's first visit, in 1836, "We have Coburgs enough." He did, however, put it to the queen that Germans smoked incessantly and were reluctant to wash their faces.

Although she remembered Albert as a sleepy, awkward young man outshone by his brother, Victoria had enjoyed his company, and she knew that he had been brought up with the notion that he would be her husband. She would not, however, be hurried. "I may not," she wrote carefully, "have the feeling for him that is requisite to ensure happiness. I *may* like him as a friend, and as a *cousin,* and as a *brother,* but not *more.*" She begged her uncle to ensure that Albert knew there was no engagement between them. "I am anxious that you should acquaint Uncle Ernest, that if I should like Albert, that I can make *no final promise this year,* for, at the *very earliest,* any such event could not take place till *two or three years hence.*" Indeed there was "no anxiety evinced in this country for such an event." She had embraced the visit of her cousins while a lonely girl at Kensington Palace, but now she was queen. "We have had the Grand Duke of Russia here for some time," she wrote a little pointedly to Albert. "I liked him extremely."

The queen's desire to escape her mother did not outweigh her passionate attachment to her independence. She loved being her own mistress, relished being answerable to no one, and was proud of her ability to make decisions. After a childhood witnessing her mother being dominated by John Conroy, she never wished to feel herself similarly cowed.

News that Albert might visit England prompted some of Victoria's male subjects to declare themselves. One Ned Hayward bombarded the Home Office with letters wondering whether Victoria might marry him. Once, when she was riding in Hyde Park, he tried to waylay her and thrust a letter into her tiny hand. He was promptly arrested and later imprisoned. The *Penny Satirist* magazine exploited the lovesick swains by printing letters purporting to be from admirers.

> *I find it hard to love a Queen. I see her lovely features so often in picture shops, and her name is too often mentioned to effect a speedy cure. I must find some retreat, where no journals come, where no picture shops are, and where her name is never, or seldom, heard. I must find some Cave, and live like a hermit, and write about her till I die, or make a perfect cure. . . . Could I only respect her as my Queen, then I should do; but her sweet lips, her pure bosom, her lovely eyes, are eternally before me.*

The queen's fine bosom was a perennial attraction. A much later satire on her invasive admirers in the weekly magazine *The Mysteries of London* featured a young boy, Henry Holford, scampering around the palace, dazzled and bewildered, smitten with Victoria's fine figure and "fantastic bust," enjoying an "unknown and unaccountable species of happiness in recalling to mind and pondering all that had fallen from her lips."

Albert seemed not to be enjoying fevered dreams about the prospect of intimacy with the queen of England. On his twentieth birthday, he wrote a characteristically pompous letter to his brother: "Let us try all the more to attain something perfect—general education, elasticity of the brain. That is what gives great men such power to rule over others. You were born to a position that required such qualities. Fate seems to have chosen me for a similar or rather more difficult position." Even though Stockmar had been diligently training him for the role of co-sovereign, the young prince was dubious about his bride-to-be. He wrote haughtily that Victoria was "said to be extremely stubborn . . . her extreme obstinacy at war with her good nature." Worst of all, she was obsessed with court frivolities. "She is said to take not the slightest pleasure in nature, to enjoy sitting up late at night and sleeping late into the day." In time, he mused to his old tutor, these "gloomy prospects" would worsen, as her bad habits became established.

Albert and Victoria were, on paper, very unsuited. She liked bustle and city life; he preferred quiet reading and country pursuits. Victoria was happy to live in public, surrounded by courtiers and friends. Albert preferred solitude. She was warm, while he was stiff and standoffish and found it impossible to be gallant in the expected way. He was utterly unused to the role of a courtier. As he had demonstrated so disastrously in 1836, he could not disguise his lack of appetite for the endless balls and dinners the young queen so adored. Still worse, he was nonplussed by England, horrified by the seeming frivolity of the upper classes and bewildered by the widespread materialism. The dreary food sickened him, the dull, rainy weather gave him a headache, and he was confused by the aggressive politics and brash newspaper culture. The king of the Belgians, who had spent the previous years fulminating about the government's plans to reduce his pension, was hardly likely to inspire his nephew with optimism about his prospective homeland. Albert was such a patriot that his uncle's attempts to awaken him to the romantic beauties of the Latin world had failed. He traveled to the Italian lakes, Milan, Venice, northern Italy, and Switzerland, and saw the places that were firing the great poets with inspiration and filling amateur travelers with the desire to write, but he remained unconvinced. Germany, he thought, was vastly superior.

Albert liked to play the stoic, and he embraced the opportunity to do so over the negotiations about the marriage. He insisted that Uncle Leopold know what a great sacrifice he was making for the Saxe-Coburg family and Germany. As he gloomily lectured his uncle, "troubles are inseparable from all human positions and . . . therefore if one must be subject to plagues and annoyances, it is better to be so for some great or worthy object than for trifles and miseries." Unfortunately for Albert, Leopold was deaf to self-pitying emotional blackmail and remained determined on his course. He needed a source of influence in the court, for his niece had proved dismayingly unsupportive of his various foreign policy schemes. Albert would marry Victoria, and it was simply a case of waiting for her to make up her mind. Meanwhile, Albert was sent off to sample the joys of Italy once more, accompanied by Stockmar. The trip also had a greater purpose: to separate him from his beloved brother, Ernest.

In Florence, Albert studied hard and allowed Stockmar to persuade him to attend balls. He made sure that everyone knew how much he was suffering. "I have thrown myself into the vortex of society," he moaned. "I have danced, dined, supped, paid compliments, been introduced to people and had people introduced to me, chattered French and English, exhausted every conceivable phrase about the weather. . . . You know my passion for this sort of thing, and must therefore admire my strength of character." Stockmar was beginning to despair over Albert's refusal to play the gallant. Victoria loved compliments and flirtation, but Albert was "too indifferent and too reserved" with women. How was he to charm the girlish English queen? "He will always have more success with men than women," sighed Stockmar. The king of the Belgians was very frustrated. As one who had worked hard when young to insinuate himself into Charlotte's heart, he was more than a little irritated by a nephew who had a glittering marriage lined up for him on a plate but who obstinately refused to cooperate, grumbling instead about Victoria's passion for balls, dinners, and late nights. Leopold, however, forged ahead, hoping that he simply had to push the two together for love to grow. The queen agreed to host her cousin, and Leopold promptly made arrangements to dispatch him, with Ernest.

On October 10, 1839, the two brothers arrived at Windsor from Dover, still suffering a little from seasickness after a rough crossing. Victoria had worked herself into a nervous frenzy while waiting. As soon as she clapped eyes on her visitor, she was delighted. "It was with some emotion that I beheld Albert—who is *beautiful*," she enthused in her diary. She was quite charmed, deciding him "so excessively handsome, [with] such beautiful eyes, an exquisite nose, and such a pretty mouth with delicate mustachios and slight but very slight whiskers; a beautiful figure broad in the shoulders and a fine waist."

The cousins' trunks had been delayed, and so Albert and Ernest found themselves without formal clothes to attend their grand dinner. They were obliged to remain in their rooms (much to Albert's satisfaction, no doubt), and Victoria was somewhat piqued. Happily, they were able to join the party after dinner.

Two days after her cousins' arrival, Victoria wrote her uncle a letter to make his heart sing. "Albert's *beauty* is *most striking,* and he is most amiable and unaffected—in short, very fascinating." Under the full beam of her admiration, Albert blossomed. He managed to talk engagingly with her in German, and even to flirt. He knew very well that his prospects otherwise were somewhat meager. If he had been born forty or so years earlier, he might have made his name fighting in the Napoleonic Wars. Now, in a time of peace, he was an insignificant minor royal.

On show to the court and indeed the world, Albert tried hard to fit in and make himself agreeable. There were no reports of fatigue or early bedtimes; instead, he danced with the queen on Friday night, "so beautifully," she told Lord Melbourne, rode with her on Saturday and sat beside her at church on Sunday. By Sunday afternoon, Victoria was quite entranced. Seeing the cousins, she said, "had a good deal changed my opinion (as to marrying)." Lord Melbourne advised her to take a week to make a decision. But Victoria, decisive as ever, told her minister on the following day that she "had made up [my] mind" to have Albert. She thought they should be engaged for a year, whereas Melbourne judged they should marry more swiftly, probably because he thought a long engagement would be unpopular with the public. "You will be much more comfortable," he said, rather tearfully. "A woman cannot stand alone for any time in whatever position she may be." He knew that he was losing his old position of being prime adviser and friend to the queen.

Victoria had enjoyed playing the role of the flirtatious virgin queen, retreating behind Lord Melbourne when she pleased. She had relished her independence. But now she was about to surrender it to a young man who had plenty of book learning but no practical experience of politics and little theoretical knowledge. She judged that Albert would be a malleable consort who would obey her and do exactly as she wished. In a sense, she wanted a wife. It is fitting that the queen praised Albert's physical beauty, rather than his mind or his strength, using words such as "fascinating," very much in the way a man might describe a woman. For in some respects she occupied the typically masculine role: She had the power, riches, and judgment and wanted a handsome young spouse to sit by her at dinner and ride out with her.

As queen regnant, Victoria could not receive a proposal. "How? I asked, for that in general such things were done the other way—which made Lord Melbourne laugh." She would have to propose to "dearest Albert" herself. The following morning, only five days after Albert's arrival, she roused her courage. At half past twelve she sent for him to come to her alone. After a few slightly awkward minutes, she managed to express herself:

> *I said to him that I thought he must be aware* why *I wished him to come, and that it would make me too* happy *if he would consent to what I wished (namely to marry me); we embraced each other over and over again, and he was so kind, so affectionate; Oh! to feel I was, and am, loved by such an Angel as Albert was too great a delight to describe! he is perfection; perfection in every way—in beauty—in everything! I told him I was quite unworthy of him and kissed his dear hand.*

The queen of England was engaged. Victoria had one stricture: Her mother must not be told.

42

〜❦〜

Passing like a Dream

Afer Mary Tudor's disastrous marriage to Philip of Spain, the country was content for Elizabeth I to remain single, pleased at the way her favorites remained just that, never in charge of policy. Queen Anne suffered fourteen failed pregnancies and a marriage so chilly that she took refuge in a close friendship with the reviled Sarah, Duchess of Marlborough. And William and Mary had been successful monarchs by any estimation, but William had essentially invaded England and demanded to be co-regent with Mary, who had the claim to the throne. In sum, the husbands of England's queens had won reputations as either aggressive invaders or cruel leeches. A man may have an unpopular wife but preserve his own reputation largely intact, pitied, if anything, for being tempted by such a shrew. But a woman cannot remain so untouched by the character of her husband. If she chooses wrongly, she is seen as weak, lacking in judgment, and worst of all, unworthy of power.

Albert's strategy of complaining that he was making a great sacrifice to marry Victoria worked well. After the queen had proposed, she sat down to write to Uncle Leopold. "I love him more than I can say and I shall do everything in my power to render this sacrifice as small as I can," she scribbled. "These last few days have passed like a dream to me, and I am so much bewildered by it all that I hardly know how to write." Albert had to retire to bed early, suffering from a violent nosebleed. Victoria was showering him with passionate words and physical displays of love, and he, who had lived in a cool world of reason since the flight of his mother, was stunned. "I am often puzzled to believe that I should be the object of so much affection," he told Stockmar. "I cannot write; I am at this moment too much bewildered to do so . . . the climax has come upon us with surprise, before we could have expected it." He was, nevertheless, not too bewildered to try to assert his authority. He was careful to cast the scene so that he was in control, dominating the young queen physically and suggesting that she confessed her love rather than asked for his consent. "Yesterday in a private audience Victoria declared her love for me, and offered me her hand, which I seized in both mine and pressed tenderly to my lips."

Resignedly, Uncle Leopold agreed not to let the news slip to his sister. "As everyone says," he wrote, "she cannot keep her mouth shut and might even make bad use of the secret if it were entrusted to her." The Flora Hastings affair had destroyed Victoria's last shreds of trust in her mother, and she was also perhaps a little keen to hurt her by keeping her engagement secret. Moreover, she wanted time to plan. She knew that the duchess was eager to remain with her daughter, even after she married, and she was determined to live without her.

The queen had a full month to bask in Albert's affection and the congratulations of those in her entourage who always praised her, whatever she did. Melbourne expressed his pleasure, and Lehzen declared herself very happy. Ernest tactfully retired to his room, complaining he had stomach fever.

The young couple relished the sensation of falling in love. They sat together in the queen's small blue sitting room, and even work became an excuse for amorous exchange. "I signed some papers and warrants etc and he was so kind as to dry them with blotting paper for me. We talked a good deal together, and he clasped me so tenderly in his arms, and kissed me again and again." Albert was playing the subservient, helpful suitor. He behaved impeccably at the great dinners and balls and willingly rode out with Victoria. When he accompanied her to review troops in Hyde Park, she noted enthusiastically that he wore white cashmere breeches with "nothing under them." He gave her a lock of his hair; she offered him more costly gifts: a ring engraved with the date of their engagement and a seal that she had worn. They stood together by the fire and asked each other, "Did you expect it?"

Albert told Victoria that he had no interest in lovely women and actually made a habit of trying to "spite" those feted as great beauties by ignoring them. Although his comment contained the unfortunate implication that she was not beautiful, the queen was jealously delighted to hear that he would be immune to the charms of the handsome women at her court. The role of king's mistress was always hotly sought after as an access to power, and indeed the king who declined to take a mistress was often unpopular with his courtiers, for a woman in such a position was a useful channel for those who wished for favors. Since Victoria, the guardian of a pure succession, could hardly take lovers, families anxious for influence would naturally hope that Albert might be tempted to at least befriend a lady at court. The queen had no desire to be humiliated on a personal level, and after the fracas and divisions created by her mother, who had set up her own separate court in her house, she intended her husband to be entirely a part of her establishment, with no favorites or special courtiers. The route to power and influence would be through her alone.

"We sit so nicely side by side on that little blue sofa; no two Lovers could ever be happier than we are!" she wrote. "He took my hands in his, and said my hands were so little he could hardly believe they *were* hands, as he had hitherto only been accustomed to handle hands like Ernest's." Albert had pressed the hands of many ladies in Bonn and elsewhere, and surely Stockmar's efforts to educate him for marriage had involved a trip to a courtesan, but he was presenting himself as a perfectly virginal lover.

Albert said anything to please, promising that he would not meddle or even involve himself in politics. Indeed, he made it seem as if he would be content to occupy the role of the wife of a king: a decorative helpmate who assisted in social matters but kept aloof from politics. Secretly, though, the great lover was a little less at ease. He complained to Stockmar of the horrors of the food (indeed, he declared that many of his party had fallen ill) and the damp climate. "I shall never cease to be a true German, a true Coburg and Gotha man," he averred.

On November 10, 1839, almost a month after the proposal, Victoria finally decided to tell her mother the news that everybody else knew. The duchess herself surely suspected, but she pretended surprise. As the queen reported, she "took me in her arms and cried, and said, though I had not asked her, still that she gave her blessing to it, and seemed delighted." She then embraced Albert, telling him "that she was *as* anxious for his happiness" as for Victoria's.

On November 14, Albert's visit came to an end, and the young queen was devastated. She kissed him over and over and "leant on that dear, soft cheek, fresh and pink like a rose," once more employing language characteristic of a man describing a woman. When he left, she abandoned herself to a luxurious grief, thrilling to her feelings in her diary. "Oh! how I love him, how intensely, how devotedly, how ardently!"

Albert put his years of book learning to good use, punctuating his trip home by writing flowery messages to his betrothed. "Your image fills my whole soul," he told her the day after his departure from Windsor. "Even in my dreams I never imagined that I should find so much love on earth. How that moment shines for me when I was close to you, with your hand in mine." The young couple wound each other up to further pitches of hyperbole. "How happy do you make me with your love!" burbled Victoria. "Oh! my Angel Albert, I am quite enchanted with it! I do not deserve such love! Never, never did I think I could be loved so much."

Now that the engagement was no longer secret, the queen was telling everybody her feelings, a little too much. "Thank God the secret is out now!" she enthused. "It makes me very happy because I can talk about you so much more, my own dearest Angel." Lord Melbourne was among those not entirely convinced by her rhapsodies. She told him that Albert had declared no interest in other women. "No," he replied, "that sort of thing is apt to come later."

Not long after Albert's departure, the duchess embarked on a campaign to ensure that the marriage would not alter her position. She demanded to live with the young couple after the wedding, informing Lord Melbourne that she was "quite a slave, in fact, and wasn't mistress of her own house or anything in the house, and now she didn't wish to go." She tried emotional blackmail, complaining that even Prince Albert's valet had known about the news before her. But Victoria remained firm, and said that her subjects did not wish the duchess to live with her after she was married. The duchess had tried to convince the young Princess Victoria to do as she wished by telling her that the people only esteemed her if she obeyed her mother, and now the queen was using the same argument to the duchess. She would have to leave.

While at Windsor, Albert had promised Victoria his subservient assistance, but ambitious Leopold wanted him to be co-ruler, and encouraged him to aspire to more. The tone of Albert's letters shifted from the sentimental to the demanding. Leopold, who regretted not accepting a title when he was betrothed to Charlotte, persuaded his young nephew to request a large allowance and a peerage, to ensure that Albert would retain power and riches if Victoria died early in the marriage. "It needs but the stroke of your pen to make me a peer and to give me an English name," Albert insisted. Victoria was reluctant, for she desired Albert to be her husband and helpmate, not a peer in his own right with a seat in the House of Lords. Only ten days after he had left Windsor, she informed him that it was impossible to meet his demands. She wrote to her uncle, making it clear that the decision to withhold a peerage from Albert had been her own. "The whole Cabinet agrees with me in being strongly of the opinion that Albert should *not* be a Peer. Indeed, I see everything against it and nothing for it; the English are very jealous at the idea of Albert's having any political power, or meddling with affairs here."

The young queen had hardly had a chance to gauge the feelings of the English people. Albert had only been gone for a week. She wrote to him suggesting he give the matter no further thought, for "some of the papers (who are friendly to me and to you) expressed a hope that you would not interfere:—now, tho' I know you never would, still, if you were a peer they would all say the Prince meant to play a political part."

The engagement had set off a battle between King Leopold and Lord Melbourne. The king of the Belgians wrote to Melbourne implying that Albert's excellent qualities would make him a great consort, and that he should be accorded the status of a king. In response, Melbourne silkily made it clear that Victoria alone was the ruler. Albert's role would be that of a wife, welcome only to "give advice on occasions of difficulty and crisis which in this country are sure to arise and in which it will be natural that the Queen should look to her husband for support and assistance." Melbourne hoped that Victoria would successfully "reconcile the authority of a Sovereign with the duty of a wife." It was quite clear which role he thought should be paramount: Victoria should be guided to make the best decisions for her kingdom, and if they did not coincide with the desires of Albert (and indeed, Leopold), then this could not be helped. The king of the Belgians was infuriated, but what could be done? The queen was the queen.

Finally Albert relented. "As regards my peerage and the fears of my playing a political part, dear beloved Victoria," he wrote comfortingly, "I have only one anxious wish and one prayer: do not allow it to become a matter of worry to you. Let the papers and people, whoever they may be, be as angry with me as they like; only do not let it cause you to mistrust my love." Secretly, he had been unsure about accepting a peerage, for he was proud of his German roots. Uncle Leopold shot off a letter to Victoria in a temper. "He appears to be nettled because I no longer ask for his advice," Victoria wrote to Albert. "Dear Uncle is given to believe that he must rule the roost everywhere." She was sending a subtle message to Albert: Their uncle would not influence her.

Victoria and Albert clashed again. She suggested he take Lord Melbourne's private secretary, Mr. Anson, as part of his household. Albert protested that Victoria was showing too much favor to Melbourne and the Whigs and implied that she was appointing people to his household as "party rewards." He had typically pompous ideas of the sort of people he expected. "Let them be either of very high rank, or very rich, or very clever, or who have performed important services for England," he decided. He wanted equal numbers of Whigs and Tories (no repetition of the bedchamber crisis for him), and above all he wished that "they should be well-educated men and of high character," a tall order since he was an unpopular German prince with only a small allowance. The queen was exasperated by the suggestion that Mr. Anson was not of sufficient rank or intelligence. "You may rely on my care that you should have proper people," she countered.

Really, Albert wanted Germans, not Englishmen. He had not been impressed by the politicking, heavy-drinking, frivolous English courtiers who seemed so ignorant of philosophy and science. He wanted to keep his old friends with him, but Victoria refused, on Melbourne's advice. Neither wanted him to establish a separate German court, which would be excessively unpopular. She told him that she would choose his people. "I am distressed to tell you what I feel you do not like, but it is necessary," she wrote. Albert was powerless. Just like the wife of a king or prince (as in the case of Princess Caroline, landed with Lady Jersey, mistress of her husband, as a lady-in-waiting), Albert would be given people he did not know and would have to make the best of it. Unsurprisingly, the groom-to-be was growing nervous. He weighed up the pros and cons, and still he felt confused. "Hope, love for dear Victoria, the pain of leaving home, the parting from very dear kindred, the entrance into a new circle of relations, all meeting me with the utmost kindness, prospects the most brilliant, the dread of being unequal to my position."

On November 23, the queen announced to the Privy Council her impending marriage. Carefully she read out the declaration written by Lord Melbourne, her hands trembling. Afterward, the Duchess of Gloucester (once Princess Mary) asked if Victoria was nervous. "Yes," Victoria replied, "but I did a much more nervous thing a little while ago." Which was? the duchess inquired. "I proposed to Prince Albert."

The Privy Council was cautious about the queen's choice of husband, and the country was largely unenthusiastic. All were keen for her to produce heirs to prevent the return of the dreaded king of Hanover, but Albert seemed too young, too inexperienced, too poor, and most of all, too German. A Prince of Orange would have been grander, and Victoria's cousin George, Duke of Cambridge, more loyal to England. Albert also suffered from his association with King Leopold, who was unloved by the English for continuing to take their money after marrying a Catholic princess. Lehzen, the scapegoat for Victoria's unpopular decisions since the Flora Hastings affair, was blamed for insinuating another German into the bosom of the English royal family.

He comes the bridegroom of Victoria's choice
The nominee of Lehzen's vulgar voice;

He comes to take for "better or for worse"
England's fat queen and England's fatter purse.

Concerns were raised over the union of cousins. There were rumors that Albert was a secret Catholic who would turn his wife Papist. Victoria was typically exasperated, complaining to Albert that the Tories were ridiculous in agitating because it was utterly impossible for her to marry a Catholic, since the very act would mean she would forfeit the Crown. The Duke of Wellington demanded in Parliament that Albert's religion be declared to reassure the English that the country was "still a Protestant state." Melbourne argued and Victoria raged.

Queen Victoria's marriage was a matter of national concern. At half past ten one December night, a would-be suitor scaled the iron gates leading to Windsor Castle, ambled across the park, and appeared at the grand entrance, pronouncing, "I demand entrance into the castle as the King of England." The porter calmly addressed him as "Your Majesty" and took him to a police inspector who was on duty. The gentleman, it was discovered, had recently been released from a lunatic asylum, and, he told his inquisitors, "like all men who wanted wives, he was looking after one." The queen, he thought, would make him an excellent housekeeper.

Other men were similarly convinced that when Victoria smiled coyly out of her portraits, she was directing her soft gaze at them. One Scotsman made a special pilgrimage to Windsor and soon became so overwhelmed by spotting his beloved at a distance that he began to behave wildly. He was arrested when he fell into a frenzy as he saw the queen appear on the terrace. A few years later, another admirer, Edmund Jones, hid in an apartment at Buckingham Palace, rolled around on the bed, and then started to pocket available items, including a sword. He had already visited once before and this time he was found under the queen's sofa, next to her bedroom. At his trial, he claimed he had been lurking around the palace for nearly a fortnight: "And a very comfortable place I've found it. I used to hide behind the furniture and up the chimneys in the day time; when night came, I walked about, went into the kitchen and got my food. I have seen the Queen and her Ministers in council, and have heard all they said." Jones boasted that he could enter the palace whenever he chose, by clambering over the wall on Constitution Hill and nipping in through a window. Then he would sleep under one of the servants' beds. He may have been lying, for he was subsequently declared insane. Still, his scandalous claims hit a nerve with the lovesick Englishmen who longed to tour Buckingham Palace and penetrate the virgin queen's apartments.

Edward Jones received three months on the treadmill in the house of correction, where he declared to the officers that they should "behave towards him as they ought, to a gentleman who was anxious to make a noise in the world." He was then sent to sea. *Punch* newspaper filled endless pages with spoof reports from the passionate devotee, the "Boy Jones." Charles Dickens, no less, later produced a joke letter in which he confessed he had sneaked into Victoria's bridal rooms three days after her wedding and been quite overwhelmed. "On Tuesday we sallied down to Windsor, prowled about the Castle, saw the corridor and their private rooms—nay the very bedchamber . . . lighted up with such a ruddy, homely brilliant glow—bespeaking so much bliss and happiness—that I, your humble servant, lay down in the mud at the top of the long walk, and refused all comfort." He and his party returned, he wrote, wearing "marriage medals" next to their hearts and with "pockets full of portraits" over which they wept "in secret."

43

※

"Monsters!"

The winter of 1837–38 had been severe. The price of bread had risen sharply, and the people in the countryside were particularly hard hit. The effects of the Poor Law reformation under William IV were hitting home. Anyone who fell on hard times had to subject his family to the harsh regime of the workhouses—cold, dirty breeding grounds for disease in which husbands and wives were separated and food was sparse. As there was no health service or system for caring for the aged or mentally ill, workhouses were full of the most vulnerable and desperate in society, sad proof of the absurdity of the notion that elderly widows, orphans, and the sick could be encouraged to "help themselves" out of poverty in an economy in which jobs were reserved for able-bodied young men. Matters were little better in the cities. London was teeming with crime, squalor, and disease: One quarter of the population of just over two million was infected with typhus. Life expectancy was thirty, and nearer twenty for a worker. Only lucky children reached the age of ten. As industrialization brought benefits to some but misery to thousands, the gap between rich and poor widened into the "two Englands" that Disraeli described in his 1845 novel, *Sybil:* the haves and the have-nots.

The middle class was generally supportive of the workhouses, believing the convenient myth that poverty was caused by laziness (it allowed them to imagine that it would not happen to them). The poor, however, were soon agitating for change, and societies such as working men's associations advocating electoral reform seized the opportunity to advance their cause. A charter was created of their demands, which included universal male suffrage (women were excluded), annual Parliaments, the abolition of the requirement that members of Parliament held property, payment of MPs, and equal electoral districts. These were radical requests. Even though there had been parliamentary reform in 1832, the House was still dominated by privileged male aristocrats who had little experience of the plight of the poor or even the working mercantile classes. Thousands of discontented workers took up the cause of electoral reform.

Such agitations meant little to Victoria and her court, enclosed in the drafty splendor of Windsor Castle and quite sure that their every act was of absolute service to the country. Then a Welsh group of Chartists led by one John Frost marched to seize Newport. Troops easily quelled the rebellion, and Frost and his deputies were arrested, but ministers began to worry. The Chartists seemed not to care about their own safety, so determined were they to attack and tear apart the fabric of English society.

In January 1840, reports began circulating that the Chartists intended to attack London and set fire to all its great buildings. In expectation of riots, the government ordered the army to be on standby. "Parties are violent, Government weak, everybody wondering what will happen," wrote Greville. "Nobody [is] seeing their way clearly before them." If unrest spread to the capital, Victoria would be a target, blamed for attempting to control the government in the bedchamber crisis. As hostility grew, Albert was increasingly cast as an impostor, a familiar of Lehzen and King Leopold, a Coburg fortune hunter come to milk England for money. Victoria, however, adored her fiancé and thought him a great thing for the country, and she was convinced that everyone would agree.

Also in January, the queen formally announced to Parliament the news of her betrothal. She wanted her husband to be accorded a status above all other English peers, including her uncles (and indeed any children she and her husband might have), but ministers disagreed. The Duke of Wellington declared that Albert should have the precedence of Prince George of Denmark, "next before the Archbishop of Canterbury." Members of Parliament were similarly infuriated by Victoria's request that Albert should receive £50,000 a year for life. It was not only an astronomical amount, it was also—unfortunately—exactly the same allowance awarded to Leopold. The radical Joseph Hume declared that Albert should receive £21,000, the same allowance as the royal dukes, particularly since so many ordinary people were starving. Finally, a compromise was reached, and Albert was offered £30,000. It was suggested that he should forfeit this sum if he was widowed and remarried a Catholic or did not reside in the country for six months a year, but the motion was defeated. The queen was furious about Parliament's refusal to give her beloved Albert £50,000. "I was perfectly frantic—this wicked old foolish Duke, these confounded Tories, oh! may they be well punished for this outrageous insult!" She vowed she would not invite the Duke of Wellington to her wedding, and cried with rage, "Monsters! You Tories shall be punished. Revenge! Revenge!"

King Leopold was incensed. "I never saw anything more disgraceful than the discussion and the vote in the Commons." He thought the Tories shockingly "vulgar and disrespectful," especially, he railed, since he himself now only took £10,000 a year of his rightful allowance. Encouraged by his stuffy, doting uncle to demand everything that he could, Prince Albert was piqued. "I am surprised that you have said no word of sympathy to me about the vote of the 28th," he sniffed to his fiancée, "for those nice Tories have cut off half my income (that was to be expected), and it makes my position no very pleasant one. It is hardly conceivable that anyone could behave as disgracefully as they have to you and me." Still, the queen had one triumph: She had secured him the high precedence she desired.

Preparations for the wedding rumbled on. Previous royal weddings— including those of George IV and also his daughter Princess Charlotte— had been private affairs that took place late in the evening. Indeed, even in the highest society, an eighteenth-century wedding was a largely hurried, often plain affair, with the minimal number of guests. Wealthy Victorians, however, were developing a taste for more ostentatious events, and Victoria, Lord Melbourne decreed, should have a riotously expensive celebration. The public would fall in love with her again, and the newspapers should be appeased. Moreover, the greater the contrast between her wedding and Princess Charlotte's, the better. Victoria wished for a more private ceremony, but she was forced to give in, grumbling how "everything was always made so uncomfortable for Kings and Queens."

The Chapel Royal of St. James's Palace was selected, after Westminster Abbey was ruled out because it would seem too much like a second coronation. Hundreds were invited, and a huge banquet was planned. The queen wanted to exclude all the Tories and only acceded to the Duke of Wellington attending after Melbourne implored her. "It is MY marriage," she apparently announced, "and I will have only those who sympathise with me." Instructions were issued that ladies should wear court dress, but without trains, to prevent overcrowding.

The determined bride sketched out ideas for the outfits of her twelve bridesmaids and planned a magnificent dress. She utterly refused to wear her royal robes for the ceremony, even though Lord Melbourne thought it might be a good idea. She decided on white silk satin, choosing a bodice with a low round neck and short full sleeves in double puffs. The waist was sharply pointed over a skirt gathered into full pleats at the front. A train was made of the same material, six yards in length, edged in sprays of orange blossom. The queen wished the entire dress to be made from British materials, and so Spitalfields silk was purchased, and Mrs. Bettans, her dressmaker, sewed the outfit. The wedding was so imminent that there was no time to make new lace, but fortunately Victoria had already ordered lace for another gown. From March to November, two hundred Devonshire lace makers and seamstresses worked on the order. The pattern was destroyed afterward so that the queen's lace could never be replicated.

One hundred cakes of various types and sizes were ordered from the confectioners of London, two to be consumed on the day and the rest to be distributed among relations, the household, foreign ambassadors, and officers of state (the grandeur of the cake to be in strict accordance with the rank of the receiver). The queen also designed an extravagant brooch to be made and given to each of her twelve bridesmaids: an eagle made of gold, covered in turquoises, with rubies for eyes, a diamond for a beak, and its claws perched on large pearls. Gold snuffboxes decorated with pictures of the bridal couple were made for the foreign ambassadors, and gold rings were designed as gifts for distribution.

"The rage is begun," sighed the journal *The Satirist*. "Bedlam is certainly let loose. We are all going stark staring mad. Nothing is heard or thought of but doves and cupids, triumphal arches and whit favours, and last, but not least, variegated lamps and general illuminations." Everyone hungered for the latest detail about the arrangements for the wedding, and more suitors crawled out of the woodwork. As *The Sun* reported under the title "Another Suitor to Her Majesty," one Thomas Richard Evans bombarded Lord John Russell with letters begging him to stop the marriage and declaring his undying love for the queen.

Meanwhile, Albert, intent on reforming the raddled and debauched English court, demanded that only daughters of spotlessly virtuous mothers could be bridesmaids. But so many aristocratic ladies in the court of George IV had taken lovers that finding twelve unmarried girls of sufficient rank with mothers of unimpeachable sexual morals was almost impossible. Victoria refused her fiancé's request, and indeed selected the daughter of the notoriously promiscuous and power hungry Lady Jersey.

Albert loved Victoria, but he distrusted many of those at her court. He wanted to spend a long honeymoon of four or even six weeks alone together in the country, so that they might be able to "retire from the public eye." Victoria could think of nothing worse than spending six weeks in the dull old country, even if it was with her beloved Albert, and besides, she had work to do. "You forget, my dearest love, that I am the Sovereign, and that business can stop and wait for nothing. Parliament is sitting, and something occurs almost every day for which I may be required, and it is quite impossible for me to be absent from London." The honeymoon would only be a few days long.

Victoria was beginning to lose patience with her husband-to-be. When she had first proposed, he had seemed so gentle and malleable, much less demanding than the Prince of Orange, or George of Cambridge, who had plenty of ideas on how things could be improved. Perhaps it was impossible to reconcile the duties of a sovereign and a wife, after all. As Greville concluded, her desire for power was "stronger than love."

On January 28, Prince Albert departed for his new home, "rather exasperated about various things, and pretty full of grievances," in the words of his uncle. Still, he was gratified by the crowds waving him off, and he knew that they would not be so enthusiastic were he simply marrying a minor

German aristocrat. His family and his people had high hopes of what he would be able to accomplish for them as consort to the queen of England. He stopped off to visit Uncle Leopold in Brussels en route, then set off for Calais, where he boarded a boat and was promptly seasick. "I never remember having suffered so long or so violently," he noted plaintively. "When we landed our faces were more the colour of wax candles than human visages." Still, he perked up when he saw that thousands had turned out on the quay to welcome him with cheers even though it was a chilly February day.

Albert finally arrived at Buckingham Palace in the late afternoon of the following day, February 8. The queen had been so agitated that she, too, had fallen ill, but then "seeing his *dear dear* face again" put her "at rest about everything." Albert enjoyed a large banquet held in his honor and managed to stay up past his habitual early bedtime. The couple whiled away the evening before the wedding by reading over the marriage ceremony and trying on the rings.

There was no precedent for a grand royal wedding, and making it run smoothly had caused difficulties. There was frantic rivalry over outfits and disagreement about position in the procession. The Chapel Royal needed seats for the three hundred visitors. Chairs were even stuffed into the armory and staircase. Meanwhile, Albert's father, Duke Ernest, had the time of his life playing the father of the groom and making any excuse to paw the court beauties, as convinced as his son that Englishwomen were easily corrupted.

On her wedding day, Victoria woke up to rain lashing at her windows. She wrote in her journal: "Monday, February 10—the last time I slept alone." Albert penned a poignant letter to his grandmother begging for her love and support, and Victoria sent him a loving but practical note. "Dearest—How are you today and have you slept well? I have rested very well and feel very comfortable today. What weather! I believe however the rain will cease. Send one word when you, my most dearly loved bridegroom, will be ready. Thy ever faithful 'Victoria R.'"

44

※

"An Everlasting Impression"

The crowds were undeterred by the downpours. They began gathering from the early morning along the route to St. James's Palace, impatient to catch a glimpse of the royal bride. Of Albert, they were less sure. Florence Nightingale, who was one of the spectators, thought he was wearing clothes "borrowed to be married in," as befitting a penniless fortune hunter.

At the palace, the unsuperstitious bride broke with tradition by greeting her beloved before the wedding, ignoring Lord Melbourne's pleas. After breakfast, with the assistance of Lehzen and her maids, she dressed in her rich white satin gown ornamented with special Devonshire lace and trimmed with orange blossom. She also donned her Turkish diamond necklace and earrings and a sapphire brooch given to her by Albert. On her head she wore a lace veil and a wreath of orange blossom, the symbol of purity. At twelve thirty, Victoria left the palace and drove through the blustery rain and the cheering crowds. At the dressing room of the Chapel Royal, she met her twelve train bearers, all lovely in white tulle with white roses, ready to carry her six-foot train. The queen was in no danger of being outshone by her attendants: As one of her Ladies of the Bedchamber, Lady Lyttleton, reported, "they looked like village girls among all the gorgeous colours and jewels."

In the chapel, pale and trembling slightly, the queen was led past the three hundred guests by Lord Melbourne carrying the Sword of State, and supported by her uncle the Duke of Sussex. Flanked by his father and brother, Albert waited at the altar, splendid in the red and gold uniform of a field marshal.

"I felt so happy when the ring was put on, and by Albert," the queen enthused. Her responses rang out clearly across the whole chapel as she promised to honor her husband, cherish him, forsake all others—and obey. The service, she thought, perhaps recalling the bleak marital history of so many of her relations, "OUGHT to make an everlasting impression on everyone who promises at the Altar to *keep* what he or she promises." Some of the spectators were quietly amused (just as at the marriage of Charlotte and Leopold) when Albert offered Victoria all his worldly goods.

Although the queen had promised to obey her husband, she was not obliged to take his name. Historical precedent allowed a queen regnant to retain her own name (and indeed, it was not always standard for a woman to take her spouse's name; there were occasions when the husbands of heiresses took the bride's).

As with the coronation, the absence of rehearsal was obvious to many of the guests. Most notably, the train was too short to accommodate all the bridesmaids. One reported, "We were all huddled together, and scrambled rather than walked along, kicking each other's heels and treading in each other's gowns." The Duchess of Kent, thought *The Times*, appeared "disconsolate and distressed" throughout. Observers noted that as the queen left the chapel, she stopped to kiss Queen Adelaide but merely extended her hand to her mother.

By five past one, the procession was making its way back to Buckingham Palace. The queen and her new husband then spent half an hour alone together. Sitting on a sofa, she gave him a wedding ring (there was no place in the service for the groom's ring), and he vowed that there should be no secret they did not share. At two thirty, they emerged to eat a sumptuous wedding breakfast with a small group including Victoria's mother, Princess

Feodora and her husband, the archbishop of Canterbury, the bishop of London, Melbourne, Palmerston, and the Duke of Coburg. The guests marveled when four men staggered in struggling under the weight of the huge wedding cake, which was nine feet in circumference and sixteen inches high, topped with a model of the royal couple surrounded by doves and attended by a faithful dog. Mr. Mawdett, chief confectioner to Her Majesty in Buckingham Palace, had been at his most inventive. "We are assured," remarked *The Times* slyly, "that not one of the cherubs on the royal wedding cake was intended to represent Lord Palmerston. The resemblance therefore pointed out . . . must be purely accidental."

"Nothing could have gone off better," Lord Melbourne decreed. The bridal couple changed into their traveling outfits. Victoria wore a white satin cloak with an edging of swan's down, and a white velvet bonnet adorned with feathers and Brussels lace. She then had a private meeting with her prime minister, without her husband. "Dearest Albert came up and fetched me downstairs, where we took leave of Mamma, and drove off at near 4, Albert and I alone, which was so delightful." Rather than indulging in a new coach, the happy couple had taken an old chariot, compounding their sin, in the eyes of Greville at least, with "postillions in undress liveries, in a very poor and shabby style." As they departed, servants were preparing a grand banquet for the wedding guests and the household.

The public were delighted to see the bridal pair. Houses along the route were illuminated with crowns and stars, and all twenty-two miles were lined with enthusiastic spectators. When the party arrived in Windsor, the queen felt quite overwhelmed by the "deafening" shouts and the tumble of horses and gigs driving alongside them. As she changed into an evening gown, she was utterly weary, not to mention a little deaf.

> *We had dinner in our sitting room; but I had such a sick headache that I could eat nothing and was obliged to lie down in the middle blue room for the remainder of the evening, on the sofa, but, ill or not, I NEVER, NEVER spent such an evening!! MY DEAREST, DEAR Albert sat on a footstool by my side, and his excessive love and affection gave me*

feelings of heavenly love and happiness I never could have hoped to
have felt before. He clasped me in his arms, and we kissed each other
again and again! . . . Oh! this was the happiest day of my life!

The queen was revivified in time for the bridal night. Her entry in her journal makes it clear that she enjoyed the experience.

"When the day dawned (for we did not sleep much) and I beheld that beautiful angelic face by my side, it was more than I can express! He does look so beautiful in his shirt only, with his beautiful throat seen." The young couple bounced out of bed early and set off walking and riding. Such behavior, Greville complained to Lady Palmerston, was "not the way to provide us with a Prince of Wales." He was wrong: The queen wrote to Melbourne telling him of her happiness after a "most gratifying and bewildering night." There has been much scholarly prurience about Victoria's emphasis on her sexual pleasure with her husband. It should be remembered that the female reproductive system was still not entirely understood, and many doctors believed that orgasm caused ovulation and thus conception. Emphasizing sexual pleasure was a way of suggesting that conception might have occurred.

An exhausted Albert collapsed on the queen's sofa within hours, while she busied herself writing letters. She was eager to share her happiness with the court. That evening she hosted a dinner party, and on February 12 she sent a message to Lord Alfred Paget demanding he organize a ball for that very evening. Prince Albert was dismayed, and the courtiers were shocked that she was putting herself on display during her honeymoon. But who could tell her that she was behaving indelicately? She was the queen.

Prince Albert crept off early from the ball to slumber on the sofa. His absence tempted the queen into what was for her an early night. She left the ball at ten minutes past midnight and awoke her sleeping prince with a kiss so that they could retire together. The next day, she was delighted as he helped her put on her stockings and she watched him shave. That evening was another dance, and then, after their three-day honeymoon, they returned to London.

Up until Queen Victoria's ceremony, weddings had generally been small affairs, staged only for family. The bride would wear her best dress, which could even be black, and white featured only infrequently for it was seen as an impractical color. For the aristocracy, the great point was not the ceremony but the round of visits and the attendance at court that followed. Victoria's extravagant wedding set a new trend, which chimed with the desire of the mercantile classes to show off their wealth. Every young girl in love wanted to be like the queen-bride Victoria.

In January 1840, just before the royal nuptials, the penny post was introduced, and Great Britain's postal system was changed forever. Previously, the recipient of a letter had to pay for postage. Now, for just a penny for each letter, correspondents could write as often as they pleased, without worrying about burdening their addressees with the cost. It was a timely innovation; nearly everyone in England, it seemed, wanted to convey their impressions of the queen's wedding.

The press was still unconvinced by Albert. Even on the morning of the ceremony *The Times* was cautious: "If the thing was not finally settled indeed, one might without being unreasonable, express a wish that the consort selected for a Princess so educated and hitherto so unfairly guided, as Queen Victoria—should have been a person of riper years and likely to form more sound and circumspect opinions." To Victoria, Albert's youth was his advantage. Surely, it seemed, he would be easily dominated and turned into a decorative and always supportive consort. "The Prince is indolent," noted Lord Melbourne, "& it would be better if he were more so, for in his position we want no activity."

Not long after the honeymoon, the pair began to disagree violently about Albert's role. The queen, rather like a king, preferred to take care of all business and simply enjoy Albert as a pleasant companion. He wished to hear about affairs of state; she desired not to talk about them after a day at the dispatch box, and if she did discuss such matters, she would only do so after she had consulted Melbourne and Lehzen. She was fully determined to cast Albert in the limited role of "help with the blotting paper." "In my home life I am very happy and contented," Albert wrote to his friend Prince William of Löwenstein three months after the marriage, "but the difficulty of filling my place with proper dignity is that I am only the husband, and not the master in the house."

Victoria admitted to Lord Melbourne that she knew the prince complained of a "want of confidence," but she was loath to address it:

She said it proceeded entirely from indolence; she knew it was wrong, but when she was with the Prince, she preferred talking on other subjects. I told her Majesty that she should try to alter this, and that there was no objection to her conversing with the Prince on any subject she pleased. My impression is that the chief obstacle in her Majesty's mind is the fear of difference of opinion, and she thinks that domestic harmony is more likely to follow from avoiding subjects likely to create distance.

Really, as she and Melbourne were too polite to say, it was not simply a case of reading out the dispatches but also translating and explaining them. As the newspapers delighted in reporting, Albert's English was still far from perfect. His wife had to correct his spelling in drafts of his letters.

Albert's attempts to secure more influence looked to be doomed to failure. The queen relied on Lehzen and Lord Melbourne for advice. She wanted her husband to remain her loyal support and domestic helpmate and no more. Then came the bombshell.

I must say that I could not be more unhappy; I am really upset about it and it is spoiling my happiness; I have always hated the idea and I prayed God night and day to be left free for at least six months, but my prayers have not been answered and I am really most unhappy. I cannot understand how one can wish for such a thing, especially at the beginning of a marriage.

The queen had discovered that she was pregnant.

45

"Children Seem to Literally Be Raining Down from Heaven"

A bout myself: really it is too dreadful," the queen informed the King of the Belgians. "I cannot in any way see the good side of this sad business. Children seem to literally be raining down from heaven this year." The first child born to a reigning monarch since the birth of George IV had been conceived sometime in February, and the queen was definitely not amused. She wanted sympathy, not congratulation for safeguarding the succession, and she would rather prefer to pretend that she was not pregnant at all and quite able to continue dancing at court balls. She told King Leopold that if she produced only a "nasty girl" at the end of her plagues, she would "drown it."

A rumor sprang up that the queen was visiting Claremont, intending to furnish it exactly as it had been when Charlotte died there, nearly twenty-five years before. Then she would lie in the same room and expire in labor. The Queen's thoughts naturally turned to her unhappy cousin, but she was assured that the mistake had been keeping Charlotte so weak through bloodletting, an exiguous diet, and no exercise. Lord Melbourne pressed her to eat well, although she never needed much encouragement.

The twenty-one-year-old queen might have been miserable, but the nation was elated by the news. The era of the lascivious, promiscuous Hanoverian dukes was finally over. The young couple would hopefully produce many more progeny, all of them pushing the king of Hanover further away from the throne.

Victoria's new condition boosted Albert's reputation. He might be a prim, humorless German, but he had fulfilled his most important duty as royal spouse. Albert himself was naturally delighted by the pregnancy and wrote sternly to his brother, who was feeling depressed: "Wedded life is the only thing that can make up for the lost relationships of our youth."

"My dearest and most beloved Victoria," wrote King Leopold. "I cannot find words *strong enough* to express to you my horror at what happened on the 10th, and my happiness and delight to see you escape from a danger which was really very great."

On June 10, 1840, at about six in the evening, the four-months-pregnant Victoria was driving up Constitution Hill with Albert in an open phaeton, keen to enjoy the last of the day's sunshine. They had hardly left the palace when Albert spotted a shabby man leaning against the railings of Green Park about six paces away from them. Horror-struck, the prince realized that he was brandishing a gun. Before Albert or Victoria had time to think, the man aimed toward them and pulled the trigger. The horses reared and stopped, and Albert grabbed Victoria's hands and asked if the fright had shaken her, but she simply laughed. The man fired again, and Victoria ducked. The second shot inspired the bystanders to action, and a group of men leaped to seize the would-be assassin.

Albert urged the postilion to move on, and they drove off at a brisk pace to visit the Duchess of Kent, who had rented Ingestre House, on Belgrave Square. On arrival, they decided to take a further drive, as Albert put it, to show the public they had not "lost all confidence in them." It was the right decision. When the queen returned to the palace, "she was received with the utmost enthusiasm by the immense crowd that was congregated on carriages, on horseback, and on foot. All the Equestrians formed themselves into an Escort and attended her back to the Palace, cheering vehemently while she acknowledged with great appearance of feeling these loyal manifestations."

The attempted assassination sent Victoria's popularity soaring. Everywhere she went she was cheered, and Albert was much admired for his coolness, even by the newspapers. "What is this strange popular mania for Queen shooting," fumed Elizabeth Barrett Browning, previously no friend of Victoria.

The failed assassin turned out to be one Edward Oxford, a sullen waiter of eighteen, the son of a Birmingham jeweler. Mr. Anson visited him in custody and concluded that he showed no remorse. Some believed that the hated king of Hanover was responsible, and there were mutterings that letters posted from Hanover were found among Oxford's possessions, but the young man was judged insane at trial and sentenced to an asylum. He was released twenty-seven years later, on condition that he emigrate.

The queen was undaunted by the experience. A special green parasol was made for her with a bulletproof chain-mail lining, but she refused to use it.

On the brink of becoming the father of the heir to the throne, Albert demanded that he should be regent over the child, in the event of Victoria's death. The royal dukes wished to be regents alone, or at the most share responsibility with Albert in a regency council, but the assassination attempt had greatly increased the prince's standing with the court and the country in general. Ministers had also noted that Victoria excluded him from politics, and they thought him pliable. Indeed, he would surely be easier to manage than a council of the aggressive and rambunctious dukes, especially if the king of Hanover felt like putting his oar in. The royal sisters, of course, were not even considered.

The queen was delighted when she found that her ministers were in agreement that Albert should be regent. The Duke of Sussex threw tantrums, but the bill was passed. Not yet twenty-one, Albert was the future de facto king of England if Victoria died. He gloated to his brother:

> *I wish you could be here and see in us a couple united in love and unanimity. Now Victoria is ready to give up something for my sake, I everything for her sake. Become as happy as we are, more I cannot wish for you. Do not think I lead a submissive life. On the contrary,*

here, where the lawful position of man is so, I have formed a prize
life for myself.

The era of Victoria and Albert had begun.

As Victoria's pregnancy advanced, the prince endeavored to increase his power. It was fashionable at the time to encourage expectant mothers to rest as much as possible, lounging on sofas, in keeping with the received wisdom that ladies were incapable of exerting themselves (less leisured women were, of course, expected to work in fields or factories, or clean and cook until labor began). King Leopold encouraged his niece to walk, declaring that insufficient exercise had contributed to Charlotte's death.

He did not press her to toil over her documents, for he wished her husband to take charge. Albert attended her solicitously to ensure that he could step in when she felt weary of official correspondence. And so, as the queen occasionally did succumb to fatigue, the prince secured access to the dispatch boxes.

"I am wonderfully well," declared Victoria to Feodora. "I take long walks, some in the highest wind, every day, and am so active, though of a *great* size, I must unhappily admit." Her baby was due at the beginning of December. The queen refused to follow the tradition that the birth should be witnessed by the eminent men of the Church and Parliament. She was no queen consort, but a ruler who had to meet such men every day, and she did not wish them to see her in labor. She arranged to be attended by an obstetrician, Dr. Locock, two nurses, and her husband, and nobody else. The Duchess of Kent was firmly excluded, as were the royal dukes.

The pains began early, on the night of November 21. Victoria struggled to shake her husband awake, and he finally sent for James Clark, who called Dr. Locock. She tried to rest, but the pains grew steadily worse, and she became fearful. When the obstetrician arrived, however, he pronounced that all was well and the baby was on the way. Unfortunately, the wet nurse was still in transit from the Isle of Wight. A page dashed off to hurry her along, while the nurses and maids hurried to prepare the birth room.

As the queen's labor began, the archbishop of Canterbury, the bishop of

London, the cabinet ministers and Lord Erroll, the Lord Steward of the Household, settled themselves into the adjoining room. Victoria desired to give birth in private, but practically, this was an impossibility. The door between the two rooms was opened, and Lord Erroll claimed he could see the queen the whole time and hear what she said. Unlike the dignitaries who had sat in the room adjoining Princess Charlotte's for hours, the ministers and bishops at Buckingham Palace did not have long to wait. On November 22 at two p.m., not much more than twelve hours after the queen had begun to feel pain, the heir to the throne was born. The baby was a fine, healthy, bouncing girl. "Never mind," said the new mother to Locock. "The next will be a Prince."

"[A] perfect little child was born," Victoria confided to her diary, "but alas a girl not a boy, as we both had so hoped and wished for. We were, I am afraid, sadly disappointed." Albert's new favorable position in the nation's affections would have been further consolidated by a son. "Albert, father of a daughter; you will laugh at me!" he wrote to his brother.

The dignitaries were less distressed. The birth had been straightforward, and when they crowded around to inspect the naked baby on a table, they decided she looked very healthy. "Both the Queen and the Prince were much disappointed at not having a son," wrote Lord Clarendon, "I believe because they thought it would be a disappointment to the country, but what the country cares about is to have a life more, whether male or female, interposed between the succession and the King of Hanover."

The queen recovered quickly. "Victoria is well and happy," Albert marveled. "It is hardly to be believed that only a few hours ago she lay in dreadful pain." A deputy was found for the wet nurse, who finally appeared at two in the morning.

Victoria was delighted with the bright-eyed Princess Royal, but not besotted. She referred to her simply as "the Child." The baby was brought to her twice a day, and in the six weeks after the birth, she only saw her bathed twice. The new mother was more preoccupied by her husband's attentions. In keeping with conventional medical thinking, she was confined to bed for a fortnight after the birth. Albert devoted himself to her, jumping to answer her every call, staying in to sit beside her, reading to her, and acting as her secretary. He refused to let anyone else lift her from her bed to her sofa or to wheel her into her sitting room. His care, the queen remarked in a rather pointed blow to the Duchess of Kent, "was like that of a mother, nor could there be a kinder, wiser, or more judicious nurse."

Like Melbourne, Albert had learned that the way to win Victoria was not to command or demand, but to flatter her not inconsiderable ego. He hoped that if he showed how eager he was to be a support, she would come to rely on him. As he told the Duke of Wellington, he meant to be "the natural head of the family, superintendent of her household, manager of her private affairs, her sole confidential advisor in politics, and only assistance in her communication with the officers of the Government," as well as "her private secretary and her permanent Minister."

Albert's efforts in taking notes and dictation, listening to endless discussions about matters large and small, and coddling his wife bore fruit. On the very day the Princess Royal was born, he represented Victoria at a meeting of the Privy Council. In early December, she gave him the keys to her confidential boxes, in which were stored all the records of cabinet business. Still, Mr. Anson's point that Albert was "in fact, tho' not in name, Her Majesty's Private Secretary" was exaggerated. His English was never of sufficient standard to read and advise as Lord Melbourne had done. Even years later, he still conversed in German with his wife and children, and he made sure that his letters were checked by his secretaries or the queen to ensure that the spelling and grammar were correct.

Albert and Baroness Lehzen had long been at odds. During the queen's pregnancy, their mutual mistrust had erupted into full-blown hatred. Mr. Anson complained that Lehzen was "taking advantage of the Queen's illness to complain of the P's conduct, at a moment when, from natural excitability it could not fail to work strongly on the Queen's mind." He accused her of being "always in the Queen's path, pointing and exaggerating every little fault of the Prince, constantly misrepresenting him."

To Albert's dismay, Lehzen kept her private doorway into the couple's room after the wedding. He was still horrified that she managed the queen's spending and every bill had to be approved by her before it was paid. He could hardly bear the humiliation of essentially asking his wife's former governess for money. He was also irate that she was in charge of the household, and thus controlled when the three most important officers of the house—the Lord Steward, the Lord Chamberlain, and the Master of the Horse—had access to the queen. His frugal German spirit was outraged by the dirty, unkempt, expensive, and disorganized palaces, and he thought Lehzen was lax. The one main improvement was the installation of gaslight in many of the rooms in 1840, but otherwise the palaces had not kept pace with the outside world. Although there were hundreds of servants, many jobs were left undone, and security was poor. Stockmar complained that many foreign dignitaries got lost in Windsor Castle. "At night, if they happen to forget the right entrance from the corridors, they wander for an hour, helpless and unassisted." Even worse, in Albert's opinion, expenses were soaring, particularly on food and entertaining. In the first three months of 1840, there had been many guests to celebrate the royal wedding, but still, 24,600 dinners served at Buckingham Palace seemed excessive.

Albert dreamed of greater efficiency. He had actually lived for very little time as an adult in palaces, as much of his maturity was spent away from the residences of Saxe-Coburg, traveling or studying. As a consequence, he was more idealistic than most about what could be achieved. "Much as I am inclined to treat the Household machine with a sort of reverence from antiquity, I still remain convinced that it is clumsy in its original construction, and works so ill, that as long as its wheels are not mended there can neither be order nor regularity, comfort, security, nor outward dignity in the Queen's Palace." He believed that there should be a proper Master of the Household who lived in the palace and oversaw all the duties. Politicians, however, were nervous of making changes that might seem to detract from the authority of the Lord Chamberlain, Lord Steward, or Master of the Horse, for these were great offices, to be occupied by distinguished peers (usually in reward for political loyalty). Albert believed that such obstacles could be overcome. Only Lehzen was blocking his path.

For Albert, no lover of women, even young and pretty ones, the middle-aged, caraway-chewing German was a she-devil. He described her as a "crazy, stupid intriguer, obsessed with the lust of power, who regards herself as a demi-God, and anyone who refuses to recognise her as such is a criminal." Victoria, he judged, "like every good pupil is accustomed to regard her governess as an oracle," and he judged that Lehzen had made the queen believe that "whatever good qualities she possesses are due to her." Unable to understand the severity of Victoria's earlier trials, he could not comprehend how Lehzen had acquired such influence. He began to grow suspicious that she aimed to take control of the Princess Royal and become her governess, as well as the queen's de facto housekeeper. Indeed, it was often the case that an old governess would stay on with a family and look after the children of her charge. Albert wished above all to ensure that this would not happen.

Lord Melbourne, always alert to domestic disputes, had warned Lehzen to allow the couple more space. "I have told her she undertook great responsibility in standing between the mother and daughter, however much circumstances may have justified her—but if she ventures, or puts herself in a position to appear so, to stand between husband and wife—she will draw down ruin on herself, entail misery on her she professes to be devoted to, and be execrated by the whole country."

Albert deluded himself that the queen had "more fear than love for the Baroness and that she would *really* be happier without her, though she would not acknowledge it." Unfortunately for him, Victoria adored Lehzen and believed her selflessly devoted to her interests. Later, in a letter to an author of a biography of Albert, she wrote of her old governess, "It was *not* 'Personal ambition' *at all* but the idea that *no one* but herself was able to take care of the Queen and also she did not perceive til later, when before leaving the Queen told her herself, that *people* flattered her and made use of her for their own purposes." Victoria never saw Lehzen without thinking of how much she owed her for protecting her against Conroy. "[Albert] cannot argue," Lord Melbourne told Anson later. "If he put it in a manner implying as the alternative that either the Baroness must go, or he would not stay in the House, looking to the Queen's obstinacy and determination of character, her reply would be 'in this alternative you have contemplated the possibility of living without me, I will shew you that I can contemplate the possibility of living without you.'" Poor, angry Albert could do nothing but fume and dub his enemy the "House Dragon."

46

※

"What a Hard Task It Is for Us Women"

For all his irritation with court life, Albert fitted cheerfully around Victoria's routine. In the morning, both worked in their private rooms, then meet to discuss business before lunch with guests at two. The queen saw ministers in the afternoon, usually with Albert. In moments of free time, they sketched, painted, or played piano duets. After the meetings were over, the couple rode out in a pony phaeton and dined at eight, always accompanied by guests, courtiers, and often ministers. Fifteen minutes after everyone, including Albert, was seated, the doors were opened by two courtiers and the little queen appeared, splendid in her court outfit and dripping with jewels. She was always served first, and dinner was over when she had finished her meal, so since she was a quick eater, many guests often left the table slightly hungry.

There had been complaints about the stultifying court conversation when the queen had been a single woman. Matters did not improve after her marriage. The prince glared at anyone he suspected of flirting and restricted himself to short, polite exchanges or observations. His mood only brightened when there was a chance to discuss practical matters such as indoor drainage. He was, as Lord Melbourne sighed, very "straight-laced and a great stickler for morality, whereas she was rather the other way." Victoria refused to exclude characters with dubious histories from her court, much to his despair. Luckily for Albert, the moral code was changing; the rakes and mistresses of the eighteenth century were out of fashion.

Albert was concerned to separate himself from his family, refusing their demands for money. He even turned down Ernest's request to pay a visit, telling him, "You so openly showed yourself against Lehzen . . . Victoria was frightened, and the fear that you might influence me against her in this month would rob her of the confidence which I must have, to do good." He wrote, "[It is] necessary for us to be on the watch constantly. You would not only be in the way, but even the political views you would be expected to have might harm me."

Poor Ernest had to content himself with yet more smug missives from the happy home. "Christmas Eve we spent very pleasantly," Albert wrote to him. "Three Christmas trees adorned the hall and everyone was merry and happy. Next year the little daughter will jump around the tree, as we did not so very long ago." The Princess Royal was turning into a little darling, blessed with lovely dark blue eyes, a fine complexion, and good health. Victoria came to love her daughter more as she grew up. She called her Pussy or Pussette and decided she was "quite a little toy for us," although she reverted to calling her "the Child" again when she was naughty. Fortunately, little Pussy was beautifully behaved when she was christened Princess Victoria Adelaide Mary Louise in the Chapel Royal, St. James, on February 10, her parents' wedding anniversary. She did not cry, instead looking about her eagerly and apparently delighted by all the lights and shiny medals on the regimental uniforms. The Duke of Wellington stood in as godfather for Ernest. Victoria had quite changed her mind about him. "The Duke is the best friend we have," she said.

Although the queen had made a marvelous recovery from childbirth and was very pleased with her daughter, she dreaded a repetition of her experience. When Leopold expressed his wish that she would have many more children, he received a characteristically sharp retort.

> I think, dearest Uncle, you cannot really wish me to be the "Mamma
> d'une nombreuse famille" for I think you will see with me the great

inconvenience a large family would be to us all, and particularly to the country, independent of the hardship and inconvenience to myself; men never think, at least seldom think, what a hard task it is for us women to go through this very often.

Unfortunately, like most aristocratic and genteel women, the queen did not breastfeed and was thus denied that natural contraceptive. Many Victorian upper-class women found themselves in an almost constant state of pregnancy. Effie, wife of John Everett Millais, one of the queen's favorite painters, produced eight children in quick succession between 1856 and 1868, the first born just over ten months after their wedding. Elizabeth Barrett Browning's mother, Mary, endured a state of near perpetual childbearing from 1806 to 1824, with gaps of only about eighteen months between births. Contraception was considered sinful, and doctors had so little understanding of the female reproductive system that they would suggest that the safest time for intercourse for those who did not wish to become pregnant was in the middle of their cycle—unfortunate advice.

In early spring, Victoria found that what she most dreaded had occurred. She was pregnant once more. Aristocratic ladies desperate for heirs envied her fertility. She, however, was miserable at the thought of growing heavy, confined to the sofa, unable to dance or ride. Her depression only increased when she realized that she would soon lose her beloved Lord Melbourne.

"We are in confusion," Albert wrote. "Ministerial crisis, breaking up of Parliament, party fights, agitation among the people etc." It looked increasingly likely that the Tories would form the next government and Sir Robert Peel would become prime minister. Prince Albert took it upon himself to be the go-between with Peel over the household to ensure there was no repetition of the bedchamber crisis. The queen agreed that she would announce the resignation of the three ladies most associated with powerful Whigs: the Duchess of Sutherland, the Duchess of Bedford, and Lady Normanby. Sir Robert made all the right noises, vowing that he would give up office rather than cause the queen any embarrassment. "Her Majesty must know how pressed I am as the Head of a powerful Party, but the impression

I wish to create in her Majesty's mind is that I am to defend her against their Encroachments."

Albert had been a poor adviser. The queen had saved face and ensured the position of most of her ladies, but she had ceded to Sir Robert the right of appointing the Lord Steward, the Lord Chamberlain, and the Master of the Horse, as well as the lord-in-waiting, grooms-in-waiting, and equerries, who were MPs or ministers. At a stroke, she lost the greatest political favors that she could offer. The monarchy was moving ever closer to occupying a ceremonial role.

In early June, a vote of no confidence in Lord Melbourne's government was defeated by one vote, but he still refused to go. He was quite convinced that a general election would confirm his power, for he believed that his government's plan to impose a duty on imported corn would rouse the landed interests in Parliament to vote for him. At the election in July, his party was overwhelmingly defeated. The queen was devastated. In September, she attended the council at which the new ministers were appointed, seven months pregnant and almost in tears. Even Greville was moved: She "conducted herself in a manner which excited my greatest admiration and was really touching to see." The chancellor of the exchequer felt weepy, and the Lord Steward was so overcome that he had to rush from the room.

The queen missed her former prime minister painfully. "After seeing him for four years, with very few exceptions—*daily*—you may imagine that I must feel the change," she wrote to her uncle Leopold. She solicited Melbourne into a private correspondence with her—an unwise move.

Low spirited, Victoria began picking fights with Prince Albert, throwing tantrums when he chided her, then following him in a fury when he tried to leave the room. Infuriated by his measured letters and words, she became ever angrier, often in an attempt to prompt a reaction from him. The arguments usually ended to Albert's advantage: She regretted her temper tantrums, and he emerged the triumphant victim. Finally, early on the morning of November 9, labor began, with Dr. Locock in attendance once more. "My sufferings were really very severe and I don't know what I should have done, but for the great comfort and support my beloved Albert was to me." Just before eleven, the baby arrived: a healthy, large boy. He was the first male heir to the throne to be born for nearly eighty years.

The English were overjoyed by the new arrival. Crowds cheered outside

Buckingham Palace, and the new Prince Albert Edward was immediately an object of passionate curiosity. He was a good-looking, robust child, with big blue eyes and a high forehead. After the euphoria had subsided, however, the queen felt low and unhappy. She had none of her usual energy, and she was not entranced by "the Boy," as she called her son. Her nerves "were so battered" after his birth that, as she later told her uncle, "I suffered a *whole year* from it." Albert began to aggrandize his position. By acting as his wife's amanuensis, drafting letters, reading to her, scouring the newspapers for important articles and clipping them out, and advising her on questions of policy, he became her indispensable helpmate. The exhausted queen had lost some of her appetite for work, particularly since she had to deal with Tories. As she wrote to King Leopold, "I own I am much happier when I need not see the Ministers."

The prince's aim was to gain his wife's trust so he could oust Lehzen. "All the disagreeableness I suffer comes from one and the same person, and that is precisely the person Victoria chooses for her friend and confidante." To his fury, Lehzen had demanded to receive the revenues of the duchy of Cornwall for nursery expenses (the duchy was traditionally the possession of the Prince of Wales). In vain, the queen told Stockmar, "I never speak to her or anybody (but you) about it now if anything new has been settled about the Nursery, I *never* go to *her* to complain." Albert would not listen. To a man who as a child had never formed an attachment to anyone other than his brother, the presence of his wife's governess was a matter of life and death. It was common for old governesses to remain with their charges and look after the next generation—but for Albert, Lehzen was no elderly servant but an awful enemy. He argued, "The welfare of my children and Victoria's existence as sovereign are too sacred for me not to die fighting rather than yield them as prey to Lehzen." In his view, he was a victim of his wife's hastiness.

> She will not hear me out but flies into a rage and overwhelms me with reproaches of suspiciousness, want of trust, ambition, envy, etc. etc. There are, therefore, two ways open to me: (1) to keep silence and go away (in which case I am like a school boy who has had a dressing down from his mother and goes off snubbed), (2) I can be still more violent (and then we have scenes like that of the 16th, which I hate).

The prince could be unkind and spiteful when he wished. One example remains: a bitter note to Victoria about the treatment of little Pussy, who was suffering from her perennial stomach trouble. "Dr. Clark has mismanaged the child and poisoned her with calomel and you have starved her. I shall have nothing more to do with it; take the child away and do as you like and if she dies you will have it on your conscience." Victoria blamed her own "irritability" for the problems between them. "I will strive to conquer it though I knew before I married that this would be a trouble; I therefore wished not to marry, as the two years and a half, when I was so completely my own mistress made it difficult for me to control myself & to bend to another's will, but I trust I shall be able to conquer it."

Albert made his wife feel guilty for her outbursts and, as she put it, saying "crass and odious things which I don't myself believe." She was trying to be a good wife. "Our position is tho' very different to any other married couples. A. is in my house and not I in his.—But I am ready to submit to his wishes as I love him so dearly." With those words, Lehzen's doom was sealed.

By September 1842, Lehzen had been quietly retired from service. The queen gave her old governess £800 a year and a carriage, and the elderly baroness crept off, early in the morning of September 30, to live with her sister in Germany. There she wrote frequent letters to her charge, who always replied. After her departure, the queen characteristically decided that she had made exactly the right decision. She looked back over her old journals of her first year as queen and decided herself fortunate to have escaped. "The life I led then was so artificial & superficial, & yet I thought I was happy. Thank God! I now know what *real* happiness means!"

In the space of a few years, Victoria had changed. The young queen had been bouncing, gay, and tempestuous, a lover of big all-night parties, jealous of her prerogative, and affectionately reliant on her beloved Melbourne, Lehzen, and a few favored ladies. Government was a personal affair, and work on dispatch boxes was bound up with discussions about palace life. By 1842, she was less energetic and more dependent on Albert's painstaking efforts at taking notes and dictation and doing filing. She felt sorry for Albert for having to occupy a position subordinate to hers, and she was eager to compensate him for what she saw as his loss by chastising herself in her diary and praising him. Interestingly, her sketchbooks contain no pictures of Prince Albert with their children. After his death, she wrote pages and pages about how she had depended on him. At the time, she preferred to cut him out of the picture.

Many years later, after his death, she wrote:

> *Nor can the Queen think now without indignation against herself, of her wish to keep the Prince waiting for probably three or four years, at the risk of ruining his prospects for life, until she might feel inclined to marry! And the Prince has since told her that he came over in 1839 with the intention of telling her that if she could not then make up her mind, she must understand that he could not now wait for a decision, as he had done when this marriage was first talked about. The only excuse the Queen can make for herself is the fact that the sudden change from the secluded life at Kensington to the independence of her position as Queen Regnant, at the age of eighteen, put all ideas of marriage out of her mind, which she now most bitterly regrets.*

The queen believed she was lucky to have such a husband. Albert's announcement that he would have broken off the agreement had she not made up her mind in 1839 seems particularly ungentlemanly. Uncle Leopold would never have allowed it, and his marriage prospects were otherwise meager, as a poor, insignificant princeling with little interest in pleasing women. Still, his typically Coburgian claims of sacrifice succeeded.

As is well known, the queen retreated into strict mourning when Albert died of pneumonia at Windsor on December 14, 1861, leaving her a widow at the age of forty-two, with nine children—and no prospect of remarriage. She continued to work through her boxes of papers and to intervene in policy, advise, and discuss, but she hid herself from the public. If she had been an ordinary woman, she would have been congratulated for her behavior, as the nineteenth-century cult of mourning expected a widow to seclude herself. Both men and women mourned for years, and many of those who could afford to do so kept the room of the deceased exactly as it was before he or she died, just as Victoria did with the chamber where Albert breathed his last.

Benjamin Disraeli, the prime minister who did so much to bring the queen back into the public eye, could not forget the intensity of her devotion. On his deathbed in 1881 at the age of seventy-six, he was asked if he would like to see the queen. "Better not," he replied wittily. "She will only ask me to take a message to Albert."

With the departure of Lehzen, the queen's final link to her childhood had gone. Melbourne had left her, Peel was in power, Albert was her adviser, and there was a male heir to the throne. It was a new royal age, which would culminate in the Great Exhibition in Victoria's thirty-second year. On November 10, 1841, *The Times* declared the queen the "model of a female sovereign." There could be no higher praise.

Epilogue

An Immense Multitude

I can think of nothing else but Jubilee," wrote a young Winston Churchill to his mother from school. It was the summer of 1887, Albert had been dead for over twenty-five years, and the queen was at the apogee of her popularity. Few could recall another sovereign. The entire country was obsessed with the golden jubilee of the woman who had ruled over Great Britain as it had gained the most magnificent empire in the world. Every town wanted a jubilee building. Thousands of medals, mugs, and souvenirs were produced, and London was bursting at the seams with visitors as the English traveled in and every dignitary who could do so arrived to pay tribute. Under Victoria's rule, Britain had moved from an economically struggling country most applauded for its military might to one that ruled the world through trade, backed up by the force of its army. The young girl who had been visited fifty years ago early in the morning at Kensington Palace by the archbishop of Canterbury and Lord Conyngham was now the empress of India and the ruler of—some said—half the world.

"The day has come and I am alone," wrote the sixty-eight-year-old Victoria on the fiftieth anniversary of her accession, June 20, 1887, although she was, she recognized, "surrounded by many dear children." She continued: "God has mercifully sustained me through many great trials and sorrows." The queen drove to Westminster Abbey, which she had not entered since she had been crowned. To the despair of many of her ministers, she refused to wear her robes of state and her crown, and so the multitudes saw their queen in her favored black dress and bonnet. They hardly cared. "The crowds from the Palace gates up to the Abbey were enormous," Victoria recorded elatedly, "and there was such an extraordinary burst of enthusiasm, as I had hardly ever seen in London before." She was delighted by the decorations festooning Piccadilly and by the viewing platforms adorning the tops of houses.

The queen was escorted by Indian cavalry and surrounded by carriages carrying various members of the royal family. A lady-in-waiting to the Duchess of Cambridge could hardly believe the "masses and millions of people thronging the streets like an anthill," along with men hanging off the chimneys. "It was one continuous roar of cheering from the moment [the queen] came out of the door of her Palace till the instant she got back to it. Deafening."

In the abbey, the queen sat on the great coronation chair of Edward I and listened to the service giving thanks for her long reign. She returned, in her grand procession, for a luncheon at the palace and the distribution of jubilee gifts in the ballroom, and then to don a jubilee gown adorned with diamonds for a dinner for visiting royalty and the diplomatic corps. In the evening, she watched a fireworks display in the park from the Chinese Room in Buckingham Palace.

The following day saw a fete in Hyde Park, with bands and streamers, at which twenty-six thousand poor children were each given a bun and a jubilee mug adorned with a portrait of the queen, then sang "God Save the Queen"—slightly out of tune, thought Victoria, who presumably was a little weary of the song. She proceeded to Eton and Windsor to unveil a statue of herself and see the students singing and cheering for her. "These two days will ever remain indelibly impressed on my mind, with great gratitude to that all-merciful Providence, who has protected me for so long, and to my devoted and loyal people," she wrote in her diary that evening.

The summer saw seemingly endless receptions, garden parties, dinners, military reviews, and presentations, while the palace staff tried to make sense of the thousands of gifts from across the empire. "If I were not old and infirm," wrote Chief Letsie of Basutoland (now Lesotho), whose father had appealed for British protection against the Boers, "I would have liked to go and see Her Majesty with my own eyes, as I hear that many kings and princes from far countries have done. . . . We hear also that her Majesty's subjects are an immense multitude, numbering more than 300 millions of people, that the sun never goes down on her empire, and that all glory in being her subjects."

The wild expense of the jubilee and issues over home rule for Ireland had caused unrest at home, but it was the queen's year of triumph. "Never, never can I forget this brilliant year," she wrote in her diary at the close of 1887, "so full of marvellous kindness, loyalty & devotion of so many millions which I really could hardly have expected." Only George III (who was mad for many years) and the medieval kings Henry III and Edward II had reigned so long.

The queen's celebrations went off perfectly. The only mistake occurred during the fireworks. The penultimate firework, the pièce de résistance, was a bouquet of flowers that burst into a huge portrait of Victoria, two hundred feet wide and a hundred and eighty feet high. There was, however, one disastrous flaw: An error meant that the right eye blinked frenziedly, so that the great widowed queen seemed to those spectating to be winking slyly at her subjects.

The golden jubilee had been celebrated with incredible enthusiasm. Few expected there to be another similar landmark, but Victoria lived to preside over a splendid diamond jubilee in 1897. "Today is the day," she wrote in her journal on September 23, 1896, "on which I have reigned longer, by a day, than any English sovereign."

The death of Princess Charlotte had changed the British monarchy forever. Had the inordinately popular princess come to the throne, the monarchy might have been allowed to retain more of its privileges. After George IV, aging without dignity, and buffoonish William IV, the public were determined on moving toward a system closer to modern parliamentary democracy.

"There never was a sovereign more jealous, or wisely jealous of the prerogatives which the Constitution has allotted to her," pronounced Disraeli of Victoria, "because she believes that they are for the welfare of her people." Despite the efforts of her ministers, the queen was sometimes resistant to accepting what Anson called "the decision of the country," or a general election or vote in the Commons. She was particularly intent to retain control of the army, even attempting to install Albert as commander in chief. As she told W. E. Forster, then minister for education, in 1874, "No one can be more truly liberal at heart than the Queen is, but she also thinks, that the great principles of the Constitution of this great country ought to be maintained and preserved and that too many alterations and changes should be avoided."

It has been suggested that the monarchy lost power under Victoria and that she was the first figurehead. Yet it was the reforms of Parliament during the reign of William IV that had impelled the monarch further toward a ceremonial role, as the expansion of the electorate meant that the government was dependent on the people for assent to its measures, rather than on the whim of the monarch. Victoria, under the tutelage of Melbourne, was the first monarch actually to embrace the diminished role. The prime minister informed the queen of her rights, and in general, she assented.

The point about Victoria was not that the monarchy finally became constitutional during her reign but that it finally became beneficial to society. She had much more in common with Elizabeth I than she liked to admit, for both had a sense of duty to their country and an ambition to fulfill the role well, not least because both had to fight to succeed. From an early age, Victoria was aware of the importance of duty, responsibility, and hard work. She conceptualized her role as one of service to the country, as opposed to seeing her realm as a playground that enabled financial, social, and often sexual self-indulgence. Unlike her uncles, she was also acutely aware of the importance of image and the key role that she played in symbolizing the monarchy by behaving in a sufficiently regal fashion. She became the first monarch to attempt to seem like an ideal head of state surrounded by her perfect family. The idea of the royal family as the ultimate British family originated with her.

Queen Victoria was the first monarch for some time to devote herself to business, having said, "I hate to be idle." The behavior of George IV and

William IV largely reflected a belief that kings had a divine right to rule, and so, since it was enough that their august presence occupied the throne, they could use their Civil List allowance to spend on parties as they pleased. Victoria signed her papers, toured the country, and, with the exception of the period of her widowhood, obeyed Lord Melbourne's stricture that she should show herself off to her public. Her predecessors had focused on charming a small aristocratic circle, but Victoria was the first to be queen of a country, appealing in particular to the mercantile classes. Although she revealed an early passion for the Whigs, she eventually became more objective. The political leanings of the previous monarchs had been clear; Victoria's was the first reign in which the monarchy derived its prestige from being above politics. Victoria was the first modern monarch, the direct precursor of the notion that the king or queen should exist to raise the morale of the people. And the legacy of her representation as a beneficent ruler remained, even though England was gripped by starvation during long periods of her reign and thousands died in overseas wars.

Victoria gained great independence—but at a price. She was always sure that her mother had not loved her. In 1861, soon after the Duchess of Kent's death, she was surprised to find that the duchess had treasured scores of items from her childhood. "Not a scrap of my writing or of my hair has ever been thrown away—and such touching notes in a book about my babyhood," she marveled to her eldest daughter.

Queen Victoria steered the monarchy through an increasingly prorepublican age, fulfilling the promise of Charlotte and Leopold so many years before. The potential of the innocent Princess had kept her people faithful throughout George IV's years of dotage and William IV's buffoonery, and her acts won them over.

Queen Victoria laid down the foundations for dutiful, non-political governance. It was a hard act to keep up and follow, as her son Prince Edward was to discover. He became an aging playboy, moodily aware of his ever-mounting record as the longest-serving heir to the throne. He finally ascended in 1901 at the age of fifty-nine, and ruled for only nine years before dying in 1910. Female sovereigns may serve their country well, but thanks to their habit of longevity, they do not make life easy for their heirs.

Acknowledgments

I have accrued many debts during my research for this book, for assistance with sources, locations, individuals, and events. I thank the staff and librarians of the Royal Collections and the Royal Archives, Windsor, the British Museum, the Public Record Office, the London Library, Historic Royal Palaces, and local record offices.

I am grateful to Lucy Worsley, Chief Curator of Historic Royal Palaces; the staff of Claremont Fan Court School; St. George's Chapel, Windsor; Ramsgate Local History Society; and Simon Sebag-Montefiore, Alison Weir, Saul David, Martyn Downer, Tracey Borman, Sarah Gristwood, Ian Kelly, Hallie Rubenhold, Julie Peakman, Sophie Edmonds, Hannah Greig, Clarissa Campbell-Orr, Juliet Gardiner, Andrew Roberts, Sir Roy Strong, John Farren, Mike Wadding, James Gray, Tanya Severn, Paul Lang, Paul Miller, Helen Harrall, and all those involved in the making of the BBC Television *Timewatch* episode "Young Victoria," Richard Foreman, Bill Locke, Richard Bradley, Malcolm Craddock, Geoff Williams, and Lucy Hayman.

I owe so much to my editor, Susanna Porter, for support, brilliance, and inspiration, and to Jillian Quint for her hard work and painstaking eye. I also wish to thank my tireless agent, John Saddler. I could not have finished the book without the inestimable and selfless help of my parents in the final months of preparation. I am very grateful to all of them.

Notes

◈

Prologue

7   "strong, large and pretty boy": James Greig, ed., *The Diaries of a Duchess: Extracts from the Diaries of the First Duchess of Northumberland, 1716–1776* (London, 1926), 47.

7   "held by their tutors": Amelia Murray, *Recollections of the Early Years of the Present Century* (London, 1868), 12.

7   "He will either be": Saul David, *The Prince of Pleasure: The Prince of Wales and the Making of the Regency* (London, 1998), 18.

Chapter 1: "The Most Distressing Feelings of My Heart"

13   "Never was there seen": *The Morning Post*, January 20, 1795.

14   "young and impetuous": Thomas Raikes, *A Portion of the Journal Kept by Thomas Raikes, Esq., from 1831 to 1847* (London, 1856–57), 2:55.

15   "irresistible seduction and fascination": Nathaniel Wraxall, *The Historical and the Posthumous Memoirs of Sir Nathaniel William Wraxall* (London, 1884), 5:353.

15   "To tell you what it has": Prince of Wales to Captain J. W. Payne, July 8, 1794, in Arthur Aspinall, ed., *The Correspondence of George, Prince of Wales 1770–1812* (London, 1963–71), 2:444.

15   The caricaturist Isaac Cruikshank: Isaac Cruikshank, "My Grandmother, alias the Jersey Jig, alias the Rival Widows" (1794).

16   "They say her passions": Queen Charlotte to Charles, Duke of Mecklenburg-Strelitz, August 1794, in Aspinall, *George, Prince of Wales*, 3:9.

16   "indelicate manners, indifferent character": Duke of Wellington to Lady Salisbury, in Flora Fraser, *The Unruly Queen* (London, 1996), 43.

17   "We are all working": Prince of Wales, in Aspinall, *George, Prince of Wales*, 2:453.

17   "Pretty face—not expressive": 3rd Earl of Malmesbury, ed., *Diaries and Correspondence of James Harris, First Earl of Malmesbury* (London, 1844), 3:153.

18   "light and flighty mind": Malmesbury, *Diaries*, 3:196.

18   "those of a very high": Malmesbury, *Diaries*, 3:200.

18   "would make an excellent": Princess Caroline to Duke of Wellington, in Carola Oman, *The Gascoyne Heiress: The Life and Diaries of Frances Mary Gascoyne-Cecil, 1802–1829* (London, 1968), 93.

19   "was very delicate": Malmesbury, *Diaries*, 3:208.

Chapter 2: "I Find Him Very Fat, and Nothing as Handsome as His Portrait"

20   The London newspapers: see *The Sun*, October 22–24, 1794, January 22, 1795; *The Times*, July 28, December 10, 1794.

21   "Harris, I am not well": Malmesbury, *Diaries*, 3:217.

21   Malmesbury promised her: see *The Times*, April 6–8, 1795; *Morning Post*, April 6 and 13, 1795; *Morning Chronicle*, April 6 and 11, 1795.

22   "Her amiable qualities will": the king to Prince of Wales, April 8, 1795, in Aspinall, *George, Prince of Wales*, 3:51n.

22   "Tell Mrs. Fitzherbert she is": Malmesbury, *Diaries*, 3:179.

22   "like a man doing a thing": Christopher Hibbert, *George IV, Prince of Wales, 1762–1811* (London, 1972) 2:147.

23   "like death and full of": Lady Maria Stuart, in Egerton Castle, ed., *The Jerningham Letters: Being Excerpts from the Correspondence and Diaries of the Hon Lady Jerningham and of Her Daughter Lady Bedingfield* (London, 1894), 1:75.

23   "the coolness and indifference": Oscar Browning, ed., *The Political Memoranda of Francis, Fifth Duke of Leeds* (London, 1884), 220.

23   "Never was public": *Bon Ton Magazine*, April 1795, 39.

23   "constantly drunk, sleeping": Princess of Wales, as reported by Lord Minto, in Aspinall, *George, Prince of Wales*, 2:460.

23   "I flatter myself that": Princess Elizabeth to Prince of Wales, May 26, 1795, in Aspinall, *George, Prince of Wales*, 3:64.

24   "The poor little Princess": Earl of Bessborough, ed., *Georgiana: Extracts from the Correspondence of Georgiana, Duchess of Devonshire* (London, 1955), 55.

24   "how should she know": David, *Prince of Pleasure*, 170.

24   "the best health": Prince of Wales to Queen Charlotte, June 26, 1795, in Aspinall, *George, Prince of Wales*, 3:69.

24   "I do not know how": Alice Greenwood, *Lives of the Hanoverian Queens of England* (London, 1911), 2:260.

25   "Such shocking outrages": Prince of Wales to Queen Charlotte, November 5, 1795, in Aspinall, *George, Prince of Wales*, 3:108.

Chapter 3: *"An Immense Girl"*

26   "The Princess, after a terrible": Prince of Wales to Queen Charlotte, January 7, 1796, in Aspinall, *George, Prince of Wales,* 3:126–27.

26   "Papa is so delighted": Princess Mary, January 7, 1796, in Flora Fraser, *Princesses: The Six Daughters of George III* (London, 2005), 157.

26   "nothing but his grandchild": Christopher Hibbert, *George III: A Personal History* (London, 1998), 329.

27   "My wife, the wife of": Prince of Wales's Will, in Aspinall, *George, Prince of Wales,* 3:132–39.

29   "Our inclinations are not": Prince of Wales to Princess of Wales, April 30, 1796, in Aspinall, *George, Prince of Wales,* 3:179.

29   "It would be now": Prince of Wales to the king, May 31, 1796, in Aspinall, *George, Prince of Wales,* 3:192.

29   "This worthless wretch": Prince of Wales to the queen, June 2, 1796, in Aspinall, *George, Prince of Wales,* 3:198.

29   "You seem to look": the king to Prince of Wales, May 31, 1796, in Aspinall, *George, Prince of Wales,* 3:194.

29   "Buck! Buck! how many": James Gillray, "Fashionable Jockeyship" (1796).

29   "Marriage has legal restraints": Isaac Cruikshank, "Future Prospects or Symptoms of Love in High Life" (1796).

30   "To be sure he has": Walter Sichel, ed., *The Glenbervie Journals* (London, 1910), 71.

30   "an amiable and accomplished": *The True Briton,* May 12, 1796.

30   "The house seemed as if": *The Times,* June 1, 1796.

30   "poor little girl": Prince of Wales to the king, June 13, 1797, in Aspinall, *George, Prince of Wales,* 3:193.

31   "I regret much": Princess Royal to Lady Elgin, October 2, 1801, in Lady Rose Weigall, *A Brief Memoir of the Princess Charlotte of Wales* (London, 1874), 33.

31   "My little charge was": Weigall, *Princess Charlotte,* 11.

31   "recovered her good-humour": Ibid.

32   "And I tell you": Prince of Wales to the king, in Aspinall, *George, Prince of Wales,* 3:378.

32   "she said that she was": Countess of Minto, ed., *The Life and Letters of Sir Gilbert Elliot, 1st Earl of Minto* (London, 1874), 3:18.

32   "God grand that you": Princess Royal to Lady Elgin, February 1798, in Weigall, *Princess Charlotte,* 20.

Chapter 4: "Fleas Are the Only Enemies HRH Has"

34   "huzzaed and kissed her hand": Thea Holme, *Prinny's Daughter* (London, 1976), 43.

34   "'Bless papa, mamma'": Princess Elizabeth to Prince of Wales, in Aspinall, *George, Prince of Wales*, 3:357.

34   "She is getting to the age": Weigall, *Princess Charlotte*, 34.

35   "passions boiling over": Charles Greville, March 17, 1829, in Lytton Strachey and Roger Fulford, eds., *The Greville Memoirs* (London, 1938), 1:271–72.

36   "vows of eternal love": Lady Bess Foster, journal, in *Dearest Bess*, edited by Dorothy Stuart (London, 1955), 207.

36   "danced with great": Princess Mary to Lady Charlotte Finch, January 2, 1803, in Fraser, *Princesses*, 200.

36   "he was to take": Horace Twiss, ed., *The Public and Private Life of Lord Chancellor Eldon* (London, 1844), 1:77.

36   "The King may attempt": Charles James Fox to Prince of Wales, August 26, 1804, in Aspinall, *George, Prince of Wales*, 5:93.

Chapter 5: The Mistress of Montague House

38   "the abundant and": Castalia, Countess Granville, ed., *Lord Granville Leveson Gower (First Earl Granville): Private Correspondence, 1781–1821* (London, 1916), 1:251.

38   "How the sea-captains": Lady Hester Stanhope, *Memoirs of the Lady Hester Stanhope* (London, 1845), 1:308.

39   "You should go out": see J. Fairburn, *An Inquiry, or Delicate Investigation, into the Conduct of Her Royal Highness the Princess of Wales*, 4th ed. (London, 1820), 65–66.

40   "From this time the drawing rooms": Fairburn, *Delicate Investigation*, 52.

42   "there have appeared": the king to Princess Caroline, January 28, 1807, in Aspinall, *George, Prince of Wales*, 6:127; Princess of Wales to Anne Hayman, February 2, 1807, in Fraser, *Princesses*, 218.

42   "monster": Arthur Aspinall, ed., *The Letters of the Princess Charlotte, 1811–1817* (London, 1949), xi.

42   "He writes day and night": Lady Bessborough to Leveson Gower, October 23, in Granville, ed., *Gower Correspondence*, 2:232.

Chapter 6: Forming the Character of a Young Princess

43   "It is quite charming": the king, February 25, 1805, in Twiss, *Lord Chancellor Eldon*, 1:481.

44   "free from all fault": Lady Elgin, in Aspinall, *Charlotte*, ix.

45   "liberty of private judgement": Hannah More, *Letters to Young Ladies* (London, 1777), 40.

45   "Where, may I ask": Aspinall, *Charlotte*, ix.

46   "I shall labour": Aspinall, *Charlotte*, x.

46   "A pretty Queen": George Thomas Keppel, Earl of Albemarle, *Fifty Years of My Life* (London, 1876), 1:300.

47   "You do not see": Princess Charlotte to Miss Elphinstone, August 11, 1814, in Aspinall, *Charlotte*, 147.

47   "Forgive me, my dearest": RA 49580, in Hibbert, *George IV* (London, 1972), 246.

49   "had all the fulness": Charlotte Bury, *The Court of England Under George IV* (London, 1896), 1:36.

50   "She is forward": Sichel, *Glenbervie Journals*, 153.

50   "I do not think": Albemarle, *Fifty Years of My Life*, 1:290.

50   "Nothing like exercise": Hon. Berkeley Paget to Sir Arthur Paget, July 15, 1810, in Lord Hylton, ed., *The Paget Brothers, 1790–1840* (London, 1918), 144.

50   "something so very": Princess Charlotte to Miss Elphinstone, March 17, 1816, in Aspinall, *Charlotte*, 233.

50   "full of mystery": Earl of Ilchester, ed., *The Journal of Lady Holland* (London, 1908), 2:41.

51   "no dark passages": Gifford to John Murray, 1815, in Samuel Smiles, ed. *Memoir and Correspondence of the Late John Murray* (London, 1891), 1:282.

51   "I think Maryanne": Princess Charlotte to Miss Elphinstone, January 22, 1812, in Aspinall, *Charlotte*, 26.

51   "I pity her": Bury, *Court of England*, 1:19.

Chapter 7: Sex, Lies, and Scandals

52   "No family was": Princess Charlotte to Miss Elphinstone, January 10, 1812, Aspinall, *Charlotte*, 23.

52   "Mrs. Clarke": Paul Berry, *By Royal Appointment* (London, 1970), 24.

53   "The sensation in": Charles Lamb, March 28, 1809, in W. C. Hazlitt, ed., *Letters of Charles Lamb* (London, 1886), 1:397.

53   "I think that": Berry, *By Royal Appointment*, 54.

53   "Prince Whiskerandos": Princess Charlotte to Miss Elphinstone, October 23, 1811, in Aspinall, *Charlotte*, 10.

54   "quite lost": Princess Charlotte to Miss Elphinstone, July 20, 1811, in Aspinall, *George, Prince of Wales*, 8:49n.

Chapter 8: Prince Regent

57   "My dearest father": Princess Charlotte to the Prince of Wales, 1811, in Aspinall, *George, Prince of Wales*, 8:193.

57   "Only to tell you": Princess Charlotte to Miss Hayman, 1811, in Weigall, *Princess Charlotte*, 53.

58   "was not a spot": Christopher Hibbert, *George IV, Regent and King, 1811–1830* (London, 1973), 6.

59   "What think you": Percy Bysshe Shelley, in R. Ingpen, ed., *The Letters of Percy Bysshe Shelley* (London, 1912), 77.

59   "Nor will it be": Ibid., 99–100.

59   "We go on": Princess Elizabeth to the Prince of Wales, September 11, 1808, in Aspinall, *George, Prince of Wales*, 6:308.

Chapter 9: The Nunnery

60   "Charlotte is not": Princess Mary to the prince regent, July 6, 1812, in Aspinall, *George, Prince of Wales*, 8:35.

61   "The same thing": Charlotte to Miss Elphinstone, October 5, 1811, in Aspinall, *Charlotte*, 7.

61   "great variety of": the queen to the prince regent, June 5, 1811, in Aspinall, *George, Prince of Wales*, 8:21.

61   "[This] was a most": Princess Charlotte to Miss Elphinstone, July 11, 1811, in Aspinall, *Charlotte*, 4.

61   "I shall regularly": Princess Charlotte to Miss Elphinstone, September 26, 1811, in Aspinall, *Charlotte*, 6.

61   "very kind to me": Princess Charlotte to Miss Elphinstone, July 11, 1811 and June 10, 1811, in Aspinall, *Charlotte*, 3, 2.

61   "3 boxes of prints": Princess Charlotte to Miss Elphinstone, September 6, 1811, in Aspinall, *Charlotte*, 5.

62   "ridiculous jokes": Princess Charlotte to Miss Elphinstone, September 25, 1811, in Aspinall, *Charlotte*, 6.

62   "George Fitz-Clarence is arrived": Princess Charlotte to Miss Elphinstone, October 11, 1811, in Aspinall, *Charlotte*, 8.

64   "At every motion": The Grand Duchess Catherine to Tsar Alexander, in Alexander I, Emperor of Russia, *Scenes of Russian Court Life*, edited by Henry Havelock (London, 1917), 222.

64   "You are grown": Princess Charlotte to Miss Elphinstone, October 3, 1811, Aspinall, *Charlotte*, 7.

64   *"shriveled lemon"*: Princess Charlotte to Miss Elphinstone, January 8, 1812, in Aspinall, *Charlotte*, 23.

64   "The Princess Charlotte rose": Buckingham and Chandos, *Memoirs of the Court and Cabinets of George the Third* (London, 1853–55), 1:239, 250–51.

65   "Weep, daughter of a": "Lines to a Lady Weeping," March 1812, Byron, *Works*, 65.

65   "which could never": Princess Charlotte to Miss Elphinstone, January 10, 1812, in Aspinall, *Charlotte*, 23.

66   "The print shops": Ibid.

67   "The Prince of Whales": "The Prince of Whales, or the Fisherman at Anchor," May 1, 1812. The poem was published six weeks earlier.

67   "There are in": Bury, *Court of England*, 1:112.

67   "I confess I": Princess Charlotte to Miss Elphinstone, August 24, 1812, in Aspinall, *Charlotte*, 27–28.

68   "all his dark": Princess Charlotte to Miss Elphinstone, October 26, 1812, in Aspinall, *Charlotte*, 32.

68   "The Bishop is here": Princess Charlotte to Miss Elphinstone, November 16, 1812, Aspinall, *Charlotte*, 38.

68   "I have seen": Princess Charlotte to Miss Elphinstone, October 20, 1813, in Aspinall, *Charlotte*, 82.

Chapter 10: "Thinking that She Has a Will of Her Own"

71   "ready to receive": Arthur Aspinall, ed., *The Later Correspondence of George III* (Cambridge, 1963) 1:202–3.

71   "I know all": Bury, *Court of England*, 1:113.

71   "If she were": J. W. Kaye, ed., *Autobiography of Miss Cornelia Knight* (London, 1861), 1:184.

72   "convenient spie": Kaye, *Autobiography*, 1:66.

72   "protracted": Kaye, *Autobiography*, 1:203.

72   "superb dress of": *The Magazine of Fashion*, February 5, 1813.

73   "opened the Ball": Princess Charlotte to Miss Elphinstone, February 7, 1813, in Aspinall, *Charlotte*, 51.

73   "The Queen and the whole pack": Ibid.

73   "the deep wounds": *The Morning Chronicle*, February 10, 1813.

73   "whether it was fit": Lord Colchester, *The Diary and Correspondence of Charles Abbot, Lord Colchester* (London, 1861), 2:421.

74   "It is quite": Princess Charlotte to Miss Elphinstone, February 16, 1813, in Aspinall, *Charlotte*, 53–54.

74   "It really came": Princess Charlotte to Miss Elphinstone, September 6, 1813, in Aspinall, *Charlotte*, 71.

74   Two of her female friends: Kaye, *Autobiography*, 1:221.

74   "If you have": Princess Charlotte to Miss Elphinstone, March 7, 1813, in Aspinall, *Charlotte*, 60.

74   "It leaves you": Princess Charlotte to Miss Elphinstone, March 2, 1813, in Aspinall, *Charlotte*, 59.

75   "ill used": Princess Charlotte to Miss Elphinstone, September 6, 1813, in Aspinall, *Charlotte*, 71.

75   "My mother was": F. Max Müller, ed., Baron E. Von Stockmar, *The Memoirs of Baron Stockmar* (London, 1872), 1:2.

75   "It is a subject": Princess Charlotte to Miss Elphinstone, September 19, 1813, in Aspinall, *Charlotte*, 74–75.

75   "without being seen": Captain Hesse to Miss Elphinstone, January 12, 1814, in Aspinall, *The Letters of King George IV, 1812–1830* (Cambridge, 1938), 1:387.

76   "She was a young lady": J. Raymond, ed., *The Reminiscences and Recollections of Captain Gronow, 1810–1860* (London, 1964), 47.

76   "most high-flown praises": Princess Charlotte to Miss Elphinstone, January 17, 1814, in Aspinall, *Charlotte*, 106.

76   "intriguantes in every": Princess Charlotte to Miss Elphinstone, August 18, 1813, in Aspinall, *Charlotte*, 67.

76   "by no means": Princess Charlotte to Miss Elphinstone, August 24, 1813, in Aspinall, *Charlotte*, 69.

76   "Young P. and her father": Henry Brougham to Thomas Creevey, in John Gore, ed., *A Selection of the Letters and Papers of Thomas Creevey* (London: John Murray, 1948), 182.

77   "His constancy is": Princess Charlotte to Miss Elphinstone, December 10, 1813, in Aspinall, *Charlotte*, 91.

77   "Charlotte must lay aside": Kaye, *Autobiography*, 1:240

Chapter 11: Violent Orange Attacks

79   "a future Queen": Princess Charlotte to Miss Elphinstone, October 15, 1813, in Aspinall, *Charlotte*, 75.

79   "the young Princess's": Henry Brougham to Thomas Creevey, in Gore, *Creevey Papers*, 198.

79   "Holland is a very odd place": Princess Charlotte to Miss Elphinstone, January 4, 1814, in Aspinall, *Charlotte*, 101.

80   "iron rod": Princess Charlotte to Miss Elphinstone, September 12, 1813, in Aspinall, *Charlotte*, 73.

80   "absolutely neither": Princess Charlotte to Miss Elphinstone, August 14, 1813, in Aspinall, *Charlotte*, 63.

81   "never be persuaded": Princess Charlotte to Miss Elphinstone, October 20, 1813, in Aspinall, *Charlotte*, 82.

81   "I see he": Princess Charlotte to Miss Elphinstone, October 19, 1813, in Aspinall, *Charlotte*, 78–79.

81   "My *torments* and": Princess Charlotte to Miss Elphinstone, November 29, 1813, in Aspinall, *Charlotte*, 87.

81   *"every argument of"*: Princess Charlotte to Miss Elphinstone, December 1, 1813, in Aspinall, *Charlotte*, 87–88.

81   "I am doing": Princess Charlotte to Miss Elphinstone, December 8, 1813, in Aspinall, *Charlotte*, 89.

82   "according to the": Princess Charlotte to Miss Elphinstone, December 13, 1813, in Aspinall, *Charlotte*, 91, 92.

82   "You make me": Ibid.

82   "I could only": Kaye, *Autobiography*, 1:266.

Chapter 12: The Rising Sun

83   "It signifies nothing": Creevey to Brougham, in Gore, *Creevey Papers*, 107.

83   "more a Dutch woman": Princess Charlotte to Miss Elphinstone, December 14, 1813, in Aspinall, *Charlotte*, 93, 94.

83   "I shall ever say": Princess Charlotte to Miss Elphinstone, December 18, 1813, in Aspinall, *Charlotte*, 95.

84   "all his anxious desire": Princess Charlotte to Miss Elphinstone, December 14, 1813, in Aspinall, *Charlotte*, 93.

84   *"such a state"*: Princess Charlotte to Miss Elphinstone, January 17, 1814, in Aspinall, *Charlotte*, 105.

84   "really oppressed": Princess Charlotte to Miss Elphinstone, January 10, 1814, in Aspinall, *Charlotte*, 102.

85   "Were anythng to": Princess Charlotte to Miss Elphinstone, January 13, 1814, in Aspinall, *Charlotte*, 104.

85   "wishes his wife": Bury, *Court of England*, 1:169.

85   "Never desert your Mother!": Holme, *Prinny's Daughter*, 152.

85   "ability to support": Earl Grey to Princess Charlotte, April 10, 1814, in Aspinall, *Charlotte*, 114.

85   "When the marriage": Princess Charlotte to the prince regent, April 15, 1814, in Aspinall, *Charlotte*, 115.

86   "Dearest Charlotte": Hibbert, *George IV, Regent and King*, 61.

86   "original and indefatigable": Egerton MSS, 3362, fol. 99, British Library.

87   "The Emperor of Russia": Bury, *Court of England*, 1:168.

87   "almost continually crowded": *The Times*, June 23, 1814.

87   "My ears are very ugly": Holme, *Prinny's Daughter*, 156.

88   "The English": Earl Stanhope, *Notes of Conversations with the Duke of Wellington, 1831–1851* (London, 1998), 10.

89   "I am sometimes": Bury, *Court of England*, 1:174.

90   "Here if you": Leopold to Sophie, April 25, 1814, in E. C. Corti, *Leopold I of Belgium* (London, 1923), 93.

91   "lest it": Kaye, ed., *Autobiography*, 1:294.

91   "elegant petticoat": *The Lady's Magazine*, June 13, 1814.

92   "*totally and for ever*": Princess Charlotte to the Prince of Orange, June 16, 1814, in Aspinall, *Charlotte*, 117.

92   "I must wholly": Princess Charlotte to the prince regent, June 18, 1814, in Aspinall, *Charlotte*, 119.

92   "Plagues you must": Duke of Sussex to Princess Charlotte, July 4, 1814, in Aspinall, *Charlotte*, 120–21

92   "Tomorrow may probably": Princess Charlotte to Miss Elphinstone, July 11, 1814, in Aspinall, *Charlotte*, 125.

Chapter 13: "The Soldiers Will Be Ordered Out"

95   "a bird set loose": Henry Brougham, *The Life and Times of Henry, Lord Brougham* (London, 1871), 2:230.

97   "it must be": Brougham, *Life and Times*, 2:231.

97   "I pressed you to my burning lips": Princess Charlotte to Miss Elphinstone, July 14, 1814, in Aspinall, *Charlotte*, 127.

98   "You have no": Princess Charlotte to Miss Elphinstone, July 14, 1814, in Aspinall, *Charlotte*, 127.

99   "vulgar in conversation": Princess Charlotte to Miss Elphinstone, July 21, 1814, in Aspinall, *Charlotte*, 133.

99   "I must say": Princess Charlotte to Miss Elphinstone, July 30, 1814, in Aspinall, *Charlotte*, 138.

100   "She decidedly": Ibid.

100   "To the Princess": Bury, *Court of England*, 2:158.

Chapter 14: A Little Turquoise Heart

101   "Great and powerful": Lewis Melville, *An Injured Queen: Caroline of Brunswick* (London, 1912), 2:318.

101   "I see no chance for you": Princess Charlotte to Miss Elphinstone, September 4, 1814, in Aspinall, *Charlotte*, 149.

102   "it would have": the king of the Belgians to Queen Victoria, May 21, 1845, RA y71/65, in Cecil Woodham-Smith, *Queen Victoria: Her Life and Times* (London, 1972), 26.

102   She was also deep in debt: See British Library Additional MS 38261, 28–29, 98.

103   "*lined* on both sides": Princess Charlotte to Miss Elphinstone, September 10, 1814, in Aspinall, *Charlotte*, 150.

103   "[The] young gentleman here": Princess Charlotte to Miss Elphinstone, September 10, 1814, in Aspinall, *Charlotte*, 151.

104 "Think only of": Ibid.

105 "I cannot tell": Princess Charlotte to Miss Elphinstone, September 15, 1814, in Aspinall, *Charlotte,* 152.

106 "I am told": Princess Charlotte to Miss Elphinstone, October 7, 1814, in Aspinall, *Charlotte,* 157.

106 "I think & think": Princess Charlotte to Miss Elphinstone, September 22, 1814, in Aspinall, *Charlotte,* 155.

106 "long, long after": Princess Charlotte to Miss Elphinstone, November 10, 1814, in Aspinall, *Charlotte,* 164.

107 "it ought not": Princess Charlotte to Miss Elphinstone, November 11, 1814, in Aspinall, *Charlotte,* 165, 166.

107 "My heart has had": Princess Charlotte to Miss Elphinstone, December 14, 1814, in Aspinall, *Charlotte,* 169.

Chapter 15: The Black Sheep

108 "too deep": Princess Charlotte to Miss Elphinstone, December 22, 1814, in Aspinall, *Charlotte,* 174.

108 "If the *plain & damning* proofs": Princess Charlotte to Miss Elphinstone, December 14, 1814, in Aspinall, *Charlotte,* 169.

108 "no consolation": Princess Charlotte to Miss Elphinstone, December 18, 1814, in Aspinall, *Charlotte,* 171.

108 "I cannot allow": Princess Charlotte to Miss Elphinstone, December 22, 1814, in Aspinall, *Charlotte,* 174.

109 "Handsome as he": Princess Charlotte to Miss Elphinstone, January 8, 1815, in Aspinall, *Charlotte,* 175.

109 "*easy, cool,* familiar": Princess Charlotte to Miss Elphinstone, January 1815, in Aspinall, *Charlotte,* 182.

109 "Amusez vous": Princess Mary's memorandum, December 31, 1814, in Aspinall, *George IV,* 1:519, 520.

110 "extreme satisfaction": The prince regent to Princess Charlotte, December 26, 1814, in Aspinall, *George IV,* 1:514.

110 "I live in a state of dread": Princess Charlotte to Miss Elphinstone, January 11, 1815, in Aspinall, *Charlotte,* 176.

110 "a nasty insignificant": Princess Charlotte to Miss Elphinstone, March 15, 1815, in Aspinall, *Charlotte,* 193.

110 "*was jealous of her*": Princess Charlotte to Miss Elphinstone, January 1815, in Aspinall, *Charlotte,* 181.

110 "What do I care": Princess Charlotte to Miss Elphinstone, January 1815, in Aspinall, *Charlotte,* 180.

111 "when common sence": Princess Charlotte to Miss Elphinstone, January 1815, in Aspinall, *Charlotte,* 179.

111   "The Leo, as I": Princess Charlotte to Miss Elphinstone, Feburary 28, 1815,
       in Aspinall, *Charlotte*, 191.

111   *"No arguments"*: Princess Charlotte to Miss Elphinstone, February 26, 1815,
       in Aspinall, *Charlotte*, 191.

111   "quite impossible": Greenwood, *Hanoverian Queens*, 2:163.

112   "It *is said*": Princess Charlotte to Miss Elphinstone, March 2, 1815, in As-
       pinall, *Charlotte*, 192.

112   "All at the Castle": Princess Charlotte to Miss Elphinstone, March 17, 1815,
       in Aspinall, *Charlotte*, 193.

112   "If we do not": Princess Charlotte to Miss Elphinstone, March 23, 1815, in
       Aspinall, *Charlotte*, 195.

Chapter 16: "Everything I Could Wish & Desire Collected in One"

113   "upon my honour": Princess Charlotte to the Prince Regent, May 2, 1815, in
       Aspinall, *George IV*, 2:60.

113   "was a subject": Princess Charlotte to Miss Elphinstone, July 22, 1815, in As-
       pinall, *Charlotte*, 199.

114   "It is so near": Princess Charlotte to Miss Elphinstone, August 21, 1815, in
       Aspinall, *Charlotte*, 203.

114   *"made sufficiently* uneasy": Princess Charlotte to Miss Elphinstone, August
       25, 1815, in Aspinall, *Charlotte*, 203.

114   "delighted, not to say charmed": Princess Charlotte to Miss Elphinstone, Au-
       gust 29, 1815, in Aspinall, *Charlotte*, 204.

114   "telling tales": Princess Charlotte to Miss Elphinstone, September 25, 1815,
       in Aspinall, *Charlotte*, 208. She later wrote to Margaret that she thought, all
       in all, that she had a lucky escape. Princess Charlotte to Miss Elphinstone,
       January 20, 1815, in Aspinall, *Charlotte*, 183.

114   "His silence to you": Princess Charlotte to Miss Elphinstone, October 25,
       1815, in Aspinall, *Charlotte*, 211.

114   "I think the best thing": Princess Charlotte to Miss Elphinstone, October 26,
       1815, in Aspinall, *Charlotte*, 212.

115   "Surely, surely": Princess Charlotte to Miss Elphinstone, December 6, 1815,
       in Aspinall, *Charlotte*, 217.

116   "The army were": Charlotte Anne Eaton, *The Days of Battle* (London, 1853), 22.

116   "The finger of": Harry Smith, in G. C. Moore Smith, ed., *The Autobiography
       of Lieutenant-General Sir Harry Smith* (London, 1902), 1:275.

116   "It is a glorious victory": Lord Stavordale, ed., *Henry, Lord Holland, Further
       Memoirs of the Whig Party, 1807–21* (London, 1905), 220.

117   "day was ushered": *The Morning Post*, January 10, 1816.

117   "No one will": Princess Charlotte to the prince regent, December 1815, in Aspinall, *George IV*, 2:140.

117   "He had a mania": The Earl of Lauderdale to the Marquess of Anglesey, in Aspinall, *George IV*, 2:136–37.

117   "quite nervous": Kaye, *Autobiography*, 2:81.

117   "Everybody talks of": Ibid.

118   "cure *that*": Princess Charlotte to Miss Elphinstone, February 23, 1816, in Aspinall, *Charlotte*, 223.

118   "I find him charming": Princess Charlotte to Miss Elphinstone, February 26, 1816, in Aspinall, *Charlotte*, 224.

118   "I think him": Princess Charlotte to Miss Elphinstone, March 1, 1816, in Aspinall, *Charlotte*, 225.

118   "took it uncommonly": Princess Charlotte to Miss Elphinstone, March 1816, in Aspinall, *Charlotte*, 237.

118   "I never saw": Princess Charlotte to Miss Elphinstone, February 26, 1816, in Aspinall, *Charlotte*, 225.

118   "Imagination cannot": Countess of Ilchester to Lady Frampton, February 26, 1816, in Mary Frampton, ed., *The Journal of Mary Frampton* (London, 1885), 267.

118   "I am quite satisfied": Princess Charlotte to Miss Elphinstone, March 1, 1816, in Aspinall, *Charlotte*, 226.

119   "I have had a good lecture": Princess Charlotte to Miss Elphinstone, March 1, 1816, in Aspinall, *Charlotte*, 225.

119   "putting him on his guard": Princess Charlotte to Miss Elphinstone, March 22, 1816, in Aspinall, *Charlotte*, 234.

119   "disapproves highly": Princess Charlotte to Miss Elphinstone, March 2, 1816, in Aspinall, *Charlotte*, 227.

119   "For God's sake": Princess Charlotte to Miss Elphinstone, March 2, 1816, in Aspinall, *Charlotte*, 227.

119   "You know how": Princess Charlotte to Miss Elphinstone, March 4, 1816, in Aspinall, *Charlotte*, 228.

119   "Never let it": Princess Charlotte to Miss Elphinstone, March 13, 1816, in Aspinall, *Charlotte*, 230.

119   "[She] surprises everybody": Archduke John of Austria to Prince Metternich, March 1816, in Corti, *Leopold*, 1:36.

121   "a smuggled wedding": Princess Charlotte to Miss Elphinstone, March 17, 1816, in Aspinall, *Charlotte*, 231.

121   "It is such a fine thing": Princess Charlotte to Miss Elphinstone, April 19, 1816, in Aspinall, *Charlotte*, 241.

Chapter 17: Mr. and Mrs. Coburg

123   "counteract the despondency": *The Augustan Review,* June 1816.

123   "I cannot say": Princess Charlotte to Miss Elphinstone, May 4, 1816, in Aspinall, *Charlotte,* 242.

125   "so infected & impregnated": Princess Charlotte to Miss Elphinstone, May 7, 1816, in Aspinall, *Charlotte,* 243.

125   "a faithful account": Princess Charlotte to Miss Elphinstone, May 4, 1816, in Aspinall, *Charlotte,* 242.

125   "handsomer": Stockmar, Müller, *Memoirs,* 1:42.

126   "very *unexpected* and *undesired*": Princess Charlotte to Miss Elphinstone, May 10, 1816, in Aspinall, *Charlotte,* 243.

126   "We have not the space": *The Times,* May 16, 1816.

126   "Long may the Noble Line": Thomas Green, *Memoirs of Her Late Highness, Princess Augusta of Wales* (London, 1818), 260.

127   "never to permit": The king of the Belgians to Queen Victoria, in A. C. Benson and Viscount Esher, eds., *The Letters of Queen Victoria, 1837–1861* (London, 1907), 1:216.

128   "Thank Heaven": Robert Huish, *Life and Memoirs of Her Royal Highness, Princess Charlotte of Saxe-Coburg-Saalfeld* (London, 1818), 231.

129   "everything that can": Stockmar, in Müller, *Memoirs,* 1:44.

129   "Come in, come in!": Kaye, *Autobiography,* 2:112.

129   "We went to see": Princess Mary to Prince of Wales, September 1816, in Aspinall, *George IV,* 1:170.

130   "He is much in love": Princess Charlotte to Miss Elphinstone, August 12, 1816, in Aspinall, *Charlotte,* 243.

130   "He is certainly": Princess Charlotte to Miss Elphinstone, September 1816, in Aspinall, *Charlotte,* 245.

130   "sometimes inclined": D. M. Stuart, *Daughter of England* (London, 1951), 247.

131   "the gayest and prettiest": Princess Charlotte to Miss Elphinstone, December 26, 1816, in Aspinall, *Charlotte,* 246.

131   "We are doing": Princess Charlotte to Miss Elphinstone, December 26, 1816, in Aspinall, *Charlotte,* 245.

131   "The people cherished": Bury, *Court of England,* 2:278–79.

Chapter 18: "Some Strange, Awkward Symptoms"

133   "Princess Charlotte is going on": Lady Holland to Mrs. Creevey, September 1817, in Gore, *Creevey Papers,* 161.

134   "I have not now a wish": Countess of Ilchester to Marchioness of Landsdownen, November 11, 1817, in Frampton, *Journal,* 299.

134   "I have it not in my power": Princess Charlotte, 1817, in Weigall, *Princess Charlotte,* 164.

135   "Nothing can be": Sir Robert Gardiner to Sir Benjamin Bloomfield, November 4, 1817, in Aspinall, *George IV,* 2:209–10.

135   "made a considerable": Sir Robert Gardiner and Dr. Sims to the cabinet minister, November 5, 1817, in Aspinall, *George IV,* 2:211.

137   "I am now quite": Stockmar, in Müller, *Memoirs,* 1:66.

137   "It really was as though": Brougham, *Life and Times,* 2:332.

137   "We never recall": *The Times,* November 6, 1817.

137   "One met in the streets": Princess Lieven, November 14–26, 1817, in Lionel G. Robinson, ed., *Letters of Dorothea, Princess Lieven During her Residence in London* (London, 1902), 34.

138   "[You] had it in your power": Queen Charlotte to the prince regent, November 7, 1817, in Aspinall, *George IV,* 2:704.

138   "It is true": Leopold to Princess Sophie, December 22, 1817, in Corti, *Leopold,* 1:169.

138   "November saw the": Stockmar, in Müller, *Memoirs,* 1:66.

140   "Princess Charlotte and the excellent man": Wilberforce in the House of Commons, April 1818, in Hansard, *Parliamentary Debates,* 38:94.

Chapter 19: "The Dregs of Their Dull Race"

143   "My attention was called": Thomas Creevey, "Notes of a Conversation with H.R.H. The Duke of Kent," December 11, 1817, in Gore, *Creevey Papers,* 163. *The Morning Chronicle,* November 7, 1817. The newspaper came to the Duke's table on about November 24.

144   "the damndest": Duke of Wellington to Thomas Creevey, reported in the latter's journal, in Gore, *Creevey Papers,* 167.

144   "Princes, the dregs": Percy Bysshe Shelley, "Sonnet: England in 1819," in *Poetical Works* (Oxford, 1970), 574–75.

144   "plum pudding faces": Princess of Wales to Anne Hayman, February 2, 1807, in Fraser, *Princesses,* 218.

144   "Hymen's War terrific": Roger Fulford, *Hanover to Windsor* (London, 1960), 24.

145   "[If the] Cabinet": Duke of Clarence to the queen, December 16, 1817, in Aspinall, *George IV,* 2:223.

146   "She is doomed": Duke of Clarence to George FitzClarence, March 21, 1818, in Arthur Aspinall, *Mrs. Jordan and Her Family* (London, 1951), 189.

146   "The Duchess of Clarence": Duke of Kent to George FitzClarence, November 21, 1818, RA ADD 39/319, in Philip Ziegler, *King William IV* (London, 1971), 126.

147   "Altho' I trust I shall be": Creevey, "Notes of a Conversation with the Duke of Kent," in Gore, *Creevey Papers,* 164.

148   "name was never uttered": Duke of Wellington, in Philip Henry Stan-
       hope, *Notes of Conversations with the Duke of Wellington, 1831–51* (Oxford,
       1938), 322.

150   "connection to": Woodham-Smith, *Queen Victoria*, 27.

150   "I am leaving": Victoire, Princess of Leiningen, to the Duke of Kent, January
       25, 1818, RA MW/25, in Monica Charlot, *Victoria: the Young Queen* (Oxford,
       1991), 24.

150   "I want you to know": Kent to Princess Victoire, January 1818, RA, M2/43,
       in Woodham-Smith, *Queen Victoria*, 28.

150   "of very great family": Creevey, "Notes of a Conversation with the Duke of
       Kent," in Gore, *Creevey Papers*, 163–64.

150   "The lady, in the Duke of Kent's eye": John Wilson Croker to Robert Peel,
       November 26, 1817, in Louis L. Jennings, ed., *The Croker Papers* (London,
       1885), 1:110.

150   "We can wish": *The Times*, April 27, 1818.

151   "They [the dukes] have insulted": Duke of Wellington to Thomas Creevey,
       reported in the latter's journal, in Gore, *Creevey Papers*, 167.

Chapter 20: *"As Plump as a Partridge"*

152   "The Duke, though a man of the world": Augusta, Dowager Duchess of
       Saxe-Coburg, *In Napoleonic Days: Extracts from the Private Diary of Augusta,
       Duchess of Saxe-Coburg-Saalfeld*, ed. The Princess Beatrice (London, 1941), 123.

152   "find in this": Augusta, Dowager Duchess of Saxe-Coburg, *In Napoleonic
       Days*, 125.

153   "Her nerves are": RA 45340, Duke of Kent to Baron de Mallet, January 26,
       1819, in Woodham-Smith, *Queen Victoria*, 27.

153   "I wish to God": Fraser, *Princesses*, 312.

155   "This evening will": Duke of Kent to Duchess of Kent, December 31, 1818,
       RA, M2/73, in Stanley Weintraub, *Victoria: Biography of a Queen* (London,
       1987), 35–36.

155   "I fear what": Duke of Kent to Baron de Mallet, March 29, 1819, in RA
       45342–3, Woodham-Smith, *Queen Victoria*, 41. The Duke was very worried
       about his former mistress. See Duke of Kent to General Knollys, April 22,
       1819, U1186 C 2/9, Kent County Archives Office.

156   "pretty little Princess": Stockmar, in Müller, *Memoirs*, 1:77.

156   "Thank God": Duke of Kent to Baron de Mallet, June 8, 1819, RA 43344–5,
       in Woodham-Smith, *Queen Victoria*, 30.

156   "Again a Charlotte": Lieutenant General Charles Grey, *The Early Years of His
       Royal Highness the Prince Consort* (London, 1867), 12.

157   "truly a model": Duke of Kent to Dowager Duchess of Saxe-Coburg, May
       24, 1818, RA M3/3, in Woodham-Smith, *Queen Victoria*, 47.

157 "I would have": Duchess of Kent to Dowager Duchess of Saxe-Coburg, June 22, 1819, RA VIC/ M3/6, in Lynne Vallone, *Becoming Victoria* (New Haven, 2001), 4.

157 "The appearance of": *The Times,* June 4, 1819.

158 "Give her the mother's name": RA M4/26, Duchess of Kent to Earl Grey, in Christopher Hibbert, *Queen Victoria: A Personal History* (London, 1997), 13.

158 "My brothers are": Stockmar, in Müller, *Memoirs,* 1:77.

Chapter 21: Alexandrina Victoria

160 "We must expect": John Stevenson, *Popular Disturbances in England 1700–1870* (London, 1979), 207.

162 "I am nursing": Duchess of Kent to Polyxene von Tubeuf, January 7–10, 1820, in Woodham-Smith, *Queen Victoria,* 57.

163 "Human help could": Duchess of Kent to Polyxene von Tubeuf, in Woodham-Smith, *Queen Victoria,* 60.

164 "He was the strongest": John Wilson Croker to Lord Lowther, January 24, 1820, in Jennings, *Croker Papers,* 1:155.

164 "In every respect": Princess Mary to the prince regent, January 25 and 27, 1820, RA, add 12/359, 361, in Woodham-Smith, *Queen Victoria,* 64.

165 "That Hercules of a man": Princess Lieven to Prince Metternich, January 25, 1820, in Peter Quennell and Dilys Powell, eds., *The Private Letters of Princess Lieven to Prince Metternich* (London, 1937), 6.

165 "The chanting": Mrs. Arbuthnot, February 16, 1820, in Francis Bamford and the Duke of Wellington, eds., *The Journal of Mrs. Arbuthnot* (London, 1950), 1:4–5.

166 "in my solitude here": Duchess of Kent to Polyexne von Tubeuf, January 1820, in Woodham-Smith, *Queen Victoria,* 64.

Chapter 22: An Idol in Kensington Palace

171 "very much indulged": Queen Victoria, in Benson, *Letters,* 1:19.

172 "*dreadfully* dull, dark and gloomy": Princess Victoria to Prince Charles of Leiningen, August 12, 1833, RA Z192/5, in Woodham-Smith, *Queen Victoria,* 67.

172 "multiply till the": Judith Flanders, *The Victorian House* (London, 2003), 76.

173 "She drives me at times": Duchess of Kent to the Dowager Duchess of Saxe-Coburg, June 22–23, 1819, RA M3/6, in Woodham-Smith, *Queen Victoria,* 520.

173 "*le roi Georges* in": Countess Harriet Granville to Lady Morpeth, August 29, 1820, in F. Leveson Gower, ed., *Letters of Harriet, Countess Granville* (London, 1894), 1:168.

174   "In the morning": Augusta, Dowager Duchess of Saxe-Coburg, *In Napoleonic Days*, 215.

174   "With you": Princess Feodora to Queen Victoria, April 15, 1843, in Benson, *Letters*, 1:18.

174   "And I may call": Weintraub, *Victoria*, 61.

175   "I have grown up": Elizabeth Longford, ed., *Darling Loosy: Letters to Princess Louise, 1856–1939* (London, 1991), 155.

175   "accustomed to the society of": Benson, *Letters*, 1:14.

175   "with her fine": Sarah Tooley, *The Personal Life of Queen Victoria* (London, 1897), 18–19.

175   "very kind but extremely shy": Benson, *Letters*, 1:14–15.

175   "My children are dead": Mary Hopkirk, *Queen Adelaide* (London, 1946), 58.

175   "very sorry to be absent": Duchess of Clarence to Princess Victoria, May 24, 1822, in Benson, *Letters*, 1:32–33.

175   George IV certainly: Duke of Wellington to Greville, September 8, 1831, in Strachey and Fulford, *Greville Memoirs*, 2:193.

176   "friendless and alone": Hibbert, *Queen Victoria*, 23. Prince Charles came to England in 1824 and was quite won over by John Conroy.

176   "What you said": Duchess of Kent to John Conroy, December 26, 1838, in Katherine Hudson, *A Royal Conflict* (London, 1994), 16.

177   "In 1823, Conroy's credit": Coutts Archive, Sir John Conroy's Account.

Chapter 23: "The Nation's Hope"

178   "From 1825, Your Royal Highness": John Conroy to Duchess of Kent, July 15, 1837, RA Z 482/1, in Hudson, *A Royal Conflict*, 56.

179   "Your immediate successor": the king of the Belgians to Princess Victoria, June 17, 1837, in Benson, *Letters*, 72.

179   "lived in a mist": Hibbert, *Queen Victoria*, 27.

179   "the basis of": "A Complete History of the Policy followed at Kensington under Sir John Conroy's guidance," memorandum by Charles, Prince of Leiningen, RA M7/67 and Add V2, in 1841, in Woodham-Smith, *Queen Victoria*, 84.

180   "Do you not": Robert Peel to John Wilson Croker, March 23, 1820, in Jennings, *Croker Papers*, 1:170.

180   "generally ends with": The king of the Belgians to Princess Victoria, February 3, 1837, in Benson, *Letters*, 1:60.

180   "those of the English Royal Family": memorandum by Charles, Prince of Leiningen, RA M7/67 and add v2, in Woodham-Smith, *Queen Victoria*, 84.

181   "*everything* down to the smallest": Hudson, *A Royal Conflict*, 72.

182   "again and again": Alison Plowden, *The Young Victoria* (London, 1981), 58.

Chapter 24: Imperial Robes

183 "The King behaved": Harriet Arbuthnot, in Bamford and Wellington, *Journal of Mrs. Arbuthnot*, 1:93.

185 "Neither at the": *The Times*, June 6, 1820.

185 "Often riding to": Stevenson, *Popular Disturbances in England*, 200.

186 "boundless rage of": Kenneth Baker, *George IV: A Life in Caricature* (London, 2005), 162.

186 "I shall support": Deidre le Faye, ed., *Jane Austen's Letters* (London, 1995), 145.

186 "punish an offence": Hansard, 2:167–68

186 "I do indeed": Bury, *Court of England*, 2:265.

186 "guns were firing": A. Cobbett to J. P. Cobbett, November 15, 1820, Cobbett Papers, Nuffield Library.

187 "Let me pass": Joanna Richardson, *The Disastrous Marriage* (London, 1960), 207–8.

187 "her Majesty put on": Grantley F. Berkeley, *My Life and Recollections* (London, 1865–66), 4:175.

187 "Do you think": Lady Anne Hamilton, *Secret History of the Court of England* (London, 1832), 2:17.

188 "gayer than it": Croker, "Diary," *The Croker Papers*, 1:201.

188 "Sir your bitterest": Stavordale, *Henry Lord Holland*, 295.

188 "His mind is clearly made up": Thomas Creevey to Miss Ord, August 27, 1821, in Gore, *Creevey Papers*, 217.

188 "He looks ghastly": Princess Lieven to Prince Metternich, January 31, 1822, in Quennell, *Private Letters*, 151.

189 "It is a rather melancholy thing": Anne to James Cobbett, in E. A. Smith, *A Queen on Trial* (London, 1993), 114.

189 "nothing but a hand": Princess Lieven to Prince Metternich, December 23, 1821, in Quennell, *Private Letters*, 200.

189 "She will be": Fraser, *Princesses*, 334.

189 "We are all": Conroy Papers, Balliol College.

190 "I want words": Duke of Clarence to King George IV, April 9, 1822, in Aspinall, ed., *George IV*, 2:523.

190 "I must confess": Duchess of Kent to Dowager Duchess of Saxe-Coburg, June 22–23, 1819, RA M3/6, in Woodham-Smith, *Queen Victoria*, 520.

Chapter 25: Living in a Very Simple Manner

192 "the governess being *entirely dependent*": memorandum by Charles, Prince of Leiningen, 1841, RA M7/67 and Add V2, in Woodham-Smith, *Queen Victoria*, 83.

192   "great difficulties": Baroness Lehzen to Queen Victoria, February 20, September 6, 1867, RA Y203/79, 80, in Woodham-Smith, *Queen Victoria,* 72.

192   "sit down to table": Hudson, *A Royal Conflict,* 65.

192   "You used to": Princess Feodora to Queen Victoria, November 12, 1842, in Harold A. Albert, *Queen Victoria's Sister* (London, 1967), 40.

192   "She never for the 13 years": Queen Victoria's Journal, November 7, 1838, in Vallone, *Becoming Victoria,* 15.

193   "We lived in a": Queen Victoria, in Benson, *Letters,* 1:13.

193   "hot rolls, swimming in melted butter": Flanders, *Victorian House,* 45.

194   "I led a very unhappy life": Queen Victoria to the Princess Royal, June 9, 1858, in Roger Fulford, ed., *Dearest Child: Letters Between Queen Victoria and the Princess Royal 1858–61* (London, 1964), 111.

194   "the brightest epoch": "I always left Claremont with tears for Kensington Palace," confessed Feodora, in Benson, *Letters,* 1:14–18, 24; Princess Feodora to Queen Victoria, in Albert, *Queen Victoria's Sister,* 38.

195   "At the very first glance": Caroline Bauer, *Posthumous Memoirs of Caroline Bauer* (London, 1884–85), 1:44.

195   "It is very hard for me": Bauer, *Posthumous Memoirs,* 1:95.

196   "Oh," he cried: Bauer, *Posthumous Memoirs,* 1:106.

197   "One of my": Albemarle, *Fifty Years of My Life,* 2:227.

197   "gigantic fairy": J. H. Leigh Hunt, *The Old Court Suburb, or, Memorials of Kensington* (London, 1902), 2:175.

198   "When I look": Princess Feodora to Queen Victoria, in Benson, *Letters,* 18.

198   "always on pins": Queen Victoria to the Princess Royal, March 4, 1858, in Fulford, *Dearest Child,* 72.

Chapter 26: "I Was Greatly Pleased"

199   "Give me your little paw": Queen Victoria, in Benson, *Letters,* 1:17.

200   "paid great attention to": Queen Victoria, in Woodham-Smith, *Queen Victoria,* 78.

200   "marry soon": John Conroy to the Duchess of Kent, July 14, 1826, RA M4/1, in Woodham-Smith, *Queen Victoria,* 79.

200   "Reasoning was of": Robert Peel to John Conroy, July 19, 1825, Peel Papers, British Library Additional MSS 40380, 142.

201   "I need not": Augustus D'Este to Princess Feodora, in Albert, *Queen Victoria's Sister,* 44.

201   "I escaped some": Princess Feodora to Queen Victoria, March 17, 1843, RA Y36/128, in Woodham-Smith, *Queen Victoria,* 81.

202   "I always see": Princess Feodora to Princess Victoria, March 4, 1836, in Albert, *Queen Victoria's Sister,* 55.

202 "I was delighted": Princess Feodora to Princess Victoria, April 23, 1828, RA Y33/3, Vallone, *Becoming Victoria*, 42.

202 "If I had": Princess Feodora to Princess Victoria, May 24, 1829, in Benson, *Letters*, 1:32–33.

202 "Look at that idiot!": Princess Lieven to Prince Metternich, June 30, 1826, in Quennell, *Private Letters*, 372.

203 "leave him the example": Fulford, *Hanover to Windsor*, 27.

Chapter 27: Educating a Princess

204 "A woman on the throne": Dorothy Thompson, *Queen Victoria: Gender and Power* (London, 1990), 93.

205 "There! there is no": Hibbert, *Queen Victoria*, 18.

206 "be unoccupied, for at first": Princess Feodora to Princess Victoria, March 6, 1835, in Albert, *Queen Victoria's Sister*, 82.

206 "We helped her": Elizabeth Gaskell, "My French Master," in Jenny Uglow, *Elizabeth Gaskell: A Habit of Stories* (London, 1993), 28.

207 "You asked me": Princess Victoria to Princess Feodora, September 4, 1829, RA VIC LB1/38, in Vallone, *Becoming Victoria*, 45.

207 "I love to": Viscount Esher, ed., *The Girlhood of Queen Victoria: A Selection from Her Majesty's Diaries* (London, 1912), 1:109.

207 "I hope never": Princess Victoria to Duchess of Kent, 1829, RA VIC Z117, in Vallone, *Becoming Victoria*, 68.

207 "very ill behaved": Good Behaviour Book, November 1, 1831, in Vallone, *Becoming Victoria*, 25.

208 "fat, ugly, wilful": Thompson, *Queen Victoria: Gender and Power*, 91.

208 "short, vulgar looking": June 25, 1831, Strachey and Fulford, *Greville Memoirs*, 2:120.

208 "She moves with": Giles St. Aubyn, *Queen Victoria: A Portrait* (London, 1991), 18.

208 "I [was] very happy to": Princess Victoria to Princess Feodora, December 20, 1835, LB 16/10, in Woodham-Smith, *Queen Victoria*, 67.

208 "the course hitherto": Duchess of Kent to the bishops of Lincoln and London, March 1, 1830, RA M5/7, in Benson, *Letters*, 15.

209 "executed with the": report of the exam of Princess Victoria by the bishops, RA M/5/10, 14, in Woodham-Smith, *Queen Victoria*, 97.

209 "chronological table": Baroness Lehzen to Queen Victoria, December 2, 1867, RA VIC Y203/81, in Charlot, *Victoria*, 51.

209 "appeared to have": note by the archbishop on a letter from the duchess to the archbishop, April 27, 1830, RA VIC Z492/20, in Vallone, *Becoming Victoria*, 101.

209 "Elizabeth was a": probably circa 1828–30, RA Vic Add/7/1A, in Vallone, *Becoming Victoria*, 121.

209 "model of perfection": Hudson, *A Royal Conflict*, 19.

210 "She never reads": Princess Victoria's composition, October 11, 1829, RA VIC Add A7/1A/30, in Vallone, *Becoming Victoria*, 52, 53–54.

210 "How cruel after": August 15, 1839, Strachey and Fulford, *Greville Memoirs*, 4:199.

211 The "babies": Princess Victoria to Princess Feodora, July 5, 1829, RA, VIC Add U 171/11, in Vallone, *Becoming Victoria*, 78.

211 "In the family": Duchess of Clarence to Duchess of Kent, January 12, 1830, RA M4/16, in Woodham-Smith, *Queen Victoria*, 122.

212 "the word *Uncle*": Princess Victoria to the king of the Belgians, November 21, 1836, in Benson, *Letters*, 1:54.

Chapter 28: Sickly Uncle King

214 "two glasses of hot ale": Mrs. Arbuthnot, April 1830, Bamford and Wellington, *Journal of Mrs. Arbuthnot*, 2:352.

214 "with an eager": Helen Cathcart, *Royal Lodge, Windsor* (London, 1966), 141.

214 "No monarch will": *The Times*, July 16, 1830.

215 "This is a damn'd": September 10, 1833, in Strachey and Fulford, *Greville Memoirs*, 2:417.

215 "little old red-nosed": J. Fitzgerald Molloy, *The Sailor King* (London, 1903), 1:224.

215 "*bon enfant*": Princess Lieven to her husband, July 28, 1830, in Robinson, *Letters of Princess Lieven*, 230.

216 "The Queen!": Hopkirk, *Queen Adelaide*, 132.

217 "I earnestly advise": Duke of Wellington to Duchess of Kent, June 30, 1830, RA, M4/21, in Charlot, *Young Victoria*, 84.

217 "Irksome as it": Duchess of Kent to Duke of Wellington, July 1, 1830, and his reply, July 2, and September 8, 1831, RA M4/22–23, in Strachey and Fulford, *Greville Memoirs*, 2:195.

217 "She is the most": Thomas Creevey to Miss Ord, November 2, 1833, in Gore, *Creevey Papers*, 345.

218 "Did I not keep this line": December 16, 1830, in Strachey and Fulford, *Greville Memoirs*, 2:92.

219 "had the permission to": Princess Victoria to Princess Feodora, 1830, RA, LB1/45, in Vallone, *Becoming Victoria*, 19.

220 "The manner in": Hansard, July 6, November 15, 1830, 1:500.

Chapter 29: Charlotte the Queen?

222 It seems peculiar: Duchess of Kent to Earl Grey, June 25, 1831; William IV to Earl Grey, June 26, 1831, RA M4/32, 35, in Charlot, *Young Victoria*, 81.

222 "ready to do that which is": Duchess of Kent to Earl Grey, January 28, 1831, RA M4/27, in Woodham-Smith, *Queen Victoria*, 105.

222 "About a year after": Princess Victoria to the king of the Belgians, November 21, 1836, in Benson, *Letters*, 1:55.

223 "was the object of interest": *Fraser's Magazine*, March 1831.

223 "how particularly anxious": memorandum by the Duchess of Kent about a conversation with the Duchess of Northumberland, February 7, 1831, RA VIC M5/19, in Woodham-Smith, *Queen Victoria*, 65.

224 "The position of": the king of the Belgians to Princess Victoria, May 21, 1833, in Benson, *Letters*, 1:36.

224 "I am very ready to furnish": Princess Victoria to the king of the Belgians, January 23, 1837, in Benson, *Letters*, 1:64.

225 "I often think": Princess Feodora to Princess Victoria, November 13, 1846, in Albert, *Queen Victoria's Sister*, 39.

225 "the most perfect": Caroline Grosvenor and Charles Beilby, ed., *The First Lady Wharncliffe and Her Family* (London, 1927), 2:78–79. By "democracy" she meant republican sentiment.

Chapter 30: "The Queen Does Nothing but Embroider Flowers"

226 "useless and ill-timed": Ziegler, *William IV*, 193. "No events of consequence," wrote Greville.

227 "I concluded he": September 8, 1831, in Strachey and Fulford, *Greville Memoirs*, 2:194.

227 "Come along directly": John Doran, *Lives of the Queens of England of the House of Hanover* (London, 1855), 2:434.

227 "In the evening": Princess Lieven to Earl Grey, September 24, 1832, in Guy le Strange, ed., *Correspondence of Princess Lieven and Earl Grey* (London, 1890), 2:64.

227 "If the Queen": Fulford, *Hanover to Windsor*, 30.

227 "wiping his nose": Grace Thompson, *The Patriot King* (London, 1932), 169.

228 "Oh never mind": July 20, 1830, in Strachey and Fulford, *Greville Memoirs*, 2:9.

228 "frightened to death": November 28, 1831, in Strachey and Fulford, *Greville Memoirs*, 2:221.

229 "no Set of men": John Cowper, "An Essay Proving that the Inclosuring of Commons and Common Field Land is Contrary to the Interest of the Nation" (1732), 18.

229 "tools": Anon., "An Enquiry into the Reasons for and Against Enclosing the Common Fields (Coventry, 1967), 6; Anon., "Cursory Remarks on Inclosures, Shewing the Pernicious and Destructive Consequences of Inclosing Common Fields &c." (1786), 22.

230 "London is like": December 1, 1830, in Strachey and Fulford, *Greville Memoirs*, 2:74.

230 "The King, the Queen": Croker to Peel, November 1831, in Jennings, *Croker Papers*, 2:133.

231 "established the rule": Charles Dickens, *Oliver Twist* (Oxford, 2002), 96.

232 "I mean Buckingham Palace": Lord Broughton, *Recollections of a Long Life* (London, 1910–11), 5:23.

233 "Lord Melbourne need not": Lord Melbourne to King William, November 1, 1834, in Ziegler, *William IV*, 251.

233 "Time flies": the king of the Belgians to Princess Victoria, May 22, 1832, in Benson, *Letters*, 1:34.

233 "I wish my": Duchess of Kent to Princess Victoria, May 24, 1832, RA VIC M5/33, in Vallone, *Becoming Victoria*, 34.

233 "I should like to know": the king of the Belgians to Princess Victoria, November 18, 1836, in Benson, *Letters*, 1:53.

234 "This Book Mamma gave me": Queen Victoria's journal, July 31, 1832, in Esher, *Girlhood*, 1:20. Victoria was an avid writer of her journal. By the end of her life, she had filled 122 volumes with observations, thoughts, emotions, and descriptions of events. Unfortunately, after the queen's death, Princess Beatrice destroyed much of the diary, believing it might compromise her mother.

234 "pink silk jackets, with black hats": Queen Victoria's journal, August 2, 1832, in Esher, *Girlhood*, 1:44.

235 "literally *flew*": Queen Victoria's journal, October 14, 1832, in Esher, *Girlhood*, 1:48.

235 "VERY VERY VERY": Good Behaviour Book, September 24, 1832, in Vallone, *Becoming Victoria*, 25.

235 "a great fright": Princess Victoria to Princess Feodora, October 14, 1836, RA VIC LB 19/a, in Woodham-Smith, *Queen Victoria*, 85.

235 "blue lights, red lights": Queen Victoria's journal, October 20, 1832, in Esher, *Girlhood*, 1:56.

235 "She hardly ever sleeps": Gervas Grovesnor Huxley, *Lady Elizabeth and the Grosvenors* (London, 1956), 38.

235 "WARMLY and ENTHUSIASTICALLY": Queen Victoria's journal, November 8, 1832, in Esher, *Girlhood*, 1:59.

235 "VICTORIA comes—": *Jackson's Oxford Journal*, November 10, 1832.

236 "singular prudence": Hudson, *A Royal Conflict*, 3.

236   "all the Ladies": Queen Victoria's Journal, December 24, 1832, in Esher, *Girlhood,* 1:62.

Chapter 31: "How Very Old"

237   "I am today fourteen": Queen Victoria's journal, May 24, 1833, in Esher, *Girlhood,* 1:75.

238   "a certain little princess": the king of the Belgians to Princess Victoria, in Hibbert, *Queen Victoria,* 39.

238   "not been able": the king of the Belgians to Princess Victoria, March 1834, RA Y61/25, in Elizabeth Longford, *Victoria R.I.* (London, 1964), 34.

238   "looking generally into": the King of the Belgians to Princess Victoria, January 23, 1832, RA Y61/14, in Vallone, *Becoming Victoria,* 65.

239   "I am very fond of": Princess Victoria to the king of the Belgians, October 22, 1834, in Benson, *Letters,* 1:39.

239   "She is a most beautiful singer": Queen Victoria's journal, April 19, 1834, in Esher, *Girlhood,* 1:93.

239   The princess became: Queen Victoria's journal, July 14, 1835, in Esher, *Girlhood,* 1:121.

239   "She is a fascinating": Queen Victoria's journal, September 11, 1835, in Esher, *Girlhood,* 1:184.

240   "spot where Nelson fell": Queen Victoria's journal, July 18, 1837, in Esher, *Girlhood,* 1:83.

240   "The whole way": Queen Victoria's journal, September 16, 1833, in Esher, *Girlhood,* 1:86.

240   "disgusted at the": July 4, 1833, Strachey and Fulford, *Greville Memoirs,* 2:388.

240   "I cannot bear Lord John Russell": Ziegler, *King William IV,* 265.

Chapter 32: "When Nobody Wishes to Change and Nobody Wants to Give In"

242   "Until you are at the age": Duchess of Kent to Princess Victoria, July 30, 1835, RA M5/78, in Woodham-Smith, *Queen Victoria,* 134.

243   "Everyone likes flattery": William Flavelle Monypenny and George Earl Buckle, *The Life of Benjamin Disraeli* (London, 1929), 453.

243   "Spie of J.C.": Queen Victoria's journal, April 18, 1838, in Longford, *Victoria R.I.,* 100.

243   "his daughters were": Queen Victoria's journal, February 27, 1839, in Hudson, *A Royal Conflict,* 74.

243   "At 8, Mama, Lady Flora": Queen Victoria's journal, December 12, 1834, in Woodham-Smith, *Queen Victoria,* 125.

244   "resentful of what must have": Stockmar to Duchess of Kent, July 4, 1834, RA M7/42, in Woodham-Smith, *Queen Victoria,* 119–20.

244   "My DEAREST sister Feodora": Queen Victoria's journal, June 5, 1834, in Esher, *Girlhood,* 1:95.

245   "I could enter into": Princess Feodora to Princess Victoria, November 5, 1834, RA Y34/11, in Woodham-Smith, *Queen Victoria,* 118.

245   "I clasped her in my *arms*": Albert, *Queen Victoria's Sister,* 34.

245   "If you do not prepare yourself": the king of the Belgians to Princess Victoria, October 18, 1834, in Benson, *Letters,* 1:37–38.

245   "different authors, of different opinions": Victoria to the king of the Belgians, October 22, 1834, in Benson, *Letters,* 39.

245   "I am much obliged to you": Princess Victoria to the king of the Belgians, November 19, 1834, in Benson, *Letters,* 1:39.

245   "clever, sharp little letter": the king of the Belgians to Princess Victoria, December 2, 1834, in Benson, *Letters,* 1:39.

246   "your sincerely devoted": the king of the Belgians to Princess Victoria, August 3, 1835, in Benson, *Letters,* 1:41.

246   "intoxicated by greatness and success": the king of the Belgians to Princess Victoria, May 21, 1833, in Benson, *Letters,* 1:45.

246   "Today is my 16th birthday!": Queen Victoria's journal, May 24, 1835, in Esher, *Girlhood,* 1:116.

247   "No one can be": Queen Victoria's journal, May 18, 1835, in Esher, *Girlhood,* 1:116.

247   "This letter, I dare say": Duchess of Kent to Princess Victoria, December 31, 1834, A VIC M5/52, in Charlot, *Victoria,* 65.

247   "Nothing could be worse": Elizabeth, Lady Holland, *Journal of Lady Holland,* 2:158.

247   "she would want all her": the king of the Belgians to Princess Victoria, August 9, 1836, in Benson, *Letters,* 1:50.

248   "frightened to death": Queen Victoria's journal, July 30, 1835, in Esher, *Girlhood,* 1:126.

248   "I felt that my confirmation": Queen Victoria's journal, July 30, 1835, in Woodham-Smith, *Queen Victoria,* 54.

Chapter 33: Victoria on Tour

249   "would necessarily become the object": King William IV to Lord Melbourne, July 28, 1835, RA MP 115/52, in Charlot, *Victoria,* 65.

249   "It requires but one step more": Duchess of Kent to Lord Melbourne, July 27, 1835, RA MP 115/56, in Charlot, *Victoria,* 65.

250   "I hope the newspapers": King William IV to Princess Victoria, August 22, 1835, RA MP 115/58, in Charlot, *Victoria,* 65. The king was dishonest, for he

told the princess that he would prevent her travels, when, in fact, he would find it very difficult to do so.

250   "If the King was another man": Duchess of Kent to Princess Victoria, September 2, 1835, RA M5/84, in Woodham-Smith, *Queen Victoria*, 126.

250   "worked hard": Prince Charles of Leiningen to Princess Victoria, June 19, 1837, RA M744, in Hudson, *A Royal Conflict*, 88.

251   "a wreath of white roses": Queen Victoria's journal, September 25, 1835, in Longford, *Victoria R.I.*, 51.

251   "well nigh dead": Queen Victoria's journal, September 22, 1835, in Vallone, *Becoming Victoria*, 82.

252   "It is an end to our journey": Queen Victoria's journal, September 25, 1835, in Hudson, *A Royal Conflict*, 89.

252   "example for all young ladies": the king of the Belgians to Princess Victoria, August 31, 1832, in Benson, *Letters*, 1:34.

252   "with beating hearts": Queen Victoria's journal, September, 29, 1835, in Esher, *Girlhood*, 1:186.

252   "You must consider me": Queen Victoria's journal, October 8, 1835, in Esher, *Girlhood*, 1:135.

253   "*very good* and *valuable*": Queen Victoria's journal, October 7, 1835, in Woodham-Smith, *Queen Victoria*, 129.

Chapter 34: Victoria's Whims

254   "Dr. Clark says that if all you report": Woodham-Smith, *Queen Victoria*, 131.

255   "dangerous illness at Ramsgate": Queen Victoria's journal, February 26, 1838, in Hudson, *A Royal Conflict*, 195.

255   "Never, since a girl": Weintraub, *Victoria*, p 365.

256   "I am much better": Princess Victoria to the king of the Belgians, November 3, 1835, RA Y88/4, in Woodham-Smith, *Queen Victoria*, 133.

256   "so unceasing in": Queen Victoria's journal, November 5, 1835, in Esher, *Girlhood*, 1:188.

257   "We instantly went upstairs,": Queen Victoria's journal, January 13, 1836, in Esher, *Girlhood*, 1:142.

257   "came to her servants": Fraser, *Princesses*, 361.

258   "poor vagrant girls": Queen Victoria's journal, August 3, 1836, in Esher, *Girlhood*, 1:168.

258   "burletta of *One Hour*": Queen Victoria's journal, February 29, 1836, in Esher, *Girlhood*, 1:149.

258   "Oh! Walter Scott": Queen Victoria's journal, November 1, 1836, in Esher, *Girlhood*, 1:175.

258   "He is too indulgent": Queen Victoria's journal August 8, 1836, in Esher, *Girlhood*, 1:164.

258   "I must say I prefer": Queen Victoria's journal, April 1837, in Hibbert, *Queen Victoria*, 43.

258   "I liked my lessons": Queen Victoria's journal, April 19, 1836, in Esher, *Girlhood*, 1:156.

258   "Oh! could I once behold": Queen Victoria's journal, circa July 6, 1836, in Woodham-Smith, *Queen Victoria*, 143.

259   "*pleasure* does more good": Princess Victoria to the king of the Belgians, April 26, 1836, in Benson, *Letters*, 1:47.

259   "I am charmed": Princess Victoria to Princess Feodora, July 6, 1835, RA Vic LBK 12, in Vallone, *Becoming Victoria*, 112.

259   "quite prepared to enter" Princess Victoria to the King of the Belgians, April 26, 1836, in Benson, *Letters*, 1:47.

Chapter 35: Crowds of Princes

260   "We have had a crowd of Princes": Hudson, *A Royal Conflict*, 118.

261   "Alexander is very handsome": Queen Victoria's journal, June 16, 1833, in Christopher Hibbert, ed., *Queen Victoria in Her Letters and Journals* (London, 1984).

261   "very very sorry": Queen Victoria's journal, July 12, 1833, in Esher, *Girlhood*, 1:82.

261   "He is very good looking": Queen Victoria's journal, April 1, 1846, in Esher, *Girlhood*, 1:53.

262   "Princess Feodora wrote": Princess Feodora to Princess Victoria, April 16, 1836, in Benson, *Letters*, 1:46.

263   "he could not allow": Woodham-Smith, *Queen Victoria*, 145.

263   "The relations of the Queen and King": the king of the Belgians to Princess Victoria, May 13, 1836, in Benson, *Letters*, 1:48.

263   "The boys are both very plain": Princess Victoria to the king of the Belgians, May 17, 1836, RA Y88/11, in Woodham-Smith, *Queen Victoria*, 146.

263   "I talk to you at length": the king of the Belgians to Baroness Lehzen, May 1, 1836, RA Add. A11/2, in Woodham-Smith, *Queen Victoria*, 151.

264   "very amiable, very kind": Princess Victoria to the king of the Belgians, May 23, 1836, in Benson, *Letters*, 1:48–49.

265   "You can well imagine": Prince Albert to Duchess Marie of Saxe-Coburg and Gotha, June 1, 1836, in Kurt Jagow, ed., *Letters of the Prince Consort, 1831–61* (London, 1938), 13.

265   "After being but a short while" Queen Victoria's journal, May 24, 1836, in Hibbert, *Letters and Journals*, 18.

265   "I am sorry to say": Princess Victoria to the king of the Belgians, May 31, 1836, in Hibbert, *Letters and Journals*, 18.

265   "All this dissipation": Princess Victoria to the king of the Belgians, May 31, 1836, RA Y88/14, in Hibbert, *Letters and Journals,* 18.

265   During the rest of the visit: Queen Victoria's journal, June 10, 1836, in Esher, *Girlhood,* 1:58.

266   "I must thank you": Princess Victoria to the king of the Belgians, June 7, 1836, in Benson, *Letters,* 1:49.

266   "A poor girl has not much": Queen Victoria to the Crown Princess of Prussia, September 6, 1859, in Fulford, *Dearest Child,* 209.

266   "At 9 we all breakfasted": Queen Victoria's journal, June 10, 1836, in Esher, *Girlhood,* 1:160.

267   "Albert is superb": Grey, *Early Years of the Prince Consort,* 32.

267   "she made no attempt": Grey, *Early Years of the Prince Consort,* 35.

268   "Everything that is pleasant, alas!": Queen Victoria's journal, August 8, 1836, in Esher, *Girlhood,* 1:165.

Chapter 36: "I Cannot Expect to Live Very Long"

269   "shrunk both in mind and body": Ziegler, *William IV,* 281.

269   "There is a very strong impression": June 5, 1837, in Strachey and Fulford, *Greville Memoirs,* 3:377.

269   "I cannot expect": August 30, 1836, Strachey and Fulford, in *Greville Memoirs,* 3:305.

270   "not only without his consent": September 21, 1836, in Strachey and Fulford, *Greville Memoirs,* 3:309–10.

271   "he had been insulted": September 21, 1836, in Strachey and Fulford, *Greville Memoirs,* 3:310.

272   "she was now quite *independent*": Huxley, *Lady Elizabeth and the Grosvenors,* 74.

272   "Today is my dearest Albert's birth-day": Queen Victoria's journal, August 26, 1836, in Woodham-Smith, *Victoria,* 232.

272   "She is an Angel": Queen Victoria's journal, September 13, 1836, in Charlot, *Victoria,* 79.

272   "talked over many": Queen Victoria's journal, September 16, 1836, in Esher, *Girlhood,* 1:166.

272   "his conduct was madness": the king of the Belgians to Queen Victoria, April 8 and 12, 1861, RA Y82/112–113, in Charlot, *Victoria,* 143.

273   "My object": the king of the Belgians to Princess Victoria, June 7 and 15, 1837, in Benson, *Letters,* 1:70–71.

273   "It is dreadful how quickly": Queen Victoria's journal, September 21, 1838, in Hibbert, *Letters and Journals,* 20.

273   "the wickedness of": Lehzen to the king of the Belgians, in Woodham-Smith, *Queen Victoria,* 159.

274 "It is highly probable": the king of the Belgians to Princess Victoria, April 11, 1837, in Benson, *Letters*, 1:64–65.

274 "I would give": Queen Victoria's journal, November 3, 1836, in Woodham-Smith, *Queen Victoria*, 163.

274 Victoria had started: Princess Victoria to the king of the Belgians, January 23, 1837, in Benson, *Letters*, 1:59.

274 "rather strong": Princess Victoria to the king of the Belgians, January 30, 1837, in Benson, *Letters*, 1:60.

274 "totally unprepared": Queen Victoria's journal, November 29, 1836, in Esher, *Girlhood*, 1:178.

274 "drew sailors": Princess Victoria to Princess Feodora, March 12, 1837, RA LB 39/7, in Vallone, *Becoming Victoria*, 165.

275 "My letter will": Victoria to Princess Feodora, January 15, 1837, RA LP, in Charlot, *Victoria*, 123.

275 "My *Operatic* and": Princess Victoria to the king of the Belgians, February 6, 1837, in Benson, *Letters*, 1:61.

275 "as well as can be": Queen Victoria to the king of the Belgians, March 14, 1837, in Benson, *Letters*, 1:62.

275 She looked forward: Ibid.

275 "The time is": Princess Victoria to Prince Albert, March 1837, RA LP, in Woodham-Smith, *Queen Victoria*, 186.

275 "dreadful, so very": Queen Victoria's journal, April 5 and 7, 1837, in Woodham-Smith, *Queen Victoria*, 153.

276 "You have been the subject": The king of the Belgians to Princess Victoria, April 11, 1837, in Benson, *Letters*, 1:64.

276 "indeed a curious": Princess Victoria to the king of the Belgians, April 12, 1837, in Benson, *Letters*, 1:65.

276 "It may *all be over*": Princess Victoria to the king of the Belgians, May 16, 1837, in Benson, *Letters*, 1:72.

276 "Felt very miserable": Queen Victoria's journal, May 19, 1837, in Esher, *Girlhood*, 1:190.

276 "youth and inexperience": copies of the letter drafted for Princess Victoria to send to King William IV, May 20, 1837, RA 7/14, 21, in Woodham-Smith, *Queen Victoria*, 163.

277 "Victoria has not": memorandum by Lehzen, in RA M7/15, in Woodham-Smith, *Queen Victoria*, 163.

277 "in a manner": Duchess of Kent to Lord Melbourne, May 21, 1837, RA M7/24, in Woodham-Smith, *Queen Victoria*, 163.

277 "It is worth": Melbourne to King William, May 21, 1837, RA M7/26, in Woodham-Smith, *Queen Victoria*, 164.

277 "with the responsibility": Lord Melbourne to Sir Herbert Taylor, May 22, 1837, in Woodham-Smith, *Queen Victoria*, 164.

277   "The King was": Queen Victoria's journal, May 22 and 23, 1837, in Woodham-Smith, *Queen Victoria*, 161.

Chapter 37: *"It May All Be Over at Any Moment"*

278   "Today is my 18th birthday!": Queen Victoria's journal, May 24, 1837, in Esher, *Girlhood*, 1:190.

278   "The demonstrations of": Ibid.

279   "The Courtyard and the streets": Ibid.

279   "anxious and harassed": Carolly Erickson, *Her Little Majesty* (London, 1997), 57.

279   "gave my beloved": Queen Victoria's journal, May 24, 1837, in Esher, *Girlhood*, 1:190.

279   "The violence which": the king of the Belgians to Princess Victoria, June 7 and 15, 1837, in Benson, *Letters*, 1:70–71.

279   "You have had some battles": the king of the Belgians to Princess Victoria, May 25, 1837, in Benson, *Letters*, 1:68–69.

280   "Uncle Leopold's greatest": Queen Victoria's journal, June 4, 1837, in Esher, *Girlhood*, 1:198.

280   "treachery, lies and fraud": Stockmar to the king of the Belgians, February 24, 1837, RA Add A11/3, in Woodham-Smith, *Queen Victoria*, 188.

280   "Do you think": Prince Charles of Leiningen to Princess Victoria, June 19, 1837, in Hudson, *A Royal Conflict*, 88.

280   "I have objected": memorandum written by Lehzen, June 6, 1837, RA M7/13, in Weintraub, *Victoria*, 93.

281   "live on outwardly submissive": Stockmar to the king of the Belgians, in St. Aubyn, *Queen Victoria*, 59.

281   "there was no advantage": Lord Palmerston, May 26, 1837, in Hibbert, *Queen Victoria*, 50.

281   "On the 10th": Stockmar to the king of the Belgians, June 8–13, 1837, RA Add A11/12, in Woodham-Smith, *Queen Victoria*, 167–68.

281   "You are still very young": Duchess of Kent to Princess Victoria, June 12, 1837, RA M7/46, in Charlot, *Victoria*, 89.

282   "The news of the King": Queen Victoria's journal, June 15, 1837, in Esher, *Girlhood*, 1:68.

282   "10 minutes to 1": Ibid.

282   "younger in intellect": Hudson, *Royal Conflict*, 129.

282   "had a highly important": Queen Victoria's journal, June 15, 1837, in Esher, *Girlhood*, 1:194.

283   "She is pressed by Conroy": memorandum by Charles, Prince of Leiningen, 1841, RA M7/67 and Add V2, in Woodham-Smith, *Queen Victoria*, 84.

283   "keep her under": Greville's report of Stockmar's conversation with Lord Granville, October 30, 1854, in Strachey and Fulford, *Greville Memoirs*, 7:70.

283   "I know that": Ziegler, *William IV,* 289.

283   "The King dies": Benjamin Disraeli to Sarah Disraeli, June 19, 1837, Benjamin Disraeli, in Ralph Disraeli, ed., *Correspondence with His Sister* (London, 1886), 66.

283   "The King's state": Princess Victoria to the king of the Belgians, June 19, 1837, in Benson, *Letters,* 1:73–74.

283   "not be hurried": the king of the Belgians to Princess Victoria, June 17, 1837, in Benson, *Letters,* 1:72–73.

Chapter 38: *"Just the Sort of Life I Like"*

287   "I never was happy": Queen Victoria, in St. Aubyn, *Queen Victoria,* 57.

287   "Since it has pleased": Queen Victoria's journal, June 20, 1837, in Esher, *Girlhood,* 1:196.

288   "Dearest Feodora, two words only": Queen Victoria to Princess Feodora, June 20, 1837, RA LP, in Charlot, *Victoria,* 86.

288   "presents his humble duty": Lord Melbourne to Queen Victoria, October 6, 1837, in Benson, *Letters,* 1:92.

288   "of COURSE quite ALONE": Queen Victoria's journal, June 20, 1837, in Esher, *Girlhood,* 1:196.

289   "place my firm reliance": Queen Victoria's Declaration, June 20, 1837, RA MP 115/111, in Charlot, *Victoria,* 83.

289   "perfect calmness and self-possession": June 21, 1837, in Strachey and Fulford, *Greville Memoirs,* 3:373.

289   "as interesting and handsome": Jennings, *Croker Papers,* 2:359.

289   "went down and said good night": Queen Victoria's journal, June 20, 1837, in Hibbert, *Queen Victoria,* 56.

290   "I am completely beaten": Juliet Gardiner, *Queen Victoria* (London, 1997), 34.

290   "I had to remind her": St. Aubyn, *Queen Victoria,* 71.

290   "In marking Sir John": Duchess of Kent to Queen Victoria, July 20, 1837, RA Z482/6, in Charlot, *Victoria,* 92.

290   "I wrote to you": Queen Victoria to the king of the Belgians, August 1, 1837, RA LP, in Hudson, *A Royal Conflict,* 191.

291   "continue to them that kindness": Prince Albert to Queen Victoria, June 26, 1837, in Jagow, *Letters of the Prince Consort,* 14.

291   "I cannot tell you how happy": Queen Victoria to Prince Albert, June 30, 1837, RA LP, in Woodham-Smith, *Queen Victoria,* 187.

291   "Whenever a question": the king of the Belgians to Queen Victoria, June 27, 1837, in Benson, *Letters,* 1:80.

291   "I must see my Ministers": Queen Victoria to the king of the Belgians, June 25, 1837, in Benson, *Letters,* 1:79.

292   "Virgin Queen": Lord Holland to Lord Granville, June 30, July 21, September 15, 1837, PRO 30/29.

292   "gracefulness of her manner": June 21, 1837, in Strachey and Fulford, *Greville Memoirs*, 3:375.

292   "Is it not sometimes": Albert, *Queen Victoria's Sister*, 90.

292   Victoria confessed that she did: Lady Cowper, in St. Aubyn, *Queen Victoria*, 87.

292   "Everybody says that I am": Queen Victoria to Princess Feodora, October 23, 1837, RA LP, in Charlot, *Victoria*, 101.

292   "Reginamania": "Topics of the Day; A New Game for Children," *The Spectator*, June 28, 1838.

292   "The Gross Outrage to Her Majesty": See *The Times*, November 7, 13, and 24, 1837.

293   "I have gone through": Queen Victoria's journal, July 13, 1837, in Esher, *Girlhood*, 1:211.

296   "I shall never forget": Duchess of Kent, July 17, 1837, in Woodham-Smith, *Queen Victoria*, 179.

296   "I prorogued Parliament": Queen Victoria to the king of the Belgians, July 18, 1837, in Benson, *Letters*, 1:86.

296   "mad with loyalty": St. Aubyn, *Queen Victoria*, 87.

296   "I cannot help feeling": Queen Victoria's journal, August 22, 1837, in Esher, *Girlhood*, 1:221.

296   "The whole went off beautifully": Queen Victoria's journal, September 28, 1837, in Hibbert, *Letters and Journals*, 27.

297   "I am *very sorry*": Queen Victoria's journal, October 4, 1837, in Woodham-Smith, *Queen Victoria*, 182.

297   "the greatest concourse of people": Queen Victoria to Princess Feodora, November 13, 1837, RA LP, in Woodham-Smith, *Queen Victoria*, 192.

297   "You have it in your power": Princess Feodora to Queen Victoria, in Albert, *Queen Victoria's Sister*, 72.

298   "would have no discussion": Queen Victoria's journal, June 28, 1838, in Esher, *Girlhood*, 1:361.

298   "It is as if the population": June 27, 1838, in Strachey and Fulford, *Greville Memoirs*, 4:69.

298   "a feeling that": Queen Victoria's Journal, June 28, 1838, in Esher, *Girlhood*, 1:363.

299   "on account of the noise": Queen Victoria's Journal, June 28, 1838, in Esher, *Girlhood*, 1:357.

300   "all the eagerness of children": Benjamin Disraeli to Sarah Disraeli, June 29, 1838, in Disraeli, *Correspondence*, 109.

301   "I have often seen": the king of the Belgians to Queen Victoria, June 23, 1837, in Benson, *Letters*, 1:78–79.

301   "The great merit": June 27, 1837, Strachey and Fulford, *Greville Memoirs,* 4:72.

301   "I shall ever remember": Queen Victoria's journal, June 28, 1838, in Esher, *Girlhood,* 1:359.

Chapter 39: "He Is of the Greatest Use to Me"

302   "He is not only a clever statesman": Queen Victoria to the king of the Belgians, June 25, 1837, in Benson, *Letters,* 1:79.

303   "Talked with Stockmar": Queen Victoria's journal, January 14, 1838, in Charlot, *Victoria,* 95.

304   "She could disband the army": Walter Bagehot, *The English Constitution* (London, 1896), 75.

305   "I have no doubt he is": September 7, 1838, in Strachey and Fulford, *Greville Memoirs,* 4:93.

306   "*sexual,* although She did not know it," May 12, 1839, in Strachey and Fulford, *Greville Memoirs,* 4:169.

306   "Lord Melbourne was there": St. Aubyn, *Queen Victoria,* 76.

306   "I have seen a great deal": Queen Victoria's journal, October 3, 1837, in Esher, *Girlhood,* 1:229.

306   "It is become his province": September 12, 1838, in Fulford and Strachey, *Greville Memoirs,* 4:92.

306   "choleric disposition": Queen Victoria's journal, February 20, 1838, in Charlot, *Victoria,* 99.

307   "Take care that Lord Melbourne": Duchess of Kent to Queen Victoria, June 20, 1837, RA M7/68, in Longford, *Victoria R.I.,* 71.

307   "his situation is certainly": Jennings, *Croker Papers,* 2:320.

308   "It's all among Workhouses": Queen Victoria's journal, April 7, 1839, in Hibbert, *Letters and Journals,* 40.

308   "reckless language": Lord Ashley, in Hibbert, *Queen Victoria,* 89.

309   "My birthday is come and gone": August 30, 1837, in Strachey and Fulford, *Greville Memoirs,* 3:393.

309   "For this reason it hurts me": Duchess of Kent to Queen Victoria, July 26, 1837, RA Z482/4, in Charlot, *Victoria,* 91.

310   "I thought you would not": Queen Victoria to Duchess of Kent, August 17, 1837, RA Z482/12, in Charlot, *Victoria,* 89.

310   "The Queen should forgive": Duchess of Kent to Queen Victoria, in Woodham-Smith, *Queen Victoria,* 183.

310   "Saw Ma and oh what a scene": Queen Victoria's journal, November 16, 1837, in Charlot, *Victoria,* 92.

310   "subjected to so much annoyance": Queen Victoria's journal, November 7, 1837, in Hibbert, *Queen Victoria,* 58.

311 "will do anything when she": Queen Victoria's journal, March 1, 1838, in Charlot, *Victoria*, 93.

311 "Before you decide on anything": the king of the Belgians to Queen Victoria, June 23, 1837, in Benson, *Letters*, 1:79.

311 "How fortunate I am": Queen Victoria to the king of the Belgians, June 25, 1837, in Benson, *Letters*, 1:79.

312 "This is most provoking": Queen Victoria's journal, May 29, 1839, in Esher, *Girlhood*, 2:190.

312 "living so much": Queen Victoria's journal, June 16, 1839, in Esher, *Girlhood*, 2:207.

312 "A queen's life is very laborious": Queen Victoria's journal, October 29, 1838, in Longford, *Victoria R.I.*, 99.

312 "I felt *how* unfit I was": Queen Victoria's journal, December 15, 1838, in Longford, *Victoria R.I.*, 99.

312 "*I* should be eating all day": Queen Victoria to the king of the Belgians, July 11, 1837, in Benson, *Letters*, 1:84.

312 "an incredible weight": Weintraub, *Victoria*, 127.

312 "*It is of no use*": the king of the Belgians to Queen Victoria, July 24, 1837, in Benson, *Letters*, 1:87.

Chapter 40: Scandal

314 "I have, alas!": Queen Victoria to the king of the Belgians, July 3, 1839, in Benson, *Letters*, 1:82.

314 "amazing spy who would repeat": Queen Victoria's journal, April 18, 1838, in Longford, *Victoria R.I.*, 100.

314 "We have no doubt": Queen Victoria's journal, February 2, 1839, in Hibbert, *Letters and Journals*, 42.

315 "protect their purity": Lady Portman's statement, March 17, 1839, in Longford, *Victoria R.I.*, 182.

315 "I said, feeling perfectly innocent": Lady Flora Hastings's statement, in Woodham-Smith, *Queen Victoria*, 200.

316 "It is our opinion": certificate of Dr. Clarke and Dr. Clark, February 17, 1839, RA Z486/1, in Hibbert, *Queen Victoria*, 79.

316 "The Court is plunged": March 2, 1839, in Strachey and Fulford, *Greville Memoirs*, 4:132.

316 "was very active": Lord Holland, in Kriegel, *Holland House Diaries*, 395. "this disgraceful and mischievous scandal": March 2, 1839, in Strachey and Fulford, *Greville Memoirs*, 4:133.

316 "dreadfully agitated": Queen Victoria's journal, February 23, 1839, in Hibbert, *Letters and Journals*, 42.

317 "The whole town has been engrossed": March 2, 1839, in Strachey and Fulford, *Greville Memoirs,* 4:132.

317 "wished to have hanged the Editor": Queen Victoria's journal, June 16, 1839 RA, in Charlot, *Victoria,* 136. The queen was convinced that she was the victim of a political attack by the Hastings family, who were strong Tories, as well as the Duchess of Kent and Conroy.

318 "Meet this crisis with that firmness": Lord Melbourne to Queen Victoria, May 7, 1839, in Benson, *Letters,* 1:194. "I am but a poor helpless girl who clings to him for support and protection," the queen wrote of Lord Melbourne. "The thought of ALL ALL my happiness being possibly at stake so completely overcame me that I burst into tears and remained crying for some time." No Tory prime minister would support her in the battle against the Hastings family.

318 "The state of agony": Queen Victoria's journal, May 7, 1839, in Hibbert, *Letters and Journals,* 45–46.

318 "I really thought my heart would break": Queen Victoria's journal, May 7, 1839, in Hibbert, *Letters and Journals,* 46.

319 The queen found Peel dry: Queen Victoria's journal, May 8, 1839, in Esher, *Girlhood,* 2:163.

319 "In all ways, his dress, his manner": February 21, 1835, in Strachey and Fulford, *Greville Memoirs,* 3:162–63.

319 "Oh—how different": Queen Victoria to the king of the Belgians, May 8, 1839, in Benson, *Letters,* 1:157.

319 "such a cold, odd man": Queen Victoria's journal, May 8, 1839, in Esher, *Girlhood,* 2:165.

320 "insisted on my giving up": Queen Victoria to Lord Melbourne, May 9, 1839, in Benson, *Letters,* 1:168.

320 "The Mistress of the Robes": Queen Victoria's journal, May 9, 1839, in Esher, *Girlhood,* 1:165.

320 "secretly longing to get back": May 11, 1839, in Strachey and Fulford, *Greville Memoirs,* 4:166.

320 "The Queen of England will not submit": Queen Victoria to Lord Melbourne, May 9, 1839, in Benson, *Letters,* 1:162.

320 "Do not fear that I was not calm": May 10, 1839, in Strachey and Fulford, *Greville Memoirs,* 4:162–63.

320 "consent to a course": Queen Victoria to Robert Peel, May 7, 1839, in Esher, *Girlhood,* 2:178.

320 "humbly returning" Queen Victoria's journal, May 10, 1839, in Longford, *Victoria R.I.,* 121.

321 "I acted quite alone": Queen Victoria to the king of the Belgians, May 14, 1839, in Benson, *Letters,* 1:219–20.

321 "She has made herself": May 11, 1839, in Strachey and Fulford, *Greville Memoirs,* 4:167.

321   "high trial of our institutions": Stockmar, May 12, 1839, in Müller, *Memoirs,*
      2:13. See also Strachey and Fulford, *Greville Memoirs,* 4:167.

321   "This day I GO OUT OF MY TEENS": Queen Victoria's journal, May 24, 1839, in
      Esher, *Girlhood,* 2:186.

321   "The Grand Duke is very strong": Queen Victoria's journal, May 24, 1839, in
      Esher, *Girlhood,* 2:188–89.

321   "Words fail me": Queen Victoria's journal, May 29, 1839, in Esher, *Girlhood,*
      2:191.

322   "Then she'll die": Queen Victoria's journal, June 16, 1839, in Hibbert, *Letters
      and Journals,* 43.

322   "Had it not been for the unlucky business": Holland to Granville, May 20,
      1839, PRO Granville papers, 30/29, box 9.

323   "I went in alone": Queen Victoria's journal, June 27, 1839, in Hibbert, *Letters
      and Journals,* 43–44.

323   "It was disagreeable": Queen Victoria's journal, July 1, 1839, in Woodham-
      Smith, *Queen Victoria,* 216.

323   "the poor thing died": Queen Victoria's journal, July 5–7, 1839, in Wood-
      ham-Smith, *Queen Victoria,* 216.

324   "The cause here advocated": "The Dangers of Evil Counsel," "Warning Let-
      ter to Baroness Lehzen by a Voice Beyond the Grave," "The Palace Martyr,"
      Conroy Papers, 1839.

324   "be immediately silenced": April 21, 1839, in Strachey and Fulford, *Greville
      Memoirs,* 4:150.

Chapter 41: *A Way of Settling It*

325   "Living but for your duty": Princess Feodora to Queen Victoria, November
      9, 1837, in Albert, *Queen Victoria's Sister,* 92.

325   "to enjoy two or three years": Queen Victoria to the king of the Belgians,
      January 24, 1838, in Charlot, *Victoria,* 158.

326   "not yet quite grown up": Queen Victoria's journal, April 17, 1839, in Hib-
      bert, *Letters and Journals,* 42.

326   "We have Coburgs enough": King William to Lord Melbourne, April 27,
      1836, in Philip Ziegler, *Melbourne* (London, 1976), 253.

326   "I may not": Queen Victoria to the king of the Belgians, July 15, 1839, in
      Benson, *Letters,* 1:177.

326   "We have had the Grand Duke": Queen Victoria to Prince Albert, June 10,
      1839, RA LP, in Charlot, *Victoria,* 163.

327   Once, when she was riding: "Edmund Hayward," *The Times,* August 10 and
      21, 1839.

327   "I find it hard to love a Queen": "The Queen's Lover," *Penny Satirist,* July 6,
      1839.

327   "fantastic bust": G.W.M. Reynolds, *The Mysteries of London*, ed. Trevor Thomas (Keele, UK, 1996), 99.

327   "Let us try all the more": Prince Albert to Prince Ernest, August 29, 1839, in Hector Bolitho, ed., *The Prince Consort and His Brother* (London, 1933), 11.

327   "said to be extremely stubborn": Sir Theodore Martin, *The Life of His Royal Highness the Prince Consort* (London, 1875–80), 1:26–27.

328   "gloomy prospects": Hector Bolitho, *The Reign of Queen Victoria* (London, 1948), 53.

329   "I have thrown myself into": Prince Albert to Prince Löwenstein, in Martin, *Life of the Prince Consort*, 1:29.

329   "too indifferent and too reserved": Stockmar, in Müller, *Memoirs*, 2:7.

329   "It was with some emotion": Queen Victoria's journal, October 10, 1839, in Esher, *Girlhood*, 2:262.

329   "so excessively handsome": Queen Victoria's journal, October 11, 1839, in Esher, *Girlhood*, 2:263.

330   "Albert's *beauty* is *most striking*": Queen Victoria to the king of the Belgians, October 12, 1839, in Benson, *Letters*, 1:237.

330   "so beautifully": Queen Victoria's journal, October 11–12, 1839, in Esher, *Girlhood*, 2:264.

330   "had a good deal changed": Queen Victoria's journal, October 13, 1839, in Esher, *Girlhood*, 2:265.

330   "had made up my mind": Queen Victoria's journal, October 14, 1839, in Esher, *Girlhood*, 2:266.

330   "How? I asked": Queen Victoria's journal, October 14, 1839, in Esher, *Girlhood*, 2:267.

331   "I said to him": Queen Victoria's journal, October 15, 1839, in Esher, *Girlhood*, 2:268; Hibbert, *Letters and Journals*, 57.

Chapter 42: Passing like a Dream

333   "I love him more than I can say": Queen Victoria to the king of the Belgians, in Benson, *Letters*, 1:238.

333   "I am often puzzled": Prince Albert to Stockmar, October 16, 1839, in Grey, *Early Years of the Prince Consort*, 225, 226.

333   "As everyone says": the king of the Belgians to Baron Stockmar, in Charlot, *Victoria*, 167.

333   "I signed some papers": Queen Victoria's journal, November 3, 1839, in Longford, *Victoria R.I.*, 143.

334   "We sit so nicely": Queen Victoria's journal, November 1, 1839, in Hibbert, *Letters and Journals*, 58.

334   "I shall never cease to be": Prince Albert to William, Prince of Löwenstein, in Jagow, *Letters of the Prince Consort*, 69.

335   "leant on that dear, soft cheek": Queen Victoria's journal, November 14, 1839, in Woodham-Smith, *Queen Victoria*, 232.

335   "Your image fills my whole soul": Prince Albert to Queen Victoria, November 15, 1839, in Jagow, *Letters of the Prince Consort*, 74.

335   "How happy do you make me": Queen Victoria to Prince Albert, November 28, 1839, in Hibbert, *Letters and Journals*, 59.

335   "Thank God the secret is out": Queen Victoria to Prince Albert, November 21, 1839, RA Z490, in Woodham-Smith, *Queen Victoria*, 233.

336   "It needs but the stroke of your pen": Prince Albert to Queen Victoria, November 23, 1839, in Jagow, *Letters of the Prince Consort*, 28.

336   "The whole Cabinet agrees": Queen Victoria to the king of the Belgians, November 26, 1839, in Benson, *Letters*, 1:198.

336   "some of the papers": Queen Victoria to Prince Albert, November 27, 1830, in Benson, *Letters*, 1:199.

337   "give advice on occasions": Lord Melbourne to the king of the Belgians, December 8, 1839, RA MP 117/6, in Charlot, *Victoria*, 179.

337   "As regards my peerage": Prince Albert to Queen Victoria, December 10, 1839, in Jagow, *Letters of the Prince Consort*, 28.

337   "He appears to be nettled": Queen Victoria to Prince Albert, December 8, 1839, in Jagow, *Letters of the Prince Consort*, 28.

337   "party rewards": Prince Albert to Queen Victoria, December 10, 1839, in Jagow, *Letters of the Prince Consort*, 37.

337   "You may rely on my care": Queen Victoria to Prince Albert, December 8, 1839, in Benson, *Letters*, 1:254.

338   "I am distressed to tell you": Queen Victoria to Prince Albert, November 26, 1839, in Benson, *Letters*, 1:207.

338   "Hope, love for dear Victoria": Prince Albert to Duchess of Kent, December 6, 1839, in Jagow, *Letters of the Prince Consort*, 45.

338   "Yes": November 26, 1839, in Strachey and Fulford, *Greville Memoirs*, 4:218–19.

338   "He comes the bridegroom": David Duff, *Albert and Victoria* (London, 1972), 155.

339   There were rumors that Albert: Queen Victoria to Prince Albert, November 27, 1839, in Benson, *Letters*, 1:252.

340   "On Tuesday we sallied down to Windsor": Charles Dickens, *The Letters of Charles Dickens, 1840–41*, ed. M. House and G. Storey (London, 1969), 2:25.

Chapter 43: "Monsters!"

342   "Parties are violent": January 14, 1840, in Strachey and Fulford, *Greville Memoirs*, 4:116.

343   "I was perfectly": Queen Victoria's journal, February 2, 1840, in Woodham-Smith, *Queen Victoria*, 238.

343   "I never saw": the king of the Belgians to Queen Victoria, January 31, 1840, in Benson, *Letters*, 1:270.

343   "I am surprised": Prince Albert to Queen Victoria, February 4, 1840, in Jagow, *Letters of the Prince Consort*, 58.

344   "everything was always": Queen Victoria's journal, February 1, 1840, in Esher, *Girlhood*, 2:311.

344   "It is MY marriage": Weintraub, *Victoria*, 139.

345   "The rage is begun": *The Satirist*, February 9, 1840.

345   As *The Sun* reported: "Another Suitor to Her Majesty," *The Sun*, January 8, 1840.

345   "retire from the public": Prince Albert to Queen Victoria, in Jagow, *Letters of the Prince Consort*, 55.

345   "You forget, my dearest": Queen Victoria to Prince Albert, January 31, 1840, in Benson, *Letters*, 1:213.

345   "stronger than love": February 19, 1840, in Strachey and Fulford, *Greville Memoirs*, 4:243.

345   "rather exasperated": the king of the Belgians to Queen Victoria, February 4, 1840, in Benson, *Letters*, 1:215.

346   "I never remember": Prince Albert to Queen Victoria, February 7, 1840, in Jagow, *Letters of the Prince Consort*, 60.

346   "seeing his *dear dear* face" Queen Victoria's journal, February 8, 1840, in Longford, *Victoria R.I.*, 151.

346   "Monday, February 10": Queen Victoria's journal, February 10, 1840, in Longford, *Victoria R.I.*, 151.

346   "Dearest—How are you": Queen Victoria to Prince Albert, February 10, 1840, in Benson, *Letters*, 1:217.

Chapter 44: "An Everlasting Impression"

347   "borrowed to be married in": Cecil Woodham-Smith, *Florence Nightingale* (London, 1951), 25.

348   "they looked like village girls": Sarah Spencer, Lady Lyttleton, *The Correspondence of Sarah, Lady Littleton, 1787–1870*, ed. Mrs. Hugh Wyndham (London, 1912), 297.

348   "I felt so happy": St. Aubyn, *Queen Victoria*, 146.

348   "We were all": The Marquis of Lorne, *V.R.I.: Queen Victoria, Her Life and Empire* (London, 1901), 120.

349   "Nothing could have gone off": Queen Victoria's journal, February 10, 1840, in Esher, *Girlhood*, 2:321.

349   "Dearest Albert came": Queen Victoria's journal, February 10, 1840, in Woodham-Smith, *Queen Victoria*, 245.

349   "We had dinner": Queen Victoria's journal, February 10, 1840, in Woodham-Smith, *Queen Victoria*, 246.

350   "When the day dawned": Queen Victoria's journal, February 11, 1840, in Hibbert, *Letters and Journals*, 64.
350   "not the way": Weintraub, *Victoria*, 142.
351   "The Prince is indolent": Stanley Weintraub, *Albert: Uncrowned King* (London, 1997), 101.
351   "help with the blotting paper": Queen Victoria's journal, February 23, 1840, in Longford, *Victoria R.I.*, 154.
351   "In my home life": Prince Albert to William, Prince of Löwenstein, May 1840, in Jagow, *Letters of the Prince Consort*, 69.
351   "want of confidence": Robert Anson, "Minutes of Conversation with Lord Melbourne and Baron Stockmar," May 28, 1840, in Benson, *Letters*, 1:224.
352   "I must say": Queen Victoria to the Dowager Duchess of Saxe-Coburg, June 4, 1840, in Hibbert, *Queen Victoria*, 130.

Chapter 45: "Children Seem to Literally Be Raining Down from Heaven"

353   "About myself: really it is too dreadful": Queen Victoria to the king of the Belgians, June 15, 1840, in Charlot, *Victoria*, 191.
354   "Wedded life is the only thing": Prince Albert to Prince Ernest, August 22, 1840, in Bolitho, *The Prince Consort*, 23.
354   "My dearest and most beloved": the king of the Belgians to Queen Victoria, June 13, 1840, in Benson, *Letters*, 1:226.
354   "lost all confidence": Prince Albert to Prince Ernest, June 12, 1840, in Bolitho, *The Prince Consort*, 19.
355   "What is this": Margaret Forster, *Elizabeth Barrett Browning* (London, 1988), 109.
355   "I wish you could be here": Prince Albert to Prince Ernest, September 15, 1840, in Bolitho, *The Prince Consort*, 30.
356   "I am wonderfully well": Queen Victoria to Princess Feodora, November 10, 1840, in Charlot, *Victoria*, 195.
357   "Albert, father of a daughter": Prince Albert to Prince Ernest, November 12, 1840, in Bolitho, *The Prince Consort*, 34.
357   "Both the Queen and the Prince": Lord Clarendon to Lord Granville, November 24, 1840, PRO Granville Papers, 30/29.
357   "Victoria is well": Prince Albert to Prince Ernest, November 12, 1840, in Bolitho, *The Prince Consort*, 34.
358   "the natural head of the family": Martin, *Life of the Prince Consort*, 2:297.
358   "in fact, tho' not in name": memorandum by Mr. Anson, December 20, 1840, RA Y54/11, in Woodham-Smith, *Queen Victoria*, 261.
359   "At night, if they happen to forget": Stockmar, in Müller, *Memoirs*, 2:118–26.
359   "Much as I am inclined": Duff, *Albert and Victoria*, 214.

359 "crazy, stupid intriguer": Prince Albert to Stockmar, January 18, 1842, RA
       Add U2/4, in Woodham-Smith, *Queen Victoria*, 273.

360 "I have told her": Lord Melbourne's conversation with Queen Victoria,
       recorded in a memorandum by Mr. Anson, May 28, 1840, RA Y54/4, in
       Woodham-Smith, *Queen Victoria*, 253.

360 "It was *not* 'Personal ambition'": Queen Victoria to Sir Theodore Martin, RA
       Y169, 57, 59, 60, in Woodham-Smith, *Queen Victoria*, 277.

Chapter 46: *"What a Hard Task It Is for Us Women"*

362 "You so openly": Prince Albert to Prince Ernest, July 29, 1841, in Bolitho,
       The Prince Consort, 44.

362 "[It is] necessary": Prince Albert to Prince Ernest, August 1, 1841, in Bolitho,
       The Prince Consort, 45.

362 "Christmas Eve we spent": Prince Albert to Prince Ernest, December 25,
       1840, in Bolitho, *The Prince Consort*, 36.

362 "I think, dearest": Queen Victoria to the king of the Belgians, January 5,
       1841, in Benson, *Letters*, 1:250.

363 "We are in confusion": Prince Albert to Prince Ernest, March 25, 1840, in
       Bolitho, *The Prince Consort*, 41.

363 "Her Majesty must know": memorandum by Mr. Anson, May 9–13, RA, in
       Woodham-Smith, *Queen Victoria*, 267.

364 "After seeing him for four years": Queen Victoria to the king of the Belgians,
       September 8, 1841, RA Y90, 32, in Woodham-Smith, *Queen Victoria*, 268.

365 "I suffered a *whole year*": Queen Victoria to the king of the Belgians, Febru-
       ary 1843, in Clare Jerrold, *The Married Life of Queen Victoria* (London, 1913),
       178.

365 "I own I am much happier": Queen Victoria to the king of the Belgians, Sep-
       tember 24, 1841, in Benson, ed., *Letters*, 1:332.

365 "All the disagreeableness I suffer": Woodham-Smith, *Queen Victoria*, 233.

365 "The welfare of my children": RA Add U2/4, Prince Albert to Stockmar, Jan-
       uary 18, 1842, in Woodham-Smith, *Queen Victoria*, 274.

366 "Dr. Clark has mismanaged the child": Prince Albert to Queen Victoria, en-
       closed in a letter to Stockmar, RA ADD U2/4, Prince Albert to Stockmar,
       January 18, 1842, in Longford, *Victoria R.I.*, 172.

366 "irritability": RA ADD, U2, Queen Victoria to Baron Stockmar, January 19,
       1842, in Longford, *Victoria R.I.*, 174.

366 "crass and odious things": Queen Victoria to Stockmar, RA Add. U 27/8, Jan-
       uary 19–20, 1842, in St. Aubyn, *Queen Victoria*, 118.

366 "The life I led then": Longford, *Victoria R.I.*, 179.

367 "Nor can the Queen think now": Grey, *Early Years of the Prince Consort*, 220.

Epilogue: *An Immense Multitude*

369   "I can think of nothing else": Weintraub, *Victoria*, 5.

369   "The day has come and I am alone": St. Aubyn, *Victoria*, 218.

372   "the decision of the country": William Anson, *The Law and the Custom of the Constitution* (Oxford, 1886), 1:57.

372   "No one can be": St. Aubyn, *Victoria*, 218.

372   "I hate to be": Esher, *Girlhood*, 1:109.

Bibliography

Albemarle, George Thomas, the Earl of. *Fifty Years of My Life*. 2 vols. London, 1876.

Albert, Harold A. *Queen Victoria's Sister: The Life and Letters of Princess Feodora*. London, 1967.

Ames, Winslow. *Prince Albert and Victorian Taste*. London, 1968.

Anson, Elizabeth and Florence, eds. *Mary Hamilton, Afterwards Mrs. John Dickenson, at Court and at Home: From Letters and Diaries, 1756–1816*. London, 1925.

Aspinall, Arthur, ed. *The Correspondence of George, Prince of Wales, 1770–1812*. 8 vols. London, 1963–71.

———, ed. *The Letters of King George IV, 1812–1830*. 3 vols. Cambridge, 1938.

———, ed. *Letters of the Princess Charlotte, 1811–1817*. London, 1949.

———, ed. *Mrs. Jordan and her Family*. London, 1951.

———, *Politics and the Press, c. 1780–1850*. London, 1949.

Authentic Memoirs of the Life of the Late Lamented Princess Charlotte. London, 1817.

Baker, Kenneth. *George IV: A Life in Caricature*. London, 2005.

Bamford, Francis, and Duke of Wellington, eds. *The Journal of Mrs. Arbuthnot*. London, 1950.

Bauer, Caroline. *Posthumous Memoirs of Caroline Bauer*. London, 1885.

Behrendt, Stephen C. *Royal Mourning and Regency Culture: Elegies and Memorials of Princess Charlotte*. London, 1997.

Belien, Paul. *A Throne in Brussels: Britain, the Saxe-Coburgs and the Belgianisation of Europe*. Exeter, UK, 2005.

Bennett, Daphne. *King Without a Crown: Albert, Prince Consort of England, 1819–1861*. London, 1977.

Benson, A. C., and Viscount Esher, eds., *The Letters of Queen Victoria: A Selection from Her Majesty's Correspondence Between the Years 1837 and 1861*. 3 vols. London, 1907.

Benson, E. F. *Queen Victoria*. London, 1935.

Bessborough, Earl of, ed. *Georgiana: Extracts from the Correspondence of Georgiana, Duchess of Devonshire*. London, 1955.

Bolitho, Hector, ed. *Letters of Queen Victoria from the Archives of the House of Brandenburg-Prussia*. London, 1938.

———. *The Prince Consort and His Brother*. London, 1933.

The Book, or the Proceedings and Correspondence upon the Subject of the Inquiry into the Conduct of the Princess of Wales. London, 1813.

Bourne, Kenneth. *The Foreign Policy of Victorian England, 1830–1902*. Oxford, 1970.

———. *Palmerston: The Early Years, 1784–1841*. London, 1982.

Briggs, Asa. *Victorian People*. London, 1954.

Brougham, Henry. *The Life and Times of Henry, Lord Brougham*. 3 vols. London, 1871.

Bury, Charlotte. *The Court of England Under George IV*. London, 1896.

Cecil, David. *The Young Melbourne*. London, 1939.

Chambers, James. *Charlotte and Leopold*. London, 2007.

Charlot, Monica. *Victoria: The Young Queen*. Oxford, 1991.

Charlotte and Leopold, an Historical Tale. London, 1818.

Cloake, John. *Palaces and Parks of Richmond and Kew*. 2 vols. Chichester, U.K., 1996.

Colley, Linda. *Britons: Forging the Nation, 1707–1837*. New Haven, Conn., 1992.

Cone, C. B. *The English Jacobins: Reformers in Late Eighteenth-Century England*. London, 1968.

Connell, Brian. *Regina v. Palmerston: The Correspondence Between Queen Victoria and Her Foreign and Prime Minister, 1837–1865*. London, 1962.

Corbett, Henry Vincent. *A Royal Catastrophe: A Modern Account of the Death in Childbirth of Her Royal Highness the Princess Charlotte Augusta, Daughter of King George IV*. London, 1985.

Corti, E. C. *Leopold I of Belgium*. London, 1923.

Crainz, F. *An Obstetric Tragedy: The Case of Her Royal Highness the Princess Charlotte Augusta, Some Unpublished Documents of 1817*. London, 1977.

Creevey, Thomas. *The Creevey Papers: A Selection from the Correspondence and Diaries of the Late Thomas Creevey*. Edited by Sir Herbert Maxwell. London, 1903.

David, Saul. *The Prince of Pleasure: The Prince of Wales and the Making of the Regency*. London, 1998.

———. *Victoria's Wars: The Rise of Empire*. London, 2006.

Dennison, Matthew. *The Last Princess: The Devoted Life of Queen Victoria's Youngest Daughter*. London, 2007.

Donald, Diana. *The Age of Caricature: Satirical Prints in the Reign of George III*. London, 1996.

Downer, Martyn. *The Queen's Knight: The Extraordinary Life of Queen Victoria's Most Trusted Confidant*. London, 2007.

Duff, David. *Albert and Victoria*. London, 1973.

————. *Edward of Kent: The Life Story of Queen Victoria's Father*. London, 1938.

————. *Victoria in the Highlands: The Personal Journey of Her Majesty Queen Victoria*. London, 1971.

————. *Victoria Travels: Journeys of Queen Victoria Between 1830 and 1900*. London, 1970.

Duff, Ethel M. *The Life Story of H.R.H. the Duke of Cambridge*. London, 1938.

Dunbabin, J.P.D. *Rural Discontent in Nineteenth-Century Britain*. London, 1974.

Dyson, Hope, and Charles Tennyson, eds. *Dear and Honoured Lady: The Correspondence Between Queen Victoria and Alfred Tennyson*. Rutherford, N.J., 1971.

Epton, Nina. *Victoria and Her Daughters*. London, 1971.

Esher, Viscount, ed. *The Girlhood of Queen Victoria: A Selection from Her Majesty's Diaries, 1832–1840*. 2 vols. London, 1912.

Farington, Joseph. *The Diary of Joseph Farington*. Edited by Kathryn Cave. 16 vols. New Haven, Conn., 1978–84.

Flanders, Judith. *Consuming Passions: Leisure and Pleasure in Victorian Britain*. London, 2006.

————. *The Victorian House: Domestic Life from Childbirth to Deathbed*. London, 2004.

Ford, Colin, ed. *Happy and Glorious: 130 Years of Royal Photographs*. London, 1977.

Foreman, Amanda. *Georgiana, Duchess of Devonshire*. London, 1997.

Forster, Margaret. *Elizabeth Barrett Browning: A Biography*. London, 1988.

Foulkes, Nick. *Dancing into Battle: A Social History of the Battle of Waterloo*. London, 2006.

Fox, Celina. *London—World City, 1800–1840*. London, 1992.

Fraser, Derek. *The New Poor Law in the Nineteenth Century*. Basingstoke, U.K., 1976.

Fraser, Flora. *Princesses: The Six Daughters of George III*. London, 2004.

————. *The Unruly Queen: The Life of Queen Caroline*. London, 1996.

Fulford, Roger, ed. *Beloved Mama: Private Correspondence of Queen Victoria and the German Crown Princess, 1878–85*. London, 1981.

————, ed. *Darling Child: Private Correspondence of Queen Victoria and the Crown Princess of Prussia, 1871–78*. London, 1976.

————, ed. *Dearest Child: Letters Between Queen Victoria and the Princess Royal, 1858–61*. London, 1964.

————, ed. *Dearest Mama: Letters Between Queen Victoria and the Crown Princess of Prussia, 1861–64*. London, 1968.

————. *Hanover to Windsor*. London, 1960.

————. *The Prince Consort*. London, 1949.

————. *Queen Victoria*. London, 1951.

————. *Royal Dukes*. London, 1933.

————, ed. *Your Dear Letter: Private Correspondence of Queen Victoria and the Crown Princess of Prussia, 1865–71*. London, 1976.

Gardiner, Juliet. *Queen Victoria*. London, 1997.

George, M. Dorothy. *Catalogue of Political and Personal Satires Preserved in the Department of Prints and Drawings in the British Museum*. London, 1949.

Gill, Gillian. *Nightingales: The Story of Florence Nightingale and Her Remarkable Family*. London, 2004.

Gillen, Mollie. *The Prince and His Lady*. Toronto, 1970.

———. *Royal Duke, Augustus Frederick, Duke of Sussex (1773–1843)*. London, 1977.

Golby, J. M., and A. W. Purdue. *The Civilisation of the Crowd: Popular Culture in England, 1750–1900*. London, 1984.

Granville, Countess Castalia, ed. *Lord Granville Leveson Gower, 1st Earl Granville: Private Correspondence, 1781–1821*. London, 1917.

Green, Thomas. *Memoirs of Her Late Royal Highness Charlotte-Augusta of Wales*. London, 1818.

Greenwood, Alice. *Lives of the Hanoverian Queens of England*. 2 vols. London, 1909–11.

Grey, Lieutenant General the Hon. Charles. *The Early Years of His Royal Highness the Prince Consort*. London, 1867.

Gronow, Rees Howell. *The Reminiscences and Recollections of Captain Gronow*. 2 vols. London, 1889.

Hamilton, Lady Anne. *Secret History of the Court of England, from the Accession of George III to the Death of George IV*. 2 vols. London, 1832.

Hansard, T. C., ed. *Parliamentary Debates from the Year 1803 to the Present Time*. 41 vols. London, 1812–20.

Harcourt, Edward William, ed. *Harcourt Papers*. 14 vols. Oxford, 1880–1905.

Hedley, Olwen. *Queen Charlotte*. London, 1975.

Hibbert, Christopher. *George III: A Personal History*. London, 1998.

———. *George IV, Regent and King, 1811–30*. London, 1973.

———. *George, Prince of Wales, 1762–1811*. London, 1972.

———. *Queen Victoria: A Personal History*. London, 2000.

———, ed. *Queen Victoria in Her Letters and Journals*. London, 1984.

Hobhouse, Hermione. *Prince Albert: His Life and Work*. London, 1983.

Hobsbawm, Eric, and George Rudé. *Captain Swing*. London, 1969.

Holme, Thea. *Prinny's Daughter: A Life of Princess Charlotte of Wales*. London, 1976.

Homans, Margaret. *Royal Representations: Queen Victoria and British Culture*. Chicago, 1999.

Home, James A., ed. *The Letters and Journals of Lady Mary Coke*. 4 vols. Edinburgh, 1889–96.

———, ed. *Letters of Lady Louisa Stuart to Miss Louisa Clinton*. Edinburgh, 1903.

Hopkirk, Mary. *Queen Adelaide*. London, 1946.

Hough, Richard, ed. *Advice to a Grand-daughter: Letters from Queen Victoria to Princess Victoria of Hesse*. London, 1975.

Hudson, Katherine. *A Royal Conflict: Sir John Conroy and the Young Victoria*. London, 1994.

Huish, Robert. *Life and Memoirs of Her Royal Highness, Princess Charlotte of Saxe-Coburg Saalfeld*. London, 1818.

———. *Memoirs of Her Late Majesty Caroline, Queen of Great Britain*. 2 vols. London, 1821.

Hunt, J. H. Leigh. *Memoirs of George IV*. 2 vols. London, 1831.

———. *The Old Court Suburb, or Memorials of Kensington*. Edited by Austin Dobson. 2 vols. London: 1902.

Ilchester, Earl of, ed. *Elizabeth, Lady Holland, to Her Son, 1821–1845*. London, 1946.

Impey, Edward. *Kensington Palace: The Official Illustrated History*. London, 2003.

Jagow, Kurt, ed. *Letters of the Prince Consort 1831–61*. London, 1938.

Jennings, Louis J., ed. *The Croker Papers: The Correspondence and Diaries of the Late Rt. Hon. J. W. Croker*. 3 vols. London, 1884.

Jerrold, Clare. *The Early Court of Queen Victoria*. London, 1913.

———. *The Married Life of Queen Victoria*. London, 1913.

Johnson, Paul. *The Birth of the Modern: World Society 1815–1830*. New York, 1991.

Kelly, Ian. *Beau Brummel: The Ultimate Dandy*. London, 2005.

Kerr, John. *Queen Victoria's Scottish Diaries*. Moffat, U.K., 1992.

Kiste, John Van der. *Queen Victoria's Children*. Gloucester, U.K., 1986.

Knight, Cornelia. *Autobiography of Miss Cornelia Knight*. 2 vols. London, 1861.

Langdale, Charles. *Memoirs of Mrs. Fitzherbert*. London, 1856.

Lee, Sir Sidney. *Queen Victoria*. London, 1904.

Leslie, Shane. *The Letters of Mrs. Fitzherbert, and Connected Papers*. London, 1940.

———. *Mrs. Fitzherbert: A Life Chiefly from Unpublished Sources*. London, 1939.

Leveson Gower, F., ed. *Letters of Harriet, Countess Granville, 1810–45*. 2 vols. London, 1894.

Lieven, Princess. *The Unpublished Diary and Political Sketches*. Edited by Harold Temperley. London, 1925.

Longford, Elizabeth, ed. *Darling Loosy: Letters to Princess Louise, 1856–1939*. London, 1991.

———. "Queen Victoria's Doctors," in *A Century of Conflict, 1850–1950*. Edited by Martin Gilbert. London, 1966.

———. *Victoria R.I.* London, 1964.

Low, Frances H. *Queen Victoria's Dolls*. London, 1894.

Macalpine, Ida, and Richard Hunter. *George III and the Mad-Business*. 1991.

Malmesbury, 3rd Earl of, ed. *Diaries and Correspondence of James Harris, First Earl of Malmesbury*. 4 vols. London, 1844.

Marples, Morris. *Wicked Uncles in Love*. London, 1972.

Marshall, Dorothy. *The Life and Times of Victoria*. London, 1972.

Maunder, Andrew, and Grace Moore, eds. *Victorian Crime, Madness and Sensation*. Aldershot, U.K., 2004.

Melville, Lewis, ed. *The Berry Papers, Being the Correspondence Hitherto Unpublished of Mary and Agnes Berry (1763–1852)*. London, 1914.

Millar, Oliver. *The Later Georgian Pictures in the Collection of Her Majesty the Queen*. 2 vols. London, 1969.

———. *The Victorian Pictures in the Collection of Her Majesty the Queen*. 2 vols. London, 1969.

Minto, Countess of, ed. *Life and Letters of Sir Gilbert Elliot, First Earl of Minto*. 3 vols. London, 1874.

Mitchell, L. G. *Lord Melbourne, 1779–1848*. Oxford, 1997.

More, Hannah. *Hints Towards Forming the Character of a Young Princess*. London, 1805.

———. *Strictures on the Modern System of Female Education*. London, 1799.

Morris, Marilyn. *The British Monarchy and the French Revolution*. New Haven, Conn., 1998.

Mullen, Richard, and James Munson. *Victoria: Portrait of a Queen*. London, 1987.

Müller, F. Max, ed. *Memoirs of Baron Stockmar by His Son, Baron Ernst von Stockmar*. Translated by G. A. Müller. 2 vols. London, 1872.

Munich, Adrienne. *Queen Victoria's Secrets*. New York, 1996.

Musgrave, Clifford. *Life in Brighton*. London, 1970.

———. *The Pictorial History of Brighton and the Royal Pavilion*. London, 1959.

———. *The Royal Pavilion*. London, 1954.

Neeson, J. M. *Commoners, Common Right, Enclosure and Social Change in England, 1700–1820*. Cambridge, U.K., 1993.

Nevill, Barry St.-John. *Life at the Court of Queen Victoria, 1861–1901*. Stroud, U.K., 1984.

Ormond, Richard. *Sir Edwin Landseer*. New York, 1982.

Pakula, Hannah. *An Uncommon Woman: The Empress Frederick*. London, 1996.

Pearce, Charles E. *The Beloved Princess: Princess Charlotte of Wales, the Lonely Daughter of a Lonely Queen*. New York, 1912.

Pemberton, W. Baring. *Lord Palmerston*. London, 1954.

Plowden, Alison. *Caroline and Charlotte: Regency Scandals, 1795–1821*. Stroud, U.K., 2005.

Pocock, Tom. *Sailor King: The Life of King William IV*. London, 1991.

Pointon, Marcia. *Hanging the Head: Portraiture and Social Formation in Eighteenth-Century England*. New Haven, Conn., 1993.

———. *Strategies for Showing: Women, Possession, and Representation in English Visual Culture, 1665–1800*. Oxford, 1997.

Ponsonby, Arthur. *Henry Ponsonby: Queen Victoria's Private Secretary, His Life and Letters*. London, 1942.

Ponsonby, Frederick. ed. *Letters of the Empress Frederick*. London, 1928.

Pope-Hennessy, James. *Queen Victoria at Windsor and Balmoral: Letters from Her Grand-daughter, Princess Victoria of Prussia*. London, 1959.

Potts, D. M., and W.T.W. Potts. *Queen Victoria's Gene: Haemophilia and the Royal Family.* Stroud, U.K., 1995.

Poynter, J. R. *Society and Pauperism: English Ideas on Poor Relief, 1795–1834.* London, 1969.

Prochaska, Frank. *Royal Bounty: The Making of a Welfare Monarchy.* New Haven, Conn., 1995.

Quennell, Peter, and Dilys Powell, eds. *The Private Letters of Princess Lieven to Prince Metternich, 1820–1826.* London, 1937.

Ramm, Agatha. *Beloved and Darling Child: Last Letters Between Queen Victoria and Her Eldest Daughter, 1886–1901.* Stroud, U.K., 1990.

Reid, Michaela. *Ask Sir James: The Life of Sir James Reid, Personal Physician to Queen Victoria.* London, 1987.

Renier, J. G. *The Ill-Fated Princess: The Life of Charlotte, Daughter of the Prince Regent, 1796–1817.* London, 1932.

Rhodes James, Robert. *Albert, Prince Consort.* London, 1983.

Ribeiro, Aileen. *The Art of Dress: Fashion in England and France, 1750 to 1820.* London, 1995.

Richardson, Joanna. *Victoria and Albert.* London, 1977.

Ridley, Jane. *The Young Disraeli, 1804–1846.* London, 1995.

Ridley, Jasper. *Lord Palmerston.* London, 1970.

Roberts, Andrew. *Salisbury: Victorian Titan.* London, 1999.

———. *Waterloo: Napoleon's Last Gamble.* London, 2005.

Robins, Jane. *Rebel Queen: The Trial of Queen Caroline.* London, 2006.

Röhl, John C. G., Warren Martin, and David Hunt. *Purple Secret: Genes, "Madness" and the Royal Houses of Europe.* London, 1998.

Romberg, J. B. *Brussels and Its Environs.* London, 1816.

Rose, Kenneth. *Kings, Queens and Courtiers.* London, 1986.

St. Aubyn, Giles. *Edward VII: Prince and King.* London, 1979.

———. *Queen Victoria: A Portrait.* London, 1991.

———. *The Royal George, 1819–1904: The Life of H.R.H. Prince George, Duke of Cambridge.* London, 1963.

Sandars, Mary. *The Life and Times of Queen Adelaide.* London, 1918.

Schor, Esther. *Bearing the Dead: The British Culture of Mourning from the Enlightenment to Victoria.* Princeton, N.J., 1994.

Sichel, Walter, ed. *The Glenbervie Journals.* London, 1910.

Smith, E. A. *Lord Grey, 1764–1845.* Oxford, 1990.

Somerset, Anne. *Ladies-in-Waiting: From the Tudors to the Present Day.* London, 1984.

Sotnick, Richard. *The Coburg Conspiracy: Royal Plots and Manoeuvres.* London, 2008.

Stanhope, Lady Hester. *Memoirs of the Lady Hester Stanhope, as Related by Herself in Conversations with Her Physician.* 3 vols. London, 1845.

Stanley, Lady Augusta. *Letters of Lady Augusta Stanley: A Young Lady at Court, 1849–63.* Edited by the Dean of Windsor and Hector Bolitho. London, 1927.

Steuart, A. F., ed. *The Diary of a Lady in Waiting by Lady Charlotte Bury*. 2 vols. London, 1908.

Stevenson, John. *Popular Disturbances in England, 1700–1870*. London, 1979.

Stewart, Robert. *Henry Brougham, 1778–1868: His Public Career*. London, 1985.

Strachey, Lytton. *Queen Victoria*. London, 1921.

Strachey, Lytton, and Roger Fulford, eds. *The Greville Memoirs, 1814–1860*. 8 vols. London, 1938.

Strickland, Agnes. *Queen Victoria from Her Birth to Her Bridal*. 2 vols. London, 1840.

Strong, Roy. *Coronation: A History of Kingship and the British Monarchy*. London, 2005.

Stuart, D. M. *Daughter of England: A New Study of Princess Charlotte of Wales and Her Family*. London, 1951.

Sudley, Lord. *The Lieven–Palmerston Correspondence, 1828–1856*. London, 1943.

Thompson, Dorothy. *Queen Victoria: Gender and Power*. London, 1990.

Tillyard, Stella. *A Royal Affair: George III and His Troublesome Siblings*. London, 2006.

Tomalin, Claire. *Mrs. Jordan's Profession: The Story of a Great Actress and a Future King*. London, 1994.

Turner, E. S. *The Court of St. James's*. London, 1959.

Twiss, Horace, ed. *The Public and Private Life of Lord Chancellor Eldon*. 3 vols. London, 1844.

Vallone, Lynne. *Becoming Victoria*. New Haven, Conn., 2001.

Van Thal, Herbert. *Ernest Augustus, Duke of Cumberland and King of Hanover*. London, 1936.

Victoria, Queen. *Leaves from the Journal of Our Life in the Highlands, from 1848 to 1861*. London, 1868.

———. *More Leaves from the Journal of a Life in the Highlands, from 1862 to 1882*. London, 1884.

Vincent, John. *Disraeli*. Oxford, 1990.

Waller, Maureen. *Sovereign Ladies*. London, 2006.

Wardroper, John. *Wicked Ernest*. London, 2002.

Warner, Marina. *Queen Victoria's Sketchbook*. London, 1979.

Watkin, David. *The Royal Interiors of Regency England*. London, 1984.

Watson, Vera. *A Queen at Home: An Intimate Account of the Social and Domestic Life of Queen Victoria's Court*. London, 1952.

Weigall, Lady Rose. *A Brief Memoir of the Princess Charlotte of Wales*. London, 1874.

Weintraub, Stanley. *Albert: Uncrowned King*. London, 1997.

———. *Disraeli: A Biography*. London, 1993.

———. *Victoria*. London, 1987.

Wharncliffe, Lady. *The First Lady Wharncliffe and Her Family*. Edited by Caroline Grosvenor and Charles Beilby. 2 vols. London, 1927.

Whittle, Tyler. *Victoria and Albert at Home*. London, 1980.

Willis, G. M. *Ernest Augustus, Duke of Cumberland and King of Hanover.* London, 1954.

Wilson, A. N. *After the Victorians.* London, 2005.

———. *The Victorians.* London, 2002.

Wilson, Frances. *The Courtesan's Revenge.* London, 2003.

Wood, Marcus. *Radical Satire and Print Culture, 1790–1822.* Oxford, 1994.

Woodham-Smith, Cecil. *Queen Victoria: Her Life and Times, Vol. 1, 1819–1861.* London, 1972.

Wraxall, Sir Nathaniel. *The Historical and the Posthumous Memoirs of Sir Nathaniel William Wraxall, 1772–1784.* 5 vols. London, 1884.

York, H.R.H. Sarah, Duchess of, and Benita Stoney. *Travels with Queen Victoria.* London, 1993.

———. *Victoria and Albert: Life at Osborne House.* London, 1991.

Yorke, Phillip, ed. *Letters of Princess Elizabeth of England.* London, 1898.

Zeepvat, Charlotte. *Prince Leopold, The Untold Story of Queen Victoria's Youngest Son.* Phoenix Mill, U.K., 1998.

Ziegler, Philip. *King William IV.* London, 1971.

———. *Melbourne: A Biography of William Lamb, 2nd Viscount Melbourne.* London, 1990.

Index

About the Author

Kate Williams is the author of *England's Mistress: The Infamous Life of Emma Hamilton* and has published widely in books and journals. Williams fell in love with the eighteenth century while an undergraduate at Oxford. She has an M.A. from Queen Mary, University of London, and a D.Phil. in history from Oxford. A lecturer and TV consultant, she has hosted two television historical documentaries and appears regularly on BBC and Channel 4. She lives in London.